AF777862

For Grainne de

In appreciation of your work on comparative human rights,

Most warmly,

David

October 2023

Revolution and Constitutionalism in Britain and the U.S.

In *Revolution and Constitutionalism in Britain and the U.S.: Burke and Madison and Their Contemporary Legacies*, David A. J. Richards offers an investigative comparison of two central figures in late eighteenth-century constitutionalism, Edmund Burke and James Madison, at a time when two great constitutional experiments were in play: the Constitution of the Glorious Revolution of 1688 and the U.S. Constitution of 1787.

Richards assesses how much, as liberal Lockean constitutionalists, Burke and Madison shared and yet differed regarding violent revolution, offering three pathbreaking and original contributions about Burke's importance. First, the book defends Burke as a central figure in the development and understanding of liberal constitutionalism; second, it explores the psychology that led to his liberal voice, including Burke's own long-term loving relationship to another man; and third, it shows how Burke's understanding of the political psychology of the violence of "political religions" is an enduring contribution to understanding fascist threats to political liberalism from the eighteenth-century onwards, including the contemporary constitutional crises in the U.S. and U.K. deriving from populist movements.

Mixing thorough research with personal experiences, this book will be an invaluable resource to scholars of political science and theory, constitutional law, history, political psychology, and LGBTQ+ issues.

David A. J. Richards is Edwin D. Webb Professor of Law at the New York University School of Law and is the author of numerous articles and over 20 books, including *A Theory of Reasons for Action* (Oxford: Oxford at the Clarendon Press, 1971); *Sex, Drugs, Death and the Law: An Essay on Human Rights and Decriminalization* (Totowa: Rowman & Littlefield, 1982); *Toleration and the Constitution* (New York: Oxford University Press, 1986); *Foundations of American Constitutionalism* (New York: Oxford University Press, 1989); *Conscience and the Constitution: History, Theory, and Law of the Reconstruction Amendments* (Princeton: Princeton University Press, 1993); *Women, Gays, and the Constitution: The Grounds for Feminism and Gay Rights* *in Culture and Law* (Chicago, IL: University of Chicago Press, 1998); *Italian American: The Racializing of an Ethnic Identity* (New York: New York University Press, 1999); *Resisting Injustice and the Feminist Ethics of Care in the Age of Obama: "Suddenly, All the Truth Was Coming Out"* (New York: Routledge, 2013); *Free Speech and the Politics of Identity* (Oxford: Oxford University Press, 1999); *Disarming Manhood: Roots of Ethical Resistance* (Athens: Swallow Press, 2003); *The Deepening Darkness: Patriarchy, Resistance, and Democracy's Future* (with Carol Gilligan) (Cambridge: Cambridge University Press, 2009); *Darkness Now Visible: Patriarchy's Resurgence and Feminist Resistance* (with Carol Gilligan) (Cambridge: Cambridge University Press, 2018); *Patriarchal Religion, Sexuality, and Gender: A Critique of New Natural Law (with Nicholas Bamforth)* (Cambridge: Cambridge University Press, 2008); *Fundamentalism in American Religion and Law: Obama's Challenge to Patriarchy Threat to Democracy* (Cambridge: Cambridge University Press, 2010); *Why Love Leads to Justice: Love across the Boundaries* (Cambridge: Cambridge University Press, 2016); *The Rise of Gay Rights and the Fall of the British Empire: Liberal Resistance and the Bloomsbury Group* (Cambridge: Cambridge University Press, 2013); *Identity and the Case for Gay Rights: Race, Gender, Religion as Analogies* (Chicago, IL: University of Chicago Press, 1999); *Boys' Secrets and Men's Loves: A Memoir* (Bloomington, IN: Xlibris, 2019); and the recent *Holding a Mirror Up to Nature: Shame, Guilt, and Violence in Shakespeare* (with James Gilligan) (Cambridge: Cambridge University Press, 2022).

Routledge Studies in Social and Political Thought

174 Making Citizenship Work
Culture and Community
Edited by Rodolfo Rosales

175 Towards a Sociology of the Open Society
Critical Rationalism and the Open Society Volume II
Masoud Mohammadi Alamuti

176 Radical Civility
A Study in Utopia and Democracy
Jason Caro

177 Science Meets Philosophy
What Makes Science Divided but Still Significant
Hans Christian Garmann Johnsen

178 Civilization, Modernity, and Critique
Engaging Johann P. Arnason's Macro-Social Theory
Ľubomír Dunaj, Jeremy C.A. Smith and Kurt C.M. Mertel

179 Liberty, Governance and Resistance
Competing Discourses in John Locke's Political Philosophy
John Tate

180 Revolution and Constitutionalism in Britain and the U.S.
Burke and Madison and Their Contemporary Legacies
David A. J. Richards

For a full list of titles in this series, please visit www.routledge.com/series/RSSPT

Revolution and Constitutionalism in Britain and the U.S.

Burke and Madison and Their Contemporary Legacies

David A. J. Richards

Routledge
Taylor & Francis Group
NEW YORK AND LONDON

First published 2024
by Routledge
605 Third Avenue, New York, NY 10158

and by Routledge
4 Park Square, Milton Park, Abingdon, Oxon, OX14 4RN

Routledge is an imprint of the Taylor & Francis Group, an informa business

Library of Congress Cataloging-in-Publication Data
Names: Richards, David A. J., author.
Title: Revolution and constitutionalism in Britain and the U.S. :
Burke and Madison and their contemporary legacies / David A. J. Richards.
Other titles: Revolution and constitutionalism in Britain and the United States
Identifiers: LCCN 2023019065 (print) | LCCN 2023019066 (ebook) |
ISBN 9781032530062 (hbk) | ISBN 9781032532226 (pbk) |
ISBN 9781003410966 (ebk)
Subjects: LCSH: Constitutional history–Great Britain. |
Constitutional history–United states. | Constitutional law–Great Britain. |
Constitutional law–United States. | Great Britain–History–Revolution of 1688 . |
Revolutions–United States–History–18th century. |
Great Britian–Politics and government–History. |
United States–Politics and government–History. |
Burke, Edmund, 1729–1797. | Madison, James, 1751–1836.
Classification: LCC K3161 .R53 2023 (print) |
LCC K3161 (ebook) | DDC 342.4102/9–dc23/eng/20230609
LC record available at https://lccn.loc.gov/2023019065
LC ebook record available at https://lccn.loc.gov/2023019066

ISBN: 9781032530062 (hbk)
ISBN: 9781032532226 (pbk)
ISBN: 9781003410966 (ebk)

DOI: 10.4324/9781003410966

Typeset in Times New Roman
by Newgen Publishing UK

For Donald Levy.

The Reason why Men enter into Society, is the preservation of their Property; and the end why they chuse and authorize a Legislative, is, that there may be Laws made, and Rules set as Guards and Fences to the Properties of all the Members of the Society, to limit the Power, and moderate the Dominion of every Part and Member of the Society. For since it can never be supposed to be the Will of the Society, that the Legislative should have a Power to destroy that, which every one designs to secure, by entering into Society, and for which the People submitted themselves to the Legislators of their own making: whenever the *Legislators endeavour to take away, and destroy the Property of the People,* or to reduce them to Slavery under Arbitrary Power, they put themselves into a state of War with the People, who are thereupon absolved from any further Obedience, and are left to the Common Refuge, which God hath provided for all Men, against Force and Violence. Whensoever therefore the *Legislative* shall transgress this fundamental Rule of Society; and either by Ambition, Fear, Folly or Corruption, *endeavor to grasp themselves or put into the hands of any other an Absolute Power* over the Lives, Liberties, and Estates of the People; By this breach of Trust they *forfeit the Power, the* People had put into their hands, for quite contrary ends, and it devolves to the People, who have a Right to resume their original Liberty, and, by the Establishment of a new Legislative (such as they think fit) provide for their Safety and Security, which is the end for which they are in Society.

John Locke, *The Second Treatise of Government (Peter Laslett ed.), pp. 412–13*

Like other tyrannies, the tyranny of the majority was at first, and is still vulgarly, held in dread chiefly as operating through the acts of the public authority. But reflecting persons perceived that when society is itself the tyrant—society collectively, over the separate individuals who compose it—its means of tyrannizing are not restricted to the acts which it may do by the hands of its political functionaries. Society can and does execute its own mandates: and if it issues wrong mandates instead of right, or any mandates at all in things with which it ought not to meddle, it practices a social tyranny more formidable than many kinds of political oppression, since, though not usually held by such extreme penalties, it leaves fewer means of escape, penetrating more deeply into the details of life, and enslaving the soul itself.

John Stuart Mill, "On Liberty", in John Stuart Mill, *On Liberty, Utilitarianism and Other Essays* (Oxford: Oxford University Press), p. 8.

American colonies, Ireland, France, and India
Harried, and Burke's great melody against it.

W.B. Yeats, *"The Seven Sages," in W.B. Yeats, The Poems (New York: Scribner, 1997), p. 245.*

Contents

Preface

Reasons for Writing This Book

American and British constitutionalism share a history, and this work is meant to address that history both in the late eighteenth century when they separated after the American revolution and thereafter, including their rediscovery of one another, their common values, and the need for new transnational and international institutions during and after World War II. What did they share, and what do they share since? Dicey addressed the latter point in an 1897 article, as the title put it, "A Common Citizenship for the English Race"[1] between England and the U.S. Is there anything to it but late Victorian racism? That is my question, or one of my questions.

The prism of the investigation of this work is a comparison of two central figures in late eighteenth-century British and American constitutionalism: Edmund Burke in Britain, and James Madison in America, when the two great constitutional experiments were in play—the British Constitution of the Glorious Revolution of 1688, and the U.S. Constitution of 1787. My focus is on how much, as liberal Lockean constitutionalists, they shared (including their Lockean belief in the right to revolution and their interests in history as a guide to constitutional construction and interpretation), and yet their quite different relationships to violent revolution. Madison, like Jefferson and Adams, never questioned the legitimacy of the American revolution. Rather, the premise of his role, as a leading founder both at the 1787 Convention and defending the convention's work in *The Federalist*, was that the constitution would give the world a more legitimate constitutionalism than the British Constitution against which the colonists revolted. In contrast, no one was more skeptical of the relationship of violent revolution to liberal constitutionalism than Burke, condemning, for example, Britain's unjust and unwise treatment of the Americans precisely because, in his view, George III and Lord North were provoking a violent revolution by the colonists, which was and would

1 Dylan Lino, "The Rule of Law and the Rule of Empire: A.V. Dicey in Imperial Contest," *Modern Law Review*, 81: 5 (2018): 739–64 at 749.

be disastrous for Britain and—as he suggested to the Americans in calling for reconciliation—for them. This was, of course, long before his skepticism about the French revolution, in particular in his classic *Reflections on the Revolution in France*, written and published in 1790–91 before the revolution took its more grisly forms (the terror of 1793 and the Napoleonic despotism that followed). What is it that he saw, and what legacy has he left us in understanding the threats, still very much with us, to liberal constitutionalism? How and why did he come to see what he saw? That is very much my reason or among my reasons for writing this book.

There are many excellent studies of Burke, from which I have learned much,[2] but none of them, in my judgment, focuses on his central contribution to liberal constitutionalism and its future, namely, his exercise and defense of the priority of liberal voice (distinctive of political liberalism) resisting illiberal injustices inflicted by Britain and others, as well as his emphasis on the importance of evidence-based interpretive history in understanding and defending liberal constitutionalism and his remarkable political psychology of the sources of the fear, terror, and violence that threatens the project of such constitutionalism in Britain, America, and France whenever it effectively betrays and wars on its deepest values, respect for universal human rights. Nor do they address how and why he came so personally both to find his liberal resisting voice and to understand the political psychology that violence wars on such voice, a central and very personal reason for my own interest in his life and work as a gay man.

My work, as both a political philosopher and a constitutional lawyer, has long been among the leading works arguing for the human rights of LGBTQ people

2 See, among others, Richard Bourke, *Empire and Revolution: The Political Life of Edmund Burke* (Princeton, NJ: Princeton University Press, 2015); F. P. Lock, *Edmund Burke, Volume I: 1730–1784* (Oxford: Oxford University Press, 1998); F.P. Lock, *Edmund Burke, Volume II: 1784–1797* (Oxford: Oxford University Press, 2006); Stanley Ayling, *Edmund Burke: His Life and Opinions* (New York: St. Martin's Press, 1988); Isaac Kramnick, *The Rage of Edmund Burke: Portrait of an Ambivalent Conservative* (New York: Basic Books, 1977); Conor Cruise O'Brien, *The Great Melody: A Thematic Biography of Edmund Burke* (Chicago, IL: University of Chicago Press, 1992); David Bromwich, *The Intellectual Life of Edmund Burke: From the Sublime and Beautiful to American Independence* (Cambridge, MA: Harvard University Press, 2014); Jesse Norman, *Edmund Burke* (New York: Basic Books, 2013); Carl B. Cone, *Burke and the Nature of Politics: The Age of the American Revolution* (Lexington, KY: University of Kentucky Press, 1957); Carl B. Cone, *Burke and the Nature of Politics: The Age of the French Revolution* (Lexington, KY: University of Kentucky Press, 1964); David Dwan and Christopher J. Insole, *The Cambridge Companion to Edmund Burke* (Cambridge: Cambridge University Press, 2012); Justin Du Rivage, *Revolution against Empire: Taxes, Politics, and the Origins of American Independence* (New Haven, CT: Yale University Press, 2017); Martti Koskenniemi, *To the Uppermost Parts of the Earth: Legal Imagination and International Power 1300–1870* (Cambridge: Cambridge University Press, 2021); Daniel O'Neill, *Edmund Burke and the Conservative Logic of Empire* (Berkeley: University of California Press, 2016).

as constitutional rights[3] and was prominently cited by the Indian Supreme Court in its recent opinion decriminalizing gay sex on the basis of a free-standing constitutional right to privacy.[4] In Chapter 1 of this book, I bring my own experience as a gay man and compelling historical evidence to bear on arguing that Edmund Burke's remarkable political liberalism in a range of domains (resisting the injustice of the British treatment of Irish Catholics, the Americans, and the Indians—the Hastings impeachment) can be plausibly understood not only in terms of his being Irish but also in terms of Burke's own long-term loving relationship to another man, Will Burke. Starting from the pathbreaking work of Isaac Kramnick on the relationship of Edmund and Will[5] and the extraordinary homophobia of eighteenth-century Britain (which I document), I make this case in two ways. First, there is Burke's astonishing 1780s speech in the House of Commons condemning the use of the pillory (proposing a law forbidding this punishment) against two convicted homosexuals, leading to one of them being murdered by a homophobic London mob (a speech eliciting homophobic insults to Burke in London newspapers because he questions a violence that any true man or woman would endorse and praise). And second, there is Burke's remarkable defense not only of political liberalism but also his analysis of the political psychology of anti-liberal violence, which culminates in the prophetic depth and insight of *Reflections on the Revolution in France*. Burke's insights into this political psychology are his central contribution to political liberalism, arising in part from his understanding of and resistance to the homophobic violence of the London mobs and that he later saw in the sometimes homophobic violence of Parisian mobs (targeting Marie Antoinette, regarded as, among other things,

3 *Sex, Drugs, Death and the Law: An Essay on Human Rights and Decriminalization* (Totowa, NJ: Rowman & Littlefield, 1982); *Toleration and the Constitution* (New York: Oxford University Press, 1986); *Foundations of American Constitutionalism* (New York: Oxford University Press, 1989); *Conscience and the Constitution: History, Theory, and Law of the Reconstruction Amendments* (Princeton, NJ: Princeton University Press, 1993); *Women, Gays, and the Constitution: The Grounds for Feminism and Gay Rights in Culture and Law* (Chicago, IL: University of Chicago Press, 1998); *Identity and the Case for Gay Rights: Race, Gender, Religion as Analogies* (Chicago, IL: University of Chicago Press, 1999); *Free Speech and the Politics of Identity* (Oxford: Oxford University Press, 1999); *Patriarchal Religion, Gender, and Sexuality: A Critique of New Natural Law* (Cambridge: Cambridge University Press, 2008); *Fundamentalism in American Religion and Law: Obama's Challenge to Patriarchy's Threat to Democracy* (Cambridge: Cambridge University Press, 2010); *The Rise of Gay Rights and the Fall of the British Empire* (Cambridge: Cambridge University Press, 2013); *Why Love Leads to Justice: Love across the Boundaries* (Cambridge: Cambridge University Press, 2015).

4 The Indian Supreme Court inferred a free-standing right of constitutional privacy in its 2017 decision in *Justice KS Puttaswamy v. Union of India*, Writ Petition (Civil) No 494 of 2012, 24 August 2017; and its 2018 opinion in *Navtej Singh Johar & Ors. v. Union of* India, Writ Petition (Civil) No. 572 of 2016, 6 September 2018, the latter of which decriminalized gay sex on the basis of the value of equal dignity, citing my work, among others.

5 Isaac Kramnick, *The Rage of Edmund Burke: Portrait of an Ambivalent Conservative* (New York: Basic Books, 1977).

an adulteress and a lesbian), and a political psychology of illimitable violence that destroyed any hopes liberals had for the French revolution as a contribution to political liberalism in Europe. In both cases, the political psychology turns on violence, including terror, unleashed on any threat to patriarchal gender roles, an argument Carol Gilligan and I make in our first book, *The Deepening Darkness*,[6] and which James Gilligan and I explore in our recent book, *Holding a Mirror Up to Nature: Shame, Guilt, and Violence in Shakespeare*[7] as in terms of the transition from the hierarchies of violent shame cultures to the equality of democratic guilt cultures. However, in this book I show the explanatory power of this political psychology in understanding political violence in some contextual detail both in the eighteenth century and over the following centuries, including our contemporary situation of constitutional crisis in the U.S. over the anachronistic ideology of originalism of a majority of the current U.S. Supreme Court (three of whom were appointed by Trump), and a comparable constitutional crisis in the politics of the U.K. Burke's argument, with its focus on his intimate personal understanding of the psychological impact of terror, prefigures the later arguments of both Hannah Arendt and the psychiatrist James Gilligan on the political psychology of twentieth-century totalitarianisms and twenty-first-century resurgent violent fundamentalisms (Islamic terrorism), imperialist ethnic nationalism (the Russian incursion into Ukraine), and the anti-liberal populist politics of Trump in the U.S. and a similar politics in Britain (Brexit).

It is another feature of the originality of my account that I question the now conventional reading of Burke as the founder of political conservatism,[8] a tradition much of which Burke would have rejected (e.g., its defense of absolutism in politics and religion and its racism).[9] It is certainly true that Burke shared the view of Adam Smith that government interference into the free market did more harm than good[10] (only Thomas Paine in this period argued for state policies directed at relieving poverty[11]), but later liberal views on such issues would reasonably change in response to new circumstances on this (as in Rawls' endorsement of the difference principle[12]) and many other issues. It is also true that

6 Carol Gilligan and David A. J. Richards, *The Deepening Darkness: Patriarchy, Resistance, and Democracy's Future* (Cambridge: Cambridge University Press, 2009); see also Carol Gilligan and David A. J. Richards, *Darkness Now Visible: Patriarchy's Resurgence and Feminist Resistance* (Cambridge: Cambridge University Press, 2018).

7 James Gilligan and David A. J. Richards, *Holding a Mirror Up to Nature: Shame, Guilt, and Violence in Shakespeare* (Cambridge: Cambridge University Press, 2022).

8 See, e.g., Yuval Levin, *The Great Debate: Edmund Burke, Thomas Paine, and the Birth of Right and Left* (New York: Basic Books, 2014); C. B. Macpherson, *Burke* (New York: Hill & Wang, 1980).

9 For a fuller discussion, see Edmund Fawcett, *Conservatism: The Fight for a Tradition* (Princeton, NJ: Princeton University Press, 2020).

10 See Bourke, *Empire and Revolution*, pp. 889–91

11 See Levin, *The Great Debate*, pp. 205–22.

12 John Rawls, *A Theory of Justice* (Cambridge, MA: Harvard University Press, 1971), pp. 75–83.

Burke valued the independence of the British-landed hereditary aristocracy, a limited franchise, and an establishment church, but so regarded them, in his historical context, as the vehicles of liberal resistance to an increasingly authoritarian monarchy and mob rule (as in France); the aristocracy, for example, was open to natural aristocrats like Burke who defended such liberal resistance. "Was Burke a conservative or a liberal? Of the historical Burke, the question is anachronistic."[13] My own view, defended at length below, is that Burke was a liberal, calling for the defense and further development of liberal constitutionalism against its enemies (including European absolute monarchy, the authoritarian monarchy of George III, and the French mobs). The center of Burke's life and work was the evidence-based construction of a liberal British constitutionalism, and his appeals to history and tradition were in service of the work in progress of the development and defense of liberal constitutionalism whether in Britain or in the U.S. His critique of the French constitutionalisms was that they were not only not evidence-based but also disastrously failed to understand the political psychology of violence they unleashed. Burke's ultimate ends were, in my view, always liberal, using whatever reliable evidence showed would lead to a more liberal constitutionalism, including his own liberal voice in criticism of Britain's and France's failures to implement and preserve liberal values of free conscience, thought, and speech. In this respect, Burke is as central to the liberal tradition as Locke, Jefferson, Madison, De Tocqueville, John Stuart Mill, and John Rawls. Not all Burke's appeals to tradition, in fact, advance liberal values,[14] but he believed that they did, which is my point about the road to liberal constitutionalism he meant to defend. It is, for Burke, always incomplete, requiring a liberal resisting voice to criticize its betrayals of liberal values, and openness to evidence-based experience to construct better forms of constitutionalism at home and abroad—a universalist humanistic project, as it was for his contemporary, Kant.[15]

Burke has been thus misread even by those like the great Anglo-Irish poet W. B. Yeats, who memorably included Burke among "The Seven Sages," an epigraph of this book:

> American colonies, Ireland, France, and India
> Harried, and Burke's great melody against it.[16]

13 Fawcett, *Conservatism*, p. 17.

14 For example, Burke's defense of the patriarchal family at threat from French liberalizing reforms cannot be justified on liberal grounds. For his arguments to this effect, see Edmund Burke, "The First Letter on a Regicide Speech," in Iain Hampsher-Monk (ed.), *Burke: Revolutionary Writings* (Cambridge: Cambridge University Press, 2014), pp. 251–334 at 310–14 (attacking French laws allowing divorce).

15 See Hans Reiss (ed.), *Kant's Political Writings* (Cambridge: Cambridge University Press, 1977).

16 "The Seven Sages," in Richard J. Finneran (ed.), *The Collected Works of W. B. Yeats, Volume I: The Poems* (New York: Scribner, 1997), p. 245.

And then Yeats went on, incoherently, to concede Burke was a Whig, but not guilty of "Whiggery," "a levelling, rancorous, rational sort of mind / That never looked out of the eye of a saint/Or out of drunkard's eye."[17] For Yeats, however, "Anglo-Ireland was associated with uncompromising intellectual achievement (Swift and Goldsmith), conservative and anti-egalitarian politics (Burke), and Neoplatonic philosophy (Berkeley, with some special pleading)—all core values held" by Yeats himself.[18] During an inter-war period when democracy seemed inadequate to the challenge of fascism and the poet was concerned with controlling violence in Ireland, Yeats reads Burke incoherently because he cannot connect Burke's astonishingly expressive and courageous liberal voice (his "great melody") to the priority of liberal values of voice over other values, exactly the values of voice at threat by the fascism to which Yeats and his friend Ezra Pound were attracted.[19] On the one hand, Yeats came to appreciate the humane ethical imagination of Burke that embraced the injustices inflicted on the dehumanized (thus "the eyes of a saint / Or out of drunkard's eye")—his "great melody"—but could not understand the egalitarian liberalism that such voice rested on and developed as a model for future generations of liberals resisting injustices that refuse to extend liberal equality to all persons, a dehumanization that provokes violence. Yet, Yeats himself, as a senator in the Irish parliament, spoke, invoking Burke's liberal voice ("We are the people of Burke"), against Catholic-intolerant censorship of literature by minorities, a violation of liberal equality.[20]

In contrast to these views, I argue that the enduring value of Burke's life and work rests on the central values of political liberalism that he advanced and defended in criticizing profound injustices others could and would not acknowledge, the central values of political liberalism that both Britain and the U.S. shared and further developed over time. In his recent compelling treatment of the history of liberalism, Edmund Fawcett focuses on three normative ideas that he traces in the history and development of political liberalism as an idea and practice: first, non-intrusion in privacy; second, non-obstruction of economic and social aspiration, or not getting "in the way of social progress and personal flourishing;" and third, "non-exclusion [which] was at root moral,"[21]

17 Ibid.

18 R. F. Foster, *W.B. Yeats: A Life II, The Arch-Poet 1915–1939* (Oxford: Oxford University Press, 2003), p. 346; Richard J. Finneran (ed.), *The Collected Works of W. B. Yeats, Volume I: The Poems* (New York: Scribner, 1997), p. 346.

19 On this point, see Foster, *W. B. Yeats*, pp. 466–95. I am indebted for understanding the complexities of Yeats' views to the advice of Alexander Bubb. See Alexander Bubb, *Meetings without Knowing It: Kipling and Yeats at the Fin de Siecle* (Oxford: Oxford University Press, 2016).

20 See Foster, *W. B. Yeats*, pp. 297–98.

21 Edmund Fawcett, *Liberalism: The Life of an Idea*, 2nd ed. (Princeton, NJ: Princeton University Press, 2018), pp. 125–29; see also Edmund Fawcett, *Conservatism: The Fight for a Tradition* (Princeton, NJ: Princeton University Press, 2020).

condemning exclusions on irrationalist grounds of race/ethnicity, religion, class, gender, sexual orientation, and the like. Two works of liberal political theory, one British, the other American, offer views of political liberalism along Fawcett's lines that I find compelling: John Stuart Mill's *On Liberty* and *The Subjection of Women* and John Rawls' *A Theory of Justice*; in a later work, Rawls, who disagrees with Mill's utilitarianism as a basis for the principles Mill defends, nonetheless acknowledges that the principles of Mill's liberalism are "quite similar to those of the well-ordered society of justice as fairness"[22] (Rawls' version of political liberalism). In both Mill and Rawls, political liberalism gives priority to the values of freedom of conscience and speech, the central values of Burke's resisting voice. The interest of Fawcett's argument is that he clearly sees and explores the tension between democracy and the liberalism of Mill and Rawls (ancient Athens may have been democratic, but, in regarding Socrates' teaching of philosophy as not a legitimate form of conscience, it wrongly intruded into a sphere of private life and thought; in excluding from citizenship those, like Aristotle, not ethnically born to an Athenian, it obstructed ambition and progress; and, in exiling women and slaves from public life, it violated non-exclusion supporting a caste system on irrationalist grounds, gender and slave status, often linked to ethnic difference and defeat in one of Athens' unjust imperialistic wars). Fawcett clearly sees some leading politicians (Gladstone in the U.K.; Lincoln in the U.S.) as rightly honored for striving to align British and American politics with liberal values, but there is nothing inevitable in the alignment. Quite the contrary. Yet both British and American constitutionalisms appeal at crucial moments in their development to a distinguished philosophical political liberal and advocate of human rights and the right to revolution, John Locke, yet their constitutionalisms took a different form, with different outcomes.

Burke's political liberalism, derived from John Locke and his defense of the inalienable right to conscience, had been the justification of the Glorious Revolution of 1688 led by aristocratic Whigs and was the inspiration of the role the Whigs played as what Justin Du Rivage calls the establishment Whigs who were the central players in British politics under the first two Hanoverian monarchs until 1760 when George III becomes king and introduced the authoritarian reforms in the British treatment of the American colonies that would provoke the American revolution. Burke served in the House of Commons for 28 years (1766–94) and played an important role as spokesperson for a group of establishment Whigs, the Rockingham Whigs, led by the Marquess of

22 See John Rawls, *Lectures on the History of Political Philosophy*, edited by Samuel Freeman (Cambridge, MA: The Belknap Press of Harvard University Press, 2007), p. 297. For a recent British defense of Rawls as offering the best normative theory of British progressive liberalism, see Daniel Chandler, *Free and Equal: What Would a Fair Society Look Like?* (London: Allen Lane, 2023).

Rockingham, one of the wealthiest men in England, until his death in 1782 and who was prime minister for two brief periods (the first of which repealed the Stamp Act, and the second of which led to the peace treaty with the U.S.). The Rockingham Whigs resisted the authoritarian reformers centered in the king, but did not support the radical Whigs, like Richard Price in England and Thomas Paine in America, who called for a more extensive franchise than the narrow property-owning franchise of late eighteenth-century Britain (expanded by reform acts in the nineteenth and early twentieth centuries to include all adults, including women). It had been precisely the independent wealth of the establishment Whigs that had been the basis for their independence from the crown and its authoritarian claims at least until they lost power under George III, as well as their independence from what they regarded as the often prejudiced views of ordinary people (e.g., the anti-Catholic prejudice of the violent Gordon riot mobs, reacting to the parliamentary attempt to emancipate Catholics, attacking Burke's home because of his sympathies for Catholics, including Irish Catholics).[23]

In the sense of those terms I have developed earlier, Britain was not in this period remotely as democratic as it was later to be, but its institutions allowed liberals, resisting monarchical absolutism, to take power and, even when they lost power, to resist George III's authoritarian reform in the British Empire (taxation without representation), and Burke's resistance exemplifies this development in resistance to British imperialist authoritarianism in Ireland, America, and India. To this extent, though Burke himself defended the ambitions of the British Empire, his liberal critique anticipates the long period of criticism of the British Empire, including, in the late twentieth century, the reasons for its collapse.[24] My interest in Burke is the view he developed and defended of the form of constitutionalism that sustains the political liberalism that places a central normative value on the equal liberties of conscience and speech, as both Mill and Rawls do, as prior to other values, and demands that a realm be preserved for the exercise of such rights based in a generalization of the argument for toleration.[25] The exercise of such core liberal rights takes the form, as it does in the life and work of Burke, of the criticism of deviations from these rights, not recognized in Ireland, America, India, or in France. Burke not only exemplifies the exercise of these rights but also offers a political psychology that the refusal to respect these equal liberties of the Irish, Americans, Indians, and French by

23 For the distinction among these various political groups in Britain and America during this period, I am indebted to the discussion of Du Rivage, *Revolution against Empire*.

24 On this point, see David A. J. Richards, *The Rise of Gay Rights and the Fall of the British Empire: Liberal Resistance and the Bloomsbury Group* (Cambridge: Cambridge University Press, 2013).

25 See David A. J. Richards, *Toleration and the Constitution* (New York: Oxford University Press, 1986); *Foundations of American Constitutionalism* (New York: Oxford University Press, 1989); *Conscience and the Constitution: History, Theory, and Law of the Reconstruction Amendments* (Princeton, NJ: Princeton University Press, 1993).

the use of unjust repression and violence itself elicits violence. Burke is a foundational liberal voice in the understanding and development of constitutional liberalism because he argues for an evidence-based account of how to develop and preserve a constitutionalism that respects such rights, including the role interpretive history must play in understanding and supporting such constitutionalism, and how he came to develop and articulate a political psychology of the real threats to such liberal constitutionalism, his enduring legacy to liberalism everywhere.

Madison shares Burke's Lockean political liberalism, both justifying the right to revolution when human rights are at threat and regarding the freedom of thought and the inalienable right to conscience as central to such liberal rights. There is also a comparable interest in political psychology, the theory of faction that Madison prominently uses in *The Federalist* No. 10, to defend the federal system, as well as an interest in interpretive history in constitutional constructivism. What is of compelling interest in comparing Burke and Madison is that, like Burke, Madison develops an argument for the importance of history in the interpretation of liberal constitutionalism, which leads in later chapters to a discussion of the appropriate role of appeals to history in both British and American constitutionalism, including criticism of the interpretive originalism that a majority of the current U.S. Supreme Court used in *Dobbs v. Jackson* and other recent cases. What Madison does not see is the threat to liberal constitutionalism that the constitution's treatment of slavery would unleash, culminating in the civil war and America's continuing struggle with its cultural racism and cognate irrational prejudices that abridge universal human rights. Was this a price worth paying? Burke thought not. Addressing that question is another reason for writing this book.

Burke endorsed the 1787 U.S. Constitution as consistent with the kind of deliberative reflection on evidence-based historical experience, including that of the British Constitution and its defense by Montesquieu and others, and I show in Chapter 2 exactly what it was in Madison's liberal constructivism that Burke came to admire, including its appeal to the political philosophy of John Locke and the right to revolution that had been so important in the development of British liberal constitutionalism in the Glorious Revolution of 1688. But Burke, like Benjamin Franklin, had wanted to reconcile the Americans with the British government and had warned the Americans prophetically that their separation from Britain might lead to internecine disaster in its politics.

Burke's argument, centering on both liberal principles and the anti-liberal psychology of violence, clarifies, so I argue (Chapter 3), both the failure of American constitutionalism to deal constitutionally with the gravest of liberal evils, slavery, non-violently as the British did abolishing slavery in 1833 (which Lincoln pointed to in indicting pro-slavery constitutionalism as betraying political liberalism and the legitimacy of the 1787 Constitution). And it clarifies as well (Chapter 4) the consequences of the British betrayal of liberalism in its unjust treatment of both the Irish and the Indians, leading to unjust violence against these peoples, and terrorism as among their responses, as Burke predicted. Only outsiders to both British and American constitutionalism, Gandhi in India and Martin Luther King, Jr. in the U.S., innovate non-violent forms of civil disobedience that advance justice by exposing contradictions between their liberal constitutionalism and Christian religion and the violence (including lynchings) directed at liberal dissent.

During the nineteenth century and later, the parliamentary system in Britain changed. Burke's late eighteenth century

> ideal was a party organization resembling a political "club" rather than a modern "machine" … whose members were not beaten by the hammer of party leadership upon the anvil of constituency opinion. Burke saw the need for more effective party machinery within parliament when few others did, and earlier than his contemporaries he was to deprive the crown of the powers that interfered with control of the government by party leaders in parliament. It is not presentism to say that the tendency of Burke's idea was toward the cabinet government of the midnineteenth century, which did not know, any more than did Burke, an independent civil service, a democratic suffrage, or mass parties.[26]

During this later period, the doctrine of parliamentary sovereignty was doctrinally defended by A. V. Dicey, and the historical role of the judiciary in protecting rights less so. Rather, parliament became the central engine in the advance of political liberalism in Britain through the expansion of the franchise in the nineteenth and twentieth centuries culminating in extending the franchise to women, as well as the emancipation of Catholics and Jews, as well as enacting welfare state liberalism and socialist ownership of major industries, in particular, when the Labour Party takes power in 1945–51. How can that development during this period reasonably be squared with the British Empire, in which the colonies (both settler and non-settler colonies) are not represented in the British parliament? Dicey, for example, had problems making sense of parliamentary supremacy since the premise of his argument, representation by the affected people, was not satisfied.[27] Democracy and liberalism here are in tension, if not contradiction, as many liberal critiques of British imperialism and its legacy argue.[28] And, I argue, Burke was among these critics, as his political

26 Cone, *Burke and the Nature of Politics: The Age of the French Revolution*, pp. 36–37.

27 See Dylan Lino, "Albert Venn Dicey and the Constitutional Theory of the Empire," *Oxford Journal of Legal Studies*, 36:4 (2016): 751–80, and "The Rule of Law and the Rule of Empire: A.V. Dicey in Imperial Contest."

28 For liberal critiques of British imperialism and its consequences, see Priya Satia *Time's Monster: How History Makes History* (Cambridge, MA: Harvard University Press, 2020); Adom Getachew, *Worldmaking after Empire: The Rise and Fall of Self-Determination*

psychology of violence explains how Britain's betrayal of its own liberal values gave rise, as it had done in America and in Ireland, to the violence and atrocity in its colonies by both Britain and colonists. And, may not the empire itself, in particular the increasingly authoritarian and militaristic rule of India defended by James Fitzjames Stephen on crudely utilitarian grounds, have legitimated a comparable reactionary argument in the U.K. that tragically undermined and defeated Gladstone's last great liberal project, home rule for Ireland (against which Stephen inveighed), a worry that preoccupied Burke and others earlier?[29] My interest in this question is another of my reasons for writing this book.

My approach to these issues in this book thus combines political theory (the political liberalism both nations share and, indeed, progressively develop into forms of economic and social liberalism) with the close study of the different constitutional institutions each nation develops to advance its liberal ends, both unsuccessfully and successfully, including the important role of political psychology in their respective failures, drawing on the important work of the psychiatrist Dr. James Gilligan with whom I have cotaught for several years at the New York University School of Law and collaborated on a recently published book on what Shakespeare's plays show us about the psychology of violence, personal and political.[30] Why does American *Marbury* judicial review fail to meet its liberal ends of protecting human rights at least until World War II, while British common law and parliamentary sovereignty are for long periods much more successful? And how should we understand the increasing post-World War II importance of the British judiciary in monitoring the administrative law of parliament enforced by the executive, and the development, still controversial in the U.K., of the role accorded the British judiciary in giving effect to the Human Rights Act of 1998 (HRA), and the weight accorded by that legislation to the judgments of the European Court of Human Rights under the European Convention of Human Rights, in whose design the U.K. played an important role in 1953. And why the institutional changes, including the European

(Princeton, NJ: Princeton University Press, 2019); Mahmood Mamdani, *Neither Settler Nor Native: The Making and Unmaking of Permanent Minorities* (Cambridge, MA: Harvard University Press, 2020); Padraic X. Scanlan, *Slave Empire: How Slavery Built Modern Britain* (London: Robinson, 2020); Roderick Matthews, *Peace, Poverty, and Betrayal: A New History of British India* (London: Hurst, 2021); Sathnam Sanghera, *Empireland: How Imperialism Has Shaped Modern Britain* (London: Penguin, 2021); Lisa Ford, *The King's Peace: Law and Order in the British Empire* (Cambridge, MA: Harvard University Press, 2021); Mark Knights, *Trust and Distrust: Corruption in Office in Britain and Its Empire 1600–1850* (Oxford: Oxford University Press, 2021); Caroline Elkins, *Imperial Reckoning: The Untold Story of Britain's Gulag in Kenya* (New York: Owl Books, 2005); Caroline Elkins, *Legacy of Violence: A History of the British Empire* (New York: Alfred A. Knopf, 2022).

29 On this point, see Eric Stokes, *The English Utilitarians and India* (Oxford: Oxford at the Clarendon Press, 1959), pp. 273–311.

30 See Gilligan and Richards, *Holding a Mirror Up to Nature*.

Convention and HRA, domestic and international, after World War II? And why are these changes now contested in Britain under the current Conservative government, and on what grounds? How and why do the U.K. and the U.S., after their long separation, rediscover their common grounds in political liberalism in the Atlantic Charter of 1941 and later institutional innovations both nations forged? Both nations discover that they had made a catastrophic mistake in not taking seriously the aggressive anti-liberal violence of fascism, and that the protection of human rights at home could not be isolated from threats abroad. Have we learned from our mistakes, or rather sometimes repeated them (Iraq)?

As I earlier suggested, liberalism and democracy are not the same (the Athenian democracy was highly democratic in ways neither British nor American representative democracies are). Liberalism rests on the political conviction that legitimate government must protect universal human rights, which includes, of course, the rights of minorities. It is a conviction, in my view, that both British and American liberalism share, which is shown by the ways in which John Stuart Mill's arguments in both *On Liberty* and *The Subjection of Women* have had such political and constitutional resonance in both the U.K. and the U.S. and elsewhere. The great historical constitutional difference between the constitutionalism of these nations has been, since the late eighteenth century when Britain and the U.S. separated, importantly over the interpretation of the British Constitution that, until that point, both peoples believed they shared. This is shown by the different institutional embodiment each nation gave to Montesquieu's normative argument for the separation of powers, which he argued the British Constitution with its balance of powers between monarchy, a democratic House of Commons and aristocratic House of Lords (both enjoying parliamentary supremacy), and independent judiciary admirably embodied.[31] Montesquieu certainly argued that judicial independence was an important aspect of the British conception of its balanced constitution, but he did not defend a role for the judiciary in checking other branches of government,[32] which would have undermined parliamentary supremacy as the ultimate check on the excesses of the monarch and his ministers, and on even the people when they violated human rights, including the right to property (a conception of British constitutionalism that was, as we shall see, central to the liberalism of Edmund Burke). In contrast, the American constitutional conception of the separation of powers, defined by the first three Articles of the Constitution of 1787, not only repudiates parliamentary supremacy but also defines separate branches of the national government (an executive presidency, a bicameral democratically elected legislature with different terms and constituencies, and a judiciary that under *Marbury v. Madison* calls for judicial review of the constitutionality

31 See M. J. C. Vile, *Constitutionalism and the Separation of Powers*, 2nd ed. (Indianapolis, IN: Liberty Fund, 1998).

32 On this point, see ibid., p. 102.

of the other branches of the national government and also state government), precisely the checking function that the British conception of an independent judiciary lacks.

It is not only the British and the Americans that take a different view of the proper role of the judiciary in a liberal constitutionalism. In the wake of World War II, forms of constitutionalism, influenced by the examples of both the U.K. and the U.S., have taken different views, based on their own experience, of the proper role of the judiciary in a constitutional democracy. Several of Britain's former settler colonies (Australia and New Zealand) reject the American in favor of the British model;[33] another (Canada) has adopted American-style judicial review subject to parliamentary override both by the national and provincial parliaments;[34] and two others (South Africa and India) have adopted either strong forms of American-style judicial review (South Africa[35]) or weaker but still significant conceptions of judicial review because of the ease of parliamentary amendment, not parliamentary supremacy (India[36]). Other constitutional democracies in the nations of Western Europe, in the European Union, and elsewhere have gravitated to American-style judicial review, which at least one comparative constitutional lawyer has questioned as to whether such judicial review serves defensible normative aims in Canada, Israel, New Zealand, and South Africa,[37] and others query whether it has been effective or the extent of its effectiveness in the U.S.[38] and India,[39] arguing less so in the U.S. but more so in India. And the political theorist Jeremy Waldron, based on British constitutional experience, both prominently defends universal human rights and argues that the British parliament has better defended such human rights, including the right of abortion, than the U.S. Supreme Court, whose opinion in *Roe v. Wade* has now been overruled whereas the right of abortion remains broadly acceptable in

33 On these points, see Cheryl Saunders, *The Constitution of Australia: A Contextual Analysis* (Oxford: Hart, 2011); Matthew S. R. Palmer and Dean R. Knight, *The Constitution of New Zealand: A Contextual Analysis* (Oxford: Hart, 2022).

34 Jeremy Webber, *The Constitution of Canada: A Contextual Analysis* (Oxford: Hart, 2021).

35 Heinz Klug, *The Constitution of South Africa: A Contextual Analysis* (Oxford: Hart, 2021).

36 Arun K. Thiruvengadam, *The Constitution of India: A Contextual Analysis* (Oxford: Hart, 2017). However, in line with the eternity clauses of the German Basic Law, the Indian Supreme Court has appealed to a basic structure jurisprudence that limits the amendment powers and undermines the basic structure of Indian democratic constitutionalism. On this point, see Samuel Issacharoff, *Democracy Unmoored: Populism and the Corruption of Popular Sovereignty* (New York: Oxford University Press, 2023), pp. 124–29, 155, 173.

37 See, e.g., Ran Hirschl, *Towards Juristocracy: The Origins and Consequences of the New Constitutionalism* (Cambridge, MA: Harvard University Press, 2004).

38 See Gerald Rosenberg, *The Hollow Hope: Can Courts Bring about Social Change?* 2nd ed. (Chicago, IL: University of Chicago Press, 2008).

39 Gerald N. Rosenberg, Sudhir Krishnaswamy, and Shishir Bail, *A Qualified Hope: The Indian Supreme Court and Progressive Social Change* (Cambridge: Cambridge University Press, 2019).

the U.K. precisely because, on Waldron's view, the parliament both reasonably debated and democratically resolved the issue.[40]

It is for this reason that my comparative investigation of British and U.S. constitutionalism will explore what have been the strengths and weaknesses of both the British and American positions, and why there is now in the U.S. perhaps more skepticism by liberals about judicial review than there has ever been at least since World War II, undoubtedly heightened by the Supreme Court's recent radically illiberal turn that I criticize at some length, and why, in contrast, in the U.K. the judiciary has been increasingly looked to right the imbalance of power in the executive no longer balanced by the kind of parliamentary independence that Edmund Burke developed, endorsed, and defended.

Both British and American constitutionalism claim to speak to future generations, and my argument (Chapter 5) compares their success at doing so along a range of dimensions of written vs. unwritten constitutionalism, social democracy, transformations of Lockean thought, culture vs. institutions, the English Civil War and the American Civil War, U.K. referenda and Brexit, representation, and the democratic objection to judicial review.

It is the alliance of Britain and the U.S. as liberal democracies at threat in World War II from aggressive fascism that gives rise in both countries to arguments for new forms of national, transnational, and international institutions that would address the European political violence leading to World War I and culminating in World War II (Chapter 6). Such constitutional constructivism in both nations illustrates a Burkean wisdom in deliberating and implementing new constitutional institutions that take seriously the role of liberal institutions in addressing the political psychology of illimitable violence that, as Burke argued, warred on liberalism.

The recent development of populist forms of political illiberalism in the U.S., Britain, and elsewhere is the subject (Chapter 7) of a critique of the role patriarchal religion has played both in recent appointments to the U.S. Supreme Court and their originalist ideology, and in the politics of the U.K. urging watering down the Human Rights Act of 1998 that gave greater weight to opinions of the European Court of Human Rights interpreting the European Convention on Human Rights in the interpretive opinions of the British judiciary. The originalist approach of the new conservative majority of the Supreme Court in *Dobbs v. Jackson*, reversing *Roe v. Wade*, critically undermines the legitimacy of the U.S. Constitution in speaking to future generations and, on examination, rests on the anti-liberal psychology that Burke argued was the major threat to any defensible liberal constitutionalism. New natural law, the vehicle of this originalism, exemplifies what Burke meant by a "political religion."

The argument ends with a concluding discussion of the importance of these issues to liberal constitutionalism.

40 Jeremy Waldron, "The Core of the Case against Judicial Review," *Yale LJ* 115 (2006): 1346–406.

Acknowledgments

This work arose from collaborative work over the years with three remarkable and generous friends to each of whom I am indebted and with each of whom I have coauthored books, namely, Nicholas C. Bamforth (Queens College, Oxford),[1] James Gilligan,[2] and Carol Gilligan.[3]

The idea of a comparative historical study of the U.K. and U.S. constitutional law arose from ongoing weekly conversations on Zoom each week between Nicholas in London and myself in New York City during the years of the pandemic. I could not have written this book without these conversations and Nick's extraordinary generosity, intelligence, humor, patience, and support. Conversations with my colleague Jeremy Waldron about his seminar on enlightenment constitutionalism (including sharing his syllabus) were also invaluable.

James Gilligan and I have cotaught a seminar at the New York University School of Law for several years on retributivism, and we recently coauthored a book on Shakespeare's insights into personal and political violence, based on Jim's pathbreaking psychological insights into the causes and prevention of both personal and political violence. It was conversations with Jim that first suggested to me that Burke had made an important contribution to understanding political violence, and this book is built on the collaborative framework arising from our work together.

Carol Gilligan and I have cotaught a seminar, "Resisting Injustice," at the New York School of Law for the past 20 years, leading to our coauthoring two books on patriarchy's threat to democracy. Her insights into the developmental psychology of girls into women, and boys into men, have illuminated my understanding of the role of the initiation into patriarchy in the development of both women and men, and the crucial importance of resistance to patriarchy both to human happiness and to justice, as Burke's life and work illustrate.

1 Nicholas Bamforth and David A. J. Richards, *Patriarchal Religion, Gender, and Sexuality: A Critique of New Natural Law* (Cambridge: Cambridge University Press, 2008).

2 Gilligan and Richards, *Holding a Mirror Up to Nature*.

3 Gilligan and Richards, *The Deepening Darkness* and *Darkness Now Visible*.

Conversations with Phillip Blumberg have also guided and illuminated my work on this book, as they have all my creative work; and I am indebted to both Tarun Khaitan and Alexander Bubb for insights into both British colonialism in general and in particular in Ireland and India, and the relevant thought and poetry of William Butler Yeats on these issues.

My work on this book profited as well from a discussion of it with Charles B. Strozier's Bloomsbury Book Club, and I am grateful to all the participants in that discussion, including Charles Strozier, James Gilligan, John Alderdice, David Lotto, Michael Vincent Miller, John Riker, Harriet Wolfe, David Terman, James Block, Marcia Dobson, James Jones, Deborah Cher, and Jeffrey Stern.

I am grateful as well to Charlie Baker and Natalja Mortensen, my editors at Routledge, for their enthusiastic support to this book project, including a reader's report that was quite helpful.

This book was researched and written during summers supported by generous research grants from the New York University School of Law Filomen D'Agostino and Max E. Greenberg Faculty Research Fund, and I am grateful to the research committee for its support, as well as the support of Dean Trevor Morrison and his successor, Dean Troy McKenzie.

A work of this sort, so rooted in my personal life, arose in loving relationship with the person closest to me, Donald Levy, to whom I have dedicated this book.

Figure 0.1 Portrait of Edmund Burke: studio of Sir Joshua Reynolds © National Portrait Gallery, London.

Figure 0.2 Portrait of James Madison by Gilbert Stuart. Courtesy National Gallery of Art, Washington, D.C.

1 Burke's Liberal Constitutionalism

My investigation starts by looking closely at Burke's liberal constitutionalism developed in his four great expressions of liberal resistance, including to the injustice of the British treatment of Ireland, to the British policies against which the American colonies successfully revolted, to British colonial policies in India (the Hastings impeachment), and finally to the failure of British and American radical Whigs (Richard Price and Thomas Paine) to understand the clear and present danger of the threat to all forms of liberal constitutionalism of the disastrous constitutional experiments following the French Revolution, culminating in the Terror and Napoleon's aggressive imperialistic wars, prefiguring the political violence of twentieth- and twenty-first-century totalitarianism.[1] I have come to think that Burke had a brilliant understanding, at least for his time and perhaps for all time, not only of political liberalism and its connection to democratic constitutionalism, but what has *not* been seen by many historians of his thought, namely, his astonishing insights into the dark side of illiberal democracy, namely, the role of the humiliations inflicted by irrational prejudices rooted in deep liberal injustices on men and women, but largely men, that express themselves both in violent revolution and the violence of lynch mobs and genocidal and imperialistic violence.

Burke's passionate liberalism arose, I have come to think, from his moral indignation at the two humiliations that he had come to experience quite personally, the first of which touches my own experience as a gay man and the liberals, like myself and many others, who have played a role in the U.K. and the U.S. in arguing for gay rights as constitutional rights; and the second such indignation arises from ethnicity and religion—his being Irish (Burke spoke with a conspicuous Irish accent) and Protestant (like his father), yet his mother and wife being suspiciously Catholic in a period of long-standing British prejudice against Catholics. Because the issue of Burke's homosexuality will be the more

1 For a fuller discussion in some depth, see Richard Bourke, *Empire and Revolution: The Political Life of Edmund Burke* (Princeton: Princeton University Press, 2015).

DOI: 10.4324/9781003410966-1

controversial of my claims, I will need not only to draw on the best work on this issue, but also situate the whole issue in the larger framework of the codes of silence and concealment regarding homosexuality in eighteenth-century Britain through which gay men would both find one another and shield themselves from the virulent and quite violent homophobia of the period, including one of its poets (Pope) and another of its greatest musicians, Handel,[2] and perhaps Burke himself.

The first humiliation is the subject of Isaac Kramnick's important book, *The Rage of Edmund Burke: Portrait of an Ambivalent Conservative*.[3] Kramnick focuses on Burke's missing years (1750–56) when he flees from his tyrannical father in Ireland to study law in the inns of court in London and undergoes a personal crisis, clearly expressed in his letters and poems written during this period, centering both on his vocation (his rejection of law, his father's profession, for becoming a public intellectual publishing two important books and later becoming a politician and member of the House of Commons) and his sexuality and love life. He meets Will Burke, not a relation, a life-long intimate friend who not only lives with Burke and his family, but collaborates closely with Burke on important writings, including one about America that explains Burke's quite realistic understanding of the American situation, and plays a generous role in giving up his own proposed seat in parliament for Burke. The relationship is, in Kramnick's view, clearly homoerotic, shown by the poems Burke wrote to Will replete with expressions of sexual desire:

> The strong and weak consumes in the same fire,
> The force unequaled, equal the desire.[4]

And also there is the expression of overcoming shame to be intimately oneself:

> Can we, my friend, with any conscience bear
> To Shew our minds sheer naked as they are,
> Remove each veil of custom, pride or Art,
> Nor stretch a hand to hide one shameful part?[5]

Burke later writes of his relationship to Will as "tenderly loved, highly valued, and continually lived with, in a union not to be expressed, quite since our boyish years."[6] Stanley Ayling, another Burke biographer, comments on Burke's

2 For a brilliant and compelling investigation of this question, see Ellen T. Harris, *Handel as Orpheus: Voice and Desire in the Chamber Cantatas* (Cambridge, MA: Harvard University Press, 2001).

3 New York: Basic Books, 1977.

4 Ibid., p. 76.

5 Ibid., p. 77.

6 Ibid., p. 72.

"blinkered attachment" to Will, despite his improvidence, "there it is: loves other than sexual may be as blind."[7] No serious biographer doubts this was one of the central loves of Burke's life, which may, as Kramnick argues, have at some point been sexual. The ethical centrality of such personal relationships to Burke is shown by the way in which he connects state abridgments of such intimate relationships to what for him defines the inhumanity of the British actions in India involving "the forced sale of children"[8] or, later on in the French Revolution, "five or six hundred drunken women, calling at the bar of the Assembly for the blood of their own children, as being royalists or constitutionalists" or "fathers to demand the blood of their sons, toasting that Rome had but one Brutus, but that they could shew five hundred."[9] In *Reflections on the Revolution in France*, these are

> the worst of these politics of revolution ... : they temper and burden the breast, in order to prepare it for the desperate strokes which are sometimes used in extreme occasion ... . Plots, massacres, assassination, seem ... a trivial price for obtaining a revolution.[10]

The personal crisis Burke undoubtedly experienced was resolved by the care of a doctor whose daughter Burke later quite happily married. Burke not only includes Will in his intimate personal circle with his wife and children and brother, living with him in a relationship that lasts throughout their lives, as Will seeks opportunities in the West Indies and in India, all while he and Edmund stay in a close personal and mutually advantageous relationship. Kramnick makes quite clear that the relationship, and perhaps others, did not go unnoticed in late eighteenth-century Britain in one of its leading politicians and member of the House of Commons. Kramnick observes:

> That Burke might have been a homosexual or showed homosexual tendencies was not an idea foreign to his contemporaries. Rumours to this effect circulated in opposition circles for years, often as part of the campaign depicting Burke as a Jesuit. Contemporary cartoons, for example, shows him a particularly effeminate Jesuit. The ever-persistent rumors were given additional fuel by events in 1780, when Burke rose in the House of Commons to protest the treatment of two homosexuals, Theodosius Read and William

7 See Stanley Ayling, *Edmund Burke: His Life and Opinions* (New York: St. Martin's Press, 1988), p. 134.

8 Bourke, *Empire and Revolution*, p. 845.

9 Edmund Burke, "The First Letter on a Regicide Speech," in Iain Hampsher-Monk (ed.), *Revolutionary Writings* (Cambridge: Cambridge University Press, 2014), pp. 253–334 at 311.

10 Edmund Burke, "Reflections on the Revolution in France," in Hampsher-Monk, *Revolutionary Writings*, pp. 3–250 at 65.

> Smith, who were sentenced, as part of their punishment for sodomy, to stand in the pillory for an hour. Smith dies a victim of mob brutality. Burke spoke eloquently in the House against this barbarity and secured a pension for Smith's widow. While sodomy was, he insisted, in his speech, "a crime of all others the most detestable, because it tended to vitiate the morals of the whole community, and to defeat the first and chief end of society," the punishment of it should be tempered with mercy, inasmuch as it was a crime "of the most equivocal nature and the more difficult to prove." Better than cruelty and fury, he suggested, were "reproach and shame." The *Morning Post* of 13 April responded to Burke.
>
> Every *man* applauds the spirit of the spectators, and every *woman* thinks their conduct right. It remained only for the patriotic Mr. Burke to insinuate that the crime these men committed should not be held in the highest detestation.
>
> Burke brought suit for defamation of character against the newspaper, and he won his case.[11]

Earlier, in 1774, Burke successfully called for exercise of the prerogative of mercy for a lieutenant of the Royal Artillery who had been sentenced to death for sodomy.[12]

We must situate all this in the larger cultural framework of eighteenth century, as it bears on our understanding of how remarkable Burke's liberal resistance may have been, which even Kramnick does not fully appreciate.

At the beginning of the eighteenth century in Britain, condemnation of homosexuality became an increasingly public matter. In the seventeenth century, a prevalent attitude in England associated the notion that homosexuality was imported from Italy with the danger of Catholicism and popery, and the execution in 1631 of the Catholic Earl of Castlehaven for sodomy and other sexual crimes must be read in the context of virulent contemporary anti-Catholic sentiment.[13]

In the first decades of the eighteenth century, however, the issue of homosexuality itself drew public attention because of

> the simultaneous development of a network of molly houses and the Societies for the Reformation of Manners. The molly houses, although

11 Kramnick, *The Rage of Edmund Burke*, p. 84.

12 See Stanley Ayling, *Edmund Burke: His Life and Opinions* (New York: St. Martin's Press, 1988), pp. 53–54.

13 Harris, *Handel as Orpheus*, p. 18. For an illuminating background on both seventeenth- and eighteenth-century British attitudes to homosexuality, including on the molly houses, see Matt Cook (ed.), *A Gay History of Britain: Love and Sex between Men since the Middle Ages* (Oxford: Greenwood World, 2007), pp. 77–144. See also Alan Bray, *Homosexuality in Renaissance England* (New York: Columbia University Press, 1995).

> many who frequented them had wives and children at home, represent a landmark in the development of a separate identity for men who engaged in same-sex acts. At the same time, the political instability of the late seventeenth century and early eighteenth centuries, including the fear of external attack and internal revolution, of popery and absolutism, led to a rise of zealous reformers … . The identification of certain establishments as molly houses made them particularly vulnerable to attack, the more so because the customers were typically members of the merchant and lower classes and the reforming societies "dared not attack the aristocracy, at least not directly." The Society for the Reformation of Manners was founded in 1690; by 1699 there were nine societies and by 1701 there was twenty in London alone.
>
> The Societies quickly began their work of rounding up sodomites for prosecution, and by 1698 a few individuals had been targeted for entrapment; 1699 saw the first successful group arrest … . In 1701 a larger raid netted … between forty and one hundred arrests. At least three of these men committed suicide.
>
> After months of preparation and infiltration, in February 1716 Mother Clap's molly house was surrounded and forty men taken in arrest. Within months about twenty other houses were raided as well. Although many of those arrested were released for want of evidence, in fifteen cases of sodomy brought to trial from the same period between 1726 and 1730 four men were hanged; eight were fined and sentenced to prison and the pillory (from which one died); and three were acquitted. These numbers can be compared to twelve heterosexual rape cases from the same period, where one was hanged, one punished, and ten acquitted.[14]

Prosecutions in the Netherlands were even worse:

> In 1730 and 1731 the Netherlands initiated a far more horrific purge in which hundreds of men were arrested for sodomy and at least sixty were publicly executed by ghastly means, such as strangling and burning, drowning in a barrel, or strangling and drowning tied to a 100-pound weight. These executions were widely publicized in London … .
>
> In 1738, with the initial blast of reformers' zeal expended and public concern over paid informers rising, the Societies for the Reformation of Manners disbanded, giving themselves the credit in their final report for "instigating the prosecution of numbers of sodomites and sodomitical houses."[15]

14 Harris, *Handel as Orpheus*, pp. 241–42.
15 Ibid., p. 241.

It is worth noting that "throughout the eighteenth century [including during Burke's life time] the assailants of convicted sodomites in London consisted largely of women who were encouraged thus to revenge the supposed insult inflicted on them by men who loved other men,"[16] precisely the mobs Burke condemned in his 1780 speech to parliament.

This level of public opprobrium in the eighteenth century affected even those not prosecuted:

> As the cases of the dramatists Isaac Bickerstaff and Samuel Foote later in the century would show, an accusation of sodomy was sufficient to ruin a career. Even the aristocratic class, traditionally less affected by an accusation or acknowledgement of same-sex desire than were artists, merchants, or laborers, was slowly retreating behind a wall of silence. Although at the end of the seventeenth century Lord Rochester could banter publicly in his writings about his same-sex loves, Lord Hervey in the eighteenth century not only avoided any public commentary about himself but when accused in 1731 of being a "pathick" (the passive partner in a sodomitical relationship) fought a duel to protect his honor before retreating into silence. When Lord Bateman separated from his wife in 1738 on account of his "male seraglio," he seems to have been spared legal action partly because he maintained a façade of silence. His wife's grandmother, the Duchess of Marlborough, wrote of him at this time: "They say Lord Bateman has consented to do great things in this separation, which, if true, shows he is very much frightened."[17]

Why such silence in the first half of the eighteenth century?—"No written record … expresses antipathy to or outrage against such extreme punishments."[18] The repressive psychology is clearly fear, whether the fear of Lord Bateman, or that of Bentham himself, clearly admitted in the unpublished papers of the English legal philosopher Jeremy Bentham (1748–1842) who had published his *Introduction to the Principles of Morals and Legislation* in 1789 defending his utilitarian theory that the object of law should be the greatest happiness of the great number. These unpublished papers contain for the first time in a major political and legal philosopher a cogent criticism not only of the criminalization of homosexuality, but also of homophobia itself.[19] But, in writing about this unpublished work and probably his reasons for not publishing, Bentham writes:

16 Ibid., p. 234.

17 Ibid., p. 240.

18 Ibid., p. 230.

19 See Jeremy Bentham, *Of Sexual Irregularities, and Other Writings on Sexual Morality*, edited by Philip Schofield, Catherine Pease-Watkin, and Michael Quinn (Oxford: Oxford University Press, 2014).

> A hundred times have I shuddered at the view of the perils I was exposing myself to in encountering the opinions of men's minds on [this] subject. As often have I resolved to turn aside from a road so full of precipices, I have trembled at the thoughts of the indignation that must be raised against the Apologist of a crime that has been looked upon by many, and these excellent men, as one among the blackest under Heaven. But the dye is now cast, & having thus far adhered with the undeviating fidelity [to] the principles of general utility I at first adopted, I will not at least abandon them for considerations of personal danger. I will not have to reproach myself with the thought that those principles which my judgment has approved, my fears have compelled me to abandon.[20]

We know with certainly who were "these excellent men" whom Bentham so feared, in particular, Blackstone, whom Bentham had heard as a law student at Oxford and was the critical object of much of Bentham's utilitarian/positivist legal philosophy. It is important to remind ourselves that for a quite long period the traditional cultural status of homosexuals in America and Britain was not, unlike people of color or women, a servile social status unjustly rationalized on racist or sexist grounds, but no space at all. It was, in Blackstone's words, "a crime not fit to be named; *peccatum illud horribile, inter christianos non nominandum*" in his *Commentaries*, vol. 4, *215—not mentionable, let alone discussed or assessed. Blackstone's *Commentaries*, published in 1765, framed the American understanding of British common law, adopted in the colonies and later in the states of the American republic, as American common law, long before it was contested in Great Britain by the Bloomsbury Group and others, linked by them to the critique of the violence of British imperial patriarchy, as I show in *The Rise and Fall of the British Empire*[21] (Britain would decriminalize consensual homosexuality in 1967). Such total silencing of any reasonable discussion rendered homosexuality in America and Britain, a kind of cultural death, naturally thus understood and indeed condemned as a kind of ultimate heresy or treason against essential moral values. The English legal scholar Tony Honoré captured this point exactly in *Sex Law* by his observation about the contemporary status of the homosexual: "It is not primarily a matter of breaking rules but of dissenting attitudes. It resembles political or religious dissent, being an atheist in Catholic Ireland or a dissident in Soviet Russia."[22]

It is against this background that we can see just how remarkable Burke's parliamentary speeches of 1780 on sodomy prosecutions were. Ellen Harris, in her

20 Quoted in Harris, *Handel as Orpheus*, p. 231.

21 See David A. J. Richards, *The Rise and Fall of the British Empire: Liberal Resistance and the Bloomsbury Group* (Cambridge: Cambridge University Press, 2013).

22 Tony Honoré, *Sex Law* (London: Duckworth, 1978) p. 89.

path-breaking study of Handel as, probably like Pope, a closeted homosexual,[23] observes, after having described Bentham's fear of going public with his indictment of British homophobia:

> On 11 April 1780, following another horrible death of a convicted sodomite in the pillory (and the permanent injury of another), Edmund Burke, in what was perhaps the first public statement on this issue in the House of Commons, proposed a bill that would have abolished this form of punishment.[24]

A London newspaper reports the events Burke condemns:

> A description of the "vast Concourse of People [that] had assembled upon the Occasion … who had collected dead Dogs, Cats, … [etc.] in great Abundance, which were plentifully thrown at them," and of the death of one of the men convicted for attempted sodomy and the horrible injuries of the other appears in *The Daily Advertiser*, 11 April 1780, p. 1, col. 2.[25]

Burke's great speech of 1780 begins with a quite precise description of these newspaper reports:

> He said, the matter which had induced him to make these reflections was the perusal of a melancholy circumstances stated in the newspapers of this morning … . The relation he alluded to, was that unhappy and horrid murder of a poor wretch, condemned to stand in the pillory the preceding day. The account stated that two men (Reed and Smith) had been doomed to this punishment; that one of them being short of stature, and remarkably shortnecked, he could not reach the hole made for the admission of his head, in the awkward and ugly instrument used in this mode of punishment; that the officers of justice, nevertheless, forced his head through the hole, and the poor wretch hung rather than walked as the pillory turned round: that previous to his being put in, he had deprecated the vengeance of the mob, and begged that mercy, which from their exasperation at his crime, and their want of considering the consequences of their cruelty, they seemed very little to bestow. That he soon grew black in the face and the blood forced itself out of his nostrils, his eyes

23 Harris' case for this, based on both a close study of Handel's life and works, is reasonable and persuasive. See Richard Taruskin in his *Music in the Seventeenth and Eighteenth Centuries: The Oxford History of Western Music* (Oxford: Oxford University Press, 2010), vol. 2, p. 340: "Many scholars now agree, Handel, a lifelong bachelor, was probably what we now call a closeted gay man."

24 Harris, *Handel as Orpheus*, p. 231. Burke's speech is given in *The Parliamentary History of England from the Earliest Period to the Year 1803* (London: Printed by T. C. Hansard, 1814), vol. 21, cols. 388–89.

25 Quoted in Harris, *Handel as Orpheus*, p. 409, n. 53.

> and his ears. That the mob, nevertheless attacked him and fellow criminal with great fury. That the officers seeing his situation, opened the pillory, and the poor wretch fell down dead on the stand of the instrument. The other man, he understood was so maimed and hurt by what had been thrown at him, that he now lay without hope of recovery.[26]

After mentioning, as earlier noted in Kramnick's quotation of the speech, what would have been in this period a "mandatory depreciation"[27] of a crime that "could scarcely be mentioned, much less defended or extenuated," Burke goes on in the speech to deal with matters not mentioned by Kramnick, but dealing with the law itself, namely, the use of the pillory "as much more severe than execution at Tyburn, as to die in torment, was more dreadful than momentary death."[28] As Louis Crompton makes clear in his more extensive discussion of these events:

> Burke then seized the occasion to propose that a bill be introduced to abolish the pillory since it was open to such abuse. Burke's brave and unprecedented raising of the issue prompted others to voice their own misgivings. Another member told how a man he had known at Bury, condemned for the same crime, has swallowed poison fearing "the populace would be so exasperated against him that they would take his life." He was exposed the next day and was "so severely treated by the populace that he dies that night in goal, and whether he died from the poison, or in consequence of his ill treatment from the mob had never been ascertained."
>
> Burke had the satisfaction of seeing the undersheriff for Surrey tried for murder; not surprisingly, the jury acquitted him. Burke himself, though complemented in the House on his humanity, suffering much abuse in the press for his stand. The *Morning Post* complained: "Every *man* applauds the spirit of the spectators, and every *woman* thinks their conduct right. It remained only for the patriotic Mr. Burke to insinuate that the crime these men committed should not be held in the highest detestation than ignominious death." Four years later, the *Public Advertiser* also attacked Burke maliciously for showing sympathy for homosexuals. In both cases Burke sued for libel and won. He was able to obtain a pension for the dead coachman's widow, a circumstance that suggests that not all levels of British officialdom were as passionately homophobic as the press.[29]

26 Quoted in Louis Crompton, *Byron and Greek Love: Homophobia in 19th-Century England* (Berkley: University of California Press, 1985), p. 32.

27 Ibid.

28 Quoted in ibid.

29 Crompton, *Byron and Greek Love*, pp. 32–33.

In contrast to Crompton (publishing in 1985), Kramnick (publishing in 1977) deals with the issue of Burke's homosexuality in the then current terms among American psychiatrists and psychoanalysts (not, notably, Freud himself) of neurosis,[30] supposedly clarifying the sometimes extravagant invocations of sexual abuse in his speeches, condemning, for example, the horrors of the British treatment of Indian women (Kramnick's book was published only four years after the Board of Trustees of the American Psychiatric Association in 1973 controversially affirmed the ruling that homosexuality should be deleted from the list of mental disorders, a view Freud himself had earlier advocated[31]). There is, in my and Crompton's view, nothing neurotic either in those speeches or in the way Burke speaks in public, even as a public man in the House of Commons, of unjust mob violence against a despised sexual minority, a mob violence, as we shall shortly see, he himself also directly experienced as an alleged Catholic sympathizer during the Gordon riots. If Kramnick and I are right about Burke's understandably repressed homosexuality, what is remarkable is that, even in such a homophobic period, he expressed his liberal indignation in public certainly against forms of irrational mob violence and was condemned for it. That is not neurosis, but a remarkable exercise of courageous liberal voice, an intimate understanding of and feeling for unjustly despised minorities that was at the psychological heart of Burke's liberal constitutionalism and his astonishing insights, as we shall see, into political violence. It also clarifies why, as we shall see, Burke distinguished liberal constitutionalism from democracy.

It is astonishing to me that although all the biographies of Burke acknowledge the love between Edmund and Will and many of them knew of Kramnick's remarkable book, none of them, except Kramnick and then through a glass darkly, *connects* his remarkable record of sometimes politically effective liberal indignation to the degree to which one of the great loves of his life was for another man, to whom Burke stayed in relationship throughout their lives (helping and supporting one another, including Edmund Burke's understanding of both America and India, in the latter of which Will was to spend some time seeking employment); Will never marries.

Burke was to move in some of the most distinguished literary and political circles of British London, a member of "the Club" including close friendships with Samuel Johnson and James Boswell, Johnson's biographer, as well as the

30 For criticism of this approach, see Kenneth Lewes, *The Psychoanalytic Theory of Male Homosexuality* (New York: Simon & Schuster, 1988). For more recent discussions along these lines, see R. W. Isay, *Becoming Gay: The Journey to Self-Acceptance* (New York: Vintage, 1966); R. W. Isay, *Being Homosexual: Gay Men and Their Development* (New York: Vintage, 1989); R. W. Isay, *Commitment and Healing: Gay Men and the Need for Romantic Love* (New York: Wiley, 2006); K. Corbett, *Boyhoods: Rethinking Masculinities* (New Haven, CT: Yale University Press, 2009).

31 See, on this point, Lewes, *The Psychoanalytic Theory of Male Homosexuality*, pp. 213–41.

painter Joshua Reynolds, and other luminaries of the period. His intellectual and expressive gifts were recognized and rewarded by the Rockingham Whigs, and his long service as their spokesperson in the House of Commons placed him at the center of British public life. He was also a committed Protestant Anglican Christian. In a cultural world framed by Blackstone's Christian homophobia, whatever homoerotic feelings Burke had for Will and Will for him could never be publicly acknowledged, but the depth of their long loving relationship, as love, is, if anything, confirmed by how, as we earlier saw, his biographer Stanley Ayling puzzles over what many regarded during Burke's lifetime as his "blinkered attachment" to Will, despite his improvidence, concluding: "There it is: loves other than sexual may be as blind."[32] And why not sexual at some point as well, as Kramnick documents? Why cannot we see and appreciate the power of love, gay or straight, in a well-lived human life in all its complexity?

It should be an important feature of our coming to honest terms with the unreasonable treatment of sexuality in general and homosexuality in particular by historical forms of Christianity[33] that we can now better understand remarkable people like Burke who had to accept such unreasonable treatment as normative, and yet still remain vitally alive in the homosexual love Burke held onto throughout his life. Having myself lived through an earlier period of my life quite like Burke's, I understand this psychology intimately and how finding and holding on to the love of another man becomes central to one's sense of a range of injustices inflicted on stigmatized minorities (afflicted by what I called a culture of moral slavery directed at people of color, Jews, women, and others[34]) even when that indignation cannot be directly expressed, as queer people, like myself, may and do express it today.[35] But, even under the repressive circumstances of the cultural homophobia under which Burke lived, Burke like other such creative men could and did. The psychiatrist Hans Loewald offers a psychoanalytic view of sublimation not as a neurotic defense against unacceptable impulses, but as a development of intellectual and emotionally mature competence and ego strength[36] that fits my own developmental experience and may fit Burke's. On this view, which questions the distinction between

32 See Stanley Ayling, *Edmund Burke: His Life and Opinions* (New York: St. Martin's Press, 1988), p. 134.

33 For a fuller discussion, see Nicholas C. Bamforth and David A. J. Richards, *Patriarchal Religion, Sexuality, and Gender: A Critique of New Natural Law* (Cambridge: Cambridge University Press, 2008).

34 For a fuller discussion, see Carol Gilligan and David A. J. Richards, *The Deepening Darkness: Patriarchy, Resistance, and Democracy's Future* (Cambridge: Cambridge University Press, 2009), pp. 10, 18–20, 72, 133–34, 197, 215.

35 On my personal history, see David A. J. Richards, *Boys' Secrets and Men's Loves: A Memoir* (Bloomington, IN.: Xlibris, 2019).

36 For Loewald on sublimation, see Hans W. Loewald, *The Essential Loewald: Collected Papers and Monographs* (Hagerstown, MD: University Publishing Group, 2000), pp. 439–520.

primary and secondary processes,[37] the experience of culturally forbidden desire is developmentally transformed from quite early on into larger cultural patterns of resisting injustice in other related areas, finding and speaking in a universalist resisting voice that, in resisting injustices to the Irish, Americans, Indians, and the French, was inspired, so I have to think, by the injustice inflicted on his own personal and political life, finding and constructing culturally confirmed interpersonal meaning through resistance. Burke's remarkably contemporary, almost anthropological focus on culture and cultural evolution, supports this interpretation. What drew me to the closer study of Burke was my sense of what his struggles were and how admirably he stood his ground, liberal resistance becoming the core of his being and his larger political and constitutional significance in the ongoing project of political liberalism. And political liberalism, for Burke and for me, has a cultural evolution and an enduring human value in any reasonable understanding of a humanism that can save us from war and violence, a point Kant saw roughly at the time Burke was writing.[38]

I believe I also understand why it was, in light of the unjust humiliations Burke experienced as a repressed homosexual (the insults directed even at his criticism of mob violence against a gay man), and as Irish and sympathetic to Catholicism (again subject to mob violence), Burke understood so well the psychology of terror, the central psychological insight of his *Reflections*, earlier discussed in *A Philosophical Enquiry into the Sublime and Beautiful*. It is what Bentham acknowledges with such honesty when he explains his fear of even writing about the issue: "A hundred times have I shuddered at the view of the perils I was exposing myself to in encountering the opinions of men's minds on [this] subject." Bentham was independently wealthy, and yet acknowledges fear leading to silence: great wealth, as in the case of William Beckford (whom Bentham had met), fled and never returned to Britain after newspapers disclosed a sexual relationship with a 16-year-old.[39] The only protection for gay men was silence, or hypocrisy (James I, an active homosexual with aristocratic lovers, "nevertheless, in his *Basilikon Doron*, ostentatiously listed sodomy as one of the of the half-dozen capital crimes that a king should never on any account pardon"[40]). Burke, in contrast, was a member of the House of Commons, and yet nonetheless publicly condemns homophobic violence facilitated by the pillory as a punishment, which brings on him homophobic insult and contempt, which no other man of this period was prepared to endure in order not to be silenced. Speaking in this way and in this context appears to have been for Burke a

37 See Hans Loeward, "Primary Process, Secondary Process, and Language," in *The Essential Loewald: Collected Papers and Monographs*, pp. 178–206.

38 See Hans Kant (ed.), "Perpetual Peace: A Philosophical Sketch," in *Kant's Political Writings* (Cambridge: Cambridge University Press, 1970), pp. 93–130.

39 See Crompton, *Byron and Greek Love*, pp. 118–20.

40 Ibid., p. 42. On Byron's similar hypocrisy, see pp. 120–21.

matter of his sense of *public* liberal responsibility as a member of the House of Commons, not a private matter.[41] Kramnick's description of the speech is worth at this point repeating:

> Burke spoke eloquently in the House against this barbarity and secured a pension for Smith's widow. While sodomy was, he insisted, in his speech, "a crime of all others the most detestable, because it tended to vitiate the morals of the whole community, and to defeat the first and chief end of society," the punishment of it should be tempered with mercy, inasmuch as it was a crime "of the most equivocal nature and the more difficult to prove."[42]

Burke's focus is on insensate mob violence, triggered, as we earlier learned, by humiliated patriarchal womanhood: "throughout the eighteenth century the assailants of convicted sodomites in London consisted largely of women who were encouraged thus to revenge the supposed insult inflicted on them by men who loved other men."[43] It is the same psychology of humiliation Burke was to anatomize in the violent Parisian mobs, including the women, as we shall see, attacking Marie Antoinette at Versailles. Such violent London mobs directed at convicted homosexuals in the pillory were to continue in Britain well into the nineteenth century; foreign visitors were reminded, when they saw street women tormenting the prisoners, of the women of the French Revolution;[44] and newspapers, as in Burke's time, urged on such populist vengeance, advocating even the death penalty.[45] The issue of such populist violence, elicited by the supposed humiliation from unconventional or unusual "unnatural" gender roles (Marie had certainly been so regarded in anti-royalist propaganda of the period,[46] including alleged adultery and lesbianism[47]), appears to be the heart of the matter, as we can see in the very terms in which the *Morning Post* condemned Burke's defense of homosexuals: "Every *man* applauds the spirit of the spectators, and every *woman* thinks their conduct right. It remained only for the patriotic Mr.

41 When the famed "Ladies of Llangollen," who lived as a same-sex couple privately in Wales, were exposed by a newspaper, they asked Burke whether to sue for libel to protect their private lives. He advised them not to sue. See Crompton, *Byron and Greek Love*, pp. 103–04.

42 Kramnick, *The Rage of Edmund Burke*, p. 84.

43 Ibid., p. 234.

44 Crampton, *Byron and Greek Love*, pp. 165–66.

45 Ibid., p. 167.

46 See Lynn Hunt, "The Many Bodies of Marie Antoinette: Political Pornography and the Problem of the Feminine in the French Revolution," in Lynn Hunt (ed.), *Eroticism and the Body Politic* (Baltimore, MD: The Johns Hopkins University Press, 1991), pp. 108–31.

47 As an example of this widespread view not only in France, Samuel Johnson's friend Hester Thrale wrote a few months before the French revolution: "The Queen of France is at the Head of a Set of Monsters call'd by each other *Sapphists,* who boast her Example; and deserve to be thrown with the *He* Demons that haunt each other likewise, into Mount Vesuvius." Quoted in Crompton, *Byron and Greek Love*, pp. 35–36.

Burke to insinuate that the crime these men committed should not be held in the highest detestation than ignominious death." The newspaper *approves* the violence and claims no one could be a true man or a true woman who did not approve the violence. Even Bentham takes seriously and rationally exposes the irrationality of the widespread homophobic view (found, for example, in the Orpheus myth as told by Ovid in his *Metamorphoses*,[48] Orpheus murdered by the Thracian women—dismembering him—because of his preference for men[49]) that homosexuality humiliates women, a view that rationalizes the violent homicidal rage of women and others in defense of patriarchal gender roles now in doubt and thus at threat.[50] The issue of enforcing patriarchal gender roles is quite clear here, indeed by illimitable violence if anyone like the "sodomites" flouts such roles or like Burke implicitly criticizes the violence enforcing such gender roles. The violence of patriarchy could not be more salient, and Burke's resistance to it more telling about the depth of his liberalism and his psychological understanding of the roots of mob violence, the subject of "Reflections on the Revolution in France."

In his path-breaking study of male violence based on his work with violent criminals in American prisons, Dr. James Gilligan observes the central role homophobia plays in the violence of such criminals inflicted on other criminals with whom they are often having sex, consensually and non-consensually.[51] Indeed, Gilligan has come to think that homophobia, expressing violence against men who love other men because they violate the norms of patriarchal manhood, is implicit in male violence generally, inflicted on anyone (male or female) who flouts patriarchal gender roles (personal communication from James Gilligan). But, women are much less prone to homicidal violence than men, so how should we understand the homophobic violence of the London and Parisian mobs, including women prominently?

When women are homicidally violent, like Medea killing her children when her lover abandons her for another woman, it arises from very extreme humiliations, a shaming, as in Euripides' play, in which, as Medea explains:

> Yes, I can endure guilt, however horrible;
> The laughter of my enemies I will not endure.[52]

48 See Ovid, *Metamorphoses*, translated by David Raeburn (New York: Penguin, 2004), pp. 385–86, 422–25.

49 On this point, see Harris, *Handel as Orpheus*, pp. 32–35, 43–45, 155, 238–39.

50 On this point, see Crompton, *Byron and Greek Love*, pp. 49–52. On the shifts in gender conceptions during this period, see Randolph Trumbach, *Sex and the Gender Revolution. Volume One: Heterosexuality and the Third Gender in Enlightenment London* (Chicago: University of Chicago Press, 1998).

51 See Trumbach, *Sex and the Gender Revolution*, pp. 76, 81, 83–84, 156–57, 164, 171, 189.

52 Euripides, "Medea," in *Medea and Other Plays*, translated by Philip Vellacott (London: Penguin, 1963), pp. 17–61 at 41.

As in many other such myths, there is a psychological reality behind them. James Gilligan, for example, has seen this pattern in contemporary Medeas[53] and suggested to me the same pattern in the London mobs (personal communication from Gilligan). In Medea's case, the humiliation was of her extraordinarily self-sacrificial love for Jason (helping him secure the Golden Fleece and then killing and dismembering her brother to distract her father following the fleeing couple[54]); and she certainly sees women's experience (giving birth) as not only on a par with but worse than men in war.[55] As she explains in the Euripides play (see above quote), such shaming of her womanhood extinguishes any inhibiting guilt she might otherwise feel. The homophobic mobs of women in London and Paris assume the gender roles patriarchy rigidly prescribes for men and women, namely that men must support women, and women's economic and personal well-being (given the limited roles otherwise available to women) requires that men must do so. But, many of the men, convicted as "sodomites," were themselves married with children, and women, as required by patriarchy as reflected in the illimitable violence of the Thracian women, violently enforce the gender roles these men are assumed to have flouted and that they believe so threaten them not only economically, but in their psyches so intimately (abandonment shaming them). It is a familiar enough feature of patriarchy reflected in Shakespeare's penetrating psychological studies of women like Lady Macbeth and Volumnia, the mother of Coriolanus, that wives like Lady Macbeth and mothers like Volumnia enforce on their husbands or sons the codes of manhood patriarchy requires, shaming them, as Lady Macbeth and Volumnia do, to fulfill their patriarchal roles, even unto their deaths.[56] Indeed, the jealousy that drives a Medea to violence when her husband betrays her with another woman may be exacerbated under patriarchy when women are, by patriarchal law and cultural convention, deemed to be threatened by men unspeakably loving other men, but less so by the heterosexual dalliances of men under patriarchy. Men's heterosexuality under patriarchy is much freer than that of women, including the eighteenth-century male libertinism in Britain and rampant prostitution in London.[57] Patriarchy may limit women's power under patriarchy to control heterosexual men; but homosexuals were an unspeakable caste apart and homophobia was culturally encouraged, indeed mandated by law (including not only the pillory, but sometimes hangings). For women in these mobs, gay men loving

53 See James Gilligan, *Violence: Reflections on a National Epidemic* (New York: Vintage Books, 1997), pp. 20, 58.

54 See htttps://en.wikipedia.org/wiki/Medea.

55 "I'd rather stand three times in the front line than bear/One child:" Euripides, "Medea," p. 25.

56 For a further discussion of both Lady Macbeth and Volumnia along these lines, see James Gilligan and David A. J. Richards, *Holding a Mirror Up to Nature: Shame, Guilt, and Violence in Shakespeare* (Cambridge: Cambridge University Press, 2022), pp. 67–77, 89–93.

57 Trumbach, *Sex and the Gender Revolution*, pp. 69–228.

men would in such a homophobic culture be experienced as men abandoning not only the indispensable support but the love women expected from men, an abandonment of devoted love that would, like Medea's abandonment by Jason, be experienced an irreparable loss and thus a shaming of patriarchal womanhood that could be and was expressed in homicidal violence against persons upon whom the legal culture itself unleashed violence. What is remarkable is that, in a culture that terrorized even Bentham not to speak his mind about the injustice of such mindless violence inflicted by law and the public, Burke spoke in a public voice (in the House of Commons no less) condemning a legal culture that encouraged such violence, and indeed connecting it, as he did, to a larger understanding of the roots of anti-liberal violence in France and elsewhere.

As I argue at greater length below, Burke's psychological argument is about the strains and vulnerabilities in a culture in transition from a shame to a guilt culture in which the emerging guilt culture, which I associate with democratic liberalism, must deal with the still powerful shame culture that it is resisting. Such shame cultures rest, as I have argued at length elsewhere,[58] on a patriarchal psychology, so clear in the Roman Republic, that violently wars on any perceived threat to its entrenched patriarchal manhood, including Rome's endless wars. When patriarchy is at threat, as it is from the emergence of a guilt culture, it reacts with irrational violence directed at the very convictions, often liberal, that challenge it. Any liberal like Burke, who in fact was brought up in such a period in transition, would experience intrapsychically such violence directed against his liberal convictions, and this is, I believe, the background of how Burke came to understand terror and its role in the repression of such convictions, including doubts about the shame culture beliefs he still shared ambivalently at least to some degree (e.g., doubts about its violent homophobia). Indeed, his parliamentary speech appeals to shame not state-enforced violence as the way to deal with sodomy, which is consistent with his ambivalence, struggling with doubt arising from internalized shame and guilt.

My reason for thinking this is precisely that even in a period when he would stand absolutely nothing to gain and much to lose from exposing in parliament his liberal horror at the London mobs tearing a gay men limb from limb, he chose to do so; and then there is as well his horror at the anti-Catholic London mobs during the Gordon riots directed at Burke largely because Burke, though Protestant, was known to be critical of Britain's illiberal policies against the Catholic Irish. Burke knew the psychology of terror intimately, and nothing was more terrifying in eighteenth-century Britain than accusations of homosexuality:

58 See Gilligan and Richards, *The Deepening Darkness*, pp. 9–120.

> So potent an instrument of terror were they that judges of the King's Bench ruled in 1779 that their use in extortion cases made the crime equivalent to highway robbery at pistol point.[59]

Burke's greatest achievement was to bring to the public mind of a culture in transition from patriarchy to liberalism the reactionary threat of violent homophobia, and the like, to political liberalism, which he apparently was the first to see and take seriously understandably in light of the culturally important transition from a shame to a guilt culture he both observed and advanced in late eighteenth-century Europe and America. It is a political tragedy that his critique was thought by many in Europe to align him with a reactionary authoritarian and absolutist monarchist culture he in fact despised.

Why the difference between Bentham and Burke? Burke was not, of course, prepared to go as far as Bentham in his critique of British homophobia, but in focusing on mob violence he is in fact publicly highlighting and exposing critically irrational homophobic violence, about which Bentham never publishes in his life time though he was the first political theorist who condemned it as well as the criminalization of homosexually so unequivocally and with such great and clarifying rational force. There is to me a salient point of the psychology that moves to resistance to injustice that explains and clarifies Burke's speech, namely, his continuing love for Will Burke that nourished and supported both of them throughout their lives both personally and politically. Only an enduring love that strong sustains, in my experience, the kind of resisting voice Burke found in himself and was moved to give voice to in the most political and public of places, the House of Commons. If liberalism means anything, it means the value and importance of that kind of voice based on the human rights of despised and outcast minorities; and if constitutional government means anything, it means a space for that voice must be constitutionally protected. On this point, Ellen Harris' comment on Handel's probable same-sex loves in a still homophobic and sexist culture is illuminating:

> Within the context of the eighteenth century, it would have been normal for Handel to share his creative and intellectual interests with men. Generally speaking, women were still not given the benefit of a serious education, so that the "marriage of true minds" could only occur between men—suggesting at least one possible reason the biblical David could say of his deceased friend Jonathan. "The love to me was wonderful, passing the love of women."[60]

59 Crompton, *Byron and Greek Love*, p. 125.
60 Harris, *Handel as Orpheus*, p. 22.

Burke was apparently quite happily married and devoted to his children, but his enduring love for Will gave him something unique, "tenderly loved, highly valued, and continually lived with, in an union not to be expressed, quite since our boyish years,"[61] a love that lasted and played a significant role in Burke's understanding of both America and India, on which he drew in two of his great acts of liberal resistance (America and India). Such a gender-bending love itself gives rise to resistance to protect not only the love itself, but, as in Burke's case, a wider resistance to other forms of injustice.[62]

The other humiliation Burke endured has been explored by Conor Cruise O'Brien's *The Great Melody*,[63] namely, the humiliation of being of Irish ethnicity with a Catholic mother and wife, combining the peculiarly British toxic brew of ethnic and religious prejudice. In contrast to his homosexuality, on this issue Burke spoke and wrote quite explicitly not only about the long-standing British injustice of ethnic and religious prejudice against the Irish,[64] but, quite prophetically, that the failure to extend the toleration required by political liberalism would lead to the Anglophobia of Irish revolutionary violence, including terrorism.[65] Burke had written of the treatment of Catholics in Ireland "no good Constitution of Governm[en]t can find it necessary for its security to form any part of its subject to permanent slavery."[66] Both because of his Irish ethnicity and Catholic family connections (in fact, Burke was a committed Anglican), Burke had experienced throughout his life in Britain the populist irrational prejudices arising from the long history of intolerance of Catholics both in England and Ireland, including, notably, both him and his London home being targeted by the violent mobs of the Gordon riots, triggered by the demagogy of Lord George Gordon protesting the measure of parliamentary emancipation of Catholics in the Catholic Relief Act of 1778.[67] Important studies by Tim Clayton of the general pattern of political caricature of this period (including some notable attacks on Burke)[68] and the study of Nicholas Robinson on caricatures of

61 Ayling, *Edmund Burke*, p. 72.

62 On this point, see David A. J. Richards, *Why Love Leads to Justice: Love across the Boundaries* (Cambridge: Cambridge University Press, 2016).

63 See Conor Cruise O'Brien, *The Great Melody: A Thematic Biography of Edmund Burke* (Chicago: University of Chicago Press, 1992).

64 On the historical roots of Irish Anglophobia, see R. F. Foster, *Modern Ireland 1600–1972* (London: Penguin, 1989).

65 On this point, see Bourke, *Empire and Revolution*, pp. 783–800.

66 Quoted in ibid., p. 409.

67 On this matter, see F. P. Lock, *Edmund Burke, Volume I: 1730–1784* (Oxford: Clarendon Press, 1998), pp. 467–66. On both Scottish and English anti-Catholic riots, see Bourke, *Empire and Revolution*, pp. 406–19.

68 Tim Clayton, *James Gillray: A Revolution in Caricature* (New Haven, CT: Yale University Press, 2022).

Burke in particular[69] prominently feature his representation as an aggressive rather feminized Catholic Jesuit, identified by his spectacles and pointed nose. One even depicts Burke, at the time of his opposition to the French Revolution, as "a Contest between two old Ladies,"[70] touching on issues of deviant gender as well as deviant religion.

Burke, as a political liberal, clearly accepted Locke's argument for a right to revolution when the state violated the human rights respect for which is a condition for the legitimacy of government.[71] What led to his publication of his most important book, *Reflections on the Revolution in France*, namely, the defense by Richard Price of the French Revolution on such grounds, was that "British defenders [like Price and others] of 1789, in interpreting the French Revolution as a reprise of [the Glorious Revolution] of 1688, had confused the glorious deliverance accomplished by William III with the tragedy of the 1640s," the English Civil War.[72] Understanding the difference between the revolution of the 1640s and of 1688 is the key to understanding Burke's constitutional liberalism.

The English Civil War was for Burke and other British liberals a tragedy, not because it was not founded on the right to revolution against Charles I's assertion of absolute monarchy, but because its leaders, Cromwell and others, successfully formed and led the New Model Army, based on a religiously informed egalitarian solidarity among its soldiers, that decisively defeated Charles' forces, but then rejected both the appeal of its soldiers for a written constitution at the Putney Debates and democratic legitimation by the still existing institutions, the Commons and Lords, left after Charles' execution.[73]

The closest the New Model Army came to reasonable deliberation on a new constitution was the Putney Debates:

> Several days were given over to debating a new, more radical document, the *Agreement of the People.* Embodying the truly novel and revolutionary concepts of the sovereignty of the people over Parliament, and a written constitution enacted by the signatures of all the freeborn men of England, it also delineated a set of key points that were to be reserved to the people alone and that no government could exercise. Without monarch or House of Lords, it envisioned a single-chamber representative model of a free state—in short a republic. Although its authority was anonymous, the *Agreement* was at one level simply the New Model's "fulfilling of our Declaration of June the 14,"

69 Nicholas K. Robinson, *Edmund Burke: A Life in Caricature* (New Haven, CT: Yale University Press, 1996).

70 See ibid., p. 136.

71 On this point, see Bourke, *Empire and Revolution*, pp. 498–506.

72 Ibid., p. 685.

73 For a fuller discussion, see Ian Gentles, *The New Model Army: Agent of Revolution* (New Haven, CT: Yale University Press, 2022).

> as its authors affirmed in their postscript. Printed on the army's own press, it was essentially an army, not a Leveller document. There was obviously Leveller input—from William Walwyn, John Wildman, Maximilian Petty and Henry Marten. But in the end if came from a "thoroughly politicised army that was capable of thinking for itself."[74]

The *Agreement* enjoyed support within the army, but was resisted by the army's leaders, Cromwell and Ireton. After the *Agreement* was read out, Ireton objected to universal manhood suffrage:

> Rainborowe, confident in his audience, took up Ireton's challenge in words that still ring in our ears after nearly four centuries: "Really I think that the poorest he that is in England hath a life to live as the greatest he; and therefore truly, Sir, it's clear that every man that is to live under a government ought first by his own consent to put himself under the government."
>
> Ireton countered with a doctrine of political rights for the propertied alone, meaning landowners and merchants: "No person hath a right … in choosing those that shall determine what laws we shall be ruled by here … that has not a permanent fixed interest in its kingdom." … .
>
> Seemingly unaware that almost the whole room was against him, Ireton stubbornly stuck to his position … . The debate dragged on until finally John Wildman exploded with anger. Contemptuous of Ireton's reverence for history, precedent and law, he demands to know what principle they have fought for if not that "all government is in the free consent of the people." Colonel Rainborowe's brother William pithily observed that human rights were more important than property rights: "my person … is more dear than my estate." Sexby, the only accredited agitator to speak that day, passionately defended the interests of the private soldiers who had borne the heat and burden of the day: "it seems now except a man hath a fixed estate in this kingdom, he hath no right in this kingdom. I wonder we were so much deceived."[75]

If there was to be no accountability to the soldiers of the New Model Army, there was little accountability either to the parliamentary institutions that continued to exist, as Cromwell essentially used military force to exclude members of parliament with whom he disagreed and insisted on the execution of Charles that few wanted and most came to regret.[76] Cromwell's militarism, in Ireland, for example, took the form of mindless retributivism against Catholics for their 1641–42 massacre of Protestants, leading to his own massacres of Catholics

74 Ibid., p. 94.
75 Ibid., p. 57.
76 Ibid., pp. 128–57.

(some 300,000)[77] and his refusal to allow the practice of Catholicism.[78] And he established the plantations in Ireland to reward his Protestant soldiers and others, setting the stage for the colonial system in Ireland at the expense of majority Catholics.[79] After the death of Cromwell, the last gasp of revolutionary militarism was the announcement by the last military junto that all previous parliamentary laws were invalid. "This was the first time in England's history that an army or any other body had even presumed to cancel an Act of Parliament."[80] Some British people may happily have welcomed back the monarchy, resenting the suppression of traditional festive culture—"Morris dancing, Christmas celebrations, Sabbath sports, bear-baiting, cockfighting, horse-racing, the theatre and alehouses," as well as, more seriously, "the ballooning expense of an increasingly bloated army … . In later centuries the New Model Army would be admired for having tamed absolute monarchy, advanced the cause of democracy and begun the long process of law reform. The other aspect of its legacy would be the enduring popular suspicion of standing armies, and an aversion to Puritanism."[81]

As we earlier saw, Burke's argument in *Reflections* was prompted by the defense of the French Revolution by a British radical Whig, Richard Price, and at the very beginning expressly connects Price's defense, both in spirit and content, to a sermon during the English Civil War of Hugh Peter,[82] "the Independent chaplain who had fortified the army before its marched on London for Pride's purge in 1648. Like Price, in preaching love to mankind, Peter is alleged to have spread hatred among fellow citizens … . It was no accident that Burke chose to juxtapose Price's sermon with the exhortations of a seventeenth-century regicide preacher."[83] How was Peter connected to the tragedy of the 1640s?

> Peter had played a notorious role in the climax of the decade, conspiring with Ireton and Cromwell to secure the execution of the king. On the eve of Charles I's death, he delivered a gruesome sermon based on Isiah 14:19–20: "thou art cast out of thy grave like an abominable branch." An address at St. James's Chapel on 28 January 1648 beseeching the saintly to "bind their *kings* with chains and their *nobles* with fetters of iron" enjoyed notoriety even after the restoration. In the fifth volume of his *History of England,* Hume cited as a favourite "among the enthusiasts of that age." It was most probably

77 Ibid., pp. 181–82, 196.

78 Ibid., p. 190.

79 Ibid., pp. 194–208.

80 Ibid., p. 301.

81 Ibid., p. 320–21.

82 See Edmund Burke, "Reflections on the Revolution in France," in Hampsher-Monk, *Revolutionary Writings*, pp. 3–250 at 12–13.

83 Bourke, *Empire and Revolution*, p. 685.

> Hume's account that put Burke in mind of a zealous chaplain whose activities during the civil war exemplified the perils of politicised religion. "No sound ought to be heard from the church but the healing voice of Christian charity," Burke asserted: "politics and the pulpit are terms that have little agreement." Religion was in the habit of polluting politics, Hume had argued. Politics was inclined to corrupt religion, Burke responded.[84]

Burke's entire argument in *Reflections* rests on the Lockean political liberalism that he shares with Price and other defenders of the French Revolution, like Tom Paine,[85] namely, the Lockean right to revolution when government violates basic human rights. For Burke, however, the way in which the right had been exercised in the English Civil War itself violated such rights in wanton violence and did not establish a more legitimate constitutionalism than the one it supplanted, becoming hostage to sectarian religion. Burke is at pains to distinguish the tragedy of the 1640s from the Glorious Revolution of 1688 that was largely non-violent and left in place the three institutions of the balanced British Constitution that Montesquieu had praised as consistent with the separation of powers, rejecting only the absolutism of the Stuart monarchy of James I, a Catholic, who threatened the rights of free religion of Protestants and was legitimately dethroned by another monarch who constrained his power by the Toleration Act of 1688 and the Bill of Rights of 1689. The Glorious Revolution thus appealed to the right to revolution not to repudiate the basic structure of the British Constitution, but to reform it legitimately because it better protected basic rights.

In contrast, the tragedy of the 1640s in Britain and of the French Revolution in 1789 was, first, their inadequate understanding of basic rights in general and the rights already protected by existing institutions on which they could build; second, the absence of any appeal to a reasonable understanding of how the historical experience of human governments should inform a constitution that aspires to protect basic human rights; and third, the disastrous, indeed catastrophic, consequence of these failures, namely, the unleashing of the wanton violence of sectarian fundamentalism, ethnic and religious nationalism, imperialism, and the terrors of totalitarianism. Burke regarded these sectarian forces as, in effect, themselves a political religion that unleashed these terrors, a sectarian political religion he believed that led to the tragedy of the 1640s and the internecine violence of the French Revolution both on fellow Frenchmen and a universal war on everyone, culminating in the dictatorship and imperialism of Napoleon. Burke's insights into this political psychology may be among his most remarkable achievements, as I aim to show, prophetic of arguments of

84 Ibid., pp. 685–86.

85 On Burke's and Paine's disagreement on this point, see Yuval Levin, *The Great Debate: Edmund Burke, Thomas Paine, and the Birth of Right and Left* (New York: Basic Books, 2014).

political psychology that were to develop in the twentieth and twenty-first centuries to understand totalitarianism, terrorism, and other forms of political violence, including aggressive war.

1.1 Real v. Unreal Human Rights

Burke draws a distinction between the "rights of man" as used in the French Assembly's Declaration of the Rights of Man and Citizen of 1789 and what he calls "the *real* rights of man."[86] It is important to remember that *Reflections* is written and published in 1790–91. The argument certainly predicts the later excesses of the French revolutionaries (the Terror of 1793, for example), which were to discredit them for the many liberals, including those in Burke's own political party, who had, like Price and Paine, acclaimed and supported the revolution. What Burke correctly sees even in the early days of the constitutional politics of the French revolutionaries is that they lack any reasonable understanding, based on experience, of how democratic politics can and should be rendered constitutionally in service of human rights.

Burke thus appeals, as examples of "the *real* rights of man," to the rights constitutionally protected under the British Constitution, "Magna Charta ... [from which] Sir Edward Coke, the great oracle of our law, and indeed all the great men who follow him, to Blackstone, are industrious to prove the pedigree of our liberties,"[87] as well as "the famous law ... of Charles I, called the *Petition of Right*" that "Selden and the other profoundly learned men" grounded not in "the general theories concerning the 'rights of men'" but "positive, recorded, *hereditary* title to all which can be dear to the man and the citizen."[88] And he goes on:

> The same policy pervades all the laws which have since been made for the preservation of our liberties. In the 1st of William and Mary, in the famous statute, called the Declaration of Right, the two houses utter not a syllable of "a right to frame a government for themselves." You will see that the whole care was to secure the religion, laws, and liberties that had been long possessed, and had been lately endangered.[89]

He concludes:

> You will observe, that from Magna Charta to the Declaration of Right, it has been the uniform policy of our constitution to claim and assert our liberties,

86 Edmund Burke, "Reflections on the Revolution in France," in Hampsher-Monk, *Revolutionary Writings*, pp. 3–250 at 59.

87 Ibid., p. 32.

88 Ibid., p. 33.

89 Ibid.

> as an *entailed inheritance* derived from our forefathers, and to be transmitted to our posterity … . This policy appears to me to be the result of profound reflection, or rather the happy effect of following nature, which is wisdom without reflection, and above it … . In this choice of inheritance we have given to our frame of polity, the image of a relation in blood, binding up the constitution of our country with our dearest domestic ties, adopting our fundamental laws in the bosom of our family affections; keeping inseparable, and cherishing with the warmth of all their combined and mutually reflected charities, our state, our hearths, our sepulchres, and our altars.[90]

"Society is indeed a contract," Burke argues. But, it must be thought of as a historical intergenerational development whose purposes are ultimately moral enlightenment:

> It is a partnership in all science; a partnership in art; a partnership in every virtue, and in all perfection. As the ends of such a partnership cannot be obtained in many generations; it becomes a partnership not only between those who are living, but between those who are dead, and those who are to be born. Each contract of each particular state is but a clause in the great primaeval contract of eternal society, linking the lower with the higher natures, connecting the visible and invisible world, according to a fixed compact sanctioned by the inviolable oath which holds all physical and all moral natures, each in their appointed place.[91]

Burke's appeal to the *real* rights protected by the British Constitution was not idealized or uncritical. To the contrary, what distinguished Burke's political achievements were his liberal resistance to the treatment of the Irish, to the war on America, and to the British Empire's abuses in India, and, at the end of his life, his resistance to members of his own Whig party who had come uncritically to admire the French Revolution. All of these achievements were, however, made possible because the British constitutional system had accorded Burke, an Irish man with a Catholic mother and wife and suspected of being gay, an important role in British politics first as the voice of the Rockingham Whigs, who took power, albeit briefly, for two short periods during Burke's 30 years in parliament, and later as a liberal voice, after Rockingham's death, opposing his own party. In his great defense of his opposition to his own party, "An Appeal from the New to the Old Whigs,"[92] Burke writes of the role in British culture and politics of a "true natural aristocracy:"

90 Ibid., pp. 34–35.

91 Ibid., p. 101.

92 Edmund Burke, "An Appeal from the New to the Old Whigs," in Isaac Kramnick (ed.), *The Portable Edmund Burke* (New York: Penguin, 1999), pp. 474–98.

> To be bred in a place of estimation; to see nothing low and sordid from one's infancy; to be taught to respect one's self; to be habituated to the censorial inspection of the public eye; to look early to public opinion; to stand upon such elevated ground as to be enabled to take a large view of the widespread and infinitely diversified combinations of men and affairs in a large society; to have leisure to read, to reflect, to converse; to be enabled to draw the court and attention of the wise and learned, wherever they are to be found; to be habituated in armies to command and to obey; to be taught to despise danger in the pursuit of honor and glory; to be formed to the greatest degree of vigilance, foresight, and circumspection, in a state of things in which no fault is committed with impunity and the slightest mistakes draw on the most ruinous consequences; to be led to a guarded and regulated conduct, from a sense that you are considered as an instructor of your fellow-citizens in their highest concerns, and that you act as a reconciler between God and man; to be employed as an administrator of law and justice, and to be thereby amongst the first benefactors of mankind; to be a professor of high science or of liberal and ingenuous art; to be amongst rich traders, who from their success are presumed to have sharp and vigorous understandings, and to possess the virtues of diligence, constancy, and regularity, and to have cultivated an habitual regard to commutative justice: these are the circumstances of men that form what I should call a *natural* aristocracy, without which there is no nation.[93]

Burke describes in this remarkable passage his own sense of the demanding role and stage and critical perspective the British Constitution had accorded him, both as a public intellectual and a politician, as the voice of a group of hereditary aristocrats, the Rockingham Whigs, with liberal views often opposing the authoritarian views of George III and his ministers, for example, over going to war with the American colonies.[94] Burke also played an important role as a Rockingham Whig both in arguing for the role of political parties in constitutional democracy, "a body of men united for promoting by their joint endeavors the national interest upon some particular principle on which they all agreed,"[95] and arguing as well for a conception of representation based on the independent conscience of the member of parliament, not the will of the electorate.[96] One of the signal differences, as we shall later see, between British and American

93 Ibid., pp. 495–96.

94 On this point, see Justin Du Rivage, *Revolution against Empire: Taxes, Politics, and the Origins of American Independence* (New Haven, CT: Yale University Press, 2017).

95 See Edmund Burke, "Thoughts on the Present Discontents," in Isaac Kramnick, *The Portable Edmund Burke*, p. 146.

96 On this point, see Edmund Burke, "Speech at Mr. Burke's Arrival in Bristol," in Isaac Kramnick, *The Portable Edmund Burke*, pp. 155–57.

liberal constitutionalism was Burke's path-breaking empirically based defense of competitive political parties as fundamental to democratic constitutionalism, whereas, much to their cost, the American Founders (notably Madison) had regarded them as "factions," incapable of democratic representation.[97]

Burke's entire program of liberal resistance against the injustices of British treatment of the Irish, the Americans, and the Indians rested on a universalist humanist moral conception of virtual representation of the interests and rights of marginalized persons unjustly treated. "According to Burke, a regime that failed to represent in any sense was illegitimate,"[98] such representation thus requiring a humane ethical sympathy that "depended on stimulating the imagination through which we could identify with the condition of our fellow creatures," "a process of imaginative identification"[99] with Indians that he vividly displayed in his criticisms of British moral atrocities in India over the years of the Hastings impeachment, in which he played a pivotal role both gathering facts and as impresario of the depiction of this moral tragedy with which he confronted the nation.

Burke well understood the difference between a natural and hereditary aristocrat: when unjustly criticized by a hereditary aristocrat, Burke indignantly rebuked him, noting how the aristocrat, unlike Rockingham and other hereditary aristocrats, had abused the privileges of wealth and status he had inherited.[100] Burke's defense of the British Constitution in *Reflections*, in contrast to the constitutional experiments of the French revolutionaries, was precisely that British culture and politics made possible, indeed nurtured natural aristocrats like himself, empowering his liberal resisting voice to the injustices inflicted by his government, voices silenced in France by the Terror. The point was not that he was always politically successful, but that his voice was heard and respected and would itself set a precedent for the expression and development of later forms of political liberalism in British politics.

It also afforded the model of thought, experience, and deliberation required for constitutional construction:

> Political arrangement, as it is a work for social ends, is to be only wrought by social means. There mind must conspire with mind. Time is required to product that union of minds which along can produce all the good we aim at.

97 For an important recent exploration of this contrast and its continuing consequences today not only in the U.K. and U.S. but much more broadly, see Samuel Issacharoff, *Democracy Unmoored: Populism and the Corruption of Popular Sovereignty* (New York: Oxford University Press, 2023). See pp. 86–87, 133 for the pivotally important role of Burke in justifying the role of competitive political parties in British democratic constitutionalism.

98 Bourke, *Empire and Revolution*, p. 370.

99 Ibid., p. 251.

100 See Edmund Burke, "A Letter to a Noble Lord," in Isaac Kramnick, *The Portable Edmund Burke*, pp. 213–32.

> Our patience will achieve more than our force. If I may venture to appeal to what is so much out of fashion in Paris, I mean, to experience, I should tell you, that in my course I have known, and, according to my measure, have co-operated with great men; and I have never yet seen any plan which has not been mended by the observations of those who were much inferior in understanding to the person who took the lead in the business. By a slow but well-sustained progress, the effect of each step is watched; the good or ill success of the first, gives light to us in the second; and so, from light to light, we are conducted through the whole series … . From thence arises, not an excellence in simplicity, but one far superior, an excellence in composition. Where the great interests of mankind are concerned though a long succession of generations, that succession ought to be admitted into some share in the councils which are so deeply to affect them. If justice requires this, the work itself requires the aid of more minds than one age can furnish. It is from this view of things that the best legislators have been often satisfied with the establishment of some sure, solid, and ruling principle in government.[101]

Burke did not believe and never argued that the historical role that a hereditary independent aristocracy had played in the development of British constitutional liberalism (resisting, for example, monarchical abuses) was a necessary condition for the legitimacy of a liberal constitution, but only that in Britain it had historically played such a role in the development of constitutional liberalism. "In the same speech [defending the role a hereditary aristocracy played in British constitutional development], he also 'recommended an imitation of the Government of the United States of America [lacking a hereditary aristocracy],' as the best model 'now existing' for the peoples of the new world."[102] Indeed, after the U.S. Constitution of 1787 was ratified, "Burke publicised his admiration for the newly constructed nation. He was satisfied that the current configuration of America meant the continuation of the kind of regulated government that he associated with old Europe. In the new world, at least, a system of civilized politics would survive."[103] The contrast, of course, was to French constitutionalism that had radically repudiated existing institutions that could have been used to develop a liberalizing form of constitutional democracy rather than institutions that, for Burke, gave rise to wanton violence and dictatorial repression of dissent and were more violative of human rights than the institutions against which they revolted, thus failing the Lockean liberal test for the legitimacy of revolution.

Three of Burke's great projects of liberal resistance (Ireland, America, India) indicted injustices of British colonialism that had become increasingly important in the British economy and politics from the 1600s forward (the British East

101 Burke, *Reflections on the Revolution in France*, pp. 172–73.

102 Bourke, *Empire and Revolution*, p. 782.

103 Ibid., pp. 921–22.

India Company was founded by royal charter in 1600). What connects all these great projects is the universalist humanism of the liberal principles to which Burke appeals in his criticism of the injustices of British colonialism: the principle of toleration central to Lockean liberalism not extended to Irish Catholics, the principle of fair representation in parliament that the Americans were denied, and the racist "geographic morality"[104] applied to India, not treating them as moral persons. Such criticisms, though not successful either in emancipating Irish Catholics or stopping the war on the American colonies or securing the impeachment of Hastings (whom the House of Lords after four years of hearings finds not guilty), defended liberal principles and arguments that were to be resonant in later British history and parliamentary practice, including the important role for political parties and independent voices in parliament in continuing liberal reform for the next two centuries.

Of the three projects, Burke's resistance to going to war with the American colonies is particularly resonant for Americans, suggesting an alternative path for American constitutional liberalism, the road not taken. Burke was always remarkable as a liberal politician for his studious attention to facts and context and thus his distrust of abstract theory not informed by facts and context. His views on America were based on quite close study reflected in his collaboration with his intimate friend, Will Burke, on *An Account of the European Settlements in America*, a compilation of various sources dealing with America, including the colonial conflicts of Britain with France, the role of the Amerindians in these conflicts, and the settlement of the east coast largely by British expatriates, bringing with them British values and institutions, including forms of colonial democracy under the authority of the British parliament[105] (Will was later to play an important role in informing Burke about India, where Will served as representative to the Raja of Tanjore). Indeed, Burke served for several years as representative of the New York Assembly in London, and, earlier, had seriously intended to emigrate to America. Burke's critiques of government policy in America—including on taxes (the Stamp Act, later repealed, only to be followed by the Townsend duties),[106] and his two great speeches to parliament against going to war with the colonies[107]—reflect his deep understanding of the moral position of the Americans and the cultural traditions they reflect—the

104 See Edmund Burke, "Speeches on the Impeachment of Warren Hastings", in Isaac Kramnick, *The Portable Edmund Burke*, pp. 388–408 at 394.

105 Edmund Burke, "An Account of the European Settlements in America," in Isaac Kramnick, *The Portable Edmund Burke*, pp. 233–45. For an illuminating discussion, see F. P. Locke, *Edmund Burke: Volume I: 1730–1784* (Oxford: Clarendon Press, 1998), pp. 125–41.

106 Edmund Burke, "Observations on a Late Publication Entitled 'The Present Stage of the Nation,'" in Isaac Kramnick, *The Portable Edmund Burke*, pp. 246–53.

107 Edmund Burke, "Speech on Taxation," in Isaac Kramnick, *The Portable Edmund Burke*, pp. 254–58, and "Speech on Conciliation with the Colonies," in Isaac Kramnick, *The Portable Edmund Burke*, pp. 259–73.

Protestantism of the Northern colonies, "all Protestantism ... [being] 'a sort of dissent,' and the Americans being 'the dissidence of dissent, and the Protestantism of the Protestant religion'"[108]) and the insistence on their rights of the Southern slaveowners, "where this [slave-owning] is the case in any part of the world, those who are free are by far the most proud and jealous."[109] The Americans are as culturally British as us, and their indignation at abridgment of their rights to fair representation on matters of taxation is as real and as well based as any such claims made in England.

> Burke was in effect accepting the legitimacy of the colonial refusal to submit to government measures since 1768 ... . Resistance had, however, had to be distinguished from rebellion. The disobedience of the colonies had been reasonable self-defence rather than assault upon the authority of Britain.[110]

Burke had such a remarkable understanding of and empathy with the Americans because he sees himself in them in sharp contrast to the attitudes of George III, Lord North, and the parliament that supinely followed their lead. It is striking that the leading American historian of the American Revolution, Gordon S. Wood, in writing of the radicalism of the revolution, describes the two American liberal leaders who, more than anyone else, justified the revolution, John Adams and Thomas Jefferson, in the terms Burke described himself: "They were, in short, still aristocrats, natural aristocrats, aristocrats of virtue and talent no doubt, but aristocrats nonetheless."[111] It takes a natural aristocrat to know another. Burke, the Irish gay outsider to mainstream British leaders, was at one with American liberalism and defended them in such terms.

In his moving "Address to the British Colonists in North America,"[112] Burke urges that the Americans to secure their just aims need Britain and that separation may have unanticipated consequences:

> That very liberty, which you so justly prize above all things, originated here: and it may be very doubtful whether, without being constantly fed from the original fountain, it can be perpetuated or preserved in its native purity and perfection, it can be at all perpetuated or preserved in its native purity and perfection. Untried forms of government may, to unstable minds, recommend themselves even by their novelty. But you will do well to remember

108 Burke, "Speech on Conciliation," p. 262.

109 Ibid., p. 263.

110 Bourke, *Empire and Revolution*, p. 473.

111 Gordon S. Wood, *The Radicalism of the American Revolution* (New York: Vintage, 1991), p. 196.

112 Edmund Burke, "Address to the British Colonists in North America," in Isaac Kramnick, *The Portable Burke*, pp. 274–82.

> that England has been great and happy under the present limited monarchy (subsisting in more or less vigour and purity) for several hundred years. None but England can communicate to you the benefits of such a constitution. We apprehend you are not now, nor for ages are likely to be, capable of that form of constitution in an independent state. Besides, let us suggest to you our apprehensions that your present union (in which we rejoice, and which we wish long to subsist) cannot always subsist without the authority and weight of this great and long-respected body, to equipoise and to preserve you amongst yourselves in a just and fair equality. It may not even be impossible that a long course of war with the administration of this country may be but a prelude to a series of wars and contentions among yourselves, to end, at length, (as such scenes have long ended,) in a species of humiliating repose, which nothing but the preceding calamities would reconcile to the dispirited few who survived them.[113]

Burke, the astute analyst of the psychology of political violence, worries that the very violence of the American Revolution (and it was much more violent on both sides than Americans like to think[114]) might be one of the seeds of its undoing, a suggestion to which I shall return in Chapter 3.

Burke had earlier followed Benjamin Franklin "in condoning the colonial position,"[115] and later, in contrasting American resistance with French insurgency, revealed

> on the testimony of Franklin with whom he had been trying to collaborate in the winter of 1774–75 … he had held "a very long conversation" in the days before he left London for Philadelphia on 20 March 1775. In the aftermath of his high-handed treatment by Wedderburn over the Hutchinson-Oliver letters, Franklin's mind was undoubtedly "soured and exasperated" with the metropolis. Nonetheless, in common with the generality of American opinion, he sought a return to imperial relations prior to 1763 rather than a dissolution of British power. The aim of the American protest was manifestly not complete autonomy, not least since that outcome was so clearly contrary to the interest of the colonies. Their goal was not power but relief, specifically relief from taxation.[116]

Franklin had long been a believer, like Burke, that the British Empire, properly understood, was a republican empire and had

113 Ibid., p. 279.

114 See Holger Hoock, *Scars of Independence: America's Violent Birth* (New York: Crown, 2017).

115 Bourke, *Empire and Revolution*, p. 450

116 Ibid., p. 494.

> used the Albany Congress in the summer of 1754 to propose an ambitious colonial confederacy. Originally conceived as a meeting between the colonies and the Six Iroquois Nations to improve relations and coordinate their response against the French, the meeting ended with a plan for colonial union … . The plan stipulated that a grand council appointed by the assemblies and a president general appointed by the Crown would meet annually in Philadelphia to pass laws and regulations for the common defense of the colonies … . What emerged from Albany was unprecedented—a supracolonial government with wide latitude to levy taxes and spend money.[117]

The proposal, though abortive, shows how close an American leader like Franklin was to Burke in reframing the British Empire to recognize the right of the colonies to tax and spend. What led him finally to break with these hopes was precisely what Burke had anticipated would happen if the British refused to extend to Americans the rights owed all other British citizens, humiliating them, eliciting revolution:

> With even North under attack for failing to uphold Britain's sovereignty, Franklin gave up on reconciliation. He was embittered by the spectacle of "hereditary legislators" with "scarce discretion to govern a herd of swine" treating colonists as "the lowest of mankind, and almost of a different species from the English." Franklin had spent sixteen of the past twenty years in Britain advocating for a political community that he believed was a source of power, justice, and prosperity. Now, he was through with the British Empire. At the end of March 1775, he boarded the *Pennsylvania Packet* for Philadelphia. He would never live in England again.[118]

After the separation of the colonies from Britain, Burke did not rule out some form of reunion and tried unsuccessfully to negotiate with Franklin "en route to Paris to negotiate with Versailles."[119] But, by that time, any attempt at reconciliation was too late.

It is striking that both Franklin and Burke agreed that, had George III and his ministers been more reasonable about taxation, not only Britain but the Americans would have been better off without the revolution and 1787 Constitution. Burke's worries are, in the light of history, prophetic: "A long course of war with the administration of this country may be but a prelude to a series of wars and contentions among yourselves, to end, at length (as such scenes have long ended) in a species of humiliating repose, which nothing but the preceding

117 Du Rivage, *Revolution against Empire*, p. 63.

118 Ibid., p. 175.

119 Bourke, *Empire and Evolution*, p. 500. For Burke's continuing correspondence with Franklin, see ibid., pp. 512, 513–14.

calamities would reconcile to the dispirited few who survived them." It was certainly arguments over the interpretation of the 1787 Constitution on the issue of slavery that led to "a series of wars and contentions" among ourselves, culminating in the civil war and its intractable legacy, persisting American racism (more about this in Chapter 3). Meanwhile, Britain had abolished slavery in England, and in 1833 parliament would without violence abolish slavery with compensation to slaveowners in the colonies, which would lead Lincoln to argue that, by the test of Lockean legitimacy, the British Constitution was superior to the American Constitution.

1.2 Appeal to Experience

As we have seen, Burke, following Montesquieu, thought of liberal constitutionalism historically, based on what cumulative historical experience showed us about its promise and perils. The central normative liberal concern, associated with the protection of "the *real* rights of man," was "*that no man should be judge in his cause*,"[120] so that under a liberal constitution the surrender of one's own right to recognize and enforce his rights must be to a constitutional order that so separates the powers of government that rights are impartially and reasonably recognized and enforced, that no one is legislator, judge, jury, and executor in his own case. Thus, the separation of powers was a central requirement of liberal constitutional government in Britain because, as Montesquieu argued, the British Constitution embodied such a separation and division of powers that impartially protected rights.

What Burke saw, quite early in the constitutional thought and practice of the French Revolution, was a failure to build on and use the traditional estates of French culture to establish a separation of powers based on Montesquieu's appeal to experience, but to accord all powers to a unicameral elected assembly who had had little or no experience in government under absolutism and some of whom, the Jacobins, distrusted, under the influence of Rousseau,[121] representative government as such, let alone the separation of powers.[122] What worried Burke in the proposed French constitutionalism of 1790–91, in particular, was the lack of a senate,[123] a weak king with little control of peace and

120 Edmund Burke, "Reflections on the Revolution in France," in Hampsher-Monk, *Revolutionary Writings*, pp. 3–250 at 60.

121 See Timothy O'Hagan, *Rousseau* (London: Routledge, 1999), pp. 87–161. For Rousseau's two attempts to design constitutions along these lines, see Jean Jacques Rousseau, *Constitutional Project for Corsica* (n.p.: Kessinger Publishing, n.d.); Jean-Jacques Rousseau, *The Government of Poland*, translated by Willmoore Kendall (Indianapolis, IN: Hackett, 1985).

122 For a comprehensive treatment, see Jonathan Israel, *Revolutionary Ideas: An Intellectual History of the French Revolution from the Rights of Man to Robespierre* (Princeton, NJ: Princeton University Press, 2015).

123 Burke, *Reflections on the Revolution in France*, p. 202.

war,[124] the lack of an independent judiciary,[125] and a military not subject to civilian control.[126]

But, what led Burke to his psychological critique was the increasing wanton violence of the Parisian mobs and their vehicle, the Commune of Paris, and, even early on, their impact on the assembly itself (ignoring the rest of France as if only Paris was France, and eventually leading the assembly, as Cromwell had done, to purge its own elected members).[127] For Burke, the attack on the king and queen at Versailles by a Parisian mob bringing them to Paris is the culmination of uncontrollable vengeance on the monarchy, humiliations of the king and "the murder of his servants, the attempted assassination of himself and his wife, and the mortification, disgrace, and degradation, that he has personally suffered."[128] In effect, the rights promised by the 1789 Declaration of the Rights of Man and Citizen had become, as Burke put it, unreal, rationalizing the violence of the Parisian mobs and eventually the Terror directed at any dissent, led by a dictator, Robespierre.

Burke had a deep interest in history, including writing a book, never completed, *An Abridgement of English History*, one part dealing with the Romans to Christianity,[129] and the other with the Anglo-Saxons and the Norman Conquest.[130] "Hume's *History of England* had started to appear in 1754, with the final installment being published in 1761."[131] Burke follows Hume on many points, "emphasizing discontinuities in the trajectory of British history, undermining the illusion of a seamless passage of freedom from the Germanic arrangements … to the triumph of parliament in the seventeenth century."[132] However, while

> Burke admired Hume's philosophical detachment and systematic view of politics, yet he regarded his religious skepticism as corrosive and prone to bigotry. Hume's disdain for superstition was a case in point. For Burke, primitive beliefs provided a basis for subsequent enlightenment. Religion was the germ of improvement, not a mental and moral corruption. "The first openings of civility have been everywhere made by religion."[133]

124 Ibid., pp. 202–08.
125 Ibid., pp. 209–13.
126 Ibid., p. 213.
127 See Burke, *Reflections on the Revolution in France*, pp. 200, 227, 245.
128 Ibid., p. 71.
129 For an illuminating discussion, see Bourke, *Empire and Revolution*, pp. 176–84.
130 See ibid., pp. 185–92.
131 Ibid., p. 181.
132 Ibid., p. 184.
133 Ibid., p. 181.

In thinking about the development of cultures, Burke took the position of a cultural anthropologist, acknowledging the importance of Christianity, in both its Catholic and Protestant forms, in the civilizing development of European culture, and, in contrast to others, like Macaulay, acknowledged the similarly civilizing role of both Hinduism and Islam in Indian cultures.[134]

But, it was not just a historically and anthropologically informed interest in cultural development that informed Burke's interest in religion as a civilizing cultural force in diverse contexts; he had come to believe that the form of egalitarian humanism, treating persons as equals, to which he often appealed in his liberal resistance to injustice, in particular, the natural moral duties of non-maleficence owed to all persons (not killing or injuring, and the like), irrespective of any institutional connection,[135] required some form of belief in terrifying divine punishment, albeit, as he put it, "humanized" by "the love of God,"[136] as by Christianity. It was a view John Locke evidently shared, on this ground not extending his principle of universal toleration to atheists.[137] Locke and Burke were wrong on this point, as Kant's deontological ethics, developed in the period of Burke's life, shows—allowing all persons to call upon their powers of rationality and reasonableness to construct and agree to reasonable principles;[138] for Kant, ethics and religion are conceptually independent (Nietzsche for this reason regards Kant as initiating the idea of the death of God in Western culture). Religion for Kant comes in not as a necessary feature of ethical deliberation and thought as such, but as a practical reason for rendering ethical demands for a universal moral community of equals (including republican democracies everywhere) more believable because only capable over time of being realized (certainly not in late eighteenth-century Europe).[139] Atheists and agnostics today can be and often are Kantians in their respect for universal human rights, all the more so when they subject conventional religious and other

134 On this point, see F. P. Lock, *Edmund Burke, Volume II: 1784–1789* (Oxford: Clarendon Press, 2006), pp. 156, 167–76.

135 On these natural duties, see David A. J. Richards, *A Theory of Reasons for Action* (Oxford: Clarendon Press, 1971), pp. 176–95.

136 See Edmund Burke, *A Philosophical Enquiry into the Sublime and Beautiful*, edited by Paul Guyer (Oxford: Oxford University Press, 2015), p. 57.

137 For a fuller discussion, see David A. J. Richards, *Toleration and the Constitution* (New York: Oxford University Press, 1986), pp. 96–97.

138 For an attempt to show this, inspired by the Kantian constructivism of John Rawls, see Richards, *A Theory of Reasons for Action*. For similar arguments along these lines, see Jeremy Waldron, *One Another's Equals: The Basis of Human Equality* (Cambridge, MA: The Belknap Press of Harvard University Press, 2017); T. M. Scanlon, *What We Owe to Each Other* (Cambridge, MA: The Belknap Press of Harvard University Press, 1998); Stephen Darwall, *The Second-Person Standpoint: Morality, Respect, and Accountability* (Cambridge, MA: Harvard University Press, 2006).

139 On this point, see Allen W. Wood, *Kant's Ethical Thought* (Cambridge: Cambridge University Press, 1999), pp. 317–20.

views, for example, on matter of gender and sexuality, to skeptical questioning on ethical grounds.

What particularly shocked Burke about the French revolutionaries was their attack not only on Catholic institutions in France (that had been anticipated in England by Henry VIII's attacks on Catholic institutions, as Burke acknowledges in *Reflections*),[140] but their attacks on religion and religious practice as such, without any sense of the role Christianity in both its Protestant and Catholic forms in particular had historically played in the development of a universalist ethical humanism; instead, the revolutionaries called for new state-sponsored rituals of a religion of reason without any respect for such historical practices and traditions, indeed repudiating them. Such an uncritical attack on religion as such, together with similar attacks on other cultural conventions, led to a moral nihilism of doubt about everything, as we shall shortly see, that unleashed the political psychology of wanton personal and political retributive violence that destroyed whatever humane ambitions that French Revolution may once have entertained. Without any ethical limits or sense of ethical limits, the people

> exercise an unnatural inverted domination, tyrannical to exact, from those who officiate in the state, not an entire devotion to their interest, which is their right, but an abject submission to their occasional will, extinguishing in all those who serve them, all moral principle, all sense of dignity, all use of judgment, and all consistency of character, whilst by the very same process they give themselves up a proper, a suitable, but a most contemptible prey to the servile ambitions or popular sycophants or courtly flatterers.[141]

Nothing could, for Burke, be more a destructive caricature of democratic constitutionalism than representatives who had, under the impact of the terror, lost any sense of their ultimate responsibility to their liberal convictions, rather supinely accepting the increasingly violent retributive commands of the Parisian mob not the democratically expressed will of the people of France.

Burke's name for this development was what he called Jacobin atheism, which had played a prominent role in unleashing this moral chaos, including the wanton murders not just against the monarchy and aristocrats, but anyone, including republicans, who expressed disagreement with Jacobin policies, in effect, political terrorism to which Burke is the first political liberal to give a name, culminating in aggressive wars. There is no doubt Burke was correct in seeing that these attacks on Catholicism would unleash violent reactionary forces (the Vendée) that the revolutionaries would come to regret, and that Napoleon would later try to remedy by his concordat with the Pope. But, what

140 See Burke, *Reflections on the Revolution in France*, pp. 120–21.
141 Ibid., p. 98.

he sees is a much deeper insight into political psychology that transcends his own beliefs connecting ethics and theism.

1.3 Political Psychology

Burke began his career as a public intellectual in Britain publishing in 1756 the *Vindication of Natural Society*, "written to ridicule and refute the specious deism of Henry St. John, Viscount Bolingbroke (1678–1751),"[142] based on an appeal to nature. There was, however, for Burke nothing natural about religion or ethics or politics, all of which rested on the ways in which humans become human through culture and cultural evolution. As he put it, "Art is man's nature."[143] His life both as a public intellectual and politician and political liberal led him to a consuming interest in how a culture develops political liberalism and how always to reform it in light of the reactionary cultural forces that are threatened by it.

It was in his second book published in 1757, *A Philosophical Enquiry into the Sublime and Beautiful*, that Burke first explores the psychology of terror and its connection to the sublime. Most of his examples are of literary works, notably Milton and Virgil, though he mentions also the role of terror in "despotic governments,"[144] a passion that "so effectually robs the mind of all its powers of acting and reasoning."[145] It is notable that Burke's account is highly gendered—terror and the sublime are decidedly masculine and serving self-preservation, whereas the contrasting pair, love and the beautiful, are decidedly marked in traditionally stereotypical feminine terms and linked to sympathy, which for Burke was the foundation of the liberal empathy of imaginative identification with unjustly treated minorities. The contrast suggests the role that gender plays in patriarchy, the masculine terror upholding gender hierarchy, the other contesting it. As Burke later turned his attention, both as an intellectual and politician, to understanding liberalism and liberal resistance, the focus of his attention, certainly in his treatment of British policies in Ireland and America, was seeing something other British leaders would not see, namely, that the failure to extend the liberal values of toleration to Irish Catholic and of fair representation to Americans in effect treated them as "subjects to permanent slavery,"[146] resting on "metropolitan pride."[147] What Burke sees that other British politicians do not see is that in both cases such humiliation will elicit violence, the American Revolution and the long history of violence by the Irish, including terrorism. Burke, as one would expect in such a student of culture, is developing, applying,

142 Lock, *Edmund Burke, Volume I*, p. 82.
143 Burke, "An Appeal from the New to the Old Whigs," p. 496.
144 See Burke, *A Philosophical Enquiry into the Sublime and Beautiful*, p. 48; see also p. 55.
145 Ibid., p. 47.
146 Quoted in Bourke, *Empire and Revolution*, p. 409.
147 Ibid., p. 449.

and deepening a cultural psychology of violence, impliedly drawing on the contrast between shame and guilt cultures, to which we must now turn in order to understand his views and insights.

1.3.1 Shame vs. Guilt Cultures

The cultural anthropologist Ruth Benedict, writing at about the same time as Erich Fromm's studies of German fascism and earlier interpretation and critique of Freud's discoveries,[148] invented the idea of a shame as opposed to a guilt culture. Americans were puzzled by the suicidal violence that Japanese soldiers showed in World War II, and Benedict, who had never been to Japan and did not read or write Japanese, had been asked to bring her cultural anthropology to bear on understanding Japanese violence. In response, she wrote her remarkable 1946 book, *The Chrysanthemum and the Sword: Patterns of Japanese Culture*.[149] Benedict, a lesbian, had experienced the injuries of patriarchy in her marriage. Once living outside such patriarchal structures in loving lesbian relationships based on mutual freedom and equality,[150] she came to an understanding of Japanese fascism as rooted in the shame culture of Japan in which men and women were defined in the terms of a rigid gender binary and a hierarchy privileging male honor, where any threat to that hierarchy elicited overwhelming shame and humiliation and thereby became a provocation for violence. The Japanese emperor cult was rigidly patriarchal with the emperor as a god-king, and the young men initiated into that system modeled themselves as men on allegiance to his commands or supposed commands, leading to a psychology acutely sensitive to any threat to their manhood, the shaming or dishonoring of manhood eliciting violence not only against others but against oneself.

Benedict is probably the first to establish what became the anthropologists' and others' use of the terms shame cultures and guilt cultures and to develop the contrast between them, that is, shame vs. guilt cultures:

> A society that inculcates absolute standards of morality and relies on men's developing a conscience is a guilt culture by definition, but a man in such a society may, as in the United States, suffer in addition from shame when he accuses himself of gaucheries which are in no way sins. He may be

148 See Erich H. Fromm, *Escape from Freedom* (New York: Henry Holt, 1965, first published 1941); *Man for Himself: An Inquiry into the Psychology of Ethics* (New York: Henry Holt, 1990, first published 1947); *The Sane Society* (New York: Henry Holt, 1990, first published 1955); *The Art of Loving* (New York: Harper Perennial, 2006, first published 1956).

149 Ruth Benedict, *The Chrysanthemum and the Sword: Patterns of Japanese Culture* (Boston, MA: A Mariner Book, 2005, originally published 1946).

150 On this point, see Richards, *Why Love Leads to Justice*, pp. 189–208.

> exceedingly chagrined about not dressing appropriately for the occasion or about a slip of the tongue … .
>
> True shame cultures rely on external sanctions for good behavior, not, as true guilt cultures do, on an internalized conviction of sin. Shame is a reaction to other people's criticism. A man is shamed either by being openly ridiculed and rejected or by fantasying to himself that he has been ridiculous. In either case it is a potent sanction. But it requires an audience or at least man's fantasy of an audience. Guilt does not.[151]

Benedict's path-breaking argument in *The Chrysanthemum and the Sword: Patterns of Japanese Culture*[152] explained to Americans their puzzlement about the suicidal levels of violence in Japanese aggressiveness in World War II in terms of the contrast between a dominantly shame culture (Japan) and a guilt culture (the U.S.), in the latter of which respect for the value of the equal right to life played a more important role. The U.S. may have been a dominantly guilt culture when Benedict wrote, but, if so, it was not unambiguously so, as the dominant culture of the antebellum American South had been quite patriarchal,[153] and, even after defeat in the civil war, these cultural patterns remained sufficiently intact to support a cultural racism that was allowed to continue there (lynchings) for a surprisingly long period. Distinctions must be among different forms of shame and guilt cultures, including mixed cases like the U.S. and others.

Benedict had earlier developed an anthropological theory implicitly of shame cultures in her discussion, based on the earlier work of her teacher Franz Boas, of the Kwakiutl,[154] an Amerindian people, who used competitive conspicuous displays of wealth and power to support an order enforcing a rigidly defined order based on the gender binary and hierarchy, rationalizing violence,[155] and the anthropologist Michelle Rosaldo later found a similar shame-based cultural pattern in the cannibalistic cultural patterns of New Guinea tribes.[156]

Rosaldo in particular called for more attention among anthropologists to a coherent theory of shame in personality and culture. She argued that "of all themes in the literature on culture and personality the opposition between guilt

151 Benedict, *The Chrysanthemum and the Sword*, pp. 222–23.

152 Ibid.

153 See Bertram Wyatt-Brown, *Southern Honor: Ethics and Behavior in the Old South* (Oxford: Oxford University Press, 2007, originally published 1982).

154 See Franz Boas, *Kwakiutl Ethnography* (Chicago: University of Chicago Ethnography, 1966). See also Franz Boas, *The Mind of Primitive Man* (n.p.: Forgotten Books, 2012, originally published 1922).

155 See Ruth Benedict, *Patterns of Culture* (Boston, MA: Houghton Mifflin, 2005, first published 1934), pp. 173–222.

156 See Michelle Z. Rosaldo, *Knowledge and Passion: Ilongot Notions of Self and Social Life* (Cambridge: Cambridge University Press, 1980).

and shame has probably proven most resilient"[157] (p. 135). Rosaldo's own description of the Ilongot, a tribe who periodically engage in group raids on neighboring tribes in which they murder and decapitate members of the other tribes, notes:

> In severing and tossing heads, Ilongot men recount, they could relieve hearts burdened with the 'weight' of insult, envy, pain, and grief; and … achieve an 'anger' that … makes shy and burdened youths … equal to their peers. (p. 137)

> Ilongot shame involves an "anger" born … in the confrontation of a would-be-peer with facts of weakness and social inferiority … "shame" is a thing that leads to striving and the shows of "anger" through which unacceptable imbalances are eventually overcome … "shame" involves awareness of deficiency or slight, a weight one is enjoined to overcome in subsequent displays of one's capacity and "anger." (p. 143)

> As children learn to speak, the verbal challenges of adults are seen to "shame" them in a way that motivates the acquisition of new skill and knowledge. Verbal wit, fine dress, productive skill are all, Ilongots claim, things that the young acquire because they envy the accomplishments of peers and would not have their fellows' excellence stand to "shame" them. Growing up and learning to behave with competence and poise requires casting off youthful vulnerability to one's fellows' taunts, and doing this means one redresses "weighty" shame with "light" displays of energy and force [e.g., headhunting]. In fact, headhunting … is in large part an angry answer to the distressing "shame" of childhood. (p. 144)

> Feelings of "weight"—whether one's grief at loss, or shame at insult, or envy at the headhunting accomplishments of peers—are what make all men think of killing … . Most youths declare that they are loathe to marry until they have taken heads for fear others will "shame" them. As novices, … they cannot work dependably, think clearly, or enjoy the company of kin because their "shame" brings sullenness, distraction, and ill-ease. But then, Ilongots claim, headhunting cures this … raids are designed to turn the vulnerable, subordinate and awkward youth into an adult peer. (p. 146)

It is equally clear, in Rosaldo's account, that the Ilongot did not experience feelings of guilt, either prior to or following these murders:

> None appeared to feel remorse for prior violent deeds, or speak of moral right and wrong when telling why they killed. (p. 137)

157 Michelle Z. Rosaldo, "The Shame of Headhunters and the Autonomy of Self," *Ethos* 11:3 (1983): 135–51, https://doi.org/10.1525/eth.1983.11.3.02a00030.

> Ilongots never speak of guilt, require punishment for wrongs, or seek displays of suffering and remorse in making up for untoward violence … . My earlier question—Do not killers suffer guilt?—is shown [to be] of questionable relevance to the Ilongot moral world … . The fact that Ilongots never speak of "guilt" in their reports of raids does not itself decide the cultural (or psychological) irrelevance of such things as self-recrimination and remorse in the experience of killers. More telling, I suggest, is the fact that Ilongots but rarely discuss actions with reference to established normative codes or formal rules of wrong and right … notions of "ought" and "obligation" appear lacking. (pp. 139–40)

Thus, Rosaldo concludes, "Ilongots may not feel guilt taking heads" (p. 142). Finally, she says, despite important differences that can be drawn between these cultures, "Ilongots … join ranks with Japanese … and Homeric Greeks as the enactors of shame morality" (p. 149).

By the time Ruth Benedict came to giving a name to a distinction that was already in wide use by her colleagues, the conceptual distinction itself (though expressed in different terminologies) had been around for a long time, not just for centuries but millennia. In fact, probably the earliest extant description of the essential difference between a shame culture and a guilt culture was made by an early Christian thinker, Augustine, in contrasting the "earthly city" (Roman shame culture) with the "heavenly city," the "city of God" (Christian guilt culture):

> The glory with the desire of which the Romans burned is the judgment of men thinking well of men. [But] virtue is better, which is content with no human judgment save that of one's own conscience. Whence the apostle says. "For this is our glory, the testimony of our conscience."[158]

The fact that there is a long tradition of social thought, going back to Plato[159] and including Aristotle,[160] St. Augustine, and Nietzsche[161] (among others), which

158 Augustine, *The City of God*, translated by Henry Bettenson (Middlesex: Penguin, 1972), p. 199.

159 Plato introduced the concept in *The Republic*, coining the word *timokratia* (i.e., timocracy—*timē* means honor and *kratein/cratos* means to rule/authority), meaning a state in which love of honor and glory is the ruling motive. The particular state he used the term to characterize was, appropriately, Sparta. See Plato, *Republic*, 8.545b, 8.547, 8.548e, 8.549c, in John M. Cooper (ed.), *Plato: Complete Works* (Indianapolis, IN: Hackett, 1997), pp. 971–1223.

160 Aristotle used the term *oligarchy* in a slightly different, though certainly not contradictory, sense to refer to a hypothetical state in which public honor is distributed according to wealth—that is, the more wealth, the more honor (and by implication, the more poverty, the more shame). See Aristotle, "Politics," in Jonathan Barnes (ed.), *The Complete Works of Aristotle, Volume Two* (Princeton, NJ: Princeton University Press, 1984), pp. 1986–2129 at 2033.

161 On ancient Greece as a shame culture in contrast to Christian culture as a guilt culture, see Friedrich Nietzsche, *On the Genealogy of Morals*, translated by Douglas Smith (Oxford: Oxford University Press, 1996).

includes concepts more or less equivalent to the one Ruth Benedict denominated "shame cultures" and "guilt cultures," suggests that the neglect of this concept, and the distinctions it encapsulates, might represent an important lacuna in our current thinking about culture and psychology. It was Dr. James Gilligan who first brought to my attention the literature on shame vs. guilt cultures and its relevance to understanding the psychology of violence. In a recent book, Gilligan has further developed the shame/guilt distinction in an important article on political violence in general, and his work has been joined by others in a path-breaking use of his work to understand political violence in a range of contexts.[162] My account here draws on Jim Gilligan's work, including distinctions he made in drafts for our earlier coauthored book, *Holding a Mirror Up to Nature*,[163] that we did not use there, but I use here; indeed, much of this section draws on his work, as I happily acknowledge.

How, then, might it be possible to conceptualize shame and guilt cultures in a way that could be applied without undue oversimplification to any culture; that would not, in other words, limit the concept to an oversimplified, all-or-nothing, either/or dichotomy incapable of taking account of the enormous variability between cultures, the almost limitless complexity within each of them, and the uniqueness of each that renders all of them incommensurable, at least in some important respects, with any of the others? At the very least, to begin with, it seems clear that we need to recognize that shame and guilt cultures vary on continua that range along two different axes, pure or homogeneous vs. mixed or heterogeneous, and extreme vs. mild. Very few cultures are pure or homogeneous, which allows for a more nuanced understanding of mixed or heterogenous, extreme or mild, cultures with features of both shame and guilt sometimes with the consequences I shall describe.

Jim Gilligan thus distinguished between relatively pure, or homogeneous, shame or guilt cultures, in which only one of these sanctions is operative to a marked degree, and the predominant moral sanction is shame only or guilt only; and "mixed" or heterogeneous cultures (such as our own) in which there are significant admixtures of both sanctions. It would be useful also to distinguish between "extreme" as opposed to "mild" shame and guilt cultures. The former would refer to societies in which exposure and sensitivity to experiences of shame or guilt, respectively, are relatively frequent, intense, and irrevocable, as opposed to ones in which individuals are relatively protected from such experiences so that they are less likely to occur or to be overwhelming or permanent. It may be seen that exposure and sensitivity to experiences of shame

162 See Roman Gerodimos (ed.), *Interdisciplinary Application of Shame/Violence Theory: Breaking the Cycle* (Cham: Palgrave Macmillan, 2022). The book is framed by the lead essay, James Gilligan, "The Role of Shame and Guilt in Political Violence: From Wars and Revolution to Genocide and Terrorism," pp. 19–38.

163 See Gilligan and. Richards, *Holding a Mirror Up to Nature*.

and/or guilt must be a function of both personality and culture. In other words, individuals themselves may vary in their sensitivity or susceptibility to shame or guilt; and cultural institutions and mores may also affect the frequency and intensity with which individuals in a society are exposed to, or protected from, life experiences capable of triggering, in the sensitive person, shame or guilt.

The term "shame culture," then, would be used to refer to societies in which the source of moral sanctions and authority is perceived to reside in other people (be they real or imaginary), in their ridicule, criticism, or contempt. "Guilt cultures," by contrast, would be those that rely on an internalized conscience and its resultant conviction of sin and absolute standards of morality.

For an example of a pure and extreme shame culture, we can turn to the Kwakiutl Indians of Vancouver Island, as documented in a series of monographs by the founder of scientific American ethnography, Franz Boas (and paraphrased by his pupil Ruth Benedict).[164] Here, to give a brief illustration of the inordinate degree to which the individuals in a culture can be preoccupied with and sensitive to shame and pride, enshrining them in their central institutions, are excerpts from her summary:

> Behavior … was dominated at every point by the need to demonstrate the greatness of the individual and the inferiority of his rivals. It was carried out with uncensored self-glorification and with gibes and insults poured upon the opponents … . The Kwakiutl stressed equally the fear of ridicule, and the interpretation of experience in terms of insults. They recognized only one gamut of emotion, that which swings between victory and shame … . Even this, however, gives only a partial picture of the extent to which this preoccupation with shame dominated their behavior. The Northwest Coast carries out this same pattern of behavior also in relation to the external world and the forces of nature. All accidents were occasions upon which one was shamed.[165]

Possibly the communities of early Christians who practiced primitive Christian communism before and during Augustine's time would have been among the best examples of guilt cultures. However, the most intensively studied guilt culture of today is in many respects similar to those communities, and in fact does practice primitive Christian communism. This is the society of the Hutterites, a Protestant (Anabaptist) religious sect numbering about 9,000 people and scattered throughout the northern Middle West and southern Canada in about 90 colonies of communal farms. One study reports that

164 See Franz Boas, *Kwakiutl Ethnography* (Chicago: University of Chicago Ethnography, 1966); see also Boas, *The Mind of Primitive Man*; Benedict, *Patterns of Culture*, pp. 173–222.

165 Benedict, *Patterns of Culture*, pp. 214–15.

> religion is the major cohesive force in this folk culture. The Hutterites consider themselves to … live the only true form of Christianity, one which entails communal sharing of property and cooperative production and distribution of goods. The values of brotherliness, self-renunciation and passivity in the face of aggression are emphasized. The Hutterites speak often of their past martyrs and of their willingness to suffer for their faith at the present time.[166]

And another study points out that, along with the stress on religion and duty to God and society and non-violence,

> there is a tendency in their entire thinking to orient members to internalize their aggressive drives. Children and adults alike are taught to look for guilt in themselves rather than in others.[167]

These authors concluded that although the Hutterites' strongly held Christian faith "gives many Hutterites a sense of great security," it "is also responsible for the high frequency of guilt feelings."[168] And an intensive study of a large number of Hutterites by means of projective tests and interviews made two relevant points. First, the tests revealed an unusually large burden of guilt (compared to American cultural norms). And second, "it clearly is aggressive impulses that seem to cause the most guilt in Hutterite society."[169] Such a propensity to guilt inhibits the violence to others characteristic of shame cultures, though it may express itself in more violence to the self (depression as a form of self-punishment).

The Hutterite culture rather clearly illustrates features in which interpersonal violence is almost wholly absent as a way of resolving conflict, and a culture of equal respect supports a shared personal and communal responsibility for one another, as equals. The contrast between the high levels of violence in the U.S. and the much lower levels in Western Europe in general and the Scandinavian democracies in particular is connected to the degree to which, in contrast to the U.S., the values of equal respect and communal responsibility and sharing support more highly developed guilt cultures in which their social democracies do not shame the dependencies of needing welfare so common in the U.S. and demonstrably linked, I believe, to the degree to which America retains features of a shame culture and thus encourages violence.[170]

166 Bert Kaplan and Thomas F. A. Plaut, *Personality in a Communal Society: An Analysis of the Mental Health of the Hutterites* (Lawrence, KS: University Press of Kansas, 1956), p. 12.

167 Joseph W. Eaton and Robert J. Weil, *Culture and Mental Disorders: A Comparative Study of the Hutterites and Other Populations* (New York: Free Press, 1955), p. 86.

168 Ibid., p. 217.

169 Kaplan and Plaut, *Personality in a Communal Society*, p. 80.

170 See James Gilligan, *Why Some Politicians Are More Dangerous Than Others* (Cambridge, MA: Polity, 2011).

What does all this have to do with violence? Pure and extreme shame cultures place a positive value on aggressiveness toward others (war, murder, torture, theft, enslavement, social and economic inequities), and a negative value on self-punishment. The Kwakiutl, for example, engaged in headhunting, cannibalism, burning slaves alive, and undiscriminating, merciless war and murder against even totally innocent, unsuspecting, hospitable, sleeping friends, neighbors, relatives, or hosts—men, women, and children. Furthermore, it seems clear that the motive for this aggressiveness was the desire to minimize or wipe out feelings of shame, humiliation, and "loss of face," and to maximize feelings of pride and social prestige, and that aggressive behavior was a recognized and honored way of doing this. For example, Benedict writes, in line with the interpretation that "all accidents were occasions upon which one was shamed," for the Kwakiutl "the great event which was dealt with in these terms was death … . Death was the paramount affront they recognized … . They took recognized means … to wipe out the shame." When a chief's son died, for example, he would kill a neighboring chief. "In this, according to their interpretation, he acted nobly because he had not been downed, but had struck back in return."[171]

Guilt cultures, by contrast, condemn aggression toward others, though they place a positive value on aggression directed toward the self. According to Eaton and Weil, there has not been a single case of murder, assault, or rape among the Hutterites since their arrival in America in the 1870s.[172] Not only is physical aggressiveness banned, but even its verbal expression: "No fighting or verbal abuse is permitted. It is expected that a Hutterite man will not get angry, swear, or lose his temper."[173] This is all the more remarkable when it is realized that the Hutterites have been constant victims of severe persecution by their neighbors everywhere they have lived. In Europe, "ghastly atrocities … during several periods brought the sect close to physical extinction;"[174] nevertheless, their martyrs are looked up to as models of correct (saintly) behavior. The Hutterites are strict, absolute pacifists, which is why emigration to North America was their only alternative to complete extinction, and since coming here many have been punished and even imprisoned for their refusal to participate in the military. They internalize their own aggressiveness in the form of feelings of guilt and sin; frequent and severe depressions; actively provoking or passively submitting to martyrdom and persecution (what Freud called "moral masochism"); shaming themselves by publicly confessing their sins; punishing themselves as penance; and occasional suicides (but, as I have said, no homicides).

171 Benedict, *Patterns of Culture*, pp. 215–16.

172 Eaton and Weil, *Culture and Mental Disorders*, p. 141.

173 Kaplan and Plaut, *Personality in a Communal Society*, pp. 19–20.

174 Ibid., p. 12.

Statistical studies of pure and extreme guilt cultures have not been possible because there are so few of them; indeed, apart from the Hutterites and a few other Anabaptist sects (the Amish, the Mennonites) it would be difficult to find any, other than, perhaps, some small, highly religious groups or sects within Judaism or Christianity, such as monastic communities of monks and/or nuns. As Freud said, no one feels guiltier than the saints; but by the same token, no one is rarer than the saints—for a variety of reasons, including the fact that they tend to become victims of individual or collective martyrdom. However, at the risk of generalizing on the basis of many shame cultures and only a few guilt cultures, and also extrapolating from what appear to the characteristics of shame and guilt as they manifest themselves in individuals, there are the following differences between pure and extreme shame and guilt cultures:

1 Shame cultures have hierarchical, authoritarian social structures and values that divide people into superior vs. inferior grades of socioeconomic status, with wide variations of social class and caste, prestige, wealth and power, often with institutionalized aristocracies and slavery. Shame cultures thus enforce the gender binary and hierarchy of patriarchy, in effect naturalizing it. These hierarchies include those of class, caste (including race/ethnicity and religion), gender (underlying sexism and homophobia), and, as Piaget saw,[175] age (gerontocracies). Its political psychology requires not only hierarchy, but always a lowest class, often held in what Carol Gilligan and David Richards have called "moral slavery," a structural injustice that rationalizes violently irrational scapegoating.[176] For example, cultures in which "sensitivity to insult is extreme" are significantly more likely to have class stratification, castes, slavery, invidious display of wealth, and possession and inheritance of private property. Guilt cultures, by contrast, are classless, democratic, and communistic, with relatively equal distributions of prestige, power, and wealth. Competition, such as it is, is more likely to be for the highest degree of humility than of prestige and honor.
2 Guilt cultures institutionalize confession of sins as a means of relieving guilt (by increasing shame). In shame cultures, exposure of transgressions of social mores is avoided, and concealment of them is sought as a means of avoiding shame, thus motivating lying, deception, and fraud.
3 Shame cultures place a negative value on needs to be loved and taken care of, and frustrate and discourage them (by one form or another of shaming); instead, they honor the development of self-reliance, activity, and achievement. For example, cultures in which "sensitivity to insult is extreme" are significantly more likely to be those in which "initial indulgence of dependency is low,"

175 See Jean Piaget, *The Moral Judgment of the Child* (New York: Free Press, 1997).
176 See Gilligan and Richards, *The Deepening Darkness*, pp. 10, 18–20, 72, 133–34, 197, 215.

> "early dependence satisfaction is low," "overall indulgence of the infant is low," "early oral satisfaction potential is low," "dependence socialization anxiety is high," and "the constancy of presence of the infant's nurturant agent is low." Other indices of shame, such as "boastfulness," "invidious display of wealth," and overall "narcissism," correlate significantly with those and other indices of negative valuation of passive dependent needs to be loved and taken care of, such as "total positive pressure toward developing both self-reliant behavior and achievement behavior in the child is high," "the child's inferred anxiety over non-performance of achievement behavior is high," "display of affection toward the infant is low," "immediacy, degree and consistency of reduction of the infant's drives is low," and so on.

Guilt cultures, by contrast, discourage aggressiveness in all forms, encourage submissiveness, patience, meekness, and humility, and thus have the effect in many spheres of behavior of discouraging activity (i.e., wherever it becomes associated with aggressiveness or self-aggrandizement rather than with nurturance or care-taking). Independence can also be guilt-inducing, where it is perceived to have the meaning of abandoning those toward whom one has an obligation.

While the Kwakiutl and many others provide examples of shame cultures, only the study of the Western tradition provides us with the opportunity to observe the transition from a shame to a guilt culture within one society. The classics scholar Eric Dodds, in *The Greeks and the Irrational*,[177] drawing on Ruth Benedict's definitions, has documented this transition in Greek history from an earlier shame culture, the society depicted in *The Iliad*, to a later guilt culture, classical Athens at the time of the tragedians and philosophers. Speaking of "the uninhibited boasting in which Homeric man indulges," Dodds says that

> Homeric man's highest good is not the enjoyment of a quiet conscience, but the enjoyment of time, public esteem [honor] … . And the strongest moral force which Homeric man knows is not the fear of god, but respect for public opinion, aidos [shame or sense of shame, sense of honor]. In such a society, anything which exposes a man to the contempt or ridicule of his fellows, which causes him to "lose face," is felt as unbearable.
>
> (pp. 17–18)

By the time the Greeks became a guilt culture, however, they worried not about experiencing too little pride and prestige, but too much—overweening pride or arrogance, up to and including violence—for which they used the term hubris. Far from being the highest good, pride by this time was called the "prime

177 E. R. Dodds, *The Greeks and the Irrational* (Berkeley: University of California Press, 1959).

evil" (*proton kakon*), as Theognis called it; the hamartia, or tragic flaw, for which, in Aristotle's analysis, Sophocles' Oedipus punished himself. It is significant that in the earlier shame culture's version of the Oedipus myth, Oedipus, far from feeling guilty and self-punitive, continued to reign in Thebes and was eventually buried with royal honors![178] Probably the individual who symbolized this transition to a guilt culture most vividly was Socrates, who declared that it was better to suffer evil and injustice than to perpetrate it, and who finally committed suicide even when he could easily have avoided doing so.

For the most extreme development of guilt in the ethos of a culture, however, we must turn to Judeo-Christian culture. Many scholars have made this observation. Freud, for example, commented that "the people of Israel … out of their sense of guilt … created the over-strict commandments of their priestly religion."[179] And Nietzsche saw that "the arrival of the Christian God … has brought with it the phenomenon of the uttermost sense of guilt."[180] And we have already noticed that the earliest extant description of the difference between a shame and a guilt culture was written by one of the early Christian thinkers, St. Augustine. The greater intensity of guilt in Christian, as compared with Greek, culture is indicated by the growth in guilt-affective tone of the word hamartia, from "tragic flaw" (the usual translation of Aristotle's meaning) to "sin," the New Testament meaning of the word, including Augustine's doctrine of original sin that rendered sexuality itself a matter of guilt. And Christ, like Socrates, became a personal symbol for the values of a guilt culture, becoming a victim rather than a perpetrator of violence (and severely chastising his followers when they were ready to defend him by means of violence). This does not necessarily indicate any great difference between early Christianity and the religious and moral values of major portions of the Jewish community at that same time, for Christianity was, after all, a Jewish sect, and 72 of the 77 verses of the "Sermon on the Mount" have rabbinical precedent.[181] In other words, Christianity was simply a subculture within the larger religious culture of the Judaism of its time.

It is worth noting, however, that the Judeo-Christian tradition, like the Greek one, began as a shame culture and only later developed into an extreme guilt culture. The earliest moral emotion mentioned in the Bible, for example, in the description of Adam and Eve, is "shame." What is unique about Judaism, however, is how early and strongly the theme of guilt emerged. Nevertheless, throughout much of the Old Testament the image of waging war successfully

178 Ibid., pp. 36, 55.

179 Sigmund Freud, "Civilization and Its Discontents" in *The Standard Edition of the Complete Psychological Works of Sigmund Freud Volume XXI (1927–1931)* James Strachey trans. (London: The Hogarth Press, 1961, pp. 59–148, 127.

180 Nietzsche, *On the Genealogy of Morals*, p. 71.

181 David Buttrick, *Speaking Jesus: Homiletic Theology and the Sermon on the Mount* (Louisville, KY: Westminster John Knox Press, 2002).

so as to humiliate the enemies of the Jewish people and put them to shame is a strong theme, alternating in a constant counterpoint with the guilt-dominated moral exhortations of the Prophets who warn against the sinfulness of pride, violence, injustice, and neglect of the poor, until the latter theme finally drowns out the former. The parallelism between Greek and Jewish culture—first a shame culture, then a guilt culture—together with the apparently much wider distribution of shame than of guilt cultures throughout the world, suggests the possibility that there is a general trend for cultures, like individuals, to be sensitive to shame before they are to guilt.

However, the history of Christianity also illustrates another possibility—the regression of a culture from a guilt into a shame culture. During its first three centuries of existence, Christianity existed under conditions that would appeal to guilt-ridden people—namely, persecution and martyrdom. Early Christianity fit Nietzsche's description of slave morality, since it identified with slaves and the qualities necessary to be slaves, such as meekness, passivity, and submissiveness in the face of domination and exploitation (advice it gave to those who literally were slaves, as well as to the free). For example, Christ said that "when you have done everything that was commanded you, you ought to say 'We are useless slaves; we have done [only] what we were obliged to do'" (Luke 17:10).[182]

Shame cultures have long been the cultural norm enforcing rigidly defined patriarchal norms that enforce the gender binary and hierarchy, the DNA of patriarchy, placing men over women, and men over other men and boys. Patriarchy is enforced by violence, arising from any challenge of the cultural definition of the gender binary and hierarchy, and structures cultural forms that foster a personal and political psychology capable of meeting its demands for violence. Roman patriarchy can be plausibly understood in these terms, as Carol Gilligan and I argue at some length, in our *The Deepening Darkness*.[183]

However, with the conversion of the Emperor Constantine early in the fourth century, Christianity became the religion of the masters, not just the slaves; and the motives for becoming a Christian changed accordingly. Thus Christianity changed from a relatively pure and extreme guilt culture to (at least) a mixed shame-and-guilt culture, capable of inspiring extremes not only of masochism, as formerly, but also of sadism; of martyrdom and murder, saintliness and savagery, piety and power, Francis of Assisi and Torquemada. It is an important feature of the conception of shame vs. guilt cultures that a political powerful shame culture like Roman imperialism may, once an ostensibly guilt culture like Christianity is made the established church of the Roman Empire, Christianity—a religion of human equality and mutual responsibility and peace—became more a Roman

182 Wayne A. Meeks, *The Moral World of the First Christians* (Philadelphia, PA: The Westminster Press, 1986), p. 38.

183 Gilligan and Richards, *The Deepening Darkness*, pp. 9–81.

shame than a Christian guilt culture, endorsing not only the Inquisition, but the wars of religion among Christians, the violence (including pogroms) of Christian anti-Semitism against the Jews, and the Crusades against Muslims. Very few cultures even today are homogenous guilt or shame cultures: the U.S. and even Britain may be largely democratic guilt cultures, but features of a shame culture were displayed by Donald Trump's victory in the U.S. and perhaps the politics of Brexit in the U.K. The earlier self-sacrificing guilt culture of Christianity survived, or was revived, in only a few atypical pockets of extreme religious fervor, such as some monastic communities and sects like the Hutterites.

Ruth Benedict's theory of shame vs. guilt cultures was developed as an explanation of one culture, that of Japan. The role of what Carol Gilligan and I call patriarchy—the gender binary and hierarchy—is implicit in her account, suggesting that historically shame cultures are dominantly patriarchal both in personal and political life. Later important works of historical psychology include, as we have seen, the work of E. R. Dodds,[184] but also that of Zevedei Barbu,[185] both of whom developed a diachronic dimension of the distinction between shame and guilt cultures. Both study, for example, the development from the dominantly shame culture of *The Iliad* (in which the shaming of manhood and violence are prominent) to the more inward guilt culture reflected in many of the Greek tragedies as well as in the emergence of Socratic philosophy (in which reflection on ethical responsibilities to self and others becomes central). Barbu prominently uses the rise and decline of patriarchy[186] as an important feature of his historical psychology, as well as the related idea of shame and guilt cultures,[187] both in his account of the development of ancient Greek culture and the development of what he calls "British national character."[188] The latter account focuses on the transition from the dominantly religious culture of medieval Britain and the growth of political absolutism, both patriarchal, to the shift to a democratic questioning of the medieval consensus and its patriarchally hierarchical chains sponsored by the impact of both the Renaissance and Reformation on British culture.

Cross-cultural research indicates that manhood has always been psychologically conflicted and fragile,[189] but the question of psychological fragility takes a different form in cultures like ours (like that of ancient Athens and Britain), which, at certain points in their history, are more democratic though still

184 Dodds, *The Greeks and the Irrational*.

185 See Zevedei Barbu, *Problems of Historical Psychology* (New York: Grove Press, 1960).

186 Ibid., pp. 7, 52, 60, 83, 91, 92, 95, 98, 110, 119, 120, 123, 179.

187 See ibid, pp. 96–122.

188 See ibid., pp. 145–218.

189 On this point, see David D. Gilmore, *Manhood in the Making: Cultural Concepts of Masculinity* (New Haven, CT: Yale University Press, 1990).

patriarchal, and which are still in transition from patriarchy to a more democratic culture.

1.3.2 Burke on the Transition from a Shame to a Guilt Culture: Moral Nihilism

It is at this juncture in the history of British liberal constitutionalism that we can better understand the path-breaking importance of Burke's insights into the psychology of political violence. Britain, at the time Burke was writing, was very much in transition from a shame to a guilt culture in view of the Glorious Revolution of 1688 that established constitutional monarchy there, and Burke plays an important role in understanding and promoting that transition. Certainly, Burke well understood the remaining features of Britain as a shame culture, monarchy, a hereditary aristocracy and rather rigid class structure, the electoral franchise for the House of Commons still quite limited, excluding Catholic and Jews and those that did not meet property qualifications, and the like. But he also well understood the role reforms of British constitutionalism had played in moving Britain culturally to more of a guilt culture, including the education and vocation it gave him as a natural aristocrat and a stage for his liberal political voice.

We can also now better understand, in light of our discussion of the cultural transition from a shame to guilt culture in ancient Greece and seventeenth- and eighteenth-century Britain, how and why Burke was so well situated psychologically and culturally to play the role he did. The very contrast that Burke drew in his most important early work, *A Philosophical Enquiry into the Sublime and Beautiful*, between terror (masculine) and love (feminine), though itself hostage to conventional patriarchal gender stereotypes of the period, also subverted them. This explains two crucial features of Burke's political liberalism: his interpretation of Christianity as a guilt culture and as a basis for a universalistic humanism that confronts imperial Britain and revolutionary France with their culpable moral wrongs, and the centering of his own life in personal love not only for his wife and family but for Will Burke, a loving relationship to another man that exposed him to insulting homophobic insinuations throughout his life. And yet through the relationship, both intimately personal and political as, again and again, they supported one another, endured and prospered, as the love of equals often does, made possible by its resistance to patriarchy.

It is these features of Burke's life and work that explain his greatest contribution to the understanding of political liberalism and its vulnerabilities to the patriarchal political psychology of the powerful shame cultures such liberalism provocatively challenges, in particular, his astonishing insights into the role terror would play in the war of patriarchy on liberalism. From his earliest reflections on terror, Burke writes: "No passion so effectually robs the mind of all it powers of acting and reasoning as fear,"[190] a theme he powerfully uses in

190 See Burke, *A Philosophical Enquiry into the Sublime and Beautiful*, p. 47.

Reflections as he indicts the French revolutionaries for having "*slain* the mind in their country."[191] As he puts it:

> The worst of these politics of revolution is this; they temper and harden the breast, in order to prepare it for the desperate strokes which are sometimes used in extreme occasions. But, as these occasions may never arrive, the mind receives a gratuitous taint; and the moral sentiments suffer not a little, when no political purpose is served by the depravation. This sort of people are so taken up with their theories about the rights of man, that they have totally forgot his nature … . Plots, massacres, assassinations, seem to some people a trivial price for obtaining a revolution. A cheap, bloodless reformation, a guiltless liberty, appear flat and vapid to their taste. There must be a change of scene; there must be a magnificent stage effect; there must be a grand spectacle to rouze the imagination, grown torpid with the lazy enjoyment of sixty years security, and the still unanimating repose of public prosperity.[192]

The use of the distinction between a guilt vs. shame culture could not be clearer. There is contempt for "a guiltless liberty," a matter of individual conscience, in favor of a shame-producing public festival in which violence is crucial, indeed required by a toxic patriarchal masculinity for which disagreement triggers repressive violence. Violence is an imperative psychological need of patriarchy under threat, and shame-driven fear and terror are how, as Burke puts it, it kills both moral conscience and heart.

Burke's earlier analyses of Britain's illiberal treatment of the Americans and the Irish was that, in unjustly degrading them from the rights owed them by liberal principles, such treatment elicits political violence. The France that give rise to the French Revolution—the France of absolute monarchy, a hereditary aristocracy, and an entrenched church supportive of both (neither the aristocracy nor church subject to taxation)—appears to be a shame culture, but now its legitimacy was in some real doubt (think of the impact on French thought of Rousseau, Diderot, Voltaire, and many others[193]); Rousseau's appeal to a bucolic state of nature apparently influenced even Marie Antoinette, creating the Petit Trianon at Versailles, her refuge from the palace.[194] Apparently some churchmen

191 Burke, *Reflections*, p. 49.

192 Ibid., p. 65.

193 For a useful set of readings of these figures, see David Williams (ed.), *The Enlightenment* (Cambridge: Cambridge University Press, 1999). One of the most brilliant among them, directly involved in constitutional debates in France during this period, was Condorcet, who went to the guillotine. See Stevens Lukes and Nadia Urbinati, *Condorcet: Political Writings* (Cambridge: Cambridge University Press, 2012). For an illuminating overview, see Israel, *Revolutionary Ideas*.

194 See "Marie Antoinette and the French Revolution," www.pbs.org/marieantoinette/life/trianon.html.

and aristocrats and many others were already in transition to a guilt culture, which is shown by their willingness to abandon their power as estates in the Estates General (two of the three estates were required to vote changes) and join one assembly as a democratic body, which would become the unicameral National Assembly that would proclaim in 1789 the Declaration of the Rights of Man and Citizen, which would, if anything, ideologically proclaim the terms of a guilt culture. It was not, however, to be. Quite the contrary.

What Burke observes and carefully analyzes in *Reflections* is that the ostensible transition from a shame to a guilt culture, which Britain had achieved over centuries of self-correcting historical experience, was in France in fact a regression to a quite dangerous modernist shame culture arising from what James Gilligan and I have called moral nihilism in our *Holding a Mirror Up to Nature*,[195] an investigation into both the personal and political psychology of violence through the study of Shakespeare's tragedies. Two of Shakespeare's plays, *Hamlet* and *Troilus and Cressida*, illustrate moral nihilism and how it gives rise to uncontrollable violence, namely, the collapse of belief in conventional values and institutions, indeed the attack on all such values and institutions, leading to the paralysis of action exemplified by Hamlet himself whose paralysis leads to the death of not only the woman he loves but also her father and brother, his two former college friends, his mother, his uncle the king, and finally himself. The transition from a shame to a guilt culture is from the shame culture of patriarchal hierarchy to the guilt culture of democratic equality, not to no authority but a new form of internalized authority that respects all persons equally. When Burke distinguishes "real" from "unreal" human rights he is exposing what came to be in France an empty ideology of moral nihilism that, in the name of equality, in time rationalized the dehumanization of not only of all classes advantaged by the monarchy including the monarchy itself but rationalized as well experiences of humiliation by those disadvantaged classes as the rationale for unleashing illimitable violence, including murders.

Instead of institutions concerned to protect human rights of minorities, the central justification of liberalism, another form of rigid hierarchy emerged culminating in dictatorship and an increasingly disciplined citizen militarism in service of the dictatorship. Moral nihilism, an understandable transition from shame to guilt cultures, reinstituted a rigid shame culture, any opposition to which elicited illimitable violence, what Burke calls terror.

Burke had earlier written about terror in his *A Philosophical Enquiry into the Sublime and Beautiful*, where he had explored why in experiencing a great tragic play we take pleasure, as Aristotle observed, pity and terror, when, if such events occurred in our lives, we would find them unendurable. He returns to this point in *Reflections* contrasting the pity and terror experienced in the tragic

195 See Gilligan and Richards, *Holding a Mirror Up to Nature*.

theater with the unimaginably worse terrors of the French Revolution beyond anything tragedians have represented.[196] How does he understand these terrors and their catastrophic consequences for our common humanity?

What Burke sees is what, some two centuries later, Hannah Arendt in *The Origins of Totalitarianism* would describe as state-enforced terror, directed at both public and private life toward the end of crushing the faculties of the human mind—thinking, willing, and judging.[197] Or, what Robert O. Saxton, one of the best students of fascism, observes about the centrality of violence to fascism: as quoted by Paxton: "'The fist,' asserted a Fascist militant in 1920, 'is the synthesis of our theory.'"[198] The fascist, quoted by Paxton, refers to "our theory," a latter-day manifestation of what Burke earlier called the abstract theory of the rights of man of the French revolutionaries. How should we understand the connections of Burke's political psychology to these later developments?

It is striking that Burke is frequently cited in the argument of Arendt's *The Origins of Totalitarianism*,[199] still the most profound study of the roots of fascist and Stalinist totalitarianism in earlier European cultural experience, including its anti-Semitism, nationalism, and imperialism. Her most trenchant and suggestive discussion of Burke comes in her empirical confirmation of his attacks on the French Declaration of Rights and Citizen:

> These facts and reflections [European failures to respect human rights] offer what seems an ironical, bitter, and belated confirmation of the famous arguments with which Edmund Burke opposed the French Revolution's Declaration of the Rights of Man. They appear to buttress his assertion that human rights were an "abstraction," that it was much wiser to rely on an "entailed inheritance" of rights which one transmits to one's children like life itself, and to claim one's rights to be the "rights of an Englishman" rather than the inalienable rights of man. According to Burke, the rights which we enjoy spring "from within the nation," so that neither natural law, nor divine command, nor any concept of mankind such as Robespierre's "human race," "the sovereign of the earth," are needed as a source of law.
>
> The pragmatic soundness of Burke's concept to be beyond doubt in the light of our manifold experiences. Not only did loss of national rights in all instances entail the loss of human rights; the restoration of human rights, as the recent example of the State of Israel proves, has been achieved so far only through the restoration or the establishment of national rights.[200]

196 See Burke, *Reflections on the Revolution in France,* pp. 82–84.

197 See Hannah Arendt, *The Origins of Totalitarianism* (New York: Harcourt Brace Jovanovich, 1973).

198 Robert O. Paxton, *The Anatomy of Fascism* (New York: Vintage Books, 2004), p. 17.

199 See Arendt, *The Origins of Totalitarianism*, pp. 4, 70, 130, 175–76, 183, 185, 207, 254, 255, 352.

200 Ibid., p. 299.

Arendt's reading of Burke is understandable in light of her own traumatic experience of statelessness after she fled Germany[201] and her celebration of the U.S. Constitution after the U.S. gave her a home[202] (her commitment to Israel was, in contrast, ambivalent at best[203]). But, the very universalism of Burke's liberal resistance to British injustices in Ireland, America, and India does not support any kind of ethnic or even religious nationalism in Burke of the sort that Arendt condemns as one of the cultural sources of totalitarianism, the analysis of which by Arendt Burke anticipates. More needs to be said than Arendt tells us about how and why the dynamic, terror, so central to her analysis of the mechanisms of totalitarianism, was first so clearly stated by Burke. The key is Burke's political psychology, which is a cultural psychology investigating the transition from a shame to a guilt culture and how moral nihilism can corrupt the transition leading to even more problematic modernist shame cultures.

Keep in mind that *Reflections* is written and published in 1790–91 well before the Terror of 1793 and yet terror is quite central to his critical analysis. What terror does he have precisely in mind? What immediately struck Burke about the unfolding events in France is the yawning gap between the emancipatory abstract promise of the French Declaration of Rights of Man and Citizen of 1789 and what was happening on the ground in 1789–91, and nothing more so than story he tells about the events of October 1789—a violently murderous Paris mob (largely women) invading Versailles and coercively demanding that the king and queen and their children come to Paris, focusing, in particular, on the humiliation and terror of Marie Antoinette, a woman he acknowledges meeting and admiring in unforgettable terms as if his beloved wife or mother:

> It is now sixteen or seventeen years since I saw the queen of France, then the dauphiness at Versailles, and surely never lighted on this orb, which she hardly seemed to touch, a more delightful vision. I saw just above the horizon, decorating and cheering the elevated sphere she just began to move in—glittering like the morning-star, full of life, and splendor, and joy. Oh! what a revolution! and what an heart must I have, to contemplate without emotion that elevation and that fall! Little did I dream when she added titles of veneration to those of enthusiastic, distant, respectful love, that she should ever be obliged to carry the sharp antidote against disgrace concealed in that bosom; little did I dream that I should have lived to see such disasters fallen upon her in a nation of gallant men in a nation of men of honour and cavaliers

201 See Elisabeth Young-Bruehl, *Hannah Arendt: For Love of the World* (New Haven, CT: Yale University Press, 1982), pp. 111–258.

202 See Hannah Arendt, *On Revolution* (New York: Penguin, 1963).

203 See, e.g., Hannah Arendt, "Zionism Reconsidered," in *The Jewish Writings* (New York: Schocken Books, 2007), pp. 343–74; Hannah Arendt, *Eichmann in Jerusalem: A Report on the Banality of Evil* (New York: Penguin, 1963).

> … . The unbought grace of life, the cheap defence of nations, the nurse of manly sentiment and heroic enterprise, is gone![204]

Mary Wollstonecraft was quite right to observe about Burke's writing here that his early essay

> the *Sublime and Beautiful* had left its mark on *Reflections on the Revolution in France.* Only a dandy, far gone in the love of sensations for their own sake, could have produced the rhapsodic description of the "unbought grace of life" that issued from Burke's memory of the queen of France in her youth. The prophecy of his early essay in aesthetics was thus borne out: the sublime is indifferent to morality.[205]

It is quite true that the role terror plays in *Reflections* is anticipated by his early essay, but Wollstonecraft fails to see, strikingly denigrating him (as others did homophobically as "[o]nly a dandy"), that, for Burke, the linkage of terror and the sublime destroys liberal political morality, as it was doing in the way the violent Parisian mob was treating the queen and would treat others. And Wollstonecraft lacks any understanding of Burke's psychological insights into violence, whether the mobs in London attacking Catholics or the London newspaper endorsing violence against "sodomites" and even against Burke himself for flouting or challenging patriarchal gender roles. The violent rage of the Parisian mobs, including the women in such mobs, was the same psychology he condemned in the London mobs, largely women, who experienced humiliation at the gay men who violated their understanding of patriarchal gender roles, or the Parisian women at Versailles humiliated by their image of Marie's "unnatural" deviance from conventional gender roles (e.g., her alleged adulteries and lesbianism[206]). It was the move from protests based on resisting injustice to illimitable violence that Burke focuses on, and his psychological brilliance is to trace its trajectory.

Wollstonecraft fails also to see that in the earlier essay terror is associated with the sublime and a fear that undermines rational and reasonable ethical

204 Burke, *Reflections on the Revolution in France*, pp. 77–78.

205 David Bromwich, *The Intellectual Life of Edmund Burke: From the Sublime and Beautiful to American Independence* (Cambridge, MA: Harvard University Press, 2014), pp. 83–84

206 See Lynn Hunt (ed.), "The Many Bodies of Marie Antoinette: Political Pornography and the Problem of the Feminine in the French Revolution," in *Eroticism and the Body Politic* (Baltimore, MD: The Johns Hopkins University Press, 1991), pp. 108–31. As an example of this widespread view of her lesbianism not only in France, Samuel Johnson's friend, Hester Thrale, wrote a few months before the French revolution: "The Queen of France is at the Head of a Set of Monsters call'd by each other *Sapphists,* who boast her Example; and deserve to be thrown with the *He* Demons that haunt each other likewise, into Mount Vesuvius." Quoted in Crompton, *Byron and Greek Love*, pp. 35–36.

thought and action, love with the beautiful and sympathy, the basis of ethical sensibility. Burke's rhapsodic prose in *Reflections* expresses love and sympathetic identification with what the queen is going through, namely, a terror that led her and others to comply with the demands of the Paris mob. Burke wants us to experience what terror is, as it is here directed at and experienced in the intimate relations of a husband, wife, and children, resting on dehumanization, "a king is but a man; a queen is but a woman; a woman is but an animal; and an animal not of the highest order."[207] For Burke, as we have seen, ethics arises from and sustains loving intimate relationships, whether they are of monarchs or commoners, and his liberal resistance thus often centers, as here, on a terror that targets intimate life and those "gallant men in nation of honour and cavaliers" who would have otherwise been expected to resist people who "have perverted in themselves, and in those that attend to them, all the well-placed sympathies of the human heart."[208] Its mechanism is fear: "No mechanism so effectually robs the mind of all its powers of acting and reasoning."[209]

Burke is describing a political ideology that dehumanizes its victims that rationalizes atrocity. Burke of course moved successfully in British aristocratic life with its hierarchies and subordinations, which he came to regard as, at least in Britain, serving political liberalism, and his special horror at the treatment of the French king and queen reflects his own aristocratic sensibilities, albeit those of a natural aristocrat. He puts his point in terms of the damage being done in France to

> our manners, our civilization, and all the good things connected with manners, and with civilization, have, in this European world of ours, depended for ages upon two principles and were indeed the result of both combined; I mean the spirit of a gentleman, and the spirit of religion. The nobility and the clergy, the one by profession, the other by patronage, kept learning in existence, even in the midst of arms and confusions, and whilst governments were rather in their causes than formed. Learning paid back what it received to nobility and priesthood, and paid it with usury, by enlarging their ideas, and by furnishing their minds. Happy if they had all continued to know their indissoluble union, and their proper place![210]

He is making a point about cultural evolution from a shame to guilt culture in which aristocrats and the clergy, in periods of "arms and confusions," sustained at least some humane learning and feeling, learning often critical of the shame culture around it, a learning that undoubtedly had introduced the doubt of

207 Burke, *Reflections on the Revolution in France*, p. 79.
208 Ibid., p. 65.
209 Burke, *A Philosophical Enquiry into the Sublime and Beautiful*, p. 47.
210 Burke, *Reflections on the Revolution in France*, pp. 80–81.

many in France, including aristocrats and clergy, about the French monarchy itself. But, his essential psychological point is about a political ideology that is destroying humanism itself, namely, treating persons equals. That point would be the same for the violence directed not at the king and his wife, but against the many republicans (men and women), some of the middle and lower classes, who, coming to resist the Jacobins, were condemned to the guillotine, let alone the many other innocents slaughtered for crimes of thought. It is the alleged crime, for example, of disagreement with the revolution's condemnation of religion that rationalized the guillotining of 16 Carmelite nuns on 17 July 1794, an atrocity so shocking that it may have ended the Terror (Robespierre was himself executed ten days later).[211]

Burke also wants us to see what could motivate this and other inhumanities, "[p]lots, massacres, assassinations,"[212] namely, "the pride and intoxication of their theories."[213] Burke is quite serious about the demonic psychological forces French revolutionaries are unleashing ("rapacity, malice, revenge, and fear more dreadful than revenge") through "the splendour of these triumphs of the rights of man, all natural sense of right and wrong."[214] By the "splendour of these triumphs," he means without argument the move to democracy they endorse, suppressing mindlessly the tension between political liberalism (respect for human rights) and democracy as such:

> Have these gentlemen never heard, in the whole circle of the worlds of theory and practice, of any thing between the despotism of the monarch and the despotism of the multitude?[215]

Or, as he points the point trenchantly later, anticipating John Stuart Mill on the tyranny of the majority:

> Of this I am certain, that in a democracy, the majority of the citizens is capable of exercising the most cruel oppressions upon the minority.[216]

Burke never argues that the French absolute monarchy was not unjust and should be reformed, nor that its abuses did not give rise to understandable

211 "Martyrs of Compiegne," httprs://en.wikipedia.org/wiki/Martyrs_of_Eompi%C3%A8gne. The psychology of the faith, doubt, and courage of these women resisting the fear central to the Terror is brilliantly and movingly explored in Francis Poulenc's remarkable opera *Dialogues des Carmelites*, recently revived at the Metropolitan Opera in New York City.

212 Burke, *Reflections on the Revolution in France*, p. 65.

213 Ibid., p. 64.

214 Ibid., p. 84.

215 Ibid., p. 128.

216 Ibid., pp. 129–30.

moral indignation, nor that its injustice does not justify a right to revolt; but he sees in the theory and practice of democracy they are promoting yet another absolutism that rather than questioning the shame culture of absolutism of Bourbon France is mindlessly replacing it with another, probably worse shame culture of absolutism, expressing itself in a trajectory to the dictatorship either of an ideological leader like Robespierre or a military leader like Napoleon enforced by terror, making of any resistance a conspiracy to be repressed by endless violence first against fellow dissenting Frenchmen and then against the dissenting world, including, as Burke came to see, the political liberalism of Britain. So, rather than marking, as the French revolutionaries and some British liberals thought, the world historical transition from a shame to guilt culture, its political psychology required a political terror based on scapegoating and demonizing dissent that destroyed "all natural sense of right and wrong," the basis of an ethics of human rights and of a guilt culture.

The very role that the appeal to abstract reason had played in French revolutionary thought, so lacking in any interest in the history and experience Burke thought was required for any serious constitutional construction, led Burke to express skepticism about reliance on abstract reason of that sort pointing to its disastrous consequences for France. His defense of prejudices must be understood not as irrationalist, but on the kind of skepticism about pure reason without experience that Immanuel Kant was developing at the same time as Burke and indeed was to use quite brilliantly in his own constitutional thought, absorbed, as Burke was, in how liberal constitutions might tame the violence of European wars.[217] For Burke, political forms must be tested by cumulative historical experience of diverse peoples over time:

> We are afraid to put men to live and trade each on his own private stock of reason, because we suspect that this stock in each man is small, and that the individuals would do better to avail themselves of the general bank and capital of nations, and of ages. Many of our men of speculation, instead of exploding general prejudices, employ their sagacity to discover the latent wisdom, which prevails in them. If they find what they seek, and they seldom fail, they think it more wise to continue the prejudice, with the reason involved, than to cast away the prejudice, and to leave nothing but the naked reason; because prejudice, with its reason, has a motive to give action to that reason, and an affection which will give it permanence.[218]

217 See, e.g., Kant, *Perpetual Peace: A Philosophical Sketch*, in Hans Reiss (ed.), *Kant's Political Writings* (Cambridge: Cambridge University Press, 1970), pp. 93–130.

218 Burke, *Reflections*, p. 90.

Burke deeply admired Montesquieu's comparative political science, and would have thought that his doctrine of the separation of powers, tested by the experience of the British balanced constitution (which Montesquieu admired and recommended), would have been for the British a historical prejudice of precisely this sort, ultimately supported, as it was, by reason although not always accepted by most people on that basis.

Burke frames his critique of the French revolutionaries very much on the model of the wars of religion, arguing that, paradoxically, the very war of the French Jacobins on religion as such was itself a kind of sectarian religion. He dramatically strikes this note by beginning his argument in *Reflections on the Religion in France* by comparing, as we have seen, Richard Price's defense of the French Revolution to the influence of a sectarian Puritan preacher, Hugh Peter, on Cromwell and Ireton in the 1640s in the English Civil War. The English Civil War was motored and ultimately won not by deliberative argument, but by the religiously inspired egalitarianism, the basis of the solidarity of the New Model Army under Oliver Cromwell's increasingly antidemocratic and dictatorial leadership. What that idealistic Puritan egalitarianism might have meant for British democratic constitutionalism was suggested at the earlier discussed Putney Debates, embodied in the proposal of the soldiers for a written constitution, the Agreement of the People. But, neither Ireton or Cromwell accept the proposal, and Cromwell uses the army to undermine whatever democratic legitimacy the existing parliament may have had in discussing and drafting a new constitution. Cromwell was for Burke not a serious constitutional thinker open to deliberative argument, but a successful military leader intoxicated, as the French revolutionaries were, by his own success and the sense of sectarian religious destiny, his success led him disastrously, for Britain, to accept. Burke, unlike Hume, was not a religious skeptic. His political liberalism rested on a universalistic Christian Humanism that extended to all persons (the Irish, Americans, Indians, even gays) whose claims to justice had been ignored or rejected by the "metropolitan pride"[219] of George III, his ministers, and the British parliament. What he saw in Cromwell and the French revolutionaries was not such universalistic humanism that protected the rights of minorities (the central object of political liberalism), but, despite claims to the contrary, the political psychology of a patriarchal shame culture shown by the fact any resistance, no matter how reasonable, was experienced as a humiliation requiring violence.

It is fundamental to the depth of Burke's insight into this political psychology that he sees it arising again and again when a state, despite its claims to the contrary (whether, as with Cromwell, religious, or, as with the French or Hitler and Stalin, secular), it unjustly fails to extend its ostensible claims of toleration or fair representation or the rights of man, to despised minorities,

219 Bourke, *Empire and Revolution*, p. 449.

scapegoating their just resistance, and thus eliciting their violent resistance (in Ireland, or America). What Burke exposes is vulnerabilities to violence in political psychology in the transition from a shame to a guilt culture, as even those, like Cromwell or the French revolutionaries or later the Russian revolutionaries, who think of themselves as agents of a world historical shift from patriarchal monarchical shame cultures to a democratic guilt culture based on equal rights, insulate themselves from any fair or reasonable democratic discussion for an absolutist patriarchal certainty shamed by and violently repressing any resistance. As Theda Skocpol observes of the Russian Revolution:

> The organized revolutionaries who claimed leadership with the revolutionary crisis were, moreover, dedicated to socialist ideals of equality and proletarian democracy. Yet the Russian Revolution soon gave rise to a highly centralized and bureaucratic party-state, which eventually became committed to propelling rapid national industrialization by command and terror.[220]

It is the regressive psychology of such a shame culture responding to moral chaos that explains both why any resistance elicits violence and why they are themselves increasingly violent and dictatorial. It is for this reason that Burke calls even the attacks on religion of the French revolutionaries, "this new religious persecution,"[221] in effect, a political religion.

It is one of the most prophetic features of Burke's analysis of 1790–91 of the French Revolution (clarifying the similar dynamics of the later Russian and Chinese Revolutions[222]) that its propensities to violence included the use of military force to enforce its aims: "As the colonists rise on you, the negroes rise on them. Troops again—Massacre, torture, hanging! These are your rights of men! These are the fruits of metaphysic declarations wantonly made, and shamefully retracted."[223] As early as 1792, when France declared war on Austria, Rouget de Lisle wrote the popular "La Marseillaise," so named because of its popularity with the volunteer army units from Marseille;[224] it is a sanguinary call to revolutionary arms leading to a conception of French citizenship and aggressive nationalism defined by mass military service, on the self-conscious model of the highly patriarchal Roman Republic that celebrated (as in the grisly painting

220 Theda Skocpol, *States and Social Revolutions* (Cambridge: Cambridge University Press, 1979, 2015), p. 206.

221 Burke, *Reflections on the Revolution in France*, p. 149.

222 For a fuller discussion of the role of militarism in the French as well as Russian and Chinese revolutionary, see Skocpol, *States and Revolutions*.

223 Ibid., p. 224.

224 See "La Marseillaise: History, Lyrics, and Translation," www.britannica,com/topic/La-Marse illaise

of Jacques-Louis David, "Oath of the Horatii") a toxic masculinity and imperialistic violence that the French effectively imitate.[225] The political psychology driving the French revolutionaries continued under the Directory, Burke saw, leading to conscription and growing militarism, expressed by Brissot in the National Assembly: "In the absence of respect for a free constitution, a free people would display its vengeances: 'la vengeance d'un people libre est lente, mais elle frappe surement.'"[226] Once the French defeated the forces opposed to it at the Battle of Fleurus,

> the Revolutionary armies went on the offensive. In the late summer of 1793 the Convention had instituted the *levee en masse*, transforming the military fortunes of the French. A citizen army of around 800,000 troops supplanted the combined force of the old line army, the national guard and the volunteers that had hitherto occupied the field. The sheer volume of fighting men available to the French could overwhelm the professional and mercenary strength of the allies. After Fleurus, republican soldiers pushed northwards into the Netherlands, threatening the strategic barriers between Britain and France, and looking forward to requisitioning the naval strength of the Dutch. The determination of the allies began to slacken.[227]

The Jacobin allegedly universalist political religion now rationalized aggressive war on the other nations of Europe, and Burke, no pacifist, now urged a defensive war against France.[228] Burke's analysis of the political psychology of the French revolutionaries was to be prophetic. Consider his words:

> In the weakness of one kind of authority, and in the fluctuation of all, the officers of an army will remain for some time mutinous and full of faction, until some popular general, who understands the art of conciliating the soldiery, and possesses the true spirit of command, shall draw the eyes of all men upon himself. Armies will obey him on his personal account. There is no other way of securing military obedience in this state of things. But the moment in which that event shall happen, the person who really commands the army is your master (that is little) of your king, the master of your assembly, the master of the whole republic.[229]

225 On the role of patriarchy in the endless wars of the Roman Republic, see Gilligan and Richards, *The Deepening Darkness*, pp. 22–52.

226 Quoted in Bourke, *Empire and Revolution*, p. 808; see also pp. 855, 857, 857, 903.

227 Ibid., p. 900.

228 See Edmund Burke, "The First Letter on a Regicide Peace," in Hampsher-Monk, *Revolutionary Writings*, pp. 251–334.

229 Burke, *Reflections*, pp. 221–22.

The French Revolution would end in Napoleon's military dictatorship and his largely successful wars on other European nations ending in defeat in Russia and later at Waterloo.

The tragedy of the French Revolution was, unlike the earlier English Civil War, not just a tragedy for the nation that lived through it, but a European tragedy at least for liberal constitutionalism and the promise that both Burke and Kant shared that it might, properly understood, tame the problem of European wars.[230] The dynamic of the political psychology of the French revolutionaries discredited whatever appeal liberal constitutionalism may once have had for Europeans, ending, as it did, in the formation of an aggressive nationalism and imperialism at war with other European nations that would persist in Europe long after Napoleon's defeat and set the stage for the competing imperialisms of Britain, France, Germany, Austria-Hungary, Russia, and the Ottomans that would culminate catastrophically in World War I, setting the stage for twentieth-century totalitarianisms and the even more catastrophic World War II.

No one saw the underlying issues of political psychology more lucidly than John Maynard Keynes in *The Economic Consequences of the Peace*,[231] as the Treaty of Versailles after World War I imposed excessive demands for reparation on the defeated as well as unreasonable demands for repayments of war debts, unleashing the political psychology of aggressive fascism to which Hitler later appealed to as "the shame of Versailles." Keynes' argument is remarkable both for its economics and its exquisitely Burkean insights into political psychology. "The psychology of society"[232] prior to World War II was brilliantly successful:

> this remarkable system depended for its growth on a double bluff or deception. On the one hand the laboring classes accepted from ignorance or powerlessness, or were compelled, persuaded, or cajoled by custom, convention, authority and the well-established order of Society into accepting a situation in which they could call their own very little of the cake that they and Nature and the capitalists were co-operating to produce. And on the other hand the capitalist classes were allowed to call the best part of the cake theirs and were theoretically free to consume it, on the tacit understanding that they consumed very little of it in practice … . The duty of "saving" became nine-tenths of virtue and the growth of the cake the object of true religion. There grew around non-consumption of the cake all those instincts of puritanism

230 See Kant, "Perpetual Peace," in Hans Reiss (ed.), *Kant's Political Writings* (Cambridge: Cambridge University Press, 1970), pp. 93–130.

231 John Maynard Keynes, *The Economic Consequences of the Peace* (New York: Harcourt, Brace and Howe, 1920).

232 Ibid., p. 19.

> which in other ages has withdrawn itself from the world and has neglected the arts of production as well as those of enjoyment.[233]

The arrangement was, however, after the war no longer viable or sustainable.

> The war has disclosed the possibility of consumption to all and the vanity of abstinence to many. Thus the bluff is discovered; the laboring classes may be no longer willing to forego so largely, and the capitalist classes, no longer confident of the future, may seek to enjoy more fully their liberties of consumption so long as they last, and thus precipitate the hour of their confiscation.[234]

Keynes attended the negotiations over the Treaty of Versailles, and closely examines how its three leading figures (Wilson for the U.S.; Clemenceau for France; Lloyd George for the U.K.) not only failed to understand the new economic situation, but so disastrously mismanaged the terms of the treaty on the generous terms to the Germans that Keynes thought were required. The key to the disaster was the American lack of understanding of European politics and economics, and the ease with which Clemenceau's view that a German was "without honor, pride, or mercy … and you must never negotiate with a German or conciliate him; you must dictate to him"[235] was allowed to prevail. The problem was Wilson did not understand the game other leaders were playing: "a game of which he had no experience at all."[236] His sensibility was "solitary and aloof, … very strong-willed and obstinate."[237] Keynes asks: "What chance could such a man have against Mr. Lloyd George's unerring, almost medium-like, sensibility to everyone immediately around him?"[238] Wilson's "thought and his temperament were essentially theological [political religion, in Burke's sense] not intellectual, with all the strength and weakness of that manner of thought, feeling, and expression."[239] His greatest weakness was his moralistic blindness to how he was being manipulated to serve narrow French and British national interests: "But this blind and deaf Don Quixote was entering a cavern where the swift and glittering blade was in the hand of the adversary."[240] Keynes concludes: "There can seldom have been a statesman of the first rank more incompetent than the President in the agilities of the council chamber."[241]

233 Ibid., p. 20.
234 Ibid., p. 21.
235 Ibid., p. 28.
236 Ibid., p. 33.
237 Ibid.
238 Ibid., p. 34.
239 Ibid.
240 Ibid.
241 Ibid., p. 35.

Keynes concludes with "pessimism. The Treaty includes no provisions for the economic rehabilitation of Europe."[242] The consequence is: "An inefficient, unemployed, disorganized Europe faces us, torn by internal strife and international hate, fighting, starving, pillaging, and lying. What warrant is there for a picture of less somber colors?"[243] At this point, Keynes' argument is quite starkly and self-consciously Burkean:

> Economic privation proceeds by easy stages, and so long as men suffer it patiently the outside world cares little. Physical efficiency and resistance to disease slowly diminish, but life proceeds somehow, until the limit of human endurance is reached at last and counsels of despair and madness still the sufferers from the lethargy which precedes the crisis. Then man shakes himself, and the bonds of custom are loosed. The power of ideas is sovereign, and he listens to whatever instructions of hope, illusion, or revenge is carried to him in the air.[244]

Zachary Carter has recently shown that "Keynes was not issuing a Marxist assault on unearned bourgeois privileges but was presenting a fundamentally conservative political position inspired by Edmund Burke,"[245] as the political psychology he sketches leading to violent revolutions show ("The power of ideas is sovereign," as in the French Declaration of Human Rights, "and he listens to whatever instructions of hope, illusion, or revenge is carried to him in the air," as in the Terror). At the time he wrote *Economic Consequences*, he thought "the flames of Russian Bolshevism seem, for the moment at least to have burnt themselves out." Of course, he was wrong about that and unfortunately right about what would happen in Germany. It is striking that Keynes framed his fears for political liberalism, unleashed by the political shame-driven psychology of humiliation of the defeated at Versailles, quite explicitly in terms of Burke's argument of how the violent revolutions in Germany and Russia might, like the French Revolution, mask the "unreal rights" of utopian or crackpot scientific ideologies of race or Marxist historical inevitability appealed to by revolutionaries and instead unleash an aggressive violence against liberal values in the violent twentieth-century totalitarianisms of fascism and Stalinism, which is exactly what happened.

242 Ibid., p. 166.

243 Ibid., p. 180.

244 Ibid. For an important recent historical exploration of American irresponsibility during this period, see Robert Kagan, *The Ghost at the Feast: America and the Collapse of World Order, 1900–1941* (New York: Alfred A. Knopf, 2023).

245 On this point, see Zachary D. Carter, *The Price of Peace: Money, Democracy, and the Life of John Maynard Keynes* (New York: Random House, 2021), p. 96.

Keynes and Burke share more than may be superficially apparent in their roles as important liberal voices: in Burke, a liberal voice arising, so I have argued, from his life-long love for a man, in Keynes, a liberal voice arising from his long experience as a sexually active gay man roughly until his marriage to the ballerina, Lydia Lopokova, but always supporting, sometimes financially, his friends and former lovers in Bloomsbury (Duncan Grant); and, both were natural aristocrats and called for a liberalism that preserved a place for liberal elites courageously exercising liberal resisting voice.[246] Indeed, it is plausible that the evidence-based politics that Burke urged in the development of constitutional liberalism in the U.K. and the U.K. may have led Keynes to his evidence-based repudiation of the classical economic liberalism that may have been so successful for Britain in the Victorian period, but was not after World War I, leading him to develop the liberal socialism he in fact came to advocate, since free markets no longer delivered what for Keynes were the ends of liberal socialism, full employment, a good life, and greater economic equality and opportunity.[247] In both cases, Keynes like Burke insisted on the primacy of political liberalism over all other values, including economic values.

Such comparable Burkean worries about the threat of mob violence to political liberalism surface as well in Lincoln's remarkable "Speech to the Young Men's Lyceum of Springfield (1838)."[248] In the wake of growing mob violence, including the 1837 killing of abolitionist printer Elijah Lovejoy by a pro-slavery mob, Lincoln argues that the threat to constitutional democracy in the U.S. "must spring up amongst us. It cannot come from abroad."[249] Rather, it comes from "the operation of this mobocratic spirit, which all must admit, is now abroad in the land."[250] This requires, Lincoln argues, a rededication to the rule of law, including obeying laws one regards as unjust but arguing for justice within the law through the exercise of liberal voice, "the *political religion* of the nation,"[251] precisely Burke's understanding of liberal constitutionalism. What was for Lincoln, as for Burke, intolerable was a violence against voice itself (the murder of Lovejoy, a printer). Lincoln is unlikely to have read Burke, but he clearly anticipates the constitutional tragedy against which Burke earlier cautioned the Americans, namely, the very separation from Britain in the name of fair representation might lead to a constitutional design that failed to deal with deeper home-grown threats to its legitimacy (violence against liberal voice

246 On this point, see ibid., pp. 98–103; see also pp. 149–53.

247 For a further discussion along these lines, see Carter, *The Price of Money*, and James Crotty, *Keynes against Liberalism: His Economic Case for Liberal Socialism* (London: Routledge, 2019).

248 See Abraham Lincoln, "Speech to the Young Men's Lyceum of Springfield (1838)," https://constitutioncenter.org/the-constitution/historic-document-library/detail/abraham-lincoln-speech-to-the-young-mens-lyceum-of-springfield-1838

249 Ibid., p. 7.

250 Ibid., p. 11.

251 Ibid., p. 13.

itself and a politics that had finally, in the election of 1860, fairly given expression to that voice, in the election of an abolitionist president, Abraham Lincoln), culminating in unconstitutional secession and civil war.

1.4 Burke's Political Psychology Today: Hannah Arendt and James Gilligan

We earlier discussed Hannah Arendt's brilliant analysis of these developments in *The Origins of Totalitarianism*, noting the connections between anti-Semitism, nationalism, and imperialism. There are several features of her analysis that are, I believe, clarified by Burke's cultural psychology of violence, which will in turn lead to better understanding of political violence after World War II and the role political liberalism can and should play in bringing it under control.

First, there is her focus on the sources of the respective ideologies of both German/Italian fascism and Soviet communism: in the fascist case, the pseudoscience of race; in the communist case, Marxist ideology. In both cases, there is "the scientificality of totalitarian propaganda,"[252] neither of which is supported by reasonable scientific argument, and both of which claim universal truth and demand the infallibility of the leader interpreting and implementing such truth.[253]

Second, there are its methods, namely, terror directed at the human psyche. A population subject to terror

> do not believe in anything visible, in the reality of their own experience; they do not trust their eyes and ears but only their imaginations, which may be caught by anything that is at once universal and consistent in itself. What convinces masses are not facts, and not even invented facts, but only the consistency of the system of which they are presumably part.[254]
>
> The ideal subject of totalitarian rule is not the convinced Nazi or the convinced Communist, but people for whom the distinction between fact and reality (i.e., the reality of experience) and the distinction between true and false (i.e., the standards of thought) no longer exist.[255]

Third, the abject loyalty to the infallible leader requires an attack on "social ties to family, friends, comrades, or even mere acquaintances,"[256] in effect, on private life as such, so that "after a few years of power and systematic

252 Arendt, *The Origins of Totalitarianism.*
253 Ibid., pp. 348–49.
254 Ibid., p. 351.
255 Ibid., p. 474.
256 Ibid., pp. 323–24.

co-ordination, the Nazis could rightly announce, 'The only person who is still a private individual in Germany is somebody who is asleep.'"[257]

Fourth, all these ideologies—whether those of the French Revolution or of Hitler or of Stalin—are in their nature hostile to political liberalism, fascism, and Stalinist communism quite explicitly, the French Revolution in fact but not in its abstract theory. It was the fact that political liberalism recognized and protected the human rights of despised minorities like the Jews and people of color and homosexuals that elicited Hitler's extraordinary levels of genocidal violence (murdering six million Jews) and starting an aggressive war killing many more millions, including Germans. And Hitler exemplified how fascism rests on forging a shame culture by pointing to the shame of Versailles as the reason for his aggressive violence against those who had defeated and humiliated Germany after its defeat in World War I. And it was the demands of political liberalism for the protection of basic rights like the liberties of conscience, free speech, intimate life, and voting rights that affronted Stalin's version of the dictatorship of the proletariat, as interpreted and enforced by his infallible judgment, that led him to war on all forms of political liberalism.

Burke's analysis of the political psychology of shame cultures explains in cultural/psychological terms what Arendt observes. Arendt's observation, for example, explains the power of the alleged universalist "scientificality" of something as abstract as the French Declaration of Rights of Man and why someone captivated by this vision has no interest in facts, but only that it "is at once universal and consistent in itself." And the way terror destroys both the mind epistemically and the heart by killing love and sympathy was exactly what Burke saw as the root of the inhumanities of the French revolutionaries, including turning murderously on one another and then on the world.

Dr. James Gilligan, a psychiatrist whose path-breaking studies of violence have influenced my analysis, has further clarified and elaborated the explanatory power of this cultural psychology in understanding persisting forms of violence in modernity.[258] His work draws upon the political psychology of the authoritarian personality developed by Adorno[259] and Altmeyer,[260] and empirically confirmed and further analyzed by Karen Stenner.[261] In his analysis, Gilligan focuses on two kinds of modernist ideologies: first, echoing Burke on political religions, he discusses three forms of religions disguised as politics: nationalism,

257 Ibid., pp. 338–39.

258 See James Gilligan, "Terrorism, Fundamentalism, and Nihilism: Analyzing the Dilemmas of Modernity," in Henri Parens, Alaz Mahfouz, Stuart W. Twemlow, and David E. Scharff (eds.), *The Future of Prejudice: Psychoanalysis and the Prevention of Prejudice* (Lanham, MD: Rowman & Littlefield, 2007), pp. 37–59.

259 T. W. Adorno, E. Frenkel-Brunswick, D. J. Levinson, and R. Nevitt Sanford, *The Authoritarian Personality* (New York: Wiley, 1950).

260 B. Altmeyer, *The Authoritarian Spectre* (Cambridge: Harvard University Press, 1996).

261 Karen Stenner, *The Authoritarian Dynamic* (Cambridge: Cambridge University Press, 2005).

imperialism, and totalitarianism; and second, one form of politics disguised as religion, apocalyptic fundamentalism. The main forms of modern violence legitimated by these ideologies are tied to nationalism, imperialism, totalitarianism, thermonuclear weapons, and apocalyptic fundamentalism (terrorism, suicide bombers). All these cases, for Gilligan, as I have earlier suggested, draw upon and perpetuated shame cultures that are at war with the guilt culture of political liberalism.

How to deal with such persisting forms of shame culture and their violence? Some forms of aggressive shame-driven violence can only be stopped by defensive war, as Burke argues, but others, notably Stalin communism, can be reasonably contained until such time as they may collapse from their own internal problems, as happened with the Soviet Union in 1991. The same policy of containment may be appropriate for China, but certainly not for Putin's aggression in Ukraine in service of a theocratic nationalism that repudiates political liberalism, or for the terrorisms of apocalyptic fundamentalism.

The great wisdom of leaders like Roosevelt and Churchill after World War II was forging new institutional structures of political liberalism both in some of the European nations defeated in World War II and at the European level, including the European Union and the European Declaration of Human Rights, in which Britain played an important role, a matter to be discussed further in later chapters. In contrast to the move of the U.S. into isolationism after World War I and refusal to join the League of Nations, the U.S. with Britain now plays an important role in designing and supporting the United Nations, as well as creating alliances with European countries (NATO) and offering them the resources of the Marshall Plan to repair their damaged economies.

What have we learned of value in understanding the British constitutionalism that Burke so brilliantly defends, as well as its relationship to American constitutionalism? To answer this question, we must turn to the constitutional liberalism of America's most important founder, James Madison, whose thought is, on the issue of constitutional interpretation, quite Burkean.

2 The Liberal Constitutionalism of James Madison

The liberal constitutionalism of Madison defends both the American Revolution and the Constitution of 1787 by the same appeal to the political liberalism of John Locke that we earlier found in our discussion of Burke's liberal constitutionalism. However, unlike Burke, Madison appeals to Locke to defend a written constitution that repudiates the role that parliament and parliamentary supremacy play in Burke's argument, but yet, in Madison's view, is consistent with Locke. I begin with a discussion of Madison's rather different appeal to Locke, but then turn to his argument about the legitimacy of a written constitution in which history plays a surprisingly Burkean role.

2.1 Locke's Political Liberalism

Locke's political theory is best understood as a generalization to politics in general of the argument for religious toleration he and Bayle pioneered.[1] That argument depended on the critical analysis of a historical rationale for religious persecution, namely, that the illegitimate political power of a dominant religion had been allowed to impose on society at large a factionalized conception of religious truth that sanctified unnatural hierarchies of power and privilege. Both Locke and Bayle condemned the political uses to which the argument had been put in the history of the West, because it had stunted and stultified the capacities of the human mind and heart to engage the emancipatory and egalitarian moral teaching of historical Christianity (an argument Burke accepted). Locke, in contrast to Bayle, generalized the scope of the argument to include the very legitimacy of political power. In effect, for Locke, injustices like religious persecution could not be localized to personal religion or even ethics: they undermined the general conditions for the legitimate exercise of political power by one person over another. When Locke wrote of the conditions that would justify revolution,

1 For a full discussion, see David A. J. Richards, *Toleration and the Constitution* (New York: Oxford University Press, 1986), pp. 89–95.

DOI: 10.4324/9781003410966-2

he thus described the pertinent convictions people would entertain: "they were persuaded in their Consciences, that their Laws, and with them their Estates, Liberties, and Lives are in danger, and perhaps their Religion too."[2]

The heart of Locke's political thinking was that the authority the inalienable right to conscience had in religion and in ethics carried over to politics. Parallel corruptions of those that had stunted and stultified that religious and moral capacities of persons carried over to people's political capacities. His political theory thus combined a normative component (respect for the inalienable human rights of persons conceived as free, equal, and rational) and a historical component (the structures of illegitimate power that had stunted our capacities to exercise religious, moral, and political freedoms consistent with these rights).

The normative component of Locke's political theory (namely, inalienable human rights) rested on the reasonable moral and political inquiry that he believed was made possible and practicable once the political force of the argument religious persecution was circumscribed by the acceptance of the argument for toleration. Such reasonable inquiry must be conducted—Locke had argued in his epistemology[3]—in light of experience, and reasonable inquiry into such experience demonstrably justified a theological ethics in which persons—understood to be made in God's image of rational creative freedom[4]—had inalienable rights, rights they could not surrender (e.g., to conscience and to life).[5] Such rights were inalienable because, as normative claims, they secured to each and every person (understood as free, rational, and equal) the final, ultimate, and non-negotiable control over the resources of mind and body that is essential to exercising our rational and reasonable powers in living a complete life as independent and morally accountable creative agents.[6] Locke's theory of political legitimacy rests on working out the consequences for politics of the objective moral and political value of such rights for persons, including their right to a politics that allowed them reasonably to know and claim such rights in both their private and public lives.

2 See John Locke, *Two Treatises of Government*, edited by Peter Laslett (Cambridge: Cambridge University Press, 1960); Locke, *Second Treatise of Government* pp. 422–23 (sec. 209). On the centrality of religious liberty in Locke's thought about politics and religion, see Richard Ashcraft, *Revolutionary Politics and Locke's Two Treatises of Government* (Princeton, NJ: Princeton University Press, 1986), pp. 483, 487–88, 494–97, 500. See also John Dunn, *The Political Thought of John Locke* (Cambridge: Cambridge University Press, 1969).

3 John Locke, *An Essay Concerning Human Understanding*, 2 vols., edited by Alexander C. Fraser (New York: Dover, 1959).

4 See John Tully, *A Discourse on Property: John Locke and His Adversaries* (Cambridge: Cambridge University Press, 1980), pp. 3–50.

5 See John Colman, *John Locke's Moral Philosophy* (Edinburgh: Edinburgh University Press, 1983).

6 See A. John Simmons, "Inalienable Rights and Locke's *Treatises*," *Philosophy & Public Affairs* 12 (1983): 175–204; Tully, *Discourse on Property*.

Post-Lockean moral thought in Britain and North America—to wit, the eighteenth-century philosophy of a moral sense[7]—questioned the theological argument of Locke, not on the ground of its conclusions about inalienable human rights, but rather, that the reasonable argument to such rights was, if anything, more direct, less intellectually circuitous, more available to all persons of common sense independent of theological conceptions of God's will. If anything, moral sense theory gave more direct and robust support for an inalienable right to conscience because the failure to respect this right (e.g., by religious persecution on the grounds of political enforcement of a sectarian view of religious truth) was now construed, by Jefferson among others, as a corruption of the moral sense itself.[8] Moral sense theorists thus both used and elaborated Locke's political theory, indeed (in Britain) in defense of the program of the Whig oppositionists, including Burke, who had supported their revolution and were so admired by Americans.

It is fundamental to the Lockean conception of political legitimacy both that a state may fail to meet the minimal benchmarks that justify the power of the state and that the question of whether it has done so much be one of which "I my self can only be Judge in my own Conscience."[9] Of course, Locke understood that the right to revolution could not always be justly and effectively exercised (Burke's Lockean argument against Price about the legitimacy of the French Revolution), and he assumed that the politics of revolution would require large numbers of reasonable people to concur in their judgments about the intolerable injustice of an existing state.[10] However, the conception of political legitimacy depended on inalienable human rights, rights of each and every person that could be surrenders to no other, and the judgment of whether a state's power met or flouted such rights could no more be surrendered to others than the rights themselves.

Locke thought of this conception of political legitimacy as arising at two distinct stages, which correspond to two distinguishable contractualist metaphors that he employed. First, because any legitimate political community must respect the inalienable right of each and every person subject to its power, the community of such persons must satisfy a criterion of unanimous reasonable consent that they wish a political community to exist. In a stable existing society, Locke believed such consent must be shown by each person's actual reasonable consent to the present form of government;[11] if such an existing society should break down, people then must unanimously decide whether they choose

7 For a fuller discussion and references, see David A. J. Richards, *Foundations of American Constitutionalism* (New York: Oxford University Press, 1989), pp. 84–85.

8 For references on this point, see ibid., p. 85, n. 37.

9 Locke, *Second Treatise of Government*, p. 300 (sec. 21).

10 See, e.g., ibid., pp. 397–98 (sec. 168), pp. 422–23 (sec. 209), pp. 435–36 (sec. 230).

11 See, e.g., ibid., pp. 349–50 (sec. 96), p. 364 (sec. 117)

to continue as a political society.[12] Second, the organization of such people into a form of government should be decided "by the will and determination of the *majority*."[13] Locke thought of majority rule in this context as the only reasonable alternative to unanimity as a *political* decision-making procedure that would respect equality and yet allow political communities to be formed on reasonable terms. He rejected unanimity because many people, on grounds of "Infirmities of Health, and Avocations of Business," would not attend "the Publick Assembly,"[14] and those who attended would have such "variety of Opinions, and contrariety of Interests"[15] that they would never agree. Because some political communities are, in fact, more consistent with respect for rights than a state of nature and because unanimity would preclude the existence of any political community, our reasonable moral interest in having a political community that respect rights require that the decision-making procedure must be by majority rule. Locke's argument does not, in fact, require majority rule, and might, in fact, require others (supermajority voting rules) if they would be superior to unanimity on the grounds Locke adduced and lead to the framing of government that were more consistent with political legitimacy, that is, that respect our inalienable human rights. Locke clearly thought of majority rule as a *faute de mieux* addressed to the narrow problem of framing constitutions and not to the substance of how those constitutions should be designed: he clearly did not believe that such majority procedures would necessarily result in a government that used majority rule, because the informed majority at the stage of framing the government might reasonably decide that the government most consistent with respect for rights would circumscribe, if not eliminate, majority rule as a principle of political decision-making. Such majority rule at the stage of governmental design must, of course, be exercised reasonably in light of our equal rights, and its resulting government, in the event it violated such rights, would be illegitimate and the justifiable object of the right to revolution.

Locke's political theory thus required political judgment by citizens at three stages: the judgment to join the political society, the judgment (if it was necessary) to frame its constitution, and the judgment to decide whether the constitution was any longer political legitimate. The capacities requisite to such political empowerment had, in Locke's view, been stunted by the same kinds of sectarian tyrannies he analyzed in his argument for religious toleration. The political power of dominant religious groups had for millennia stultified the reasonable exercised of people's religious and ethical judgment, laying the intellectually and morally corrupt foundations of an unjust edifice of entrenched hierarchy and

12 For a useful discussion of these exegetical points, see Ruth W. Grant, *John Locke's Liberalism* (Chicago: University of Chicago Press, 1987), pp. 110–28.

13 Locke, *Second Treatise of Government*, p. 349 (sec. 96).

14 Ibid., p. 350 (sec. 98).

15 Ibid., pp. 350–51.

privilege (e.g., absolute monarchies) with a power that depended on the unjust disenfranchisement and disempowerment of others. The brilliance of Locke as a democratic political theorist was his deepening of this insight into a view of the corruptions of political power and the corresponding need to rethink political legitimacy in ways that would constrain such power (e.g., constitutional monarchy).

If Locke's theory of religious toleration addressed a history of the abusive uses of political power that undermined the intellectual and moral foundations of the exercise of the inalienable right to conscience, his political theory engaged the more general injustice of the abusive uses of political power to undermine the foundations for the exercise of inalienable rights If much traditional religious teaching was morally bankrupt because it was supported by illegitimate religious persecution, then the same could be said for traditional teaching in politics. "Learning and Religion shall be found to justify"[16] the worst political tyrannies, "and would have all Men born to, what their mean Souls fitted them for, Slavery."[17] Locke's theory of political legitimacy was thus directed at establishing a new conception of political argument, which would as much prohibit political imposition of a sectarian religious as political argument. Political power must be justified in a way that does justice to persons who have inalienable human rights, persons understood to have reasonable powers of thought, deliberation, and action, and to be capable of governing their lives accordingly.

Religious persecution was, for Locke, a kind of paradigm of political illegitimacy because it subverted our very capacities for thinking reasonably about essential issues of a well-lived life by the political imposition of an irrationalism that read all issues of religious truth through the Manichean lens of fixed sectarian convictions. The argument for toleration ruled out such a use of political power because such power subverted the inalienable right to conscience, undermining the intellectual and moral foundation for reasonable forms of public discussion and deliberation that were not subordinate to fixed sectarian commitments. We have seen that Locke thought of the ultimate questions of political legitimacy (including the right to revolt) as addressed to the conscience of each and every person, and the subversion of the integrity of conscience was thus, for him, an irrationalist attack on political legitimacy itself. Locke's political theory of legitimacy sought to define an alternative conception of free public reason as accessible to all, as free of factionalized sectarian distortion, as justifying political demands to the reasonable capacities of each and every person, whose inalienable rights to exercise those capacities were immune from political compromise or bargaining. To do so, political power must be and be

16 Ibid., p. 345 (sec. 92).

17 Ibid., p. 444 (sec. 239)

seen to be in the service of a just impartiality root in respect for the equality of all persons.

The normative component of Locke's theory required that no legitimate political power could be exercised over our inalienable human rights because those rights were, by definition, subject to the power of no other person. The state could, however, play a normatively justifiable role if it assisted in or promoted equal respect for our rights, including the security of our right to conscience, our right to life, and the like. In fact, in the absence of an organized political power, Locke argued that each person or the persons associated with them (e.g., family, clans) had a moral right to enforce such claims, but that our historical experience had been that such enforcement was radically unjust: Persons were legislators, prosecutors, judges, and juries in their own cases, and the distortions of self-interest, bias, and vindictiveness results in either inadequate or excessive punishment of the guilty or punishment of the innocent.[18] The state performed a politically legitimate role when its institutions ensured a more just distribution of such punishments and of the rights and goods such punishments protect, because such a distribution better secured our equal rights and interests as persons.

Locke was, for a seventeenth-century British political theorist, remarkable for his lack of interest in historical arguments about the ancient British Constitution[19] and for his evident hostility to the reasoning of the common lawyers of his age.[20] His theory of political legitimacy quite clearly rested on a morally independent and objective conception of justice (including equal human rights), and political arrangements were subject to criticism on grounds of that conception. However, Locke brought to his political theory an acute sense of the ways in which objective moral values had been historically corrupted (e.g., the psychology of religious persecution), and he used it in defining appropriate political principles (e.g., the theory of religious toleration). Locke's constitutionalism equally rested on historically informed convictions about those structures of political power more likely to secure such ends or moral and political principle and even used anthropological data to define the relevance of historical change to constitutional structures.[21] He defended institutions calling for fair representation in the

18 Ibid., p. 293 (sec. 13).

19 See, e.g., J. G. A. Pocock, *The Ancient Constitution and the Feudal Law* (Cambridge: Cambridge University Press, 1957), pp. 46, 187–88, 235–88, 348, 354–61.

20 See, e.g., Locke, *Second Treatise of Government*, p. 293 (sec. 12), where Locke compares the clarity of the natural law to "the phansies and intricate Contrivances of Men, following contrary and hidden interests put into Words;" cf. ibid., pp. 299–300 (sec. 2). See also Locke's "Fundamental Constitutions of Carolina," secs. 79 and 80, which provide that all statute laws shall be null after a century, and that no comments on the constitutions shall be permitted, in *The Works of John Locke*, vol. 10 (London: Thomas Tegg, 1823), pp. 191–92.

21 For a commentary on this point, see Richard Aschcraft, *Locke's Two Treatises of Government* (London: Allen & Unwin, 1987), p. 145.

legislature, for example, because he construed such a constitutional arrangement as more likely to protect people's rights to property on fair terms;[22] furthermore, his defense of the separation of powers expressed the judgment that, at least in the later historical stages of a society (after the introduction of money),[23] separation of the powers of the legislature and the executive (in which Locke included the judicial power) would tend to secure a more impartially just distribution of punishments.[24] There is no reason to believe that Locke supposed that his own appeal to "experience … in Forms of Government"[25] was exhaustive, and—in view of his strong views about the corruption of "Learning and Religion"[26] of these matters—he invited a kind of historical and empirical inquiry, which was not subordinate to sectarian politics, in order better to assess these matters. Later American appeals to the best political science then available are very much in the spirit of Locke's constitutionalism, and it is not surprising that, from the more informed later American perspective, Locke's exploit in framing a written constitution (namely, the Fundamental Constitutions of Carolina[27]) should appear, as it did to John Adams, "a signal absurdity."[28]

2.2 Madison's Liberal Constitutionalism

We earlier saw that Burke's defense of the British Constitution in *Reflections on the Revolution in France* began with an argument that British liberals like Richard Price and others, who defended the French Revolution, misconstrued how and why the Glorious Revolution of 1688 legitimately rested on Locke. The Glorious Revolution rested on Locke's right to revolution, but its dethroning of James II and limitations on the powers of the monarchy were constitutional reforms that kept the framework of the British balanced constitution but changed it better to secure the protection of basic rights that James II's absolutism had threatened. Burke appeals to British historical experience to show how and why the British Constitution had progressively better protected what he called "real" rights, and that the British parliament had rendered the constitution even more legitimate because it reasonably advanced this project. Burke works within the framework of Locke's argument at the second stage that parliament, representing the people, may by majority rule reasonably reform the constitution, as he argued

22 See Locke, *Second Treatise of Government*, pp. 378–81 (secs. 138–42).

23 See ibid., pp. 356–57 (sec. 107), pp. 359–60 (sec. 110), pp. 360–61 (sec. 111).

24 See ibid., pp. 382–98 (secs.143–68). Locke separates government powers into legislative, executive (in which he includes the judiciary), and federative (foreign policy).

25 Ibid., p. 356.

26 Ibid., p. 345 (sec. 92).

27 See *Works of John Locke*, vol. 10, pp. 175–99.

28 See John Adams, "A Defence of the Constitutions of the Government of the United States of America," in Charles Francis Adams (ed.), *The Works of John Adams* (Boston, MA: Little, Brown, 1851), vol. 4, p. 463.

it had in 1688. In contrast, the assembly in Paris may justly have appealed to the right to revolution, but its lack of experience in thinking about constitutions had resulted in democratic forms that violently abridged human rights and thus were less legitimate than the government it supplanted.

In contrast, Burke had, as we saw, come to admire and even praise the U.S. Constitution of 1787. Why? As we saw in the Chapter 1 , he notably led the Rockingham Whigs in parliament to challenge the taxes George III and his ministers had gotten parliament to impose on the Americans and criticized as well going to war with the Americans. He believed, as apparently Benjamin Franklin did as well, that peaceful reconciliation would be better for Britain and for the Americans, prophesying that the Americans after separation might end up going to war with one another, as they did in the Civil War largely over the issue of slavery, once they were outside the British Constitution (Britain would abolish slavery in its colonies in 1833). However, once the 1783 peace treaty between Britain and America was signed, Burke came to admire both the experience the American colonies had had with democratic politics under the empire, and the elaborate reflections on both history and political science Madison among others drew upon in designing the 1787 Constitution, including their use of Montesquieu's theory of the separation of powers and David Hume's theory of faction.[29] Burke thought that the existence in Britain of a hereditary aristocracy had been an important historical feature in the development of British liberal constitutionalism, as the aristocracy's independence of the monarch has empowered the Whig resistance that led to the Glorious Revolution of 1688. But, he did not regard such an aristocracy as an indispensable building block for a liberal constitution, though he thought the French revolutionaries had made a disastrous mistake in not building upon rather than repudiating the estates in France for a form of unicameral democracy that unleashed the political psychology of a shame culture and its mindless violence against the human rights of anyone who disagreed with them. America, however, lacked either a hereditary monarch or a hereditary aristocracy, and Burke came to see the various countervailing powers at the national level (executive, bicameral Congress, and independent judiciary) as well as the federal division of powers between the national government and the states as creating the institutional equivalent of the British balanced constitution and thus a liberal constitutionalism that was both democratic and respectful of human rights. The 1787 Constitution indeed expressly protected some human rights against abridgment both by the states and national government, and the Bill of Rights of 1791 protected an expansive conception of human rights from national (not state) abridgment, many modeled on the "real" rights protected by the British Constitution (e.g., liberty of conscience, free speech and many others).

29 For a fuller discussion, see Richards, *Foundations of American Constitutionalism*, pp. 18–88.

There was, however, one important difference between the British and U.S. constitutionalisms, namely, the authority for the Glorious Revolution of 1688 derives from a bicameral parliament (the democratically elected House of Commons and the hereditary House of Lords), both constitutionally supreme over the monarch and the courts. In this, ultimate constitutional authority, parliamentary supremacy, rests on Locke's second stage and the role he accords majority rule by such a representative body concerned better to protect human rights. The Americans, many of the leaders of whom regarded themselves as British constitutional lawyers and brilliant ones at that (e.g., Thomas Jefferson of Virginia and John Adams of Massachusetts), had come to believe that the exercise of British parliamentary supremacy over the colonies on issues of taxation and war was itself a violation of constitutional principles of fair representation, as the Americans were not represented in parliament.

The American revolutionary and constitutional minds framed their enterprises on the basis of Lockean political theory, but the constitutional debates leading to the ratification of the U.S. Constitution transformed American thinking about Lockean political legitimacy into a new conception of constitutional argument, one not tethered to parliamentary supremacy. Americans had supposed themselves to be invoking Lockean political principles not only in their revolution but also in their framing of the early state and federal constitutions. The claims on the American colonies made by the parliament in the name of the British Constitution were politically illegitimate, and the colonies had validly and successfully invoked their Lockean right to revolt. In Lockean terms, consent to the existing form of government had properly been withdrawn, and Americans were now a political community in the sense of Locke's first unanimous contract, free to decide whether to continue as a political community and to frame a new form of government or to disband. Americans, of course, enthusiastically invoked their Lockean right to frame constitutions and—consistent with his argument—used the most easily available procedures of majority rule to frame their constitutions, namely, either the already existing provincial congresses or committees that exercised political powers (Connecticut, Rhode Island, South Carolina, Virginia, New Jersey) or elections of such bodies to frame constitutions and to exercise ordinary legislative powers (New Hampshire, North Carolina, and Georgia) or elections of bodies mainly to frame constitutions (Delaware, Pennsylvania, Maryland, New York). The members of the continental congress, who were chosen by the state legislatures, drafted the Articles of Confederation, which was approved by the state legislatures.[30]

Experience under these constitutions led many Americans, however, to question the very legitimacy of them as forms of government, in particular, the dominant political authority many of them accorded legislatures, which was a

30 For further discussion and references, see ibid., p. 91.

criticism that echoed their earlier rejections of British constitutional arguments of parliamentary supremacy. It was a wholly natural step for American constitutional thought to resolve its sense of crisis over the legitimacy of the early state and federal constitutions by a new level of deliberation over and ratification of constitutions. The basic idea was forged in the crucible of Massachusetts constitutional politics. Various towns had objected, in principle, to the idea that either the legislature could properly draft or would approve a constitution meant to be supreme over the legislature,[31] and, in the wake of the massive rejection by the towns of the proposed state constitution of 1778, the "first true constitutional convention in Western history, a body of representatives elected for the exclusive purpose of framing a constitution, met in Cambridge on September 1, 1779:"[32] its draft constitution would go into effect when independently ratified by the towns. The result, the Massachusetts State Constitution of 1780, was the work of John Adams,[33] and was proposed to and ratified by the people of Massachusetts in a way that made possible a new conception of constitutional deliberation and justification.

Americans could now conceive of the task of deliberation over and justification of a constitution as wholly distinct from normal politics, indeed as authoritative over such politics because it rested on firmer foundations of Lockean political legitimacy. Locke had thought of framing a government as a process of reasonable deliberation through majority rule on the structuring of political power in ways more consistent with its legitimate exercise, namely, its respect for inalienable human rights. Americans had learned from bitter experience that this process could not reasonably be interpreted—consistent with the aims of Lockean constitutionalism—as a kind of ordinary majoritarian legislation (Locke had never suggested it could be). Americans now saw that the deeper Lockean point of the constitutionalism over which they had fought a revolution was the quality of the reasonable deliberation it demands about the proper scope and limits of judicial power. The people of Massachusetts concluded that legislative supremacy could not do it justice, and independent thinking—of the caliber displayed in *The Essex Result*'s criticism of the proposed constitution of 1778[34]—must be cultivated, extended, and deepened through new institutional forms that would make the requisite reasonable deliberation possible and practicable.

31 See Willi Paul Adams, *The First American Constitutions*, translated by Rita and Robert Kimber (Chapel Hill: University of North Carolina Press, 1980), pp. 87–90

32 Ibid., p. 92.

33 See Adams, *Works of John Adams*, vol. 4, pp. 213–67.

34 See Theophilus Parsons, "The Essex Result," in Charles S. Hyneman and Donald S. Lutz (eds.), *American Political Writing during the Founding Era 1760–1805* (Indianapolis, IN: Liberty Press, 1983), vol. 1, pp. 480–522.

John Adams later wrote his monumental *A Defence of the Constitutions of Government of the United States of America*[35] to explain to Europeans the quality of deliberation that he believed the American people had now shown could be brought democratically to bear on the issue of framing a constitution. Adams's book is long, turgidly burdened with long extracts from all the writers Adams deemed pertinent, and often carelessly expressed in ways that obscured for Americans his essential argument, namely, that an upper house and independent executive were necessary to prevent aristocratic domination, which would be inconsistent with a Lockean respect for equal rights.[36] However, the approach of the work to the task of constitutional liberation brilliantly exemplified how Adams and the people of Massachusetts had come to understand its requirements not only institutionally (constitutional convention and ratification by the people), but also substantively.

People gathered their deliberative forces in a constitutional convention and in ratification debates to reflect on and decide on a constitutional framework for the exercise of political power that was consistent with human rights. Americans had learned "that neither liberty nor justice can be secured to the individuals of a nation, nor its prosperity promoted, but by a fixed constitution of government, and stated laws, know and obeyed by all."[37] If Americans were concerned only for their own time and place in a still largely unpopulated agricultural society, they could perhaps thrive

> under almost any kind of government, or without any government at all. But it is of great importance to begin well: misarrangements now made, will have great, extensive, and distant consequences; and we are now employed, how little soever we may think of it, in making establishment which will affect the happiness of a hundred millions of inhabitants over time, in a period not very distant. All nations, under all governments, must have parties; the great secret is to control them.[38]

Constitutional design thus required that people look at political life and forms from a more abstract point of view, garnering perhaps from the kind of comparative political science that Adams (following the example of Montesquieu and Hume) conspicuously displayed in his monumental treatise. Moreover, they must consider the likely pattern of social and economic developments in the society and the impact of political forms on such developments, including on

35 See Adams, *Works of John Adams*, vols. 4–6.

36 See R. R. Palmer, *The Age of the Democratic Revolution* (Princeton, NJ: Princeton University Press, 1959), vol. 1, p. 275.

37 Adams, *A Defence*, p. 401.

38 Ibid., pp. 587–88.

their posterity. If they or their posterity should later suffer from the oppressions of untrammeled political power:

> It will be entirely the fault of the constitution, and of the people who will not now adopted a good one; … for what consolation can it be to a man, to think that his whole life, and that of his son and grandson, must be spent in unceasing misery and warfare, for the sake only of a possibility that his great grandson may become a despot![39]

Adams construed Americans' sense of constitutional responsibility to be an exercise of collective democratic deliberation on the corruptive and distributive tendencies of political power such that he regarded ratification of a constitution like that of Massachusetts as the endorsement of a constitutional structure that would be control power over many generations of social and economic change consistent with enduring respect for human rights.

The Massachusetts Constitution of 1780 exemplified the kind of pattern Adams proposed, a governmental structure that would best control power over many generations of social and economic change consistent with enduring respect for human rights.[40] The legislature was bicameral with power balanced between a house of representatives representing the people and a senate of 40 with a membership that was proportioned to districts according to the amount of taxes paid by inhabitants. An ascending scale of property holding and residence set the qualifications for the three branches of the legislature: the house, the senate, and the governor. The governor was the most powerful executive of any state, and was separately elected by the people and had a suspensive veto over legislation (subject to override by a two-thirds majority in each house). Judges, most of whom were appointed by the executive, retained their offices indefinitely "during good behaviour."[41] A lengthy Bill of Rights preceded the constitution, in which the principle of separation of powers was spelled out in detail. It was an exemplary constitution, features of which the 1787 convention would use in their design of the U.S. Constitution.

The Massachusetts Constitution, though widely admired in the 1780s,[42] was inadequate in controlling Shays' Rebellion,[43] and American constitutional thinkers, notably Madison, had concluded that the quality of deliberation and argument, which had been brought to the constitutional task in Massachusetts,

39 Ibid., vol. 5, p. 426.

40 For a fuller description, see Gordon W. Wood, *The Constitution of the American Republic, 1776–1787* (New York: W. W. Norton, 1969), pp. 434–35.

41 Adams, *First State Constitutions*, p. 269.

42 See Wood, *Creation of the American Republic*, pp. 434–35.

43 For a pertinent commentary, see Forrest McDonald, *E Pluribus Unum* (Indianapolis, IN: Liberty Press, 1965), pp. 244–57.

would remain imperfect and incomplete until it had been brought to bear on the general problem of constitutionalism in America, including the relative powers of state and federal governments. If the legitimacy of the early state constitutions was now in dispute because of the political hegemony of the state legislatures, then such disrepute extended equally to the powers of the state legislatures over the continental congress under the Articles of Confederation; the legislatures elected representatives to the Congress and retained effective discretion over whether to pay requisitions (taxes) and any state could veto a proposed amendment to the Articles (and needed amendments had been rejected).[44] When compelled to address the claim that the constitution's ratification procedure violated the Articles, Madison refused to take it seriously,[45] an impatience rooted in the Lockean theory of political legitimacy that he assumed. Citing the Declaration of Independence,[46] Madison reminded Americans of the "transcendent and precious right of the people to 'abolish or alter their governments as to them seem most likely to effect their safety and happiness,'"[47] a remark that suggests issues about the Lockean political illegitimacy of the Articles of Confederation themselves. If so, Madison's argument was, in effect, that the constitutionalism for which Americans had fought a revolution was not the Articles and that Americans now should be accorded the deliberative opportunity to reject it (precisely because it failed adequately to protect rights and secure the public good) and to achieve a better understanding of their Lockean constitutionalism.[48] That understanding was crucially expressed for Madison by both the quality of deliberation that the constitutional convention made possible and the kind of deliberative ratification by the people at large (not the state legislatures) that it required.

Americans naturally interpreted this new conception of constitutional deliberation and argument in terms of the Lockean constitutionalism that some of them (e.g., James Wilson of Pennsylvania) had earlier used in justifying the sovereignty of the British Constitution over parliament. When Wilson—now one of the leading founders—rose at the Pennsylvania ratifying convention to characterize the authority the constitution would have when ratified, he recalled how Americans, like himself, had rejected in the revolutionary debates Blackstone's doctrine of parliamentary sovereignty, and announced that Americans finally

44 See in general Merrill Jensen, *The Articles of Confederation* (Madison: University of Wisconsin Press, 1970); Jack N. Rakove, *The Beginnings of National Politics: An Interpretive History of the Continental Congress* (Baltimore, MD: Johns Hopkins University Press, 1979).

45 See Jacob E. Cooke (ed.), *The Federalist* (Middletown, CT: Wesleyan University Press, 1961), p. 263.

46 Ibid., p. 265.

47 Ibid.

48 For notable references to the revolution in *The Federalist*, see ibid., pp. 89, 250, 297, 309, 320.

had found a practicable institutional form to express the alternative conception of political legitimacy for which they had fought:

> The supreme, absolute, and uncontrollable authority *remains* with the people … . The practical recognition of this truth was reserved for the honor of this country. I recollect no constitution founded on this principle. But we have witnessed the improvement, and enjoy the happiness, of seeing it carried into practice. The great and penetrating mind of Locke seems to be the only one that pointed towards even the theory of this great truth.[49]

The authority of the ratified constitution was thus identified with a Lockean interpretation of popular sovereignty. The authority of constitutional argument thus understood was supreme over all political bodies and agencies, which explains why Wilson and many others rejected any idea that it would be regarded as a kind of contract between one political body and another (e.g., the British conception of Magna Charta as a contract between the monarch and the barons).[50] The constitution was contractualist only in Locke's sense, namely, a contract among the people, not between rulers and ruled.[51] In effect, under the American doctrine of the supremacy of the constitution, no political body was or could be sovereign, because the constitution's supremacy rested on the judgments it embodied about political legitimacy, which subordinated all political power to the demands of reasonable justification to persons understood as free and equal bearers of human rights.

Americans had finally discovered a new way of thinking about constitutionalism that explained their grievances under the British Constitution and their criticisms of the earlier state and federal constitutions. Constitutional law has to move to a new level of deliberation and justification, and new institutional forms had to be invented that were more adequate to the supremacy of such arguments over ordinary politics. The need for institutional innovations—moved by the demands of abstract political argument, their own experience with democracy as colonies, and sophisticated comparative political science—led such a historically minded people to reclaim for future generations the Harringtonian idea of the founders of "an immortal commonwealth."[52]

The self-conscious sense of the founders, as founders, was perhaps their most remarkable use of history, because it represented their choice to identify the

49 Merrill Jensen (ed.), *Documentary History of the Ratification of the Constitution*, vol. 2 (Madison: State Historical Society of Wisconsin, 1976), p. 472.

50 For Wilson's rejection, see ibid., pp. 555–56; see in general Wood, *Creation of the American Republic*, pp. 541–42, 601–02.

51 See Wood, *Creation of the American Republic*, p. 601.

52 See James Harrington, "The Commonwealth of Oceana," in J. G. A. Pocock (ed.), *Political Works of James Harrington* (Cambridge: Cambridge University Press, 1977), pp. 209, 321–22.

American constitutional tradition with Harrington's aspiration to cut Britain free of its corrupt "Gothic model"[53] of balanced classes in the service of a republican aspiration to "an immortal commonwealth"[54] using Machiavelli's political science of Roman republicanism in service of that aspiration.[55] However, Harrington argued, in contrast to Machiavelli's limited hopes to retard corruption, that the proper use of such science could achieve "a commonwealth rightly ordered … as immortal, or long-lived, as the world."[56] However, this could be accomplished only if "first … the legislator should be one man, and secondly … the government should be made altogether, or at once."[57] Harrington sharply distinguished, as did Adams and later Madison, the normal psychology of people in politics from the normative role of a republican written constitution. A founder should not display true political virtue because it was often corrupted by faction,[58] or religious virtue because it would "reduce a commonwealth unto a party."[59] A point that was fundamental to the thinking of the American founders was bluntly put by Harrington:

> "Give us good men and they will make us good laws" is the maxim of a demagogue … . But "give us good orders, and they will make us good men" is the maxim of a legislator and the most infallible in politics.[60]

The normative end of a commonwealth was "an empire of laws and not of men,"[61] reasonable treatment of all persons as equals under the "law of nature,"[62] and Harrington no more doubted the objective truth of such moral and political values than did Adams or later Madison. The constructivist project of a founder was to take seriously such values, their corruption by normal political psychology, and the need to invent constitutional forms to channel such political motivations to achieve the ends of egalitarian public reason. In language that anticipated Madison's defense of the separation of powers,[63] Harrington

53 See James Harrington, "The Prerogative of Popular Government," in Pocock, *Political Works of James Harrington*, p. 563.

54 Harrington, *Commonwealth of Oceana*, p. 209.

55 For an illuminating study, see Zera S. Fink, *The Classical Republicans* (Evanston, IL: Northwestern University Press, 1945). For a further discussion of Harrington's argument, see Richards, *Foundations of American Constitutionalism*, pp. 97–100.

56 Harrington, *Commonwealth of Oceana*, p. 321.

57 Ibid., p. 207.

58 See ibid., pp. 173, 202, 206, 676.

59 Ibid., p. 204.

60 Ibid., p. 205.

61 Ibid., p. 170.

62 Ibid., p. 171.

63 "But the great security against a gradual concentration of the several powers in the same department, consists in giving to those who administer such department, the necessary constitutional means, and personal motives, to resist encroachments of the others" (*The Federalist*, p. 349).

called for a constitutional structure "that there can be in the same no number of men, having the interest, that can have the power, nor any number of men can have the power, that can have the interest, to invade or disturb the government."[64] The Harrington approach to constitutional design was exemplified by the analogy of dividing a cake: the way to insure justice in distribution was not to expect justice in politics, but to structure a political process of choice (you cut the cake first, and I choose my piece second) likely—given normal human motives in politics—to result in equal shares.[65] Harrington's proposals in *Oceana* were unbelievably complex.[66] To simplify, writing in a pre-capitalist society, Harrington used land as the criterion of wealth and political power, and he imposed an agrarian law that would reduce large landholdings to ensure more nearly equal patterns of land distribution and thus more nearly equal political power;[67] his voting procedures combined elements of both a lottery and voter selection,[68] and political power was subject to regular rotation to ensure broader participation in government through a diverse and non-recurring political leadership.[69] Under Harrington's proposals, voting by all citizens (in contrast to servants[70]) was structured through successive intermediate representative bodies culminating in a bicameral legislature: a small branch of lords or senate (indirectly elected by popular vote) that could only deliberate and propose laws, and a larger house of representatives (directly elected) that could only adopt or refuse. He aimed to ensure the deliberative use of public reason through a refining process of representation[71] by "a natural aristocracy"[72] (similar to the later usage of Adams and Jefferson[73]) accountable to the electorate in ways that would tend to assure equal protection of all. Politics had to be thus structured because—in terms that prefigure Madison's point about the corruptibility even of Socratic conscience by the politics of "a mob"[74]—Harrington observed that "the body of a people, not led by the reason of the government, is not a people, but a herd."[75]

64 James Harrington, "The Art of Lawgiving," in Pocock, *Political Works of James Harrington*, p. 658.

65 Ibid., p. 172.

66 For a clear exposition of the proposals, see Fink, *Classical Republicans*, pp. 52–89.

67 See Pocock, *Political Works of James Harrington*, pp. 62–63.

68 Harrington adapted the Venetian ballot that combined such elements; see *Commonwealth of Oceana*, pp. 241–44. On the Venetian republic and its impact on Harrington's thought, see Fink, *Classical Republicans*, pp. 28–29.

69 See Pocock, *Political Works of James Harrington*, pp. 69–72.

70 See Harrington, *Commonwealth of Oceana*, pp. 212–13.

71 Harrington summarized the aims of his constructivist politics in terms of "the soul or faculties of a man … refined or made incapable of passion" ("A System of Politics," in Pocock, *Political Works of James Harrington*, p. 838).

72 Ibid., p. 173.

73 Harrington thinks of this aristocracy as one of merit. See, e.g., Harrington, *Art of Lawgiving*, p. 677.

74 *The Federalist*, p. 838.

75 Harrington, *System of Politics*, p. 838.

Harrington had insisted that the design of such a constitution be done by one person, which reflected his distrust of the shallow empiricism of people in general who tended to fall back on immediate historical experience (e.g., of the British Constitution of balanced hereditary and other classes). In contrast, Harrington's proposal for an immortal commonwealth rests on what he regarded as an empirical rigorous comparative political science and the use of imaginative political intelligence in the construction of new kinds of political orders in the service of reflective republican values. That kind of judgment would, he assumed, require the possibly ruthless Machiavellian man of genius. *Oceana*, published in 1656, is dedicated to Cromwell.

Americans had either read Harrington (Adams, and possibly Madison[76]) or absorbed his ideas from thinkers in Britain, notably, David Hume, who discusses his proposal in an essay that clearly influenced Madison's thought about the design of the federal system.[77] Many of his recommendations were rejected as either inappropriate in American circumstances or unwise, including his ideas of expansionist military heroism. But, the idea that a written constitution (in contrast to Britain's unwritten constitution) that would frame an immortal commonwealth struck a responsive chord in Americans and in Adams and Madison in particular.[78]

2.3 Madison on the U.S. Constitution in History

American constitutional thinkers, like Harrington, had despaired of the British Constitution and its evolving historical conventions. Harrington's acute use of political science in the attempt to emancipate British constitutional from what he believed was its unimaginative historicism had a resonance for Americans, who had found British appeals to the historically evolving British constitutional of parliamentary supremacy so inexcusably vapid and insulting and they naturally identified their situation with the abortive constitutional proposals made during

76 In his important 1776 essay on American constitutionalism, "Thoughts on Government," Adams appealed to Harrington as an authority and indeed used his description of the ends of government, "an empire of laws, not of men," as the definition of a republic. See Adams, *Works of John Adams*, vol. 4, p. 194. In *A Defence*, Adams quoted a long excerpt from Harrington's discussion in *Oceana* of cake division, calling his arguments "eternal and unanswerable by any man" (Adams, *Works of John Adams*, vol. 4, p. 410); see also William T. Hutchinson and William M. E. Rachal (eds.), *The Papers of James Madison 1783* (Chicago: University of Chicago Press, 1969), vol. 6, pp. 410–13. Madison included Toland's edition of Harrington's works in his 1783 *Report on Books for Congress*; see p. 85 (at no. 148).

77 See David Hume, "Idea of a Perfect Commonwealth," in *Essays Moral, Political, and Literary* (Oxford: Oxford University Press, 1963), pp. 499–515.

78 On the importance of Harrington for American constitutional thought, see Edmund S. Morgan, *Inventing the People: The Rise of Popular Sovereignty in England America* (New York: W. W. Norton, 1988), pp. 86, 157, 248, 251, 291.

the English Civil War and interregnum, including Harrington.[79] Harrington's particular proposals appealed to American constitutionalists because his methods and ambitions were so congruent with their sense of their own extraordinary historic opportunity and their responsibility to bring to it the full scope of emancipated religious, moral, and political intelligence in which they took such natural pride. However, that intelligence could only realize itself if it were not subverted by the corruptive religious, moral, and political traditions that had shackled the natural scope of reasonable freedom.

This sense of historic opportunity and responsibility led the Americans to bring to their deliberations the interpretive uses of history, including the analysis of such history in light of the comparative political science of Machiavelli, Harrington, Montesquieu, Hume, and the contemporary Scottish social theorists.[80] Montesquieu, for example, wrote for a "legislator"[81] who, in felicitous circumstances, could use the normative and empirical insights culled from Montesquieu's idealization of the British Constitution to frame such a constitution or a similar such constitution in the appropriately supportive cultural, demographic, and climatic circumstances identified by Montesquieu's comparative political science. A text of this sort would understandably have enormous appeal in 1787, because it addressed, clarified, and indeed defined the kind of historic opportunity and task that the founders had before them; the founders, themselves trained in the British constitutional tradition and largely emigrants from Britain (England, Scotland, Wales, and one, Paterson of New Jersey, from Ireland), identified their circumstances as precisely those most favorable to acting on the kind of reflective wisdom that Montesquieu urged on the "legislator." Although Hume, like Burke, defended the British Constitution on the ground of long-standing tradition, he had allowed himself the utopian luxury of reflecting on an ideal Harringtonian extended republic, which he offered for a time when "an opportunity might be afforded of reducing the theory to practice, either by a dissolution of some old government, or by the combination of men to form a new one, in distant part of the world." The American founders found themselves, miraculously, in precisely such a situation, and Madison, in particular, found Hume's advice as well as his theory of faction quite useful in the argument of No. 10, *The Federalist*, for the federal system.[82]

79 See in general Francis D. Wormuth, *The Origins of Modern Constitutionalism* (New York: Harper & Row, 1949); also Edmund S. Morgan, *Inventing the People: The Rise of Popular Sovereignty in England America* (New York: W. W. Norton, 1988), pp. 55–93.

80 For a comprehensive discussion, see Richards, *Foundations of American Constitutionalism*, pp. 18–77.

81 Baron de Montesquieu, *The Spirit of the Laws*, translated by Thomas Nugent (New York: Hafner, 1949), vol. 2, p. 156.

82 For a fuller discussion, see Richards, *Foundations of American Constitutionalism*, pp. 32–39.

The American constitutionalists tested, refined and elaborated their critical political intelligence (based on their experience with democracy as colonies) in light of such political science because, like Harrington, they had learned to distrust the shallow historicist empiricism of their now shattered faith in the British Constitution: they knew also that the test of their exercise of emancipatory political intelligence would be their capacity for moral independence and reasonable criticism of the traditions that had so stunted and stultified the human heart and mind into acceptance of unnatural hierarchies of power and privilege. Such exercise of critical intelligence included an independent stance from the comparative political science they had found so illuminating. Americans thus used Montesquieu, sometimes critically, for precisely the Harringtonian purposes (an immortal commonwealth) he deplored, and they used Hume's own brilliant political science of the psychology of groups in politics (the theory of faction) and the search for political impartiality in service of a Lockean theory of political legitimacy that Hume rejected. Furthermore, Americans were certainly absorbed by Harrington's methods and ambitions, but they could not subscribe to the conception of Machiavellian political science as kind of alternative organon to ultimate religious and moral truth (e.g., laying the foundations of an Erastian civil religion of the state that Jefferson and Madison both rejected when they pioneered anti-establishment in Virginia and later in the First Amendment of the Bill of Rights).[83] Americans were absorbed by Harrington for reasons of their own, namely, as a model for the quality of deliberation that was required by their great historic opportunity and responsibility in service of protecting the inalienable human rights that were fundamental to the legitimacy of political power. Consistent with this political theory, they needed a conception of themselves not as Harrington's ruthless man of genius but as participants in a great collective democratic deliberation over a new conception of constitutional argument that would dignity all Americans of their generation in the light of history.

Importantly, "the ends" of such constitutional argument, as Madison put it at the constitutional convention, "were first to protect the people agst. their rulers; secondly to protect [the people] agst. the transient impressions into which they themselves might be led."[84] The authority of such arguments was that their "ends" were those of a "people deliberating in a temperate moment, and with the experience of other nations before them, on the plan of Govt. most likely to secure their happiness."[85] That authority was crucially in play in *The Federalist* No. 49 when Madison defended the founders' conception of a long-enduring

83 See, in general, Leo Strauss, *Thoughts on Machiavelli* (Chicago: University of Chicago Press, 1984); Mark Hulliung, *Citizen Machiavelli* (Princeton, NJ: Princeton University Press, 1983).

84 Max Farrand (ed.), *Records of the Federal Convention*, vol. 1 (New Haven, CT: Yale University Press, 1966), p. 421.

85 Ibid.

constitution against Jefferson's idea of a written constitution more easily amendable by each generation.[86]

Madison's argument was an appeal to the extraordinary sort of liberty, opportunity, and reflective capacity that were collectively and democratically brought to the framing and ratification of the U.S. Constitution. The authority of the framers' conception of a written constitution was precisely that it was not the product of routine democratic politics in which competitors for political power brought to all disputes their factionalized perceptions of issues of both principle and policy. Madison thought of the legislative debates of such normal politics as "so many judicial determinations, not indeed concerning the rights of single persons, but the concerning the right of large bodies of citizens,"[87] namely, as a substantive debate about justice in which all parties interpret such claims of justice filtered their factionalized commitments as creditors or debtors, farmers or manufacturers, Quakers or Anglicans, and so on. The authority of the constitution, in contrast, was in the impartiality brought to bear on the construction of constraints on power and the provision of reasonable substantive and procedural arguments limiting the exercise of such routine politics, consistent with a larger Lockean conception of justice, equal rights, and the effective use of collective power to advance the public good. Madison's objection to Jefferson's view of a written constitution was that the sense of a written constitution that was too easily changed or modified eroded the distinctive authority of the framers' intent and undermined its distinctive virtue of constitutional impartiality by the factionalized perceptions of constitutional argument that necessarily arise in normal politics. However, that would unleash yet again Hamilton's "demon of faction,"[88] which it was the very point of the written constitution to tame and civilize. For this reason, the very impartiality of the written constitution must place it beyond any change resembling normal democratic politics. That deeper impartiality expressed a conception of the collective reasonableness of the constitution itself. Furthermore, Madison argued that amendments must be so designed to approximate the same sort of collective exercise of deliberative reflection on enduring constitutional design.[89]

Madison's argument about the authority of the constitution was contractualist in Locke's sense: namely, the legitimacy of political power was tested against a

86 Madison referred to Jefferson's draft Virginia Constitution of 1783, which he had appended to his *Notes on the State of Virginia*. See Thomas Jefferson, *Notes on the State of Virginia*, edited by William Peden (New York: W. W. Norton, 1954), pp. 209–22, in which Jefferson advocated that whenever two branches of a government should by two-thirds vote concur, a constitutional convention of the people shall be called to amend the constitution. See ibid., p. 221.

87 *The Federalist*, p. 59.

88 Ibid., p. 444.

89 Ibid., pp. 341–43.

political ideal of the acceptability of such power to the free, rational, and equal persons subject to such power. The legitimacy of the constitution was the way in which it imposed constraints on the power of the state and the power of the people that could be and often were publicly justified to all persons subject to them as reasonable such limits. It was therefore essential, as founders like Wilson and Madison insisted at the convention,[90] that the constitution be ratified by one of the most inclusive deliberative processes that any republican government had ever seen; such ratification had normative force because it gave authoritative political expression to the deeper Lockean judgment of reasonable justification.

The authority of an enduring written constitution was, Madison argued, the impartial reasonableness of its written constraints on the power of both the state and the people. However, Madison thought of these constraints as an enduring heritage to posterity, namely, constitutional argument based on the impartially conceived republican morality enforceable against both the state and the people; further, he and others founders certainly shared Jefferson's bitterly realistic Machiavellian prophecy about the probable direction of America away from its original Lockean aspirations and his view of the responsibilities of American constitutionalists in light of that anticipated declension from republican virtue:

> They should look forward to a time, and that not a distant one, when corruption in this, as in the country from which we derive our original, will have seized the heads of government, and be spread by them through the body of the people; when they will purchase the voices of the people, and make them pay the price. Human nature is the same on every side of the Atlantic, and will be alike influenced by the same causes. The time to guard against corruption and tyranny, is before they shall have gotten hold on us. It is better to keep the wolf out of the fold, than to trust to drawing his teeth and talons after he shall have entered.[91]

The future integrity of republican morality and the inalienable rights it protected would depend on the quality of constitutional argument that the American people could sustain. Madison had no doubt about the objective truth of that morality (centering on respect for the inalienable right to conscience), and "a nation of philosophers" might, as Jefferson probably believed, rediscover it in each generation. However, in a passage Burke could have written, Madison opines:

90 See, e.g., Farrand, *Records of the Federal Convention*, vol. 1, pp. 122–23 (Madison), p. 123 (Wilson), p. 127 (Wilson); vol. 2, p. 92 (Madison), pp. 468–69 (Wilson), p. 469 (Madison), pp. 475–76 (Madison), p. 477 (Wilson), pp. 561–62 (Wilson).

91 Jefferson, *Notes on the State of Virginia*, p. 121.

> The reason of man, like man himself is timid and cautious, when left alone; and acquires firmness and confidence, in proportion to the number with which it is associated. When the examples, which fortify opinion, are *antient* as well as *numerous*, they are known to have a double effect. In a nation of philosophers, this consideration ought to be disregarded. A reverence for the laws, would be sufficiently inculcated by the voice of an enlightened reason. But a nation of philosophers is as little to be expected as the philosophical race of kings wished for by Plato.[92]

Madison here anticipates remarkably the normative role that the historical commitment to a written constitution (and its founders) would play in constituting American as an enduring republican community over generations. The constitution has been self-consciously conceived in this way: in the words of the Preamble, to "secure the blessings of liberty to ourselves and our posterity," and all sides to the debates over the constitution—Federalist[93] and anti-Federalist[94]—appealed to the effects on posterity as a crucial test of the legitimacy of the constitution. Madison's point—against Jefferson—was that the aspiration to such an enduring written constitution could best be achieved by self-consciously using the deeply human sense of history and tradition to maintain in the people at large the capacity for deliberative constitutional argument in service of Lockean political legitimacy. The idea of the founders would play a role in the American constitutional tradition not as a point of reference for ruthless Machiavellian genius but for a quality of public argument and vision among a free people that, as it dignified their generation, might dignify theirs.

History and tradition must, however, themselves be interpreted by later generations, and their interpretive processes would, as Federalists and anti-Federalists both saw, be absorbed by study of the founders. We need to understand—consistent with the premises of Lockean political legitimacy that motivated the Constitution—how such interpretation should be understood. Two founders, James Madison and James Wilson, addressed this issue in ways that merit attention. Madison was concerned with the kind of legitimacy to which an enduring constitution must make claim; Wilson, as a justice of the U.S. Supreme Court, suggested how such claims of legitimacy must shape the interpretive practice of the supreme constitution over time. America's Lockean constitution for posterity must—consistent with the legitimacy of its ratification—be

92 *The Federalist*, p. 340.

93 See, e.g., *The Federalist*, pp. 89, 145, 210–11, 213, 276–77; John Dickinson, "Letters of Fabius," in Paul Leicester Ford (ed.), *Pamphlets on the Constitution of the United States Published during Discussion by the People 1787–1788* (Brooklyn, NY: n.p., 1888), pp. 165–216 at 200–01.

94 See, e.g., Herbert J. Storing (ed.), *The Complete Anti-Federalist* (Chicago: University of Chicago Press, 1981), vol. 1, pp. 96, 105, 117, 155, 227, 249, 326, 363–64, 372; vol. 3, pp. 14, 21, 39, 67, 86, 97, 105, 165; vol. 4, pp. 18, 20, 64; vol. 6, pp. 130, 141–42.

interpreted over time to justify only those exercises of political power that can be justified to the people of each generation in the same way that it was justified at its ratification.

Madison had been compelled to address the issue of the amendability of a written constitution during a correspondence with Jefferson that carried to new depths their earlier disagreement. Jefferson, who represented America in France, had become absorbed in discussions among the French revolutionaries about whether the ancient debts of the French monarchy should be valid against the new constitutional order then in process of formation,[95] and he took the occasion of a brief illness to write Madison an unusually philosophical letter dated September 6, 1789 about what he took to be the "self-evident" principle governing these matters, namely, "'*that the earth belongs in usufruct to the living*': that the dead have neither powers nor rights over it."[96] Every generation, speaking through a majority, had, according to this view, a natural right to start anew on a clean slate unencumbered by the obligations of a previous generation. On the basis of Jefferson's actuarial calculations of the length of lives of a majority of people at the time aged 21, 19 years should be "the term beyond which neither the representatives of a nation, nor even the whole nation assembled, can validly extend a debt."[97] Jefferson's pre-occupation was the scope of obligation of old national debts, but he generalized the principle memorably thus:

> On similar grounds, it may be proved that no society can make a perpetual constitution, or even a perpetual law. The earth belongs always to the living generation … . Every constitution then, and every law, naturally expires at the end of 19 years.[98]

Madison responded in a letter of February 4, 1790—predictably in view of *The Federalist* No. 49—and questioned whether, as a practical matter, Jefferson's revisable constitutions would "become too mutable to retain those prejudices in its favor which antiquity inspires, and which are perhaps a salutary aid to the most rational government in the most enlightened age."[99] He went on to raise two points of political principle. First, a present generations does not write on a morally clean slate, because it may incur obligations to previous generations: "The *improvements* made by the dead form a charge against the living who take the

95 See the editorial note in Julian P. Boyd (ed.), *The Papers of Thomas Jefferson 1789*, vol. 15 (Princeton, NJ: Princeton University Press, 1958), pp. 384–91.

96 Ibid., p. 392.

97 Ibid., p. 394.

98 Ibid., p. 396.

99 Julian P. Boyd (ed.), *The Papers of Thomas Jefferson 1789*, vol. 15 (Princeton, NJ: Princeton University Press, 1958), p. 148.

benefit of them."[100] Second, Jefferson's insistence that his principle required the expiration of constitutions and laws would create violent struggles over reviving or revising them, which could only be satisfactorily avoided by assuming tacit consent of each generation to continue obeying pre-existing constitutions and laws. Madison amplified the importance of this concept:

> May it not be questioned whether it be possible to exclude wholly the idea of tacit consent, without subverting the foundation of every civil Society—on what principle does the voice of the majority bind the minority? It does not result I conceive from the law of nature, but from compact founded on conveniency. A greater proportion might be required by the fundamental constitution of a Society if it were judged eligible. Prior then to the establishment of this principle, *unanimity* was necessary, and strict Theory at all times presupposes the assent of every member to the establishment of the rule itself. If this assent can be given tacitly, or be not implied where no positive evidence forbids, persons born in Society would not on attaining ripe age be bound by acts of the Majority; and either a *unanimous* repetition of every law would be necessary on the accession of new members, or an express assent must be obtained from these to the rule by which the voice of the Majority is made the voice of the whole.[101]

Madison concluded, somewhat inconsistently, that his "observations are not meant however to impeach either the utility of the [Jefferson's] principle in some particular cases or the general importance of it in the eye of the philosophical Legislator,"[102] and "that our hemisphere must be still more enlightened before many of the sublime truths which are seen thro' the medium of Philosophy, become visible to the naked eye of the ordinary Politician."[103] However, in fact, his argument—to the extent it rested on the Lockean conception of political legitimacy that was fundamental to America's new constitutionalism—quite undercut Jefferson's simplistic claim of a recurring 19-year natural right of constitutional majoritarianism.

Madison probably sympathized with the spirit of Jefferson's argument because its principle at least interpreted Locke's claim "*that a Child is born a Subject of no Country or Government* ...; nor is he bound up, by any Compact of his Ancestors."[104] Locke had made the argument against Filmer's patriarchal

100 Ibid.

101 Ibid., p. 149.

102 Ibid., p. 150.

103 Ibid.

104 John Locke, "The Second Treatise of Government," in Locke, *Two Treatises of Government*, p. 365 (sec. 118). For a useful commentary on Locke's opposition to Filmer's historicism, see Ashcraft, *Locke's Two Treatises of Government*, pp. 60–79.

historicism, that is, the claim that political legitimacy today had be traced lineally to the authority of the original father of the human race. Locke, in contrast, argued that no such past figure could have a legitimate claim on his or her ancestors, because the normative basis of political legitimacy was not history, but respect for the inalienable human rights that protected the spheres of reasonable self-government of free people. For this reason, no past government (including the founders) could, in and of itself, bind a present generation. Madison sympathized with Jefferson's principle as a way of making this Lockean point.

However, Madison could not agree with the doctrinaire way Jefferson had chosen to state this Lockean view because it failed to observe Locke's crucial distinction between two levels of consent. Locke interpreted this requirement that politics must respect inalienable human rights by requiring that all persons who are subject to its power must have consented in fact to live under a polity; furthermore, from this benchmark of legitimate political community, a majority of such had the authority—should the issue properly arise—to decide on that particular form of government most likely in their view to respect equal rights and pursue the public good. If that government should fail to respect rights, then the people have a right to overthrow it: they may then decide (unanimously) whether they should continue as a community and (by majority rule) on their new form of government. Jefferson conflated the two issues and, in Madison's clear-eyed view, thus undercut the deeper foundations of the entire conception of political legitimacy. That conception rested on respect for inalienable human rights, and Locke gave that point political expression through the requirement of unanimous consent, which could not, in principle, be given by any reasonable person if it involved abridgment of their inalienable human rights. Reasonable unanimity was a way of making the deeper point of political legitimacy. However, Jefferson's interpretation of the point spoke of majority rule, to which Madison brilliantly responded that even majority rule—on deeper grounds of Lockean political legitimacy—had legitimate political force only if it was, as it may not always be, the best *political* decision-making procedure for designing a government to protect inalienable human rights.

Madison's point had particular force in respect to constitutionalism because Jefferson's idea demanded an expiration of constitutions and a majoritarian reframing of them in a completely doctrinaire way that might often result in constitutions less politically legitimate than the one they supplanted. However, Locke's claim had been that revolution was justified when existing constitutions violated inalienable human rights, not that people have some abstract right to the abolition and reframing of their constitutions notwithstanding their justice and wisdom. Locke's drafting of the Fundamental Constitutions of Carolina expresses this view exactly; his stipulation that the constitutions "shall be and remain the sacred and unalterable form and rule of government of Carolina for ever"[105] presumes that subsequent generations would tacitly consent to the continuing justice and wisdom of the constitutions and the legal relations (e.g., property relations) under them; if his presumption were correct (i.e., later generations did consent on good normative grounds), the constitutional order would be legitimate and fully binding them. Madison found Jefferson's contrary doctrine "dangerous"[106] and not simply because it fundamentally misinterpreted Lockean constitutional legitimacy. It subverted the authority of America's new experiment in Lockean constitutionalism—a political order that more powerfully embodied the ends of Lockean political legitimacy than had any government in human history, and that offered a path-breaking model for how history and traditions might be used constructively to constitute a political community based on a consensus permanently committed to this type of enlightened government. Jefferson's bad Lockean theory was in this instance subverting America's excellent Lockean practice.

Madison's theory of that practice gave posterity the basis for useful appeals to the founders. These appeals did not rely on Filmer's specious reasons of natural patriarchal authority, but relied on reasons of Lockean constitutionalism. This interpretive practice, suitably understood, could constitute a continuing political community with a legitimacy based on its aspiration to satisfy the Lockean requirement of unanimous reasonable consent in each generation. We already discussed how the American constitutionalists self-consciously recaptured the Machiavellian and Harringtonian idea of the founders, transforming it from ruthless political genius into a historically unique exercise of collective democratic political intelligence of a free people deliberating about the permanent ambitions, structures, and values of Lockean constitutionalism. Ratification of the U.S. Constitution by constitutional conventions elected by the people was fundamental to confirming the Lockean legitimacy of the constitution. The point was not that everyone in fact consented to ratification (an unrealistic procedure, as Locke saw), but that the deliberative and democratic character and focus of the ratification process would contain political power in ways that respected equally the rights and interests of all. Because the constitution treated people as equals in this way, it could be offered to and accepted by all as, in principle, reasonable and therefore, on Lockean grounds, legitimate. We must now inquire into the implications of such legitimacy for continuing interpretive practice.

At the Pennsylvania ratifying convention, James Wilson also characterized the legitimacy of the new constitution in Lockean terms: "The great and penetrating mind of Locke seems to be the only one that pointed towards even the

105 See John Locke, *The Fundamental Constitutions of Carolina, The Works of John Locke*, vol. X (London: Thomas Tegg, 1823), p. cxx at 19.

106 Julian P. Boyd (ed.), *The Papers of Thomas Jefferson 1789–1900*, vol. 16 (Princeton, NJ: Princeton University Press, 1961), p. 149.

theory of this great truth."[107] Wilson had prominently invoked that theory in his constitutional arguments about the British Constitution in the pre-revolutionary period, and he was to give final observance to it in the 1790–91 *Lectures on Law* that he delivered as a justice of the U.S. Supreme Court.[108] The latter argument clarifies the kind of interpretive practice that makes the best sense of the founders' thinking about the political legitimacy of the constitution for both their own and future generations.

Wilson argued that Americans had brought into play a new conception of law that sharply contrasted with Blackstone's positivism. Americans as revolutionaries had rejected Blackstone's theory of British constitutionalism, and they must now decisively reject its position as the theory of both American law in general and constitutional law in particular.[109] Blackstone's positivism rested on a theory of sovereignty, whereby the law was defined by the requisite sovereign in a particular community. He had defined sovereignty in Great Britain in terms of the legislative sovereignty of parliament,[110] a sovereignty that American pre-revolutionary constitutional thought rejected. Wilson argued, as he had in 1774,[111] that Blackstone's supposition of a supreme lawgiving power in government "has never been evinced to be true. Those powers and rights were, I think, collected to be exercised and enjoyed, not to be alienated and lost."[112] All such views had, for Wilson, corrupted sanctified an "implicit deference to authority, ... the bane of science, ... the yoke of that intellectual tyranny, by which, in many ages and countries, men have been deprived of the inherent and inalienable right of judging for themselves."[113] However, this simple truth of the matter, available to a democratic common sense emancipated from such tyranny, was that "the dread and redoubtable sovereign, when traced to his ultimate and genuine source" is not parliament or any political body, but "the free and independent man."[114] In contrast to Blackstone, the point of legitimate government was not to surrender all our rights[115] but to protect them, in order to maintain the ultimate sovereignty of independent conscience over government. Respect for our inalienable human rights, like conscience, enabled us to exercise

107 Jensen, *Documentary History*, p. 472.

108 See James Wilson, "Lectures on Law," in Robert Green McCloskey (ed.), *The Works of James Wilson*, 2 vols. (Cambridge, MA: The Belknap Press of Harvard University Press, 1967).

109 For the core of Wilson's argument against Blackstone, see *Lectures on Law*, vol. 1, pp. 168–96.

110 See William Blackstone, *Commentaries on the Laws of England*, vol. 1 (Chicago: University of Chicago Press, 1979), pp. 91, 156–57.

111 James Wilson, *Considerations on the Nature and Extent of the Legislative Authority of the British Parliament* (1774), reprinted in Robert Green McCloskey (ed.), *The Works of James Wilson*, vol. 2 (Cambridge, MA: The Belknap Press of Harvard University Press, 1967).

112 Ibid., p. 174.

113 Ibid., vol. 2, p. 502.

114 Ibid., p. 81.

115 See ibid., pp. 585–86, 588–89.

the reasonable moral capacities available to all persons (the "moral sense"[116]) to know, understand, and implement as free and equal persons the principles of justice ("the law of nature"[117]). The legitimacy of law arose, for Wilson, from the consent of free and equal persons thus understood, a consent "give in the freest and most unbiassed [*sic*] manner"[118] to the principles that best secured our equal rights and the common interests of all.

Wilson understood such consent broadly:

> The consent may be authenticated in different ways: in its different stages of existence, it may assume different names—approbation—ratification—experience: but in all its different shapes—under all its different appellations, it may easily be resolved in this proposition, simple, natural, and just—All human laws should be founded on the consent of those, who obey them.[119]

However, Wilson clearly thought that consent "given originally" or "given in the form of ratification" was inferior to "what is most satisfactory of all, consent given after long, approved, and uninterrupted experience. This last, I think, is the principle of the common law."[120] Wilson had defined the British Constitution in 1774 in terms of a set of principles consensually validated by the history of the common law, and he held parliament's assertion of powers of taxation over the colonies to be unconstitutional on that basis. What is of interest is that Wilson, after playing a pivotal role both in insisting (with Madison) on broadly democratic ratification at the convention[121] and in participating in the actual debates over ratification of the constitution in Pennsylvania,[122] would prefer the common law in 1790 as a better model for the kind of consent that conferred Lockean legitimacy on law.

The key to understanding this is Wilson's picture of the common law process very much in line with Burke's appeal to the "real" rights of British constitutionalism, namely, as a cumulative pattern of deliberative experiments over time that protected rights:

> a system of experimental law, equally just, equally beautiful, and, important, as Newton's system is, far more important still. This system has stood the

116 See, e.g., ibid., vol. 1, pp. 124, 142, 225, 378–79.

117 Ibid., p. 125.

118 Ibid., p. 102.

119 Ibid., p. 180.

120 Ibid.

121 See, e.g., Farrand, *Records of the Federal Convention*, vol. 1, pp. 122–23 (Madison), p. 123 (Wilson), p. 127 (Wilson); vol. 2, p. 92 (Madison), pp. 468–69 (Wilson), p. 469 (Madison), pp. 475–76 (Madison), p. 477 (Wilson), pp. 561–62 (Wilson).

122 See, e.g., Jensen, *Documentary History*, vol. 2, pp. 167–72, 229–63, *et passim*.

> test of numerous ages: to every age it has disclosed new beauties and new truths. In improvement, it is yet progressive; and what has said poetically on another occasion, may be said in the strictest form of asseveration on this—it acquires strength in its process. From this system, we derive our dearest birthright and richest inheritance.[123]

The common law, as experiments in the protection of freedom,[124] had thus not only been deliberatively tested over a longer period by larger numbers of people, but its requirements also reasonably adjusted to changing circumstances.[125] Finally, custom had continuing force in the protection of liberty that ratification might lack:

> The regions of custom afford a most secure asylum from the operations of absolute, despotick power. To the cautious, circumspect, gradual, and tedious probation, which is law, darted from custom, must undergo, a law derived from compulsion will never submit.[126]

Wilson, like Madison, quite clearly saw that even a ratification as free and deliberative as that of the U.S. Constitution would be of little continuing effect if the interpretation of the constitution over time did not comparably elaborate its experiment in freedom using this type of common law basis in ways that could be justified to the community at large with at least as much force as its ratification. He pointed out the continuing need to renew the original principles of the constitution and thought of both bicameralism[127] and judicial review[128] as constitutional institutions aimed at this end. Presumably, such needed interpretive practices over time must, if the political legitimacy of the constitution was to be preserved, themselves be politically legitimate in the same way. The natural inference from Wilson's argument would indeed be that they must prove their legitimacy in a more complete and pervasive way. Whereas the constitution was ratified on the basis of contestable judgments about its likelihood to meet better the demands of Lockean political legitimacy in the abstract, its elaboration over time must prove its political power to the community subject to that power on terms of equal respect for rights and pursuit of the common interests of all. The political legitimacy of the constitution would, in effect, have been deliberatively tested over a longer period by large numbers of people in changing circumstances, and such long-standing and cumulatively successful

123 Ibid., vol. 1, p. 183.
124 See also ibid., pp. 356–57; see also vol. 2, pp. 560–65.
125 Ibid., vol. 1, pp. 354, 360.
126 Ibid.
127 See ibid., pp. 290–92, 414–17, 432–33.
128 Ibid., pp. 326–31.

interpretive practices would exercise a powerful customary constraint over abuses of political power and be further legitimated on that basis.

If Madison suggests that the understanding of constitutional interpretation over time must make sense of a pattern of Lockean reasonable consent over time, Wilson suggests the further methodological guide that our analysis proceed in two steps: first, giving the best account that can be given of the Lockean legitimacy of the constitution in 1787–88, and second, giving an account of the interpretation of the constitution over time is at least as legitimate as the founders' project. To begin with, then, we must give the best interpretation that can be given to the deliberative ratification of the constitution by the American generation of 1787–88. It was, of course, one of the most broadly democratic and deliberative processes in the political history of both the nation and the world to date,[129] and its point was conceived by that generation as political action of a qualitatively different kind from ordinary legislation. Indeed, it was that difference that would—consistent with the Massachusetts example—give American constitutionalism the status of supreme law over all others kinds and forms of ordinary political activity, including legislation. Ratification must have a political force more deeply legitimate than ordinary legislation, and mere numbers (e.g., larger democratic majorities) could not make the difference.

The ratification process was a natural political expression of the ideal that the constitutional structures to be ratified could sensibly be regarded as having passed the test required by Lockean legitimacy, or at least have passed a better test of such legitimacy than the ordinary legislative processes in which Americans had rightly lost constitutional faith. The ratification process had authority for Americans not as an expression of will but of judgment, namely, the judgment that the constitutional structures of federalism, separation of powers, and judicial review had, in effect, so divided, channeled, and constrained political power that Lockean Americans had made and expressed the deliberative judgment that these structures could be reasonably justified to all as securing uses of political power that would respect the equal rights of all and advance the common interests of all alike.

In effect, American constitutionalists created a new kind of political process as a reinterpretation of the moral point of Locke's first stage of unanimous reasonable consent. Locke had regarded that stage as crucial to any legitimate political community, and then regarded majority rule as the only available political procedure that could frame a government consistent with it. However, Locke's argument was problematic at both the normative and constitutional stages. Locke's normative theory of unanimous consent was subject to the kind of

129 On the comparative broadness of American suffrage during this period, see Donald S. Lutz, "The First American Constitutions," in Leonard W. Levy and Dennis J Mahoney (eds.), *The Framing and Ratification of the Constitution* (New York: Macmillan, 1987), pp. 71, 76–77.

decisive objection Hume had made,[130] namely, that a weak requirement of actual consent (i.e., veto by possible exit), could not adequately measure what Locke wanted it to measure: the demands of respect for inalienable rights. Furthermore, the Lockean view confused the deliberation appropriate to framing constitutions with the deliberation appropriate for legislation. Americans certainly had found Locke's view of the second constitution-making stage inadequate to the purposes of the first legitimacy-making stage, and therefore quite naturally elided the distinction between the two stages into a conception of framing a constitution much closer to the underlying normative theory of political legitimacy that was fundamental to the first stage.

Americans were sometimes no clearer than Locke about the ambiguity in his first stage between a tacit actual consent of all and a reasonable benchmark of respect for the inalienable human rights of all; Madison himself elided the two ideas in his response to Jefferson. However, American constitutional practice rests on a level beyond Locke in the understanding of how constitutionalism might secure the ends of just government, including respect for the rights of all. The authority of the ratification process for Americans like Madison cannot be sensibly understood on the model of the actual consent of all but only in terms of a more demanding normative conception of justifiability to all that is a distinctive American contribution to constitutionalism. The object of the ratification process was not a judgment of actual consent, but of constructive reasonable consent: the institutions could, in principle, be reasonably justifiable to all persons who were subject to political power because these institutions rested on reasonable deliberations about the permanent nature of political power (the political psychology of faction), about the inalienable rights of human nature in terms of which the legitimacy of all power must be tested, and about the enduring structures for the exercise of political power that might best harness it to legitimate ends. Ratification thus legitimated the constitution because it was the best available deliberative, free, and broadly egalitarian *political* decision-making procedure that could fairly be interpreted authoritatively to have made such a judgment of legitimacy, namely, that the constitution was a reasonably justifiable structure of political power for both the present generation and

130 Hume made a cogent objection to the Lockean inference of both the freedom and rationality of consent from mere facts of actual submission to authority:

> Can we seriously say that a poor peasant or artisan has a free choice to leave his country, when he knows no foreign language or manners, and lives, from day to day, by the small wages he acquires? We may as well assert that he may, by remaining in a vessel, freely consent to the dominion of the master, though he was carried on board while asleep, and must leap into the ocean and perish the moment he leaves her.
>
> (David Hume, "Of the Original Contract," in *Essays Moral, Political, and Literary* (Oxford: Oxford University Press, 1963), p. 462)

future generations because it secured respect for the rights and interests of all, and would and should be interpreted accordingly to require the justification by public (nonsectarian) reason of state power in terms of each generation's understanding of their inalienable human rights and interests (Chapter 7).

My argument has, to this point, focused on Madisonian liberal constitutionalism at the founding, but the real contemporary question is how later generations should interpret such an intergenerational project, and how, in contrast to what Burke defended as the liberal constitutionalism of the British Constitution, has it fared in comparison to Britain? Comparisons are in order, starting with the Burkean themes in Madison, and the Madisonian themes in Burke.

3 Burke on Violent Revolution and Its Legacy for Madisonian Constitutionalism

We have been exploring a late eighteenth-century period in the constitutional history of Britain and the U.S. when they were first united in a common imperial system under the unwritten British Constitution, followed by a surprisingly successful colonial revolution culminating in the 1787 written U.S. Constitution, to be followed in turn by the 1789 French Revolution and its experiments in constitutionalism. If there was ever a moment in human history when the question of democratic revolution and constitutionalism took center stage, it was during this period; and I have tried in the previous two chapters to put two central players in the British and American constitutional systems, Burke and Madison, in the best light I can in terms of the two remarkable things they share, a Lockean belief in the right to revolution and the human rights, in particular, the inalienable human rights of conscience they share, the abridgment of which may justify revolution; and second, a belief that the understanding and progressive development of the legitimacy of a liberal constitution justified in this way requires close study of interpretive history to understand and develop those institutions that better align democracy with liberalism. It makes sense against this background that Burke, such a profound critic of the French experiments, should have found the U.S. Constitution so promising. It was decidedly not the British unwritten constitution, and it repudiated the parliamentary supremacy central to that system. And it was very much a written constitution developed, as we have seen, on the basis of models for such written constitutions that had first been developed in Britain in the civil war period (notably, proposals of the Levellers and Harrington), and shared the ideological ambitions of the advocates of such written constitutions for future generations. What apparently impressed Burke about the U.S. Constitution, in contrast to the French experiments, was, as we saw at length in Chapter 2, the close study by Adams and Madison and others (natural aristocrats like himself) of the history of political institutions over time very much in the spirit of Montesquieu and his strong support for the British Constitution as the best liberal government feasible in modern circumstances in contrast to the ancient democracy of Athens and republic of Rome, and certainly preferable

DOI: 10.4324/9781003410966-3

to Bourbon absolutism in France. The American founders do not follow the model of British separation of powers, as Montesquieu described and defended it, but they create very much a simulacrum with a strong executive (elected, of course), a bicameral legislature with a more democratically accountable and another less democratically accountable branch, and an independent judiciary with powers of judicial review. The essence of Burke's defense of the British Constitution—competing institutions that check and balance one another so no one is judge in his own case—is preserved, and regular democratic elections are required. America did not have the hereditary aristocracy that, in Burke's view, had engineered the Glorious Revolution of 1688 and the liberal governments that followed, but he did not believe it was always necessary if comparable independent liberalizing forces had a place in the constitutional structure.

In her book, *On Revolution*,[1] Hannah Arendt argued that both the American Revolution and its resulting constitutionalism showed, in contrast to the disastrous French Revolution and its equally disastrous impact on later European politics, an alternative model for political philosophers like Arendt, namely, participation as citizens in democratic debate about politics and public affairs as the highest use of our human faculties. Arendt, herself a distinguished German philosopher once devoted to the conception of high German philosophy of her teacher and lover, Heidegger, was traumatized as a Jewess by his supine complicity with Hitler,[2] and she turned from an essentially Platonic and Aristotelian contemplative conception of philosophy to the alternative she found in the nation that, after a long period of statelessness, gave her a home, the U.S.[3] *On Revolution* is a tribute to American constitutionalism as showing to Europeans an alternative to Marxism,

> the politically most pernicious doctrine of the modern age, namely that life is the highest good, and that the life process of society is the very center of the very center of human endeavor. Thus the role of revolution was no longer to liberate men from the oppression of their fellow men, let alone to found freedom, but to liberate the life process of society from the fetters of scarcity so that it could swell into a stream of abundance. Not freedom but abundance became now the aims of revolution.[4]

1 Hannah Arendt, *On Revolution* (New York: Penguin, 1963).

2 See Young-Bruehl, *Hannah Arendt*, pp. 1–110; for Arendt's own comments on his philosophy, see Hannah Arendt, "Heidegger at 80," in *Thinking without a Banister: Essays in Understanding 1953–1975* (New York: Schocken, 2018), pp. 419–31.

3 For Arendt's argument for a turn from a contemplative to a politically engaged philosophy, see Hannah Arendt, *The Life of the Mind* (San Diego: A Harvest/HBJ Book, 1971); Hannah Arendt, *Lectures on Kant's Political Philosophy*, edited by Ronald Beiner (Chicago: University of Chicago Press, 1992); Hannah Arendt, *Responsibility and Judgment*, edited by Jerome Cohn (New York: Schocken, 2003).

4 Arendt, *On Revolution*, p. 54.

For Arendt, European thought and politics had experienced in effect a long period of moral nihilism after the French Revolution had discredited the democratic liberalism of its declaration of the human rights of man and citizen, a liberalism that had been defended by Immanuel Kant, the philosopher, more than any other, who influenced and shaped Arendt's version of political liberalism.

It was a nihilism with which some of Europe's best minds conspicuously struggled, notably, Nietzsche, an important influence on Arendt's teacher, Heidegger. For example, Nietzsche's turn to moral nihilism arose from his critique of Kant's ethical and political liberalism, in particular, Kant's rather incoherent advocacy of strong retributivism (murder requiring a death penalty, etc.) irrespective of consequences (lowering homicide rates). This and other problems in Kant's ethical theory led Friedrich Nietzsche to argue in his most philosophically important work, *On the Genealogy of Morals*,[5] that Kant's strong retributivism reflected a long history of repelling Christian thought in Aquinas and Tertullian that took pleasure in the punishment of the damned. Such endorsement of cruelty in Tertullian, Aquinas, and Kant expressed, on Nietzsche's penetrating pre-Freudian understanding of the unconscious, not reasonable argument, but the return of the repressed (repressed violence—indeed, Christian non-violence—now expressing itself in wantonly cruel violence). For Nietzsche, the whole theory of strong retributivism rests on the repressive guilt morality that Christianity had put in place after the long dominant shame morality of the Pagan world, in particular, the ancient Greek world of *The Iliad* and *The Oresteia* he adored. Nietzsche's critique was never directed against Jews whose cosmopolitanism he admired (he rejected German anti-Semitism precisely because it was a form of ethnic nationalism), but against what he analyzed as the slave guilt morality that Christianity had imposed on the Western ethical mind.[6] Nietzsche may very well have been a repressed homosexual,[7] and Lou Salome, who knew him as well as anyone (Nietzsche once fell in love with her and proposed marriage, which she rejected), offers an insightful analysis of this deeply neurotic and brilliant man: at the end of life, before his madness, Nietzsche was deeply alone, abandoned by his family and friends (including Richard Wagner as well as Salome) and obsessed by the traumatic loss of his Christian minister father as a boy (the father, like his son, went mad); that loss was psychologically filled by Nietzsche's incarnating himself (thus, the eternal

5 Friedrich Nietzsche, *On the Genealogy of Morals*, translated by Douglas Smith (Oxford: Oxford University Press, 1996).

6 For a compelling analysis of Nietzsche's views along these lines, see Julian Young, *Friedrich Nietzsche: A Philosophical Biography* (New York: Cambridge University Press, 2010).

7 For a compelling argument to this effect, see Joachim Kohler, *Zarathustra's Secret: The Interior Life of Friedrich Nietzsche* (New Haven, CT: Yale University Press, 2002). For a contrary view, see Julian Young, *Friedrich Nietzsche: A Philosophical Biography* (New York: Cambridge University Press, 2010).

return) in his father's image of Jesus but as himself the new savior (Zarathustra), sacrificing all (any personal happiness or love in his own life) for humankind,[8] high priest of an anti-Christianity repudiating the sexual and emotional repression of his homosexuality. This explains his repudiation of the sexual and emotional asceticism he thought Christianity had imposed on Western culture, both religious and philosophical (e.g., in Kant's strong retributivism).[9] Nietzsche argued that Kant's death of God has led to moral nihilism because Kant and others did not credibly offer an empirically based alternative, but rather a perpetuation of a form of guilt morality that rested on unjust sexual and emotional repression of our human bodies and our animal instincts (Nietzsche was immensely influenced by Darwin's compelling scientific case for our animality[10]). I, like many others (including many contemporary Christians and others), agree with this aspect of his implicit critique of the unjustly patriarchal Pauline repressions of both sexuality and gender, but view it as consistent with, indeed required by, a humane understanding of the ethical imperative, treating persons as equals, central to many forms of Christianity and other religions as well as secular views (as Burke saw).

I mention Nietzsche here because he gave perhaps the most influential expression of late nineteenth-century moral nihilism, and proposed an alternative to the guilt morality of Kant in terms of a regressive return to the shame morality of ancient Greece. So far from questioning patriarchy, as I do, Nietzsche rejected the guilt morality of treating others as equals for a modern reintroduction of the shame morality of the ancient Greeks, rejecting both democratic liberalism and feminism because inconsistent with the linchpins of patriarchy, the gender binary and its hierarchy. Nietzsche, as we have seen, despised German anti-Semitism, but his views were interpreted by Hitler to give expression to a genocidal political anti-Semitism and aggressive violence against all forms of democratic liberalism and, of course, feminism. When Arendt confronted the consequences of this view in Hitler's politics (including Heidegger's complicity with Nazism), she forged an alternative based on a critique of the French Revolution contrasting it with the American Revolution and its constitutionalism.

Arendt certainly shares with Burke a critique of the French Revolution as a clear and present danger to political liberalism. But, her critique is based on its turn to the sphere of economics instead of the sphere of political and civil

8 See Lou Salome, *Nietzsche*, translated by Siegfried Mandel (Redding Ridge, CT: Black Swan Books, 1988). Salome does not bring up Nietzsche's repressed homosexuality, but she did take that view of one of Nietzsche's closest friends, Paul Ree. On this point, see Julian Young, *Friedrich Nietzsche: A Philosophical Biography* (New York: Cambridge University Press, 2010), pp. 212–13.

9 For his critique of asceticism, see Friedrich Nietzsche, *On the Genealogy of Morals*, translated by Douglas Smith (Oxford: Oxford University Press, 1996), pp. 77–136.

10 On this point, see Julian Young, *Friedrich Nietzsche: A Philosophical Biography* (New York: Cambridge University Press, 2010).

liberties. Burke certainly argued that the economic policies of the French revolutionaries were disastrous, but his focus is on the political psychology that unleashed illimitable violence on quite elementary human rights to life and security and the terror that rationalized such inhumanity. More importantly, Arendt does not engage Burke's central psychological insight that violent revolution as such is unlikely to lead to secure liberal constitutionalisms.

But, America had in fact had a quite violent revolution, as Holger Hoock documents in his *Scars of Independence*:[11]

> Because to modern eyes the absolute numbers involved look small, it is easy to forget that with an estimated 6,800 to 8,000 Patriot battle deaths, 10,000 killed by disease in camps, and up to 16,000 or even 19,000 who perished in captivity, the number of Patriot soldiers killed in the Revolutionary War would be well over 3 million in terms of today's population … and significantly more than that if we consider Patriot deaths as a proportion of only the Patriot population in 1775 or 1783. More than ten times as many Americans died, per capita, in the Revolutionary War as in World War I, and nearly five times as many as in World War II. The death rate among Revolutionary war-era prisoners of war was the highest in American history. In addition, at least 20,000 British and thousands more American Loyalist, Native American, German, and French lives were lost. The Revolution exacted further human sacrifice when at war's end approximately 1 to 40 Americans went into permanent exile, the equivalent of 7.5 million today.[12]

Moreover, the violence included the persecution and torture by Patriots of Loyalists,[13] British soldiers massacring enemy soldiers and raping colonial women,[14] prisoners starved on disease-ridden ships and in subterranean cells,[15] African Americans held in slavery fighting for or against independence suffering disproportionately,[16] and Washington's army waging a genocidal campaign against the Iroquois.[17]

In Britain, Burke protested the government's suspension of *habeas corpus* for British captive Americans, "All the ancient, honest juridical principles, and institutions of England, are so many clogs to check and retard the headlong course of violence and oppression."[18] He went on, appealing to equality for all citizens:

11 Holger Hoock, *Scars of Independence: America's Violent Birth* (New York: Crown, 2017).
12 Ibid., p. 17.
13 Ibid., pp. 23–54.
14 Ibid., pp. 151–77, 243–71.
15 Ibid., pp. 211–40.
16 Ibid., pp. 299–311.
17 Ibid., pp. 275–95.
18 Cited at ibid., p. 227.

> Liberty, if I understand it all, is a *general* principle, and clear right of all the subjects within the realm, or of none. Partial freedom seems to me a most invidious mode of slavery. But, unfortunately, it is the kind of slavery the most easily committed in terms of civil discord.[19]

And when British commissioners made an offer of settlement that the Americans refused, and with "a deep sense of the insults they have received," issued a manifesto threatening "by every means in our power, [to] destroy or render useless a connection contrived for her [Great Britain's] ruin."[20]

> Edmund Burke, once again, raising his voice as the conscience of the House, argued that the manifesto forewarned of nothing less than Britain abandoning the customary "lenity" and "humanity" as dictated by the laws of war. Instead, it held out the specter of inexcusable "extremes of war and the desolation of a country."[21]

As we earlier saw, in his futile attempt to conciliate the Americans, Burke had warned of the consequences of leaving the British Constitution:

> But you will do well to remember that England has been great and happy under the present limited monarchy (subsisting in more or less vigour and purity) for several hundred years. None but England can communicate to you the benefits of such a constitution. We apprehend you are not now, nor for ages are likely to be, capable of that form of constitution in an independent state. Besides, let us suggest to you our apprehensions that your present union (in which we rejoice, and which we wish long to subsist) cannot always subsist without the authority and weight of this great and long-respected body, to equipoise and to preserve you amongst yourselves in a just and fair equality. It may not even be impossible that a long course of war with the administration of this country may be but a prelude to a series of wars and contentions among yourselves, to end, at length, (as such scenes have long ended,) in a species of humiliating repose, which nothing but the preceding calamities would reconcile to the dispirited few who survived them.[22]

The phrase "a species of humiliating repose" describes rather precisely the state of the nation after the revolutionary war at least when understood in the context of the skepticism, based on his political psychology about the tragedies in constitutionalism that followed the violent revolutions of the English Civil War and

19 Cited at ibid.
20 Cited at ibid., pp. 248–49.
21 Ibid., p. 269.
22 Ibid., p. 279.

the French Revolution. The apparent difference is that, in contrast to both, the Americans engage, as seen in Chapter 2, in a deliberative process including the judicious use of history (modeled by Montesquieu) constructing a simulacrum to the British Constitution, and Burke endorsed it for that reason.

It is a notable feature of Madison's constitutional constructivism that he used Hume's theory of faction as the empirical background of political psychology that a liberal constitution must take seriously in designing structures meant to align democratic politics with liberal values of respect for human rights, including the rights of minorities. The whole argument of his classic defense in No. 10, *The Federalist*, is that the two features of the federal system, delegation and representation, reasonably assume the political psychology of faction will thrive under democracy, namely, that groups will organize themselves around economic or ideological convictions that may regard outsiders to the group as not fully human, and thus neither their rights nor their interests are given the weight that justice requires. The argument of *Federalist* No. 10 is that the diversity of such factions is the key to aligning democracy with liberalism. In particular, what may be a majority faction at the state level and thus hostile to the rights and interests of minorities, will be a minority at the national level and, in order to achieve its political ends, factions will break down in order to achieve a broader democratic consensus and pass laws using majority rule. The great problem with this argument is that certain factions, resting on race/ethnicity (being white) or on religion (dominant Christianity), may be factions at both the state and federal level and nothing in the argument limits the threats to human rights that such superfactions might impose (e.g., anti-Semitism, or racism). If so, this might explain the role that the U.S. Supreme Court has played, at least after World War II, in addressing these issues through its powers of judicial review respecting the rights of racial/ethnic and religious minorities.

So, Madison, as a constitutional constructivist, took seriously political psychology, that is, how groups act as groups in vying for political power in a democracy. And as a Lockean liberal, his whole argument for liberal constitutionalism was, as Burke also argued, to so divide and separate the constitutional structures through which groups operate that they will tend to be less able to achieve their factionalized ends and be more likely to achieve the normative ends of political liberalism, respect for human rights and the public interest, including the rights and interests of minorities. And just to be clear, Madison like Jefferson was a slave-owner who, as a liberal, condemned slavery as the most serious abridgment of human rights and urged its abolition, and also quite clearly acknowledged at the Federal Convention of 1787 that "the mere distinction of colour made … a ground of the most oppressive dominion ever exercised by man over man,"[23]

23 Cited in Richards, *Conscience and the Constitution*, p. 24.

was the worst faction. For this reason, it is plausible to think that Madison's private views, expressed in a letter to Jefferson, about the constitution's defects,[24] may well have extended to its role in not limiting the worst faction, racism, though in public he agreed to the provisions of the constitution that protected the slave-owner's property interests in slaves.[25] It now appears reasonably clear that the intrinsic wrongness, on liberal grounds, of slavery was shared by many in the founding generation, a critique which antedated the American Revolution, which makes the hypocrisy of the constitution's putative liberal justification all the more evident today.[26] If so, the constitution was indeed illegitimate in the terms of its own Lockean liberal ambitions.

But, the problem that Madison may himself have seen lies deeper if we bring Burke's political psychology to bear on the foundation of American constitutionalism, namely, the ideological ambitions of the American revolution to give the world a better liberal constitution than the British Constitution against which the Americans had successfully revolted. The American revolution was, as we have seen, unbelievably violent on both sides, but the terms of the antagonist parties were defined by their common British white ethnicity, and indeed the humiliations that led even so reasonable a republican imperialist like Franklin to revolt were, as we have seen, quite clearly along the lines of humiliating a fellow English man:

> With even North under attack for failing to uphold Britain's sovereignty, Franklin gave up on reconciliation. He was embittered by the spectacle of "hereditary legislators" with "scarce discretion to govern a herd of swine" treating colonists as "the lowest of mankind, and almost of a different species from the English." Franklin had spent sixteen of the past twenty years in Britain advocating for a political community that he believed was a source of power, justice, and prosperity. Now, he was through with the British Empire. At the end of March 1775, he boarded the *Pennsylvania Packet* for Philadelphia. He would never live in England again.[27]

Britain was not the republican imperial power Franklin, like Burke, had imagined it to be, and we should at this point remember that the grounds of Burke's four great expressions of liberal resistance (over Ireland, America, India, and France) were all over the failure of Britain and France to understand and give effect to their own liberalism, treating people as equals. In all these cases, Burke had

24 On this point, see ibid., pp. 22–23.

25 For an attempt to understand how Madison might have viewed these protections as consistent with the long-term abolition of slavery, see ibid., pp. 24–27.

26 For an argument along these lines, see Edward J. Larson, *American Inheritance: Liberty and Slavery in the Birth of a Nation, 1765–1795* (New York: Norton, 2023).

27 Du Rivage, *Revolution against Empire*, p. 175.

appealed not just to the injustice of not treating people as equals, but to the underlying forms of irrational prejudice that degraded and humiliated them, and that therefore elicited violence. That is his cautionary warning to political liberalism, to take seriously when it violates its own egalitarian principles that it may unleash illimitable violence. Failure to listen to Burke's warning to the British over America exemplifies this consequence, and the failure of Americans to listen to Burke exemplifies yet again this consequence as the American revolution, far from the idealized Athenian agora Arendt imagines, leads to violence not just with the British, but with fellow Americans, as well as African Americans held in slavery and Amerindians.

When seen in this way through the prism of Burke on the political psychology of violence, the very way the American Revolution was brutally fought reinforced and strengthened existing irrational prejudices not just against loyalists, but against African Americans and Amerindians, all in violation of liberal principles of treating persons as equals. It was bad enough unjustly to degrade persons in this way in war, but it was a tragedy for American constitutionalism when the written constitution, justified by Madison as aligning democracy with liberalism, and meant to be a model for future generations of Americans, effectively writes these prejudices into the constitution.

In her important book, *Caste*,[28] Isabel Wilkerson defines eight pillars of caste: divine will and laws of nature, heritability, endogamy and the control of marriage and mating, purity versus pollution, occupational hierarchy, dehumanization and stigma, cruelty as means of social control, and inherent superiority versus inherent inferiority.[29] Wilkerson then explores the rigid hierarchy of caste in three caste systems: America, India, and Nazi Germany. I am particularly interested in the caste systems that have been constructed in constitutional democracies like the U.S. and Britain in which the protection of human rights of citizens has often proudly been proclaimed. What distinguishes caste in these nations is the dehumanizing treatment of differences (including differences of race, ethnicity, religion, class, gender, and sexual orientation) in two ways: first, the disfavored group is denied the basic human rights accorded others (rights of conscience, free speech, intimate life, and work); and second, such abridgment is rationalized, in a viciously unjust circle, by the dehumanizing stereotypes that draw whatever rationalizing support they have as a consequence of the abridgements of basic rights.

Caste, as I use and develop it in the comparison of British and American constitutionalism, centers on race in the U.S. What strikes me is the comparative ease with which British institutions, common law and parliament, dealt with and indeed abolished slavery both in Britain and in its colonies, an

28 Isabel Wilkerson, *The Origins of Our Discontents* (New York: Random House, 2020).
29 Ibid., pp. 99–166.

institution rationalized by racism.[30] Racism was arguably an influence in the different treatment within the British Empire of settler, largely white colonies (Australia, New Zealand, Canada) and largely non-white non-settler colonies (South Africa and India), but it apparently was not strong enough to defeat the abolition of slavery in Britain and its colonies, as it certainly was in the U.S. One important difference is that slavery existed as an important, quite large, and profitable institution not in foreign climes (as in the U.K.) but in the U.S. itself, and Southern states, as a condition of agreeing to the U.S. Constitution in 1787, insisted and got agreement to allowing the slave trade to the U.S. to continue for a longer period than other states preferred, and accorded the South express protections for return of fugitive slaves who had escaped to the North and gave states retaining slavery an additional 3/5 representation for each slave (the consequence is that the South largely politically dominated all the federal institutions—executive, legislative, and judicial until the civil war). There were no comparable protections of slavery in the colonies under the British Constitution, nor additional representation for slave-owners. The best that can be said of this ugly American deal is that both Madison and Jefferson (themselves slave-owners), who believed slavery must on liberal grounds eventually be abolished, is that they may have believed that, under their leadership, the Southern states would abolish slavery just as all American states had abolished established churches by 1833. But, any such liberal sentiments in the South were overwhelmed by President Jackson's racist populism, and Calhoun's pro-slavery constitutionalism, which the Supreme Court would endorse in *Dred Scott v. Sanford*.[31] The consequence is that American cultural racism, certainly not addressed by the 1787 Constitution and 1791 Bill of Rights, became politically powerful in the South and even in the North, so, in contrast to the U.K., the greatest human rights issue of the nineteenth century (the abolition of slavery) would not be addressed within the terms of the constitution, the American constitutional tragedy, when the U.K. had been able to address it under the terms of its unwritten constitution. It required a fratricidal civil war to end slavery in the U.S., and the resulting racism of a defeated South, like the fury of the defeated Germans after World War I (under the leadership of Hitler demonizing the Jews as scapegoats, creating yet another caste to rationalize genocide), left racism more powerful in the South and even the North than it had ever been before the civil war. It still remains a powerful force in American politics.

It would be a great mistake to think that Britain was entirely free of the racism that was to corrupt American constitutionalism until after World War II. New immigrants to Britain—people of color from the Caribbean, as well as South Asians,

30 On this point, see Kwame Anthony Appiah, *The Honor Code: How Moral Revolutions Happen* (New York: W. W. Norton, 2010). But, for ongoing British debate about the abolition of slavery, see Christopher L. Brown, "Later, Not Now," *London Review of Books* 43:14 (2021): 25–28.

31 *Dred Scott v. Sanford* 19 How. (60 U.S.) 393 (1857).

many of whom were Muslim—were both objects of racist violence by the British police, and exploded in violence in 1981 to race riots in Brixton, Manchester, and Liverpool, leading to an important report by Lord Scarman,[32] and the 1984 Police and Criminal Justice Act. And under the Blair government, the killing of a black youth, Stephen Lawrence, by a white boy and the failure of the police to deal with the matter fairly led to yet another report in 1993, the MacPherson Report, which condemned and sought to remedy institutional racism.[33]

But, the legacy of slavery and a fratricidal civil war over slavery make the issue of racism, including both private and police violence against people of color, a much more profound feature of American politics and constitutionalism than in the contemporary U.K. (violence against colonial resistance under the British Empire is a quite different matter, as I argue in Chapter 4). American politics, in contrast to the legislative actions of the British parliament to address British racism against new immigrant people of color, did not address the violent lynchings of people of color in the U.S. after the Reconstruction Amendments until a quite recent 2022 law making it a hate crime. Racist populism in the U.S. has a long history, and persists today, as Trump's appalling politics illustrates.[34]

Burke's warning about how violent revolutions can undermine liberal constitutionalism may well explain the American culture that, in the name of "We, the People," could, in violating its own liberal principles, unleash not only the violence of the civil war, but the violence inflicted on African Americans (lynchings) and on Amerindians (genocide) and the appalling levels of violence that today distinguish the U.S. among other nations. Idealizing the American Revolution and constitutionalism is an understandable matter particularly by new immigrants, like Arendt, but idealization often covers loss, in Arendt's case the traumas of a German Jewess seeking an alternative vision of politically engaged philosophy in democratic debate about justice and the common good. In Arendt's case, it led to one of the very few grave mistakes in her critiques of American politics, "Reflections on Little Rock,"[35] in which her rigid categories of the political vs. social led her not to understand the depth of the injustice of American racism in both personal and political law, and the indispensable role non-violence played in resisting this injustice so effectively. Not to understand the roots of American racism in the formation of the American Constitution is not to understand America.

32 See Scarman Report, https://en.wikipedia.org/wiki/Scarman_Report.

33 See Sir William MacPherson of CLUNY, *The Stephen Lawrence Inquiry Cm4262-I* (London: The Stationery Office, 1999), https:/assets.publishing.service.gov.uk/uploads/attachment_datafile/27111/4262.pdf.

34 See Jefferson Cowie, *Freedom's Dominion: A Saga of White Resistance to Federal Power* (New York: Basic Books, 2022).

35 See Hannah Arendt, *Responsibility and Judgment* (New York: Schocken, 2003), pp. 193–213.

4 Burke on the Political Psychology of Violence in the British Empire

Ireland and India

We have seen that Burke shared Benjamin Franklin's belief in the republican imperialism of the British Empire, namely, that the rights of the colonies to democratic self-government would under the British Constitution be respected and that both Britain and its colonies would not only share or come to share political liberalism but the commerce and prosperity thus made possible.[1] For Burke, the projects of advancing political liberalism and economic prosperity were closely connected, and the tragedy for him of the separation of the American colonies from the British Empire was that it set back both projects to the damage, as he saw it, of both Britain and the U.S. Burke's arguments along these lines can and have been interpreted as laying the foundation for the later reactionary and illiberal development of British imperialism, but there is an interpretive problem in ascribing to Burke writing in an eighteenth-century context anything like endorsement of the development of such imperialism "in the years after the Indian Mutiny down to post-war decolonization (1857–1953),"[2] some of which involved violent atrocities he would certainly have condemned (consider his condemnation of the dehumanizing "geographic morality" of not condemning Hastings' atrocities in India). More importantly, Burke brought to his critique of both the British and Americans insights into political psychology such critics ignore, namely, that both the failure to respect persons as equals and their unjust stigmatization and humiliating dehumanization elicit illimitable violence, features, as we have seen, of the American Revolution with a legacy for its flawed liberal constitutionalism that set the stage for a catastrophic civil war from which American constitutionalism has not yet recovered.

Burke's critiques on this ground were directed not only against British imperialism in its American colonies, but critiques of such imperialism in Ireland and

1 On Burke's view of the empire, see Jennifer Pitts, "Burke and the Ends of Empire," in David Dwan and Christopher J. Insole (eds.), *The Cambridge Companion to Edmund Burke* (Cambridge: Cambridge University Press, 2012), pp. 145–55.

2 Daniel J. O'Neill, *Edmund Burke and the Conservative Logic of Empire* (Oakland, CA: University of California Press, 2016), p. 169.

DOI: 10.4324/9781003410966-4

India, and in both cases Burke's argument illuminates the political violence its policies unleashed. I begin with Ireland, and then turn to India, which brings us forward to the nineteenth and the twentieth centuries.

The issue for the British in Ireland was, at bottom, religion (the Catholicism of most of the Irish), which brings us to the different constitutional treatments of religion in U.S. and U.K. constitutionalism.

Religion is the subject, more than any other in early liberalism, that gave rise to the central tenet of political liberalism that the alignment of religion and political authority in Europe had given rise to the unjust violence of the wars of religion as well as to the dominance in Europe of forms of autocratic monarchy (the divine right of kings, supported by established religions)—Catholics against Protestants, Protestants against one another, both against Jews (both Christian anti-Semitism and racist anti-Semitism), and both against Muslims (the Crusades), and all against philosophical dissenters to all forms of religion (Spinoza). The central task of early liberalism, Locke in Britain (*A Letter Concerning Toleration*[3]), Pierre Bayle in France, was to articulate and defend a principle of toleration as the basis for legitimate government[4] Locke, unlike Bayle, connects this argument to a general theory of democratic liberalism in *The Second Treatise of Government*, and is for this reason the central philosophical liberal in the foundation of both British and American constitutionalism, which share, because of Locke, both respect for human rights as requirement for the legitimacy of democratic political power, and the structuring of such power by the division of legislative, executive, and judicial powers.

Neither Locke nor Bayle, however, extend the scope of toleration to Catholics and atheists, which, in the British case, confirms the observation of Linda Colley in *Britons: Forging the Nation 1701–1837*[5] that for long historical periods the only basis for any sense of being British was anti-Catholic Protestantism (thus, the long-standing problem with Catholic Ireland). In contrast, the First Amendment of the U.S. Bill of Rights of 1791 prominently guarantees not only a right of free exercise, but forbids an established church, and both guarantees have under the Fourteenth Amendment been extended to the states. When Jefferson drafts the Virginia Bill for Religious Freedom that states the anti-establishment principle that Madison later puts in the First Amendment, he clearly states "but where he [Locke] stopped short, we may go on,"[6] and the American constitutional principle has not been limited in the way Locke defends (allowing for an established

3 See John Locke (ed.), "A Letter Concerning Toleration," in *A Treatise of Civil Government and Letter Concerning Toleration* (New York: Appleton-Century-Crofts, 1937, originally published 1690).

4 On this point, see Richards, *Toleration and the Constitution*, pp. 89–98.

5 See Linda Colley, *Britons: Forging the Nation 1701–1837* (New Haven, CT: Yale University Press, 2020).

6 Quoted in Richards, *Toleration and the Constitution*, p. 112.

church, which Britain still has). And the anti-establishment principle may be the most brilliant innovation of American constitutionalism based not only on the premise that religion has, since Constantine, corrupted politics and condemned liberal democracy, but, much more important for Jefferson and Madison, the linkage of sectarian religion to politics has corrupted religion, in particular, Christianity (rationalizing the Inquisition, the wars of religion (including the Crusades), and Christian anti-Semitism).

It is notable that, in the U.S. Bill of Rights (1791), the religion clauses come first before the guarantees of freedom of speech and press, and, certainly in the conception of the religion clauses prominently defended by both Jefferson and Madison in the early republic, the most protected speech was religious speech, including proselytizing speech, because the censorship of the advocacy of religious minorities was so likely to be censored by majoritarian religious authorities. Accordingly, it is a remarkable feature of the American conception of civil liberties that the prosecution of both heresy and blasphemy are forbidden, for both such prosecutions require the state to take as the measure of enforcement dominant majoritarian religious views.[7] In contrast, the private blasphemy prosecution brought by Mrs. Whitehouse against the *Gay Times* for publishing a poem that depicted Jesus as having sex, among others, with his disciples was allowed by the British courts[8] and the European Court of Human Rights held it consistent with the Convention as well.[9] The common offense was, however, abolished by parliament in the Criminal Justice and Immigration Act, 2008.

The American constitutional skepticism about state judgments of good or bad religion has made the prosecution of religious fraud in the U.S. constitutionally difficult, because, as Justice Douglas worried in *United States v. Ballard*,[10] jury judgments of religious fraud were likely to confuse sincerity with jurors' views on religious truth, views that the state is forbidden to enforce under the anti-establishment clause. For this reason, the American religion clauses have generated a number of religions invented in the U.S., including Mormonism, Christian Science, and even Scientology, which American officials have found it very difficult to prosecute for fraud.[11] Indeed, the very protection of the free exercise of religion has often taken the form of the protection of religious speech,

7 For an illuminating historical study, see Leonard Levy, *Blasphemy: Verbal Offense against the Sacred, from Moses to Salman Rushdie* (Chapel Hill: University of North Carolina Press, 1993).

8 *Whitehouse v. Lemon*, [1979] 2 WLR, or *Whitehouse v. Gay News Ltd.* [1979] AC 617, HL. The common offense was, however, abolished by parliament in the Criminal Justice and Immigration Act, 2008.

9 *Gay News Ltd. and Lemon v. United Kingdom* [Eur Comm HR] 5 EHRR 123 (1982), App. No. 8710/79.

10 322 U.S. 78 (1944).

11 On this point, see Lawrence Wright, "The Apostate: *Paul Haggis v. The Church of Scientology*," *New Yorker*, February 14 and 21, 2011.

for the underlying respect for the inalienable right to conscience requires as well protection of the attempts to share with others one's religious convictions.

The two religion clauses of the First Amendment of the U.S. Bill of Rights, anti-establishment and free exercise, protect from different threats to the underlying inalienable right to conscience. The guarantee of free exercise protects already established convictions, condemning any attempt by the state to burden free exercise, requiring, as the Elizabethan Religious Settlement did, that all citizens attend Anglican services, or forbidding a religious practice (like the sacrifice of chickens by Santeria believers[12]). Such protection is limited, as Locke argued, by a harm principle forbidding human sacrifice, which Locke argued did not extend to animal sacrifice. American constitutional law follows Locke closely here.

The anti-establishment clause protects the process of acquiring or changing such religious or ethical convictions, forbidding state incentives by sectarian religions to acquire their beliefs or to incentive conversion to their beliefs (in the U.S. the acquisition of religion is regarded as a matter for parents, linking religious free exercise to constitutional privacy). As Jefferson put the point, people may choose their own religious or other teachers, but the state may not itself be such a teacher or endorse one sectarian teacher over another. Accordingly, the jurisprudence of anti-establishment has limited state support of primary and secondary religious schools only to secular components of such education, and forbidden requirements of school prayer or the teaching of a sectarian view of science (creationism) or putting up the Ten Commandments that contain a number of purely religious instructions in public primary and secondary schools. The holding of the European Court of Human Rights upholding the constitutionality under the Convention of Italy's display of crucifixes in schools[13] would clearly violate the anti-establishment clause in the U.S. And the U.S. Supreme Court has extended anti-establishment to the public sphere, questioning whether a holiday like Christmas may include a state-sponsored purely sectarian religious scene (a creche) that endorses the Christian doctrine of the incarnation (God becoming man), in which not all Christians and most non-Christians do not believe.

There are also constitutional prohibitions in the text of the Constitution of 1787 on religious tests for any official serving in the any of the branches of the national government.[14] And these prohibitions have now been extended to comparable state officials.[15]

12 On this point, see *Church of the Lukumi Babalu Aye v. City of Hialeah*, 508 U.S. 520 (1993).

13 See *Lautsi & Ors v. Italy*, [2011] ECHR Application No. 30814/06 (18 March 2011).

14 See U.S. Constitution, Article VI, paragraph 3.

15 See *McDaniel v. Paty*, 435 U.S. 618 (1978) (state disqualification of clergyman from serving in state legislature held unconstitutional).

This close connection between free exercise and free speech has, in the course of the development of both the judicial interpretation of the religion clauses and of free speech, extended well beyond Locke's and Bayle's conception of the limits on the argument for toleration. No religion can any longer be regarded in the U.S. as outside the scope of the principle of toleration, including Catholics and Jews and Buddhism (without any conception of a personal deity) or the various forms of agnosticism and atheism that are for increasingly large numbers the basis of their ethical convictions of value in personal and interpersonal life (cf. Kant on defending an ethics of universal human rights independent of religion). And the remarkable scope of the American protection of free speech, including now subversive advocacy, extends well beyond religion, to any conscientious convictions critical of not only of the state (thus, the protection of subversive advocacy), but critical of dominant institutions and practices.

Nonetheless, it must be acknowledged that the constitutionalisms of both Britain and the U.S.—written and unwritten—are historically connected to their dominant Protestantism of *sola scriptura* and the weight Protestantism or, more precisely, the more radical forms of Protestantism of both Locke and Bayle have accorded the right to conscience. I also should acknowledge that some Protestants, notably Luther, were much less tolerant, indeed violently anti-Semitic and sometimes violently opposed to Protestant radicals (he called for killing the peasants during the Peasant Revolt), than the Catholic humanist Erasmus, an altogether more attractive liberal figure.[16] The tolerant humanist Catholic Montaigne also comes to mind in this connection, as well as the excommunicated Jew Spinoza's advocacy of the most expansive scope of toleration advocated by anyone in the seventeenth century, including by Locke and Bayle.[17] The legacy of Henry VIII's break with Rome and the papacy's excommunication of Henry and Elizabeth I and other British monarchs, legitimating political violence against and assassination of British Protestant monarchs, gives the whole Protestant–Catholic division in this period a character closer to the Cold War between democracy and communism or to Al-Qaeda and the West than to such intra-Christian religious divisions today, in particular, in light of Vatican II's liberalization of Catholicism on central issues like its repudiation of Augustinian intolerance and Christian anti-Semitism in the wake of the Holocaust.[18]

16 On this point, see Michael Massing, *Fatal Discord: Erasmus, Luther, and the Fight for the Western Mind* (New York: Harper, 2018).

17 On this point, see Carol Gilligan and David A. J. Richards, *The Deepening Darkness: Patriarchy, Resistance, and Democracy's Future* (Cambridge: Cambridge University Press, 2009), pp. 139–40.

18 On this point, see Bamforth and Richards, *Patriarchal Religion, Sexuality, and Gender*, pp. 12–14.

Nonetheless, the centrality of the religion clauses to the American conception of basic rights is in stark contrast to Britain's established church, with the monarch as the head of the Church of England, linking political and religious authority in the way American law forbids. Similarly, the long British limitation of the exercise of state power to Anglicans, excluding other Protestants, as well as Catholics, Jews, and others violates long-standing American views forbidding any religious tests. Also, the British view that its great universities, Oxford and Cambridge, were religious in nature, requiring teachers to be Anglican and even celibate, decidedly would be forbidden by the American anti-establishment tradition. Jefferson and Madison, in particular, call for great public universities (the University of Virginia), but demand they must be secular.

Despite the different constitutional arrangements regarding religion in the U.S. and the U.K., there were violent anti-Catholic movements in the U.K., including the Gordon Riots against Catholic emancipation, brilliantly portrayed in Dickens' *Barnaby Rudge*,[19] and, in the U.S., the antebellum Know-Nothing Party (American Party), arising after the collapse of the Whig Party (Lincoln was a Whig) based on anti-Catholic immigrant feeling (great numbers of Irish come to the U.S. in response to the potato famine),[20] but collapses into Republican Party that, under Lincoln's leadership, wins the election of 1860 and, more surprisingly, the election of 1864. And the lynchings of the K.K.K. after the collapse of Radical Reconstruction focused not only on people of color, but Catholic immigrants (Italians) and Jews.

Politics in the U.K. and the U.S. are thus less different than their constitutional arrangements would suggest, but their constitutional arrangements could not be more different, as we have seen. My question is how these arrangements advance or retard liberal values.

Religion linked to race (colorism), as one marker of caste, is familiar enough from the Indian caste system, but also plays a role both in the links between religion and race/ethnicity in Britain (the Irish) and in the animus in the U.S. against Catholic immigrants from Southern Europe and Jewish Immigrants from Eastern Europe that took the form of federal legislation stopping immigrants from these nations for a long period, even, shockingly, during World War II when European Jews were being murdered by Hitler's genocidal fascism, which the U.S. was ostensibly fighting.[21] There is also in the U.S., as there was in Nazi Germany, a close relationship between religion and racism: for example, when people of color were first brought to the American colonies as slaves, the fact that they were not Christians was a ground for enslavement; but when they converted to

19 See Charles Dickens, *Barnaby Rudge* (London: Penguin, 2003).

20 For an illuminating discussion, see Peter Canellos, *The Great Dissenter* (New York: Simon & Schuster, 2021), pp. 86, 88, 89, 100, 101, 110, 125.

21 See Daniel Okrent, *The Guarded Gate: Bigotry, Eugenics, and the Law That Kept Two Generations of Jews, Italians, and Other European Immigrants Out of America* (New York: Scribner, 2019).

Christianity, as they did, the religious difference no longer rationalized slavery, but became racism.[22] German anti-Semitism starts as a form of Christian anti-Semitism from the populist excesses of which the Catholic Church often tried to protect Jews, but later, even if Jews convert, it transmogrifies into a scientific racism that rationalizes genocide in a form that shocked Christians.[23] The failure of the European churches to resist Hitler in Germany and Mussolini in Italy is one of the reasons that so discredited religion among Europeans, resulting in much more secular societies than previously existed.

Burke condemned the British treatment of the great majority of the Irish people, who were Catholic, who had endured Cromwell's genocidal militarism[24] and been penalized since the Glorious Revolution.[25] The Nine Years War (1688–97) was about ideas: absolutism versus constitutionalism, and Catholicism versus Protestantism, or more accurately, religious uniformity versus religious toleration, and pitted the France of Louis XIV against a Grand Alliance that included Britain now, after the Glorious Revolution, with William III of the Netherlands as its constitutional monarch. In the summer of 1689, Louis backed an invasion of Ireland by the Catholic James II, who had been deposed. Oppressed Catholic Irish peasants flocked to his cause. In the summer of 1690 William defeated James at the Battle of the Boyne.

> This defeat resulted in the ruthless suppression of the Catholic-Irish population by Protestant landowners. The Irish Penal Code, passed over the next 40 years, forbade the Catholic-Irish from voting, holding office, sitting in Parliament, attending university, practicing law, purchasing land, inheriting land from Protestants, bearing arms or wearing swords (a mark of gentility), or owning a horse worth more than 5 pounds. The Catholic-Irish were forced to divide bequests among all their heirs (partible inheritance), thus leading to the gradual elimination of large land holdings. As a result, by 1727, the Catholic Irish amounted to four-fifths of the population but owned only one-seventh of the land.[26]

The Irish parliament, subject to the British parliament, placed political power in the Protestant Ascendancy,[27] as it was called, namely, the Protestants who had settled in Ireland, as well as converts to Protestantism, like Burke's father

22 On this point, see Richards, *Conscience and the Constitution*, pp. 84–85.

23 For a fuller discussion, see Gavin I. Langmuir, *Toward a Definition of Antisemitism* (Berkeley: University of California Press, 1990).

24 See Foster, *Modern Ireland 1600–1972*, pp. 101–16.

25 See ibid., pp. 153–63.

26 Robert Bucholz, *Foundations of Western Civilization II: A History of the Modern Western World Course Guidebook* (Chantilly: Teaching Company, 2006), p. 78.

27 See Foster, *Modern Ireland*, pp. 138–94.

and Burke himself. Burke himself regarded such treatment as a form of slavery, not only depriving Irish Catholics of the basic rights of English citizens, but stigmatizing them as subhuman. Consistent with his political psychology, he already saw indications among the Catholic Irish of resistance, and was especially concerned that, inspired by the French Revolution, such resistance would become self-destructively violent. In fact, the year after his death, the Irish Rebellion of 1798 exploded,[28] followed by continuing British unjust treatment (including the famine[29]), giving rise over time in the late nineteenth and twentieth centuries to what the leading historian of Ireland calls "an almost psychotic Anglophobia,"[30] exploding in violent civil war and terrorism, the latter of which continues after Catholic Ireland becomes a republic and Protestant northern Ireland remains in Britain.[31] What Burke predicted happened: British irrational prejudice against the Catholic Irish gave rise to the countervailing prejudice of Anglophobia, both of which were illimitably violent.

Ireland was arguably the British Empire's first colony, and many of the issues that were later to arise in empire's relationship to its other colonies, in particular, the non-settler colonies, were anticipated in its treatment of the Irish, leading to the patterns of violence by both colonials and by the British brilliantly documented by Caroline Elkins in her important book, *A Legacy of Violence*.[32] British political liberalism had by the late Victorian period of Dicey been justified by the expansion of the franchise, in time including all citizens including women. It was because the increasingly dominant House of Commons embodied fair representation of all that it was supposed to align democracy with liberalism. But, the colonies were not represented in the British parliament, putting a strain on any conception of liberal legitimacy at least when it came to the British Empire defended in terms of the self-contradictory idea of liberal imperialism. Dicey himself proudly defended it in precisely the terms Burke had used of the French revolutionaries: "Imperialism is to all who share it a form of passionate feeling." It was "a political religion … a form of patriotism which has a high absolute worth of its own, and is both excited and justified by the lessons of history."[33] In effect, he constitutionally rationalized what Elkins calls the "legalized lawlessness"[34] of British violence in response to the Indian Mutiny, Jamaica's Morant Bay Rebellion, Indian resistance (the Amritsar massacre), Boer resistance (concentration camps for women and children), and

28 See ibid., pp. 278–82.

29 See ibid., pp. 318–44.

30 Ibid., p. 316.

31 For an illuminating treatment, see ibid.

32 See Caroline Elkins, *Legacy of Violence: A History of the British Empire* (New York: Alfred A. Knopf, 2022); see also Caroline Elkins, *Imperial Reckoning: The Untold Story of Britain's Gulag in Kenya* (New York: Henry Holt, 2005).

33 Quoted in ibid., p. 96.

34 Ibid., p. 15.

other atrocities. The underlying motivating racism was sometimes strikingly explicit: to optimize gold production in South Africa, the high commissioner expressed the willingness "to sacrifice 'the nigger' absolutely."[35] Some atrocities had been contested in Britain by British liberals like John Stuart Mill (protesting Morant Bay), but Mill, Britain's leading philosophical liberal (author of *On Liberty* and *The Subjection of Women*), followed his father as an official of the East India Company (for India), and "advocated for a 'paternal despotism' to tutor the empire's children"[36] (Indians); neither Mill nor his father had ever been to India, or understood its diverse languages. Burke had spoken in a very different liberal voice in condemning the racist "geographic morality"[37] applied to India, not treating them as moral persons, during the Hastings impeachment he abortively led in late eighteenth-century Britain.

It is, I believe, a tribute to British political liberalism that it was not a Briton, but an Indian, Gandhi, who lived and studied in Great Britain becoming a barrister in India, who was once again to speak in Burke's liberal voice but as an analyst of the political psychology of British violence, and innovating a non-violent strategy, Satyagraha, that was to work against British imperialism in India as it was later to work under the leadership of Martin Luther King, Jr. in the U.S. against American cultural racism. In *Disarming Manhood*,[38] my study of both Gandhi and King and their progenitors (William Lloyd Garrison and Leo Tolstoy), I explore the common gender-bending relational psychology they all share deriving from maternal figures who espouse an anti-patriarchal interpretation of religious texts (e.g., the Sermon on the Mount of Jesus) quite different from dominant interpretations of those texts that marginalize non-violence. Gandhi shares this psychology (including his life-long admiration of Jesus of Nazareth), but would not have come to Satyagraha as a strategy against British imperialism in India (he had earlier developed a form of in in South Africa) without his years in Britain, closely studying both British constitutionalism and the British people.

What he saw was, I believe, what Burke saw: a people and a constitutionalism living in contradiction, a shame culture prone to violence against outsiders, and also a guilt culture supported by a constitutionalism that respected what Burke would have called "real" human rights and a Christian guilt culture in which the teachings of Jesus of Nazareth (including the Sermon on the Mount) were prominent features. Satyagraha called for resistance to injustice, sometimes breaking laws regarded by the resisters as unjust, but Gandhi believed that

35 Quote in ibid., p. 92.

36 Ibid., p. 51.

37 See Edmund Burke, "Speeches on the Impeachment of Warren Hastings," in Isaac Kramnick (ed.), *The Portable Edmund Burke* (New York: Penguin, 1999), pp. 388–408 at 394.

38 See David A. J. Richards, *Disarming Manhood: Roots of Ethical Resistance* (Athens: Swallow Press/Ohio University Press, 2005).

non-violence, exposing oneself to possible violence for breaking laws, might appeal to the underlying guilt culture of both Britain's political liberalism and Christianity. The key was an appeal to an underlying political liberalism that both the protesters and those protested share, exposing the contradictions to deliberative reflections bringing people to a sense of guilt in terms of a morality they shared, certainly not a "geographic morality." Non-violence was the key because the willingness to accept unjust violence directed at resistance dramatized in a politically powerful way that the underlying racism itself rested on irrational violence and only violence and had nothing to be said for it in terms of liberal values. Gandhi was to this extent taking the critical position to the British imperial system that Burke had earlier taken, liberal resistance to imperialist injustices. But, he, unlike Burke, had found a collective strategy through non-violence to penetrate the imperialist carapace resting on fear of outsiders, speaking to the heart and mind of its underlying humanist universalism as Burke did in all his acts of liberal resistance. Only someone who believed in British political liberalism could have innovated such a strategy, which is why Gandhi's non-violence draws upon, as Burke did, an outsider's understanding of British culture that Britons did not themselves possess. Outsiders to a liberal culture, precisely because they have personally experienced liberal injustices that the culture does not yet see, sometimes, it appears, play pivotal roles in giving effect to liberal principles.

Martin Luther King, Jr. in the U.S. closely studied Satyagraha in a visit to India after Gandhi's murder. The U.S., like Britain, also lived in contradiction: its shame culture of racist violence in tension with the political liberalism of its democratic constitutionalism and its dominant Christianity, Protestant and Catholic. And through non-violence the Civil Rights Movements, met by racist violence, dramatized that racism rested on nothing but irrational violence, enabling Americans to appeal to their underlying political liberalism and Christianity that they and the movement shared. King's movement achieved politically through non-violence what many had previously thought was unimaginable: Congressional passage of the Civil Rights of 1964 and the Voting Rights Act of 1965.

The impact of both Gandhi in India and Martin Luther King, Jr. in the U.S. can be understood, in their respective contexts of the contradictions in their respective cultures, Britain and the U.S., cultures still in transition from the shame cultures still in play in the British Empire and in the racism of the American South, innovating a new kind of non-violent liberal voice appealing to the liberal conscience of both the political liberalism of their respective constitutionalism and their religion, the Christianity of the Sermon on the Mount. Its underlying psychology is very much in line with Burke's insights into this transition, the insights of outsiders to the dominant culture aggrieved by its propensities to repressive violence against claims of justice based in treating persons as equals and through non-violence exposing to the public mind of their respective liberal democracies the dignity of their claims and persons and bringing citizens to a long delayed sense of culpable guilt calling for responsible action, Britain leaving India, America passing the path-breaking civil rights acts of 1964 and 1965. That such transitions are both painful and often incomplete is shown by the fact that the leaders of both movements, Gandhi and King, were murdered by reactionary advocates of the shame culture they had both brilliantly resisted, and that the British, long having used a strategy of divide and conquer (Muslims vs. Hindus) to rule India, did not take seriously the legacy of this strategy, preferring one religious group over another, shaming one at the expense of the other, leading to the illimitable religious violence that followed Britain's irresponsibly precipitous partition and exit that set the stage for the wars between Pakistan and India as well as the violence in both nations against religious minorities that is, if anything, worse today than it has ever been.

5 A Constitution for the Ages?

Constitutionalism in the U.S. and Britain

Burke's defense of the British Constitution included a belief in its imperial system, both as defensible forms of liberal constitutionalism, and his resistance to its treatment of the Irish, the Americans, and the Indians appealed precisely to the liberal values that he believed each form of imperialism had flouted. It was precisely because such injustices degraded whole groups of persons as sub-human that such humiliation, not treating them as equal persons, would illicit illimitable violence, a legacy that would threaten liberal constitutionalism in Britain itself. Burke thought, however, of constitutionalism in a culturally evolutionary sense, and his interest in comparing the British Glorious Revolution of 1688 to the disastrous political religions of the English Civil War and the French Revolution was that British history reflected a progressive self-correcting system that had reformed British institutions in a more liberal direction retaining the institutions that worked. Such reform had been made possible by the aristocratic Whig elites resisting the monarchy, but also by the important role they accorded natural aristocrats like Burke, including his liberal resistance to what he argued were illiberal policies of the British government in Ireland, America, and India. Burke thus thought of the British Constitution as an important contribution to human culture that would itself change over time as British institutions had changed in the past. His own role in the development of British constitutionalism was his conception of independent political parties organized around common principles and his defense of the independent role of representatives in expressing their own convictions, even when his constituents did not agree and, as happened to him in his criticism of the French Revolution, about which his own party disagreed.

Burke's endorsement of the U.S. Constitution of 1787 shows that he did not regard Britain's unwritten constitution as the only legitimate form of liberal constitutionalism, but he certainly thought the British model was a legitimate model for others, as Montesquieu had himself argued. As we saw in Chapter 2, the Madisonian ambition for a written constitution quite self-consciously thought of it as a constitution for the ages, one which would have

DOI: 10.4324/9781003410966-5

weight for later generations of Americans. Both Burke and Madison thought of their respective constitutionalisms as models for others. The question thus naturally arises how each constitutionalism—unwritten vs. written—has in fact dealt with the remarkable changes in each nation since the late eighteenth century. I will explore this question along several dimensions using British and American experience as a focus: written vs. unwritten constitutions, social democracy, the reinterpretation of Locke as each nation faces new circumstances, culture vs. institutions, the significance of the English Civil War and American Civil War, referenda (Brexit in the U.K.), representation and political parties, and the democratic objection to judicial review as it bears on the legitimacy of judicial review and judicial independence, focusing on the contemporary constitutional crisis in both the U.S. and the U.K. arising from populist threats to the role of the judiciary in both nations in protecting human rights.

5.1 Written vs. Unwritten Constitutionalisms

In her important recent book, *The Gun, the Ship, and the Pen,*[1] Linda Colley puts the popularity of written constitutions in a broad historical perspective, not always or often linked to political liberalism as I have studied it in this book. The written constitutions she studies exhaustively, many of them certainly not in the mainstream of constitutional scholarship, are often democratic, but not particularly liberal. For example, the Japanese experiment with written constitutions after the Meiji restoration was never in service of liberalism, but, like many other such written constitutions she discusses and that the Japanese admired (Germany, in particular), concerned with mobilizing Japanese men in the aggressive imperialistic wars that were ultimately to destroy imperial Japan as they would destroy Germany.[2] It is a tragic story of democracy gone wrong familiar from ancient Athens that is destroyed by its propensity for the imperialist wars that were popular with the Athenian demos (the protests of Socrates and others notwithstanding[3]), but what is new and rather appalling for liberals is how often written constitutions have been used in the retelling of this tragic story, including the role of the U.S. Constitution denying rights to indigenous peoples.[4] On Colley's telling, the only constitutional tradition that

1 Linda Colley, *The Gun, the Ship, and the Pen: Warfare, Constitutions, and the Making of the Modern World* (New York: Liveright, 2021).

2 See ibid., pp. 357–400.

3 Socrates voted against the unjust procedure used to condemn defeated Athenian generals to death. For a discussion, see John Laws, *The Constitutional Balance* (Oxford: Hart, 2021), p. 30.

4 For a pertinent discussion, including its background in both Locke and British common law, see Martin Loughlin, *Against Constitutionalism* (Cambridge, MA: Harvard University Press, 2022), pp. 168–71.

stands apart is the alternative history of the proudly unwritten constitution of the U.K.,[5] and we now must inquire how the ostensibly liberal written constitution of the U.S. compares on liberal grounds with the unwritten constitution of the U.K.

But, how unwritten is the British Constitution? John Laws, a British judge, has distinguished constitutional statutes from ordinary legislation, including, among such constitutional statutes, "the Magna Carta, the Bill of Rights 1689, the Act of Union, the Reform Acts which distributed and enlarged the franchise, the [Human Rights Act, 1998] the Scotland Act 1998 and the Government of Wales Act 1998."[6] Laws concedes any of these could be explicitly repealed by parliament (Brexit, for example, ended the European Communities Act of 1972, which the House of Lords had earlier interpreted as according European Community law supremacy over parliamentary laws).[7] Laws lists the Communities Act as one of these constitutional statutes (limiting parliamentary supremacy), regarding them as having a deeper authority than ordinary legislation, which suggests that the normative foundations of British constitutionalism rest on something deeper than parliamentary sovereignty as such. Laws elsewhere invokes three normative fundamentals in British constitutionalism: reason, fairness, and the presumption of liberty,[8] against which all British institutions must be assessed for their legitimacy, both common law and parliament, requiring a balance dictated by these normative demands and the different competences of institutions to meet them. These demands are, of course, those of political liberalism. And Laws goes on to argue that they justify three constitutional principles: (1) a presumption of liberty that individuals are free to do whatever is not illegal; (2) the anti-tyranny principle that, for public bodies, and notably government, everything that is not forbidden is allowed; and (3) the principle of minimal interference that every intrusion by the state upon the freedom of the individual stands in need of objective justification.[9]

The unwritten constitution of the U.K., so understood, and the written constitution of the U.S. must be tested by the political liberalism, rooted in Locke, they share. My argument shows that, at least for a long period from the U.S. Constitution of 1787 and Bill of Rights of 1791 to the end of World War II, the U.S. Constitution, justified by giving the world a better constitutionalism than that of the U.K. against which they revolted on Lockean grounds, fails rather miserably. The controlling issue for this normative assessment is the interlinked issue of American slavery and the racism that rationalized it, which led to a civil war that, if anything, deepened American racism. Such racism, as a cultural

5 See Colley, *The Gun, the Ship, and the Pen*, pp. 415–16.

6 Laws, *The Constitutional Balance*, p. 112.

7 See *R (Factortame Ltd) v. Secretary of State for Transport (No. 2)* [1991] 1AC 603.

8 Laws, *The Constitutional Balance*, p. 8.

9 See ibid., pp. 80–83.

force, not only outlived the abolition of slavery by the 13th Amendment in 1865, but was allowed to prosper by both the Supreme Court (*Plessy v. Ferguson,*[10] and similar opinions) and the mainstream political parties after 1877. The tide of reactionary American cultural racism that had flooded the U.S. after the civil war, North and South, became hegemonic after the withdrawal of federal troops in 1877,[11] burying the constitutionally promised rights of people of color in order for white North and South to find common ground as Americans join to fight an imperialistic war, the Spanish–American War, and enter the even more disastrous World War I—which Wilson's mishandling of the Versailles Treaty and inability to get the U.S. to join the League of Nations rendered even more catastrophic (the "shame of Versailles"—Hitler's words—from the onerous treaty at the end of the war provoking the aggressive political anti-Semitism that rationalized his aggressive wars and the murder of six million innocent Jews and millions of others and ordering the destruction of Germany at the end of the war).[12]

Another comparative point against U.S. constitutionalism, in contrast to the U.K., is that the American judiciary invoked its *Marbury* powers on unjustified grounds to invalidate equality as a reasonable ground for just redistributive legislation[13] whereas, in the U.K., parliament, once the Labour Party took power in 1945, could pursue such policies without impediment. In the U.S., such legislation required a constitutional crisis, ending with a change in the view of at least one justice, and the appointment of others.

The very flexibility of Britain's unwritten constitution, in contrast to the inflexibility of the U.S.'s written constitution, is part of its appeal, giving rise to a constructive ambiguity in the interpretation of constitutional institutions and principles (over, for example, jurisdictional power and the exercise of those powers), one that learns from and changes in light of experience (e.g., the shift from judicial common law-making to parliamentary legislation). In his critical study of Dicey on British constitutionalism, Paul Craig puts Dicey's point as

10 *Plessy v. Ferguson,* 163 U.S. 537 (1896) (upholding the constitutionality of racial segregation).

11 On this point, see C. Van Woodward, *Reunion and Reaction: The Compromise of 1877 and the End of Reconstruction* (New York: Oxford University Press, 1966).

12 On these points, see David W. Blight, *Race and Reunion: The Civil War in American Memory* (Cambridge, MA: The Belknap Press of Harvard University Press, 2001); Woodward, *Reunion and Reaction*; for the prophetic prediction that the onerous terms of the Versailles Treaty would provoke a political reaction in Germany, see Keynes, *The Economic Consequences of the Peace*; on Hitler's use of the slogan "the shame of Versailles" to rationalize aggressive political violence, see Michele Caimmi, "When Hitler Ordered the Destruction of Germany," https//medium.com-wgat-i-ve-learned/when-hitler-ordered-the-destruction-of-germanyb3454 0ea1500

13 See, e.g., *Lochner v. New York*, 198 U.S. 45 (1905) (invalidating state law limiting hours of work in bakery).

one of self-correction through democratic politics,[14] the external limit of electoral preferences aligning with the internal limit of the majority in the House of Commons, but then observes that Dicey's theory does not fit British constitutionalism when he wrote and certainly later, failing to take seriously the role of a law-making, rights-protecting common law judiciary historically independent of parliament and its continuing role recently as well as, after the franchise was extended broadly, the increasingly important role of executives leading party politics at the expense of parliament's traditional representative role, all at the expense of the rights of minorities.[15] Craig elsewhere argues that the interpretation of parliamentary sovereignty as a statutory monopoly of law-making, so common law courts can only act with parliamentary consent, in fact does not fit British constitutional experience in which the common law has played such an important role in protecting rights independent of parliament and an increasingly important role recently. Craig accepts that "common law rules remain 'vulnerable to legislative abrogation,'"[16] but accepts as well "the classic model of continuing sovereignty, which has at its core Parliament's ability to amend, repeal, and change," including a power of correction through democratic politics illustrated in 1945 when the British people corrected the disastrous politics that led to World War II.[17] We can see this flexibility in the reforms of the British civil service starting with the Northcote-Trevelyan Report of 1854[18] and the upgrading of the British civil service with credentials now the same as lawyers and judges,[19] regarded now as often more competent than the ministers they serve; see the popularity in the U.K. of the series, "Yes, Minister."[20] We can see this as well in the innovation within British parliamentary politics of the increasing use of select committees in the U.K. since 1979 some of which have overseen the work of government departments and agencies.[21] These select committees have existed in Britain since the Tudor period, and Burke played a prominent role in such committees in the investigations into wrongdoing during the Hastings impeachment. The system of committees was further

14 See A. V. Dicey, *Introduction to the Study of the Law of the Constitution* (Indianapolis, IN: Liberty Fund, 1982).

15 See Paul Craig, *Public Law and Democracy in the United Kingdom and the United States* (Oxford: Clarendon Press, 1990), pp. 12–79.

16 See Paul Craig, *UK, EU and Global Administrative Law: Foundations and Challenges* (Cambridge: Cambridge University Press, 2015), p. 151.

17 See Peter Hennessy, *Never Again: Britain 1945–1951* (New York: Pantheon, 1993).

18 See "Northcoe-Trevelyan Report," https://en.wikipedia.org/wiki/Northcote%E2%80%93Trevelyan_Report.

19 On this point, see Stephen Sedley, *Lions under the Throne: Essays on the History of English Public Law* (Cambridge: Cambridge University Press, 2015), pp. 34–37, 53–56, 97, 107–08.

20 See "Yes Minister", https://en.wikipedia.org/wiki/Yes_Minister

21 For a fuller discussion, see "Select Committee (United Kingdom)," https://en.wikipedia.org/wiki/Select_committee_(United_Kingdom).

developed during the mid-1960s by Richard Crossman as leader of the House of Commons.[22]

The problem, of course, is that, without a written constitution that mandates federalism between the states and federal government, separation of powers at the national level, and *Marbury*-style judicial review protecting human rights, there are limited grounds for resistance to abusive powers by the executive within the constitutional system, and the very flexibility of the unwritten constitution may lead to the reactionary politics of a Margaret Thatcher and Brexit, or the mistake of Blair ratifying Bush's incursion into Iraq, or Cameron's disastrous misreading of the sentiments of many British people, manipulated by demagogues, about Brexit. There is no analog within the British system for the powers of the U.S. Supreme Court in *Youngstown Sheet & Tube Co. v. Sawyer [The Steel Seizure Case]*[23] to stop a president (Truman) from abusing his war powers by ordering the seizure of steel mills better to fight the Korean War, or the similar abuse of a later president (Nixon) to stop publication of the Pentagon Papers that exposed the abuse of presidential war powers in the conduct of the Vietnam War stretching back over many administrations, Democratic and Republican,[24] or, for that matter, powers within Congress to limit executive abuses, or powers of the states within the federal system to question and sometimes resist federal abuses. Devolution in the U.K. of political powers to Scotland, Wales, and Northern Ireland remains subject to parliamentary limits and repeal, and executive erosion of parliamentary powers is a growing concern in the U.K., eroding, as it does, the separation of powers between executive and legislative powers. For these reasons, Linda Colley has recently argued that Britain may now need a written constitution.[25]

Yet, on close examination, liberal political theory (both British, John Stuart Mill, and American, John Rawls) clarifies developments in both jurisdictions, whether in Britain's common law and parliamentary supremacy or America's judicial review. Americans have learned, at least since World War II, that judicial review can and now is justified by protecting human rights in a way in which other American institutions have not. And British liberals, increasingly aware that the separation of powers has broken down because of the executive's control of parliament, are reviving the common law that has always been a central feature of British constitutionalism's central normative value, the rule of law. The recent U.K. Supreme Court decision in *R (Miller) v. The Prime*

22 On the importance of the development of such institutions from the perspective of comparative constitutionalism, see Mark Tushnet, *The New Fourth Branch: Institutions for Protecting Constitutional Democracy* (Cambridge: Cambridge University Press, 2021).

23 343 U.S. 579 (1952).

24 See *New York Times Co. v. United States [The Pentagon Papers Case]*. 403 U.S. 713 (1971).

25 See Linda Colley, "The Radical Constitutional Change Britain Needs," *New York Times*, September 13, 2022, at A22.

Minister and Cherry v. Advocate General for Scotland,[26] striking down a prime minister's proroguing of parliament to avoid parliamentary debate about Brexit, shows how and why such common law judicial power is needed to preserve the sovereignty of parliament over executive abuses.[27] Both the authority of parliament and the judiciary are now increasingly assessed from this overall normative perspective reflected in John Laws' "balance." Parliament has served the British well, certainly in comparison with U.S. institutions, as an institution with a remarkable record of realizing human rights in changed and changing circumstances. It is now more open to comparative constitutionalism than it has ever been, and the common law has played an increasingly important role in this process. If the test is the effective protection of human rights David Dyzenhaus seems to me surely correct: "Nor is it at all obvious that legal orders in which there is parliamentary supremacy do a worse constitutional job in maintaining these statuses [the protection of human rights]."[28] America, like Britain, today has a better understanding of the crucial role of an independent judiciary in any constitutionalism grounded in respect for human rights. Perhaps, that is what strikes me as something both these constitutionalisms share, and may explain, despite all their differences, why they remain so influential as other peoples strive in their circumstances to forge democratic constitutionalisms grounded in respect for human rights.

5.2 Social Democracy in the U.K. and the U.S.

I have already observed that the U.K.'s unwritten constitution, precisely because it accords parliament the constitutional powers it does, has allowed the progressive redistributive politics of social democracy much more scope than the comparable U.S. politics once the Labour Party won free and fair elections, as it did in 1945 and has done subsequently. The consequence has been that the policies of Labour governments have achieved two remarkable social democratic objectives not yet achieved in the U.S.: first, the National Health Service (NHS), and second, opening up education not only to the middle but to the lower classes. If class has been the central caste problem in the U.K. and race in the U.S., Britain's constitutionalism has gone much further than the U.S. in responsibly deconstructing class than the U.S. has in deconstructing race.

The creation of the NHS in the U.K. can be traced to William Beveridge's "celebrated report on social insurance in December 1942":[29]

26 [2019] UKSC 41.

27 For a fuller defense, see Paul Craig, "The Supreme Court, Prorogation and Constitutional Principle," *Forthcoming in Public Law*, Oxford Legal Studies Research Paper No 57/2019.

28 David Dyzenhaus, *The Long Arc of Legality: Hobbes, Kelsen, Hart* (Cambridge: Cambridge University Press, 2022), p. 278.

29 Hennessy, *Never Again*.

> Stripped to its core the Beveridge Report was targeted on "Five Giants on the Road to Recovery" which he identified in bold, capital letters—"WANT, DISEASE, IGNORANCE, SQUALOR and IDLENESS." To defeat them, Beveridge designed a comprehensive welfare system ... based on three "assumptions"—a free national health service, child allowances, full employment ... . That all this struck such a vibrant chord in the nation at war was, as Beveridge's biographer noted, a matter of luck and partly of careful calculation. The report was published a few days after the battle of Alamein, which to many people seemed like a turning-point in the war; and Beveridge was fortunate in that his mingled tone of optimism, patriotism, high principle and pragmatism exactly fitted the prevailing popular mood. It suited also the feeling of national solidarity that seems to have been engendered in all sections of the community by the Second World War.
>
> Nevertheless the groundwork for the reception of the report had been carefully and consciously prepared for many months before. Beveridge himself throughout 1942 had referred in numerous articles and broadcasts to the need for "equality of sacrifice" and the possibility of abolishing poverty after the war. And without precisely "leaking" advance information, he had contrived to create the expectation that his Report would be far-reaching in scope and radical in tone.[30]

The NHS, enacted in 1948 after in 1945 the Labour Party won one of the most overwhelming electoral victories in British history, offered the first health system in any Western society covering free medical care for the entire nation, paid for by the state out of tax monies. It is

> the nearest Britain had ever come to institutionalizing altruism. It is ... "the only service organized around an ethical imperative." Aneurin Bevan knew its core philosophy transcended mere notions of socialist planning and progressive administration. "Society," he wrote when piecing together his new scheme, "becomes more wholesome, more serene, and spiritually healthier, if it knows that its citizens have at the back of their consciousness the knowledge that not only themselves, but all their fellows, have access, when Ill, to the best that medical skill can prove."[31]

Other parts of the Labor Party's legislation during this period (e.g., state ownership of many industries) were not to survive, but the NHS has commanded cross-party support, with some changes (in 1980 Thatcher allowed private health options), marking institutionalizing an ethical imperative of social democracy,

30 Ibid., pp. 73–74.
31 Ibid., p. 132.

a right of all as equals to medical care irrespective of other differences of class and the like.[32]

Just as remarkable, parliament has opened up the educational system. Secondary school education for all is supported by the state. And red brick universities, alternatives to Oxford and Cambridge opened up, and, for long periods, British students paid no fees to any of them, nor to secondary schools, though fees have been now been introduced, but they are capped at lower levels than such fees in the U.S.[33] In the U.S., both in public and private universities, substantial fees are requirements of attendance, so a recent commentator in *The Economist* writes of the "great reversal," "Is Britain becoming more meritocratic than America?"[34] I share Michael Young's democratic skepticism about meritocracy,[35] but the U.K.'s breaking down of its long-standing educational caste system[36] seems quite just as a reasonable deconstruction of class as caste in the U.K. I hope the U.S. may some day be similarly inspired to deconstruct educational barriers that have long supported race as caste in the U.S., and still do so.

The British unwritten constitution has thus allowed and facilitated social democratic politics, many enjoying cross-party support, that remain unthinkable in the current state of U.S. politics in which the very word, "socialism," is one among the terms that strike irrational fear in the hearts of many voters who would gain from more social democratic policies aimed at the growing economic and social inequalities of American life.[37]

Britain's progress on deconstructing the caste of class can be contrasted with continuing difficulties in the U.S. of even recognizing the degree to which race as caste has long dominated and continues to dominate American politics. Though the U.S. judiciary has played a pivotal role in opening the matter to political discussion, American politics, as in the victory of Trump and his period in office, illustrates how far the U.S. has yet to go in addressing responsibly its cultural racism.

32 For the current state of the British healthcare system, see Jonathan Montgomery, *Health Care Law*, 2nd ed. (Oxford: Oxford University Press, 2013).

33 See "Tuition Fees in the United Kingdom," https://wikipedia.org/wiki/Tuition_fees_in_the_United)Kingdom

34 See "Bagehot: The Great Reversal," *The Economist*, August 7–13, 2021, p. 47.

35 See Michael Young, *The Rise of Meritocracy* (New Brunswick, NJ: Transaction, 2008).

36 For a critique of the role the educational system played in legitimating class as caste in the U.K. (leading to Britons in different parts of the nation not understanding the English both spoke), see R. H. Tawney, *Equality*, 4th ed. (n.p.: Capricorn, 1961).

37 For an illuminating historical background of this American view, focusing on fears of communist-style controls, see Gary Dorrien, *American Democratic Socialism: History, Politics, and Theory* (New Haven, CT: Yale University Press, 2022).

5.3 Beyond Locke on "Property"

The discussion of social democracy in the U.K. and the U.S. raises the question of how the liberalism of both nations, including the increasing importance of social democratic liberalism in both nations, can be squared with Locke's liberalism in which the protection of "Property" is the test of liberal legitimacy. There is, first, a lexical point to make: namely, "Property," for Locke, is a term for what belongs to one as an individual, in particular, our rights (life, liberty, and property),[38] including the right to conscience that was, in fact, central to his liberalism based on the argument for toleration, as we earlier saw, a liberalism Jefferson shared when he redefined this aim as life, liberty, and the pursuit of happiness, and in fact made the argument for toleration central to the American understanding of inalienable human rights that Madison enshrined in the religion clauses of the First Amendment to the U.S. Bill of the Rights. The pro-slavery constitutionalism of Calhoun, which the Supreme Court constitutionalized in *Dred Scott v. Sanford*,[39] endorsed without moral compunction the idea of property rights in slaves, and it is this very lack of moral compunction that outraged both radical and moderate abolitionists. As Lincoln, a moderate abolitionist, put the point, "If slavery is not wrong, nothing can be wrong."[40] It was axiomatic for Lincoln, as it was for Jefferson and Madison, that Lockean liberalism condemned slavery because it abridged basic human rights without justification (Locke's own views on slavery were, surprisingly, based on a questionable theory of forfeiture, more equivocal[41]). The civil war was, at bottom, over this question. It is a tribute to the British Constitution, in contrast to the U.S. Constitution, that these issues were resolved democratically, whereas the U.S. could only address them in a self-destructive civil war, whose legacy has haunted the U.S. ever since.

Liberalism, as a theory and a practice, is not historically static. It is certainly historically true that in the U.K. voting was premised on the ownership of property, land, in particular, but the ownership of land was the source of the power and rights of the Whig aristocrats and their sense of their political independence of the monarchy, the basis of their resistance and political actions "to secure the people's freedom"[42] through passage of the Reform Act of 1832, which later

38 On the expansive understanding of "Property" for Locke, Locke is himself quite clear: "He … is willing to join in Society with others for the mutual preservation of their Lives, Liberties, and Estates, which I call by the general name, *Property*;" quoted in Albert Boni et al., *The Compact Edition of the Oxford English Dictionary* (Oxford: Oxford University Press, 1971), vol. II, P-Z, p. 1471, at Locke, Gov't ii, ix.

39 *Dred Scott v. Sanford* 19 How. (60 U.S.) 393 (1857).

40 Quoted in Richards, *Conscience and the Constitution*, p. 62.

41 See ibid., pp. 73–74. See also Kevin C. O'Leary, *Madison's Sorrow: Today's War on the Founders and America's Liberal Ideal* (New York: Pegasus, 2020), pp. 14–17.

42 Colley, *Britons*, p. 345.

reform acts were to expand. Later experience has deepened understanding of the implications of liberalism as societies, like the U.K. and the U.S., faced developments, including the Industrial Revolution, that did not confront Britain at the time of its Glorious Revolution in 1688 or the U.S. in the period of the American Revolution of 1776–1801 or the U.S. Constitution of 1787. Concern with these new economic and social development expressed itself in a development within British liberalism to take seriously the injustices inflicted on the working classes as a caste. John Stuart Mill was certainly one such social liberal. But, other British liberal philosophers, notably T. H. Green, raised profound philosophical objections to Mill's utilitarianism rooted in Kantian deontological liberalism, and articulated a form of social liberalism concerned with poverty and economic inequality and the class system in Britain, which in turn shaped the social liberalism of Leonard Hobhouse and T. H. Marshall and John Hobson's critique of British imperialism,[43] all of which shaped the policies of the Liberal Party in the U.K. in the late nineteenth and early twentieth centuries and, with the collapse of the Liberal Party, the Labour Party.[44] And contemporary investigations of the philosophical basis for property law persuasively argue that, to the extent a highly conventional institution like property is or can be just, it must meet and satisfy human needs.[45]

The novels of Dickens, George Eliot, and many others reflect a growing concern with the role the evil of class as caste played out in British life during the Industrial Revolution and later, and expressed itself in a development within British liberalism to take seriously the injustices inflicted on the lower classes as a caste. John Dewey in the U.S., inspired by the writings of T. H. Green and other British social liberals, urged a similar rethinking of Lockean liberalism,[46]

43 See T. H. Green, *Lectures on the Principles of Ethics*, edited by Paul Harris and John Morrow (Cambridge: Cambridge University Press, 1986), and *Prolegomena to Ethics* (Oxford: Oxford at the Clarendon Press, 1883, 2012). Green argues against utilitarianism (Bentham, Mill) that the best justification for social liberalism is some form of Kantian deontology, anticipating Rawls and Dworkin. See also F. H. Bradley, *Ethical Studies* (Oxford: Clarendon Press, 1876, 1988), probably not liberal but, like Green, very able critic of utilitarianism. See also Leonard Hobhouse, *Liberalism and Other Writings*, edited by James Meadowcroft (Cambridge: Cambridge University Press, 2006); T. H. Marshall and Tom Bottomore, *Citizenship and Social Class* (London: Pluto, 1992); John Atkinson Hobson, *Imperialism* (Cambridge: Cambridge University Press, 1902, 2010).

44 See George Dangerfield, *The Strange Death of Liberal England* (Stanford, CA: Stanford University Press, 1935, 1997).

45 For a probing argument on this point, see J. W. Harris, *Property and Justice* (Oxford: Oxford University Press, 1996).

46 For an excellent and illuminating discussion, see Alan Ryan, *John Dewey and the High Tide of American Liberalism* (New York: W. W. Norton, 1995), in particular pp. 85–100, 309–10, 356. For an important statement of Dewey's social liberalism, see John Dewey, "Individualism, Old and New," in *The Later Works of John Dewey*, edited by Jo Ann Boydston (Carbondale: Southern Illinois University Press, 2008), vol. 5, pp. 41–123.

and the formation of a party in the U.S. like the Labour Party in the U.K., regarding the New Deal as insufficiently social democratic[47] (Dewey voted for the socialist, Norman Thomas). It is an important question why political skepticism of unregulated capitalism should have taken deeper political roots in the U.K. than the U.S. much to America's cost. An important distinction is that in Britain the Labour Party was organized by and around unions and parliamentary supremacy allowed the Labour Party, when it took power in 1945–51, to impose democratic socialism. There is no comparable development in the U.S. Indeed, a leading American democratic socialist, Eugene Debs, is imprisoned during World War I for resisting the war.[48] Nonetheless, progressive liberal constitutionalists in the U.S. have persuasively argued that whatever progress the nation made under Franklin Roosevelt's New Deal is normatively incomplete, on social liberal grounds, until we fill out our conception of human rights with the Second Bill of Rights (including minimal welfare rights) Roosevelt called for in his State of the Union Address of 1944.[49]

More recently, however, both in the U.S. and Britain, the whole conception of political liberalism has been reframed by John Rawls' *A Theory of Justice* and Ronald Dworkin's use of Rawls in insisting that judicial review, whether British or American, crucially makes reference to human rights and is required to some extent in any democracy that takes rights seriously, as both the U.K. and Britain do. What is quite original about Rawls is not only his liberal theory of human rights (governed by his first principle of justice), but his argument for the difference principle (a form of which is implicit in T. H. Green and Leonard Hobhouse and John Dewey) that requires that the distribution of wealth and status must make worst off classes better off. For this reason, Daniel Chandler has recently persuasively argued that Rawls' theory of justice gives the best normative understanding of British progressive liberalism, and calls for its self-conscious use in better implementing liberal values in contemporary Britain.[50] Yet, Rawls himself does not regard the difference principle as justiciable by courts, suggesting why it is that in Britain parliament formed a cross-party political consensus expanding the state's role in the economic and social arenas, at least, from the period of the Labour Party's government in 1945 to 1951 and succeeding Labor and Conservative or coalition governments until Margaret Thatcher, and perhaps thereafter. But, does not the experience of judicial review

47 See Ryan, *John Dewey and the High Tide of American Liberalism*, pp. 292–95.

48 See Gary Dorrien, *American Democratic Socialism: History, Politics, Religion, and Theory* (New Haven, CT: Yale University Press, 2021).

49 See, e.g., Cass R. Sunstein, *The Second Bill of Rights: FDR's Unfinished Revolution and Why We Need It More Than Ever* (New York: Basic Books, 2004).

50 See Daniel Chandler, *Free and Equal: What Would a Fair Society Look Like?* (London: Allen Lane, 2023.

over such issues in South Africa, India, and elsewhere suggest a rethinking of this matter from which both the U.K. and U.S. might learn?[51]

The development of social liberalism in Britain has another aspect, an underground movement that was slowly bringing to the surface arguments for gay rights. I bring it up at this point because T. H. Green at Balliol College, Oxford University was a close friend of John Addington Symonds, and indeed marries the sister of Symonds. Symonds was a gay man and an important figure in the development of arguments for gay rights,[52] whose life and work anticipate the Bloomsbury Group.[53] Symonds, most of whose work is on the art and politics of the Italian Renaissance, writes two path-breaking studies in gay rights.[54] Under the thumb of his demanding father, Symonds marries unhappily with daughters ("the great mistake—perhaps the great crime of my life, was my marriage"[55]), and eventually settles down in Venice with a gondolier, Angelo Fusato, who is married with children, but who apparently loved and cared for Symonds, just as E. M. Forster's married policeman lover and his wife cared for Forster at his death.[56]

The development of social liberalism feeds into the politics of the Labour Party, which was decisively to take power in 1945 to 1951, and transform Britain into a social democratic welfare state. There was during this period a conflict within the left over whether the Soviet Union was a better alternative for Britain than its parliamentary politics. Beatrice and Sidney Webb, important figures in the development of British socialism,[57] increasingly looked for inspiration to the Soviet Union.[58] Certainly, the Labour Party's advocacy of state ownership of the means of production reflected classic Marxist arguments, which leading

51 On this point, see Sandra Fredman, *Human Rights Transformed: Positive Rights and Positive Duties* (Oxford: Oxford University Press, 2008).

52 See Phyllis Grosskurth, *John Addington Symonds: A Biography* (London: Longmans, 1964); Amber K. Regis, *The Memoirs of John Addington Symonds: A Critical Edition* (London: Palgrave Macmillan, 2016); Naomi Wolfe, *Outrages: Sex, Censorship, and the Criminalization of Love* (London: Chelsea Green, 2020). For a recent perceptive but highly fictionalized novel on Symonds and his relationship to Havelock Ellis, who coauthored *Sexual Inversion* (published in 1897 two years after Symonds' death), see Tom Crewe, *The New Life: A Novel* (New York: Scribner, 2023). The novel confabulates an obscenity trial of a novel, much to the credit of Symonds and discredit of Ellis.

53 See David A. J. Richards, *The Rise of Gay Rights and the Fall of the British Empire: Liberal Resistance and the Bloomsbury Group* (Cambridge: Cambridge University Press, 2013).

54 See John Addington Symonds, *A Problem in Greek Ethics* (n.p.: Pen House Editions, 1901), and *A Problem in Modern Ethics* (Frankfurt am Main: Outlook Verlag, 2020).

55 Amber K. Regis, *The Memoirs of John Addington Symonds: A Critical Edition* (London: Palgrave Macmillan, 2016), p. 363.

56 See Richards, *The Rise of Gay Rights and the Fall of the British Empire*, p. 138.

57 See, e.g., Sidney Webb and Beatrice Webb, *Industrial Democracy: New Edition in Two Volumes Bound in One* (n.p.: Alpha Editions, 2020).

58 See Beatrice and Sidney Webb, *Soviet Communism: A New Civilization?*(New York: C. Scribners' Sons, 1936).

intellectuals of the left were later, as we shall see, to repudiate in favor of other redistributive measures.

Why the rethinking of socialism? Any idealized picture of the U.S.S.R., as a model for Britain, was decisively challenged by disclosures of Stalin's totalitarianism, and had been anticipated by the remarkable challenge to the British left's love affair with the Soviet Union by the novelist and essayist George Orwell, who had once shared such views but, having fought in the Spanish Civil War in favor of a putatively liberal government allied with Communists (supported by the Soviet Union) against the fascist Franco (supported by fascist Germany and Italy), came to see communism as little better than fascism,[59] both exhibiting what Hannah Arendt was later to call a totalitarianism that warred on democracy and human rights,[60] the heart of liberalism for Orwell. Perhaps, the most remarkable essay by Orwell on the nature and future of British democratic socialism was an essay published early in World War II (1941), "The Lion and the Unicorn: Socialism and the English Genius,"[61] which argues that socialism is an organic development within British culture and prophetically anticipates that, in the wake of World War II, it will come to power, which it did. There is little or no revolutionary Marxist ideology in Orwell's argument, but rather a brilliant anticipation that British democracy would through its parliamentary politics and free and fair elections support, in the wake of World War II, the redistributive socialism that would be required to address deconstructing the injustice of the British caste system of class, including the NHS and opening up the educational system to the middle and working classes. Ownership of the means of production had been a classic Marxist policy, and Britain would adopt a form of it, but later experience led socialist intellectuals to argue and the Labour Party to accept that the better way to the redistributive justice and equal respect socialism called for was not ownership of the means of production, but other redistributive measures, some of which were enacted when Labour returned to power.[62] John Maynard Keynes himself evidently supported neither state ownership of the means of production nor capitalism, defending rather a liberal socialism "under an economic system designed to generate sustained full employment, substantial economic growth, and a more egalitarian society."[63]

In 1930 John Dewey in the U.S. drew upon the views of the British social liberals in his important essay, "Individualism, Old and New," arguing that

59 For this development in Orwell's life and writing, see Bernard Crick, *George Orwell: A Life* (London: Sutherland House, 1980); D. J. Taylor, *Orwell: The Life* (New York: Henry Hold, 2003).

60 Hannah Arendt, *The Origins of Totalitarianism* (Orlando, FL: A Harvest Book, 1976).

61 See George Orwell, "The Lion and the Unicorn: Socialism and the English Genius," in *Essays*, introduction by John Carey (New York: Everyman's Library, 1996), pp. 291–348.

62 See, e.g., Anthony Crosland, *The Future of Socialism* (London: Constable, 1956, 2006); J. E. Meade, *Efficiency, Equality and the Ownership of Property* (New York: Routledge, 2020).

63 Crotty, *Keynes against Capitalism: His Economic Case for Liberal Socialism*, p. 374.

the old Lockean liberalism of possessive individualism reflecting an agrarian economy must give way, in light of the Industrial Revolution, to a new individualism that takes seriously

> our inability to grasp the psychological and moral consequences of the precarious condition in which vast multitudes live. Insecurity cuts deeper and extends more widely than bare unemployment. Fear of Loss of work, dread of the oncoming old age, create anxiety and eat into self-respect that impairs personal dignity.[64]

I also observed in the U.S. the development in 1971 of the powerful liberal political of John Rawls that, in addition to preserving the basis human rights of conscience, association, and equal opportunity, argues for a difference principle quite normatively similar to the arguments of social liberalism of T. H. Green, Leonard Hobhouse, T. H. Marshall in the U.K., and John Dewey in the U.S., requiring that issues of economic and social justice must be assessed in terms of whether worst off classes are made better off than they would be under more egalitarian arrangements.

On reflection, contemporary liberalism takes as its focal normative conception not property and not utilitarian pleasure or pain either, but the Kantian value of dignity, a value Dewey appeals to when he condemns injustices that "eat into self-respect that impairs personal dignity," a value central to the liberalisms of Rawls, Dworkin, and Waldron and to the judicial opinions in diverse jurisdictions (South Africa and India) that have recognized gay rights as constitutional rights in two cultures in which a transformative constitutionalism self-consciously seeks to undo racial apartheid (South Africa) and a racialized caste system (India) . The Constitutional Court of South Africa has produced three key decisions on LGBT matters. First, in *National Coalition for Gay and Lesbian Equality v. Minister of Justice*, the court held that common law and statutory provisions criminalizing sodomy between two men and sexual acts between men when more than two people were present were incompatible with the two express rights, as well as privacy.[65] Secondly, in *National Coalition for Gay and Lesbian Equality v. Minister of Home Affairs*, section 25(5) of the Aliens Control Act 96 of 1991, which excluded same-sex life partners from benefits extended to (opposite-sex) spouses, was found to discriminate due to sexual orientation and marital status and to breach sections 9 and 10.[66] Thirdly, in *Minister of Home Affairs v. Fourie*, the court held that the exclusively opposite-sex definition of marriage at common law and in section 30(1) of the Marriage Act 1961 was under-inclusive and unfairly discriminatory, and again violated

64 See Dewey, "Individualism, Old and New," p. 68.
65 CCT 11/98, 1999 (1) SA 6.
66 CCT 10/99, 2000 (2) SA 1, paras [57], [97].

sections 9 and 10.[67] And the Indian Supreme Court inferred a free-standing right of constitutional privacy in its 2017 decision in *Justice KS Puttaswamy v. Union of India*,[68] and its 2018 opinion in *Navtej Singh Johar & Ors. V. Union of India*,[69] the latter of which decriminalized gay sex on the basis of the value of equal dignity. Undoing caste has been reasonably extended, as a matter of principle, to homosexuality as caste, in particular, Blackstone's view of unspeakability that the Indian Supreme Court rightly criticizes as a moralistic imposition by Britain on the complex pluralism of Indian culture. Even John Stuart Mill, who retained his allegiance to his father's utilitarianism throughout his life, implicitly uses the Kantian value of dignity in his most important contribution to political liberalism, *On Liberty*.[70] Dignity is the value ascribed to what Kant called "the fact of reason,"[71] namely, our intellectual and emotional capacity nurtured by our interpersonal relationships to think and act reflectively about our ends, prudential and ethical, and accord a like respect to this competence in other persons. Political liberalism in its nature gives priority to conscience, speech, association, and opportunity as basic rights the state must respect, but it gives weight as well to the distribution of wealth and status, making the worst off better off than would be the case under equality (Rawls' difference principle), including in the measure of "better off" not only wealth, but self-respect, which may be undermined by inequalities that humiliate the less well off. It may be this latter impulse that is the moral basis in Britain of the NHS, according to all equally a good like access to health services that respects life itself. The failure of American politics to guarantee this good in some form is a glaring defect in its political liberalism.

5.4 Culture vs. Institutions

Because British constitutionalism depends so heavily on parliament, there is, in contrast to the U.S., much less of a gap between culture and constitutional law in the U.K., and a resulting politics of compromise that supports parliamentary recognition of new constitutional rights. We can see this in the emergence of gay rights in the U.K., as the culture allowed, in contrast to the U.S. during the

67 Cases CCT 60/04 and 10/05, 2006 (1) SA 524, paras [78], [79], [82], [114], [117], [118], [120] (Sachs J); see also [164] (O'Regan J); for analysis, see Pierre de Vos, "A Judicial Revolution: A Court-Led Achievement of Same-Sex Marriage in South Africa," *Utrecht Law Review* 4 (2008): 162–74. The connection with *National Coalition for Gay and Lesbian Equality v. Minister for Home Affairs* was highlighted in paras [51]–[55].

68 Writ Petition (Civil) No 494 of 2012, 24 August 2017.

69 Writ Petition (Civil) No. 572 of 2016, 6 September 2018

70 See John Stuart Mill, "On Liberty," in *On Liberty, Utilitarianism, and Other Essays* (Oxford: Oxford University Press, 2015), pp. 5–112, in particular ch. 3, pp. 55–72.

71 Immanuel Kant, "Critique of Practical Reason," in Mary J. Gregor (ed.), *Practical Philosophy* (Cambridge: Cambridge University Press, 1999), pp. 133–272 at 164.

same period, at least discreet resisting voices to be heard, eventually achieving more public acceptance and support, culminating in the 1967 decriminalization.[72] Only with Northern Ireland has British politics been riven by the ghosts of Protestant prejudices against Catholics.

The British politics of compromise also leads to a cross-party consensus, for example, on social democracy until Thatcher, and even then the NHS remains intact and the reversal of state ownership of many industries as well the greater regulation of labor unions are not reversed by later Labour governments. Some of Labour's former policies (state ownership) are themselves criticized, as we have seen, by important Labour politicians in favor of other policies of economic and social redistribution.[73] And Thatcher's homophobic section 28 was reversed by later Labour governments, reflecting Craig's view of the self-correcting features of the U.K. parliamentary democracy. Thatcher's remarkable political success (the longest serving prime minister in the modern period) was ended by her inflexible demand, infatuated by her self-proclaiming identity as "the iron lady," for a poll tax that was regressive, alienating the British people and her own party, who ended her rule. However, it is hard to believe that Thatcher's and Reagan's détente with Gorbachev, leading to the end of the Soviet Union, would have been initiated by more liberal political leaders, just as Nixon's and Kissinger's opening to China was acceptable precisely because Nixon had been such a conservative cold warrior and Kissinger such an amoral realist in international politics (consider the bombing of Cambodia and the murder of Pinochet in Chile). Illiberal politicians in constitutional democracies have their uses when they serve liberal ends, as they have in both the U.K. and the U.S. And whether liberal or illiberal in their politics, Britain has elected three woman prime ministers, the U.S. none. That is a tribute to British liberalism, in which women like Mary Wollstonecraft and Virginia Woolf have played such an important role in a feminism rooted in the understanding that patriarchy undermines liberal democracy.

At least since World War II, the American judiciary has taken wholly justified and long overdue liberal positions on race, gender, and sexual orientation that are often critical of the cultural racism, sexism, and homophobia that has existed in the U.S.—supported for long periods both by the judiciary and political parties—for far too long. The consequence is a politics more divided by absolutist positions, supported by religious minorities protected by the religion clauses of the First Amendment and by other reactionary forces that were empowered, as we earlier saw, by Republican politicians attempting to limit the achievements of the progressive resistance movements that transformed American culture and law. And sometimes, these reactionary movements have

72 For a fuller discussion, see Richards, *The Rise of Gay Rights and the Fall of the British Empire*.
73 See Crosland, *The Future of Socialism*.

sponsored changes in constitutional interpretation (Second Amendment protection of gun rights that are constitutionally dubious[74] and, more recently, the overruling of *Roe v. Wade*), which I shall shortly discuss at greater length (Chapter 7). Recent judicial appointments by former President Donald Trump, supported by the reactionary forces his election supported and mobilized, have led to yet further erosion of constitutional rights like abortion, more likely precisely because the *Marbury* powers of the judiciary now enjoy support on the ground that the powers have served liberal ends and those powers, because of the politics of judicial appointments under Trump, draw on such support though, paradoxically, they may now serve illiberal ends with which a majority of Americans may disagree. The judiciary of the U.K., lacking such *Marbury* powers, would face reversal by parliamentary democracy, better serving liberal ends and principles. Indeed, the whole issue of judicial appointments in the U.K., in contrast to the U.S., has a less politicized character,[75] which serves the ends of judicial impartiality and independence in its liberalism.

The increasingly polarized character of democratic politics in the U.S. may be at least part of the price Americans pay for the liberalism of judicial review since World War II, as the court, in contrast to the British parliament, does not reflect but sometimes rejects the racist culture that has, in violation of constitutional guarantees of basic rights and equal protection, dominated American politics and the main political parties for far too long. It is a price well worth paying, but there is an alternative exemplified by the British institutions that the Americans rejected in 1776 and 1787. For, British constitutionalism rests on much less of a gap between culture and constitutional law, and yet has been respectful of human rights, arguably more respectful than the U.S.

5.5 The English Civil War and the American Civil War

It is a striking fact about the history of democratic constitutionalism in the U.K. and the U.S. that the idea of a written constitution first arose in Britain during the period of the successful English Civil War of 1642–51 and its aftermath Cromwell's Puritan Commonwealth.[76] The idea of a written constitution, in origin English, was abandoned in the U.K. in the Glorious Revolution of 1688 for an unwritten constitution. It is the American colonists during the period from 1688 to their revolution in 1776 who keep the idea of a written constitution alive and use it in the design of their state constitutions as well as the

74 See *District of Columbia v. Heller*, 554 U.S. 570 (2008) (dissents of Justice Stevens and Justice Breyer); *McDonald v. City of Chicago*, 561 U.S. 742 (2010) (dissent of Justice Stevens).

75 See "Judicial Appointments Commission," https://en.wikipedia.org/wiki/Judicial_Appointments_Commission

76 See Michael Walzer, *The Revolution of the Saints* (Cambridge, MA: Harvard University Press, 1965); A. S. P. Woodhouse (ed.), *Puritanism and Liberty* (London: Dent, 1938).

federal constitution of 1787.[77] Yet, it is the temporizing over slavery, a clear Lockean abridgment of basic human rights, in the Constitution of 1787 that sets the stage for the turn away from Lockean political liberalism in the populist racism of Andrew Jackson and the pro-slavery constitutionalism of John Calhoun, constitutionalized in *Dred Scott v. Sanford*, culminating in a fratricidal civil war leading to the abolition of slavery in the 13th Amendment (1865), which in turn worsened American cultural racism, as we earlier saw.

There are important questions about this contrast between the roles of the English Civil War and the American Civil War in their respective constitutionalisms. At least one not implausible view of the English Civil War in British historical memory is worry that a written constitution would be too associated with a Puritan ideology not shared by many people (not least, perhaps, its mindless hatred of the theater, an absurd view in a nation that gave the world, among others, Shakespeare[78]), and might lead to yet another violent civil war. In contrast, the Glorious Revolution of 1688, justified on Lockean grounds, leads to an unwritten constitution, including constitutional monarchy, which preserves yet modifies long-standing institutions, including the enhanced powers of parliament with the flexibility to both reflect and change constitutional arrangements over time. There is perhaps here an experienced based skepticism about violent revolutions as a basis for constitutional democracy, one Burke voices in his skepticism about the likely trajectory of the quite violent French Revolution into, as it turned out, Robespierre's judicial murders of his political enemies, and later, Napoleonic imperialist despotism that discredits democracy throughout Europe (except the U.K.). Neither the violence of the French Revolution and of the Russian Revolution later led to constitutionalisms that either respected human rights or supported democracy. Quite to the contrary.

The U.S. written constitution arises out of a violent revolution against the British Constitution on the ground that the U.K. unwritten constitution had violated its own principles in taxing colonists not represented in parliament, and claimed it would give the world a superior written constitution. It did not. Indeed, defects in the written constitution on the issue of slavery set the stage for a violent and destructive fratricidal civil war that, if anything, exacerbated American cultural racism as a legacy for future generations cursed by its pervasiveness in American culture, which only the judiciary responsibly addressed after World War II and even that, after Trump, is under threat. Perhaps, in light of this history, we should be skeptical not about written constitutions as such, but such constitutions that, contrary to its Lockean aspirations, so hard wire a

77 See Bernard Bailyn, *The Ideological Origins of the American Revolution* (Cambridge, MA: Harvard University Press, 1967).

78 On Shakespeare's astonishing contributions to both art and science, see Gilligan and Richards, *Holding a Mirror Up to Nature*.

rights-denying institution like slavery into the written constitution that it cripples the capacity of constitutional government democratically to address and rectify an institution like slavery. Or, perhaps we should be skeptical about the role of American-style judicial role as a model for liberal democratic constitutionalism generally: its problems, as a vehicle for political liberalism in the U.S., may extend to other jurisdictions.[79] Certainly, "'weak' or even no judicial review exist in consolidated traditional democracies: in the United Kingdom, Australia, New Zealand, Japan, Canada, Scandinavia."[80] It is the tragedy of American constitutionalism that, born in Lockean revolution, its institutions should so fatally betray Locke. Violent revolutions, even when based in the Lockean right to rebel, are, as the U.S. shows, not likely to secure an enduring constitution that respects human rights. Martin Luther King, Jr. achieved more justice through non-violence than Malcolm X's celebration of violent revolution did or could.[81] Is Canada, which did not join Americans in revolting against Britain, perhaps an example that the lack of violent revolution leads nonetheless to a quite liberal form of democratic constitutionalism not haunted and compromised, as the U.S. is, by a racism reinforced by its disastrous civil war?[82]

5.6 U.K. Referenda and Brexit

This picture of a closer relationship between culture and constitutional law in the U.K. than the U.S. has recently been disrupted by the increasing use of referenda in the U.K. by all political parties when in power, culminating in Brexit. The politician, the then Prime Minister David Cameron who called the referendum on Brexit, clearly had misjudged British culture that he mistakenly believed would follow his leadership in opposing Brexit. In effect, Cameron had permitted intra-party divisions over the European Union to undermine not only his own judgment about the politics of Brexit but his constitutional judgment about referenda. In fact, I believe and will argue that such referenda should at least be problematic in constitutional democracies like the U.K., as Lawrence G. Sager has argued in the U.S.[83]

Referendums in the U.K. have been occasionally held at the national, regional, or local levels. National referendums can be permitted by an Act of

79 For a recent argument along these lines, see Martin Loughlin, *Against Constitutionalism* (Cambridge, MA: Harvard University Press, 2022).

80 Wojciech Sadurski, *A Pandemic of Poulists* (Cambridge: Cambridge University Press, 2022), p. 140. Sadurski goes on to observe that the adoption of more aggressive judicial review in transitional democracies like Poland and Hungary has been turned to illiberal ends.

81 For Malcolm X on violent vs. non-violent revolution, see Louis Menand, *The Free World: Art and Thought in the Cold War* (New York: Farrar, Straus, and Giroux, 2021), pp. 639–40.

82 I am grateful for this thought to conversations with James Gilligan.

83 See Lawrence G. Sager, "Insular Minorities Unabated: *Warth v. Seldin and City of Eastlake v. Forest City Enterprises*," *Harvard Law Review* 91 (1978): 1373–425.

Parliament but by tradition are extremely rare due to the principle of parliamentary sovereignty "meaning that they cannot be constitutionally binding on either the Government or Parliament, though they usually have persuasive effect … . Until the latter half of the twentieth century the concept of a referendum was widely seen in British politics as 'unconstitutional' and an 'alien device.' As of 2021, only three national referendums have been held across the whole of the United Kingdom,"[84] in 1975 (over membership of the European Union), 2011 (over the proposal to use the alternative vote system that was part of the Conservative–Liberal Coalition Agreement), and 2016 (continued membership in the European Union).

I agree with John Laws that referendums in the U.K. are and should be impermissible, if not unconstitutional.[85] If there is any sense in parliamentary supremacy at all, at least as the British have practiced it over time, it is in the argument that legislative power in a democracy should be based on fair representation in a deliberative process in which all voices are heard and based on reasonable judgments about the circumstances of the matter.[86] It was a point Madison made in No. 55 of *The Federalist*, in favor of representative democracy over Athenian mass assemblies, namely, that it would respect inalienable human rights like freedom of conscience and free speech:

> In all very numerous assemblies, of whatever characters composed, passion never fails to wrest the sceptre from reason. Had every Athenian citizen been a Socrates; every Athenian assembly would still have been a mob.[87]

Freedom of speech is the correlative right that protects the crucial role of expression (linguistic and non-linguistic) in the interpersonal relationships that make us human and in questioning and resisting unjust patriarchal and other demands. The judicial murder of Socrates was not only a crime against conscience, but against free speech, which must extend in a constitutional democracy to the full range of convictions critical not only of politics, but, in contrast to Athens, constitutional democracy itself.[88] As Madison observed, calling for a Senate in which free speech would be respected in No. 63, *The Federalist*:

84 "Referendums in the United Kingdom," https://en.wikipedia.org/wiki/Referendums_in_the-United-Kingdom

85 John Laws, *The Constitutional Balance* (Oxford: Hart, 2021), pp. 34–36.

86 For further reasons to the skeptical role referenda have played in anti-constitutional populist politics, see Samuel Issacharoff, *Democracy Unmoored: Populism and the Corruption of Popular Sovereignty* (New York: Oxford University Press, 2023), pp. 52–53, 60, 89, 134, 181.

87 Alexander Hamilton, James Madison, and John Jay, *The Federalist*, edited by Terence Ball (Cambridge: Cambridge University Press, 2007), p. 270.

88 On this point, see David A. J. Richards, *Toleration and the Constitution* (New York: Oxford University Press, 1986), pp. 165–230.

> What bitter anguish would not the people of Athens have often escaped, if their government had contained so provident a safeguard against the tyranny of their own passions? Popular liberty might then have escaped the indelible reproach of decreeing to the same citizens the hemlock on one day, and statues on the next.[89]

It was John Stuart Mill's signal contribution to the discourse of free speech to connect the kind of muscular conception of free speech he advocated to exposing and questioning explicitly the role patriarchy had, in his view, historically played in the deformation of ethical thinking, as it may well have played in the death of Socrates (the fury of patriarchal men shamed by his invention of a moral philosophy, reflecting an emerging guilt culture based on conscience, that challenged much conventional authority).

Referendums could perhaps be justified if the structure of representative democracy is itself flawed by unfair representation, which is more plausible in the U.S., as we shall shortly see, than it is in Britain. Even if referenda can sometimes be justified as advancing constitutional democracy in some contexts, as Tushnet and Bugaric have recently argued,[90] even they concede "the Brexit referendum failed to satisfy a central element of thin constitutionalism—that the views of a current majority of citizens be reliably determined."[91] It is precisely the separation of representatives from the people they represent that preserves the Burkean justification of representation as imposing duties on the representatives to support justice and the common good, as they see it in their independent judgment, not polls and the like.[92] If John Laws is right that the normative foundation of British constitutionalism is reason, fairness, and the presumption of liberty, referendums unleash populist political forces, manipulated by demagogic politicians (as they did in Brexit), that are not supported by reason, fairness, or the presumption of liberty. They are inconsistent with the idea of deliberative democracy and respect for rights that justify British constitutionalism of the common law and parliamentary supremacy.

5.7 Representation and Parties in the U.K. and the U.S.

The U.K. and the U.S. share a constitutional conception of fair representation; indeed, the ground for the American Revolution was the unfairness of a parliament that taxed the Americans but did not give them representation in the institution that taxed them. Both the U.K. and the U.S. share a first-past-the-post

89 Hamilton et al., *The Federalist*, p. 307.

90 See Mark Tushnet and Bojan Bugaric, *Power to the People: Constitutionalism in the Age of Populism* (Oxford: Oxford University, 2021), pp. 130–38, 232–36, 259–69.

91 Ibid., p. 132.

92 See Laws, *The Constitutional Balance*, pp. 29, 34.

system of elections though it leads to results in British and American elections that are larger for the victorious party than the numbers of people who actually voted for them. This has led to arguments for proportional representation by the Liberal Party in the U.K. and the 2011 referendum that they lost.[93] There is in my view much to be said for proportional representation both as matter of fairness and for the coalition governments to which it often leads, which in the U.S. would lead to much more inter-party cooperation than currently exists in America's highly polarized politics. It might also render the British electoral system more fairly representative of the people, including of minorities.

But, the most important contrast between the U.K. Burkean unwritten constitution and the U.S. Madisonian written constitution is the central role Burke himself played, on the basis of evidence-based arguments based on experience, in defending Britain's competitive party system and independent representation, as central to constitutional democracy.[94] In contrast, "one indicator of the age of the American Constitution is the absence of any formal recognition for political parties."[95] Other twentieth-century written constitutions take a very different view. For example, "Article 21 of the German Constitution, adopted after World War II, places parties front and center in the organization of democratic politics, and it commands that 'parties participate in the formation of the political will of the people' … . In the period of ascendancy of democratic constitutions in the 20th century, political parties enjoyed privileged constitutional status as the galvanizing force of democratic politics."[96]

The contrast to the thinking of the American Founders could not be sharper: "the framers of the U.S. Constitution equated parties with factions and aimed for a democratic politics that would rise above sectional concerns, immediate gratification of wants, and the risk of succumbing to the passions of greed and envy."[97] On this point, the Founders ignored to their cost the democratic experience of Great Britain, to which Burke, the greatest defender in Parliament of the Americans' increasingly revolutionary protests of unfair taxation by Britain, had appealed in defending Britain's competitive political parties because they could be and had been capable of representing both human rights and the public good, as his own Whig Party had in eighteenth-century British politics opposing, not always successfully, the Tory Party (e.g., over America). Indeed, it is a striking feature of Britain's unwritten constitution that it has institutionalized the role of a competitive party system "in the shadow cabinet the United Kingdom, designated at 'Her Majesty's Loyal Opposition.'"[98] The

93 On this point, see Bob Watt, *UK Election Law: A Critical Examination* (London: Routledge, 2016), pp. 190–92.

94 On this point, see Issacharoff, *Democracy Unmoored*, pp. 86–7, 133.

95 Ibid., p. 57.

96 Ibid., p. 47.

97 Ibid.

98 Ibid., p. 201.

American framers themselves soon discovered the need for political parties: "as early as the first contested presidential election in 1796, the founding generation discovered the need to coordinate national candidacies in furtherance of a political program."[99] But, the failure to take political parties seriously in the design of the U.S. Constitution—depending instead on federalism, the separation of powers, and judicial review—myopically failed to take seriously that American-style political parties themselves can and have undermined the values of political liberalism, as both history (executive domination of Congress[100]) and contemporary populism illustrate.[101] Even U.K. constitutionalism is now open to this threat (Brexit), but that, as I have argued, is a ground for criticism not endorsement.

In addition, the U.K.'s system of representation, including dealing with gerrymandering by an impartial commission, seems altogether more just than the American system.[102] Whatever the historical justification for the Senate's representative structure in 1787 (2 senators per state) when people thought of themselves more as New Yorkers or Virginians than as Americans, a representative system that Wilson and Madison questioned at the constitutional convention as violating the basic democratic principle of proportional representation,[103] it makes no sense today and has resulted in an unrepresentative political process that is both unjust and against the public interest, as many now acknowledge, frustrating much needed national policies supported by democratic majorities.[104] And the American system has led in turn to controversies over elections, like the Bush–Gore controversy that, unsurprisingly, do not occur in the U.K. I see little to be said for the American representatives system today, nor for the constitutional system that leaves the conduct of voting largely to the states, nor for the Supreme Court's refusal to take seriously the case for reasonable regulation of and limits on money buying political power[105] in contrast to the U.K.'s

99 Ibid., p. 57.

100 On this point, see Daryl Levinson and Richard Pildes, "Separation of Parties, Not Powers," *Harvard Law Review* 119 (2006): 2311–86.

101 This point has been ably made and defended, appealing not only to constitutional developments in the U.K. and the U.S. but also to comparable developments in many other nations; see Issacharoff, *Democracy Unmoored*.

102 On this point, see Watt, *UK Election Law*, pp. 192–215.

103 On this point, see Kevin C. O'Leary, *Madison's Sorrow: Today's War on the Founders and America's Liberal Ideal* (New York: Pegasus, 2020), pp. 31–33, and James Madison, *Notes of Debates in the Federal Convention of 1787 Reported by James Madison* (Athens: Ohio University Press, 1966), pp. 219–37.

104 "Policymaking at the national level in the United States has been stymied by 'gridlock' resulting from having too many veto gates:" Mark Tushnet and Bojan Bugaric, *Power to the People: Constitutionalism after Populism* (Oxford: Oxford University Press, 2021), p. 24. For a discussion of alternative solutions in the American context, see pp. 148–77, 208–70.

105 See *Buckley v. Valeo*, 424 U.S. 1 (1976), and *Citizens United v. Federal Election Commission*, 558 U.S. 310 (2010). For a critique, see Richards, *Toleration and the Constitution*, pp. 215–19.

reasonable regulation of campaign expenditures.[106] The British treatment of these issues is preferable on the ground of political liberalism.[107]

5.8 The Democratic Objection to Judicial Review in the U.K. and the U.S.

The democratic objection to judicial review in the U.S. takes two forms: the court skeptical view that the better understanding of human rights is not produced by courts, but by more representative democratic institutions, like the British parliament; the rights skeptical view denies, following Jeremy Bentham on utilitarian grounds, that rights exist at all, and therefore the judiciary plays no sound judicial role (since rights don't exist), and all issues should be left to a representative legislature whose majoritarian structure better approximates to the utilitarian principle. Court skeptics like Jeremy Waldron are not rights-skeptics, since he accepts a dignity view of human rights that is counter-utilitarian, requiring that human rights be respected that trump utilitarian aggregates to the contrary. Nonetheless, he argues that British parliamentary democracy shows that democratic institutions are better at recognizing and protecting human rights than the judiciary.[108] My argument might plausibly be taken to support Waldron's view at least when comparing the record of the U.K. and the U.S. in protecting human rights.

Rights-skepticism is the more devastating democratic objection to judicial review because, if true, it would lead a great American lawyer and judge, Learned Hand, to argue that the judiciary had no legitimate power to strike down legislation on the grounds that the law violated human rights because such rights do not exist.[109] There is little to be said, on liberal grounds, for rights-skepticism. The classic response of Herbert Wechsler to this argument was to distinguish the arguments of principle that are required for judicial review but not required to justify legislative policy-making.[110] But, arguments of principle, for Wechsler, have no normative content, and thus, not addressing Hand's rights-skepticism, why should such principles have appeal when they are in service of evil ends? Hitler's rather rigidly consistent pursuit of genocidal anti-Semitism is not redeemed by its consistency, but is more damnable.

John Rawls' *A Theory of Justice*, published in 1971, was so path-breaking to liberal political theory because it showed, on the basis of a reconstruction of

106 See Watt, *UK Election Law*, pp. 123–51.

107 On the British system, see ibid.

108 See Jeremy Waldron, "The Core of the Case against Judicial Review," *Yale Law Journal* 115 (2006): 1346–406.

109 See Learned Hand, *The Bill of Rights* (New York: Atheneum, 1968).

110 See Herbert Wechsler, "Toward Neutral Principles of Constitutional Law," *Harvard Law Review* 73 (1959): 1–35.

Kant's political theory of dignity, that utilitarianism was not the best theory of liberal equality, but that there was a better theory that defended the priority of principles of equal liberty (conscience, speech, intimate life, opportunity) and a difference principle (allowing economic inequalities only if worst off classes were made better off than under equality), both prior to utilitarian aggregation.

It was, on the basis of Rawls' liberal theory, that Ronald Dworkin developed his theory of the interpretation of laws (both public and private law), making sense of the work of great ("Herculean") judges (like Holmes, Brandeis, and Cardozo) who articulated arguments of principle to justify retrospective and prospective principles that fit the case law, and when fit did not work, appealed to normative arguments of human rights that, in their nature as rights that each person enjoys as equals, are extended to all persons by arguments of principle, and are only compromised when there is a heavy burden of justification (e.g., in the American law of free speech, a clear and present danger of a secular harm).[111] Dworkin's interpretive theory was, in its nature, anti-positivistic, since judicial interpretation did not separate law and morals (as positivists believed) but rather appealed to arguments of principle that depended on normative values of dignity and the human rights owed each person.

Dworkin, like Rawls, was a political liberal, and his interpretive theory justified much of the work of the U.S. Supreme Court after World War II in the areas of basic rights (free speech, religious liberty, and intimate life) and the guarantee of equal protection of laws (both suspect classifications, which condemn the prejudiced stereotypes that arise from a long cultural history that rationalizes the abridgment of the human rights of whole classes of person in a viciously unjust circularity on the basis of the consequences of the abridgment, and fundamental rights). Dworkin thus defended the distinctive American view that hate speech laws violate the guarantee of free speech.[112] Dworkin's interpretive theory brilliantly justified the liberalism of the Supreme Court by giving a rights-based interpretation to the arguments of principle that were regarded as a normative requirement for the legitimacy of *Marbury* judicial review in the U.S. Judicial review was justified precisely because it protected the human rights of minorities whom majoritarian politics ignored or even stigmatized. The court's role, at least since World War II, was thus justified precisely because it insured that human rights were respected, the rationale to which Chief Justice Marshall appeals in justifying *Marbury*.

John Hart Ely developed an alternative to Dworkin's appeal to human rights by appealing to a procedural theory of fair representation that argued that

111 See Ronald Dworkin, *Taking Rights Seriously* (Cambridge, MA: Harvard University Press, 1977), and *Law's Empire* (Cambridge, MA: Harvard University Press, 1986).

112 On this point, see David A. J. Richards, "Dignity and Free Speech," in Salman Khurshid, Lokendra Malik, and Veronica Rodriguez-Blanco (eds.), *Dignity in the Legal and Political Philosophy of Ronald Dworkin* (New Delhi: Oxford University Press, 2018), pp. 277–99.

judicial review was justified when the unjust treatment of a minority was based on their deprivation of fair political representation, and the court could remedy such injustice, rendering this process more democratic because more fairly representative. On this ground, Ely defended both *Brown v. Board of Education* (the product of racist infringement of voting rights), and affirmative action (because a majority sought through such plans both to acknowledge and rectify such injustices); and Ely defended the reapportionment decisions because they rendered American politics more fairly representative.[113] The procedural character of Ely's view refused to acknowledge substantive arguments of human rights (e.g., the religion clauses, constitutional privacy, and much of free speech that was non-political): only injustices afflicting groups not fairly represented politically registered as worthy of judicial remedy, which led him to argue that, once women were fairly represented (getting the vote), the judiciary could not legitimately protect them, as they could achieve their ends through democratic politics. Though Ely, as a progressive democrat, argued abortion should not be illegal, he criticized, as we shall see later, *Roe v. Wade*, because decriminalization could be achieved politically.

The democratic objection to judicial review takes a different form in the U.K. because judicial interpretation of the common law is not based on American-style *Marbury* judicial review, but is subject to reversal by parliament if the reversal is explicit. In fact, as have seen throughout this book, the British parliament has itself protected human rights, abolishing slavery in England and the colonies, and, in the twentieth century, abolishing the death penalty and decriminalizing contraception, abortion, and gay sex. And there are some cases, for example, the Police and Criminal Evidence Act, 1984, approved under Thatcher, in which the procedures parliament put in place are superior to those the judiciary would require. So, it is quite wrong to assume that the courts always give a better reading of human rights than parliament. The Police and Criminal Evidence Act is only one example to the contrary, and there is another such notable judicial opinion. In a remarkable and much criticized case, the House of Lords in a 1961 opinion, *Shaw v. Director of Public Prosecution*,[114] held, even though parliament had expressly decriminalized commercial sex in 1959, a common law charge of conspiracy to corrupt public morals was allowed against Shaw, who had published "the Ladies' Home Directory," which advertised the services of commercial sex workers to interested clients. In this case and others,[115] the conservative bent of British judges certainly would provide no aid or comfort to the reform movements now active in British political culture.

113 See John Hart Ely, *Democracy and Distrust* (Cambridge, MA: Harvard University Press, 1968).

114 House of Lords [1962] A.C. 220.

115 See, e.g., *Regina v. Brown*, [1993] UKHL 19 (holding consensual S&M to be a criminal assault). For a critique, see Nicholas Bamforth, "Sado-masochism and Consent," *Criminal Law Review* (1994): 661–64.

However, as other cases like *Wednesbury*,[116] *Anisminic*,[117] *Ridge v. Baldwin*,[118] and many others, illustrate, British courts have revived common law doctrines that more closely scrutinize administrative actions by ministers and other officials for reasonableness in meeting legislative standards. The concern evidently is that the increasing concentration of power in the executive without the parliamentary oversight that was traditional in the U.K. compromises the ideals of the Rule of Law, or what Laws calls reason, fairness, and the presumption of liberty, the normative justification for British institutions, the independence of the judiciary and parliamentary sovereignty.[119] In these and other cases, it is an independent U.K. judiciary that may be protecting a proper understanding of the democratic basis of parliamentary supremacy and its traditional role in protecting human rights.

A form of the democratic objection to judicial review has thus arisen in the U.K. in response to these developments. Dworkin's interpretive theory, really designed for U.S. constitutional interpretation, has played a part in these arguments, including T. R. S. Allan's defense of the judiciary on the grounds of Dworkin's interpretive theory[120] and John Laws' similar justification of judicial review as Kantian and parliament as utilitarian.[121] These distinctions, which make sense in the American context, may not have the same force in the context of a British parliamentary supremacy that has often been more liberal than the judiciary would be, which suggests that what Dworkin means by arguments of principle sometimes more clearly justify parliamentary liberalizing action than judicial opinions hostile to such liberalizing.

This seems quite clear when we consider the British parliament's legislative decriminalization of contraception, abortion, and gay sex long before the U.S. Supreme Court addressed these issues on the ground of a judicially inferred free-standing constitutional right to privacy. There are two striking aspects to a comparison of these legislative vs. judicial developments in the U.K. and the U.S. First, in both cases, it is John Stuart Mill's argument of political theory in *On Liberty* that justifies both developments. And second, in both cases, the argument rest on a principle of political liberalism that Mill states with great force as applicable to any constitutional democracy that respects the right of minorities.

Mill's great argument for both a robust and muscular protection of speech and for decriminalization of acts that cannot be justified on any ground of justice or

116 *Associated Provincial Picture Houses Ltd. v. Wednesbury Corporation* [1948] 1 KB 223.

117 *Anisminic v. Foreign Compensation Commission* [1969] 2 AC 147.

118 [1964] AC 40.

119 For a fuller discussion along these lines, see Sedley, *Lions under the Throne*.

120 See T. R. S. Allan, *Law, Liberty, and Justice: The Legal Foundations of British Constitutionalism* (Oxford: Clarendon Press, 1993); *Constitutional Justice: A Liberal Theory of the Rule of Law* (Oxford: Oxford University Press, 2003); *The Sovereignty of Law: Freedom, Constitution, and Common Law* (Oxford: Oxford University Press, 2013).

121 See Laws, *The Constitutional Balance*.

any harm to others or to self is motivated by his worries about the tyranny of the majority that had, in Britain, become quite real in virtue of its achievements of a genuine representative democracy in which the vote was extended to all irrespective of wealth or gender. But, such democratic majoritarianism gives rise, Mill argues, to a tyranny of the majority based on shared moral opinions that regard their being shared as sufficient for social condemnation and criminalization when they reflect irrational prejudice that has not been exposed to free debate and in fact is both unjust and harms no one. The argument of *On Liberty* is closely connected to Mill's remarkable argument in *The Subjection of Women* that argues that sexism is as unjust as racism.[122] The criminalization of contraception illustrates the force of his argument, as encouraging fertility (by condemning contraception) makes no secular sense as overpopulation is a central concern and fails to take seriously that women's control of when and whether they will have children not only harms no one, but dignifies their choices free of justly sexist patriarchal controls that are unjust. That is an argument of liberal political principle, and the British parliament quite rightly in my view applied it to contraception, abortion, and gay sex (the latter of which was examined in depth in Chapter 3).

John Stuart Mill's argument in *On Liberty* has the same explanatory and normative force in understanding the U.S. Supreme Court's development and elaboration of the free-standing constitutional right to privacy first as applied to contraception,[123] then abortion,[124] and finally gay/lesbian sex.[125] It is striking that both Justice Douglas, writing for the court, and Justice Harlan (relying on his earlier opinion in *Poe v. Ullman*[126]) appeal to the constitutional right to marry, which Harlan quite correctly argues was historically regarded by the Founders as a fundamental right not expressly listed in the Bill of Rights because the Bill applied only to the federal government, which had no authority over marriage that was regarded as a state matter. However, once the Fourteenth Amendment of the Reconstruction Amendments extended federal judicial protection of basic rights to the states on the basis of the Privileges and Immunities Clause of the Fourteenth Amendment (appealing to the metric of human rights in the Privileges and Immunities Clause of Article IV, section 2 of the 1787 Constitution), then the court quite properly extended to the states' judicial protection not only to the rights explicitly listed in the Bill of Rights but to those fundamental rights, like marriage, which the states under slavery had abridged

122 See John Stuart Mill and Harriet Taylor Mill, *Essays on Sex Equality*, edited by Alice S. Rossi (Chicago: University of Chicago Press, 1970).

123 See *Griswold v. Connecticut*, 381 U.S. 479 (1965).

124 See *Roe v. Wade*, 410 U.S. 113 (1973); *Planned Parenthood of Southeastern Pa. v. Casey*, 505 U.S. 833 (1992).

125 See *Lawrence v. Texas*, 539 U.S. 558 (2003).

126 367 U.S. 497, 523 (1961).

(forbidding slaves to marry, thus facilitating the sale of blacks south irrespective of family relationships).[127] The Founders had identified as, among inalienable human rights, the right to intimate family life--what Frances Hutcheson called "the natural right each one to enter into the matrimonial relation with anyone who consents." Indeed, relevant historical materials suggest that the right should be more abstractly stated; for example, John Witherspoon (a signatory to the Declaration of Independence), whose lectures James Madison heard at Princeton, followed Hutcheson in listing as a basic human and natural right a "right to associate, if he so incline, with any persons or persons, whom he can persuade (not force)—under this is contained the right to marriage."[128] It is the right to intimate association, thus understood, that the U.S. Supreme Court appeals to not only in striking down laws criminalizing contraceptive sale and use in and outside marriage, but laws criminalizing the decision of women whether and when to have children (forcing an intimate relationship to children on women they sometimes do not want) and laws criminalizing as well the intimate sexual lives of gay men and lesbians. In all these cases, aspects of the right to intimate life, an inalienable human right, has been subject to criminal penalties, and there is no compelling argument of justice or of harm to others and self that justified such abridgment. I have already shown this in the case of the criminalization of contraception. The right to abortion services rests on the same right of intimate association (whether and when a woman will form the relationship to a child) and there is no secular consensus that an early term fetus is a person on a par with a born child, and thus the abridgment of the right is not supported by either an argument of justice or harm to self and others. And, the loving sexual relationships of gay men and women, often today quite long term, play the role that marriage has traditionally played for others, and there is no argument of justice or of harm to self or others that could justify criminalization. Quite to the contrary, Blackstone's overwrought claim of its unspeakability, based on anachronistic sectarian views that have no place in a secular society (that homosexuality caused earthquakes[129]), has inflicted both injustice and a kind of soul murder on gay people whose psyche, like that of all persons, centers itself in and is nourished by love and maimed by its absence.[130]

The American judiciary must justify its *Marbury* powers on grounds of principle. A basic constitutional right like conscience or free speech or intimate law, being based in a human right that all humans claim as equals, must be extended

127 For a fuller defense of this argument, see Richards, *Conscience and the Constitution*, pp. 224–32.

128 For references, see ibid., p. 226.

129 On this as a ground for condemning homosexuality, see *Novella 77* of Justinian, quoted in D. S. Bailey, *Homosexuality and the Western Christian Tradition* (London: Longman, 1955), pp. 73–74.

130 On these harms, see Omar G. Encarnacion, *The Case for Gay Reparations* (New York: Oxford University Press, 2021).

to all persons equally as a matter of principle, and the principle can be only be abridged when there is a clear and present danger of harm, or a compelling secular interest. Both the inference and elaboration of the constitutional right to privacy by the U.S. Supreme Court in the cases I have discussed are justified by such a principle, which is best shown by how the argument has developed over time, starting in the right to marriage it ends in extending the right to marriage, as a matter of principle, to a once despised and stigmatized minority, indeed, a caste, like the untouchables in India, so stigmatized that it is outside caste, the untouchable, the unspeakable, namely, gay persons.[131]

So it is misleading to suppose that the legislative decriminalization in the U.K. rests on different grounds than the constitutional decriminalizations in the U.S. Both appeal to the basic principles of political liberalisms stated and defended by John Stuart Mill, and both rest on arguments of human rights recognized by the institutions in the U.K. and the U.S. whose authority, at least in significant part, rests on the role they have played in recognizing and vindicating the rights of minorities. What is remarkable, from a comparative perspective, is how far each nation's constitutional institutions both depend on common arguments and have been inspired by a liberal political theory.

There is a similarly fascinating comparison to be made between the ways in which the U.K. and the U.S. have dealt with rights-based arguments of dying with dignity in cases dealing with the discontinuation of life-sustaining procedures for persons in a persistent vegetative or other state, and others dealing with physician-assisted suicide. In the U.K. litigation, *Airedale NHS Trust v. Bland*,[132] three courts (the High Court Family Division, Court of Appeal, and the House of Lords Judicial Committee) held that it was not a taking of life under the criminal law to discontinue life-sustaining procedures in such a case, appealing to the distinction between life and the value of life that one of the justices in the Court of Appeal, Lord Hoffman, had developed in conversation with the philosophers Ronald Dworkin and Bernard Williams.[133] When it came, however, to physician-assisted suicide, the British courts have taken a different view. Noel Conway was a lecturer from Shrewsbury, England, and in 2014 he was diagnosed with motor neuron disease and wanted the right to an assisted death. All forms of assisted suicide are currently illegal in the U.K., and doctors found to be assisting a suicide can be jailed for up to 14 years, under the Suicide Act, 1961. Conway challenged this law in the High Court in 2017 on the grounds of human rights, claiming that law against physician-assisted suicide in the U.K. interferes with his "right to respect for private and family life," protected under Article 8 of the European Convention of Human Rights. The High Court rejected his view, as did the Court of Appeal in May 2018,

131 See *Obergefell v. Hodges*, 576 U.S. 644 (2015).
132 [1993] AC 789.
133 See ibid., pp. 824–26.

stating that parliament was a better place to rule on the issue, and concerns were raised over whether safeguards proposed by Conway were adequate to protect vulnerable people. The Supreme Court rejected his argument in 27 November 2018. In 2014, the Director of Public Prosecutions clarified the likelihood of prosecution against medical professionals (the law would be applied only to medical professionals directly involved in the patient's care), and guidelines had also been issued by the DPP in February 2019 (prosecution would be unlikely when victim had reached a voluntary and informed decision, and that the suspect was wholly motivated by compassion). Proposals to change the law on this issue have been introduced in parliament, but none have passed. Approximately 46 Britons a year go abroad to Dignitas in Switzerland for a physician-assisted suicide.[134]

In the U.S., the Supreme Court addressed the same two issues as the British courts had, but in terms of yet another aspect of the free-standing constitutional right to privacy, here, not the right to intimate life, but the right to life itself, including in contemporary circumstances the right over the timing and circumstances of one's death. *Cruzan v. Director, Missouri Dept of Health*[135] recognized a constitutionally protected right of a competent adult to refuse medical treatment, but required, when the patient was comatose, that there be clear and convincing evidence shown by a living will that the person did not want such medical treatment when comatose. The issue for the 5–4 majority, written for the court by Chief Justice Rehnquist, was the compelling case of the secular good of preserving life as a justification for abridging the right, including worries about making mistakes when such a good was a stake. And, in *Washington v. Glucksberg*,[136] Rehnquist, again writing for the court, refused to strike down a prohibition on physician-assisted suicide because the risks of mistake were so large, but five justices (Justices O'Connor, Ginsberg, Breyer, Stevens, and Souter) observed in their opinions that any more particularized challenge to such a law in the circumstances of the doctor, with the consent of patient and family, facilitating the death of a terminally ill patient in terrible pain might lead to a different result, striking down such an application of the prohibition as unconstitutional.

The judiciary retains in the U.K. its powers of judicial independence on grounds of human rights, but parliament continues to play a significant role in advancing the aims of political liberalism, including human rights (shown by its passage of the Human Rights Act, 1998). There is today more of a tension between the judiciary and parliament with parliament retaining its power explicitly to reverse judicial interpretation, but both held in what Laws calls "the

134 All these points are discussed in "Assisted Suicide in the United Kingdom," https://en.wikipedia.org/wiki/Assisted_suicide_in_the_United-Kingdom

135 497 U.S. 261 (1990).

136 521 U.S. 702 (1997).

constitutional balance" of the competence of the judiciary in some areas, and the competence of parliament in others.[137] What makes parliamentary sovereignty still attractive is that it allows parliament to take account of changing circumstances and thus to revise and even reject traditional British views (e.g., Blackstone's homophobia), in effect, parliament being a kind of continuing constitutional convention.

137 For the ongoing debates in the U.K. over the relationship of judicial review to parliamentary supremacy, see Christopher Forsyth (ed.), *Judicial Review and the Constitution* (Oxford: Hart, 2000).

6 The Common Challenge to the Political Liberalism of British and American Constitutionalism in World War II

Institutional Change and New Challenges, Domestic and International

This comparative study of British and American constitutionalism began in what they share: a Lockean political liberalism that justified both the Glorious Revolution of 1688 (establishing the U.K. unwritten constitution with enhanced powers of the parliament) and the American Revolution of 1776–81 (leading to the written constitution of 1787 and Bill of Rights of 1791). The U.K. and U.S. share a common Lockean political liberalism but, because the Americans regarded the U.K. unwritten constitution's lack of colonial representation in parliament as a betrayal of its liberalism, they set themselves to use the idea of a written constitution, which had been proposed during the earlier English Civil War but abandoned by the U.K. in the Glorious Revolution of parliamentary supremacy, to create a constitution with textual guarantees of federalism between the national government and the states, separation of powers at the national level, and *Marbury* judicial review to protect constitutionally protected rights. The great shift in British constitutionalism was the gradual expansion of the franchise (culminating in 1928 when all women get the vote) with the balance between the common law and parliamentary supremacy shifting to parliament. All these changes took place in, from an American perspective, a remarkably stable structure of parliamentary supremacy that allowed the Labour Party to come to power in 1945–51 and establish a social democracy that was to enjoy cross-party support until Thatcher's government and to enjoy cross-party support thereafter (all parties pledge allegiance, for example, to continuing the NHS). The U.S. Constitution, in contrast, could not address within its written terms, at least as those terms had come to be interpreted by the pro-slavery constitutionalism adopted by the U.S. Supreme Court in *Dred Scott v. Sanford*, ending the liberal obscenity of slavery as leading Founders had hoped, leading to a fratricidal Civil War and Reconstruction Amendments, themselves misinterpreted by the Supreme Court and the dominant political parties to entrench the obscenity

DOI: 10.4324/9781003410966-6

of the American caste system of racism, enforced by racist violence (lynchings) for a long period until well after World War II.[1]

My argument has been that, until this point, the political liberalism of the U.K., with the notable exception of the British Empire, was much more in accord with political liberalism than the U.S. I recognize that for many the British Empire itself should at least tilt the liberal balance toward the U.S., and it is surely difficult to square the rather admirable liberalism of the U.K. at home with some of its injustices in its colonies and their legacy.[2] Hobson explained its political psychology as "partly the dupery of imperfectly realized ideas, partly a case of psychical departmentalism. Imperialism has been floated on a sea of vague, shifty, well-sounding phrases which are seldom tested by close contact with fact."[3] If racism is in fact the key here, American racism during this period, including lynchings in the U.S., was arguably worse. And American irresponsibility at negotiations over the Treaty of Versailles after World War II (which Keynes had condemned) and its later nescience in dealing with the fascist menace in Germany, Italy, and Japan set the stage for the catastrophe of World War II.[4]

But these two experiments in liberal constitutionalism, joined for a period and then separated for a long period by a violent revolution and the different trajectories of their institutions, come into a much closer, even intimate relationship as they faced jointly the aggressive genocidal fascism of Germany (a form of anti-liberal state terror that, as we saw, Burke's political psychology, explains; see Chapter 1) as Britain desperately needed American assistance against the projected German invasion, after the fall of other allies. As Paul Kennedy recently observed, "It was, even for those two historical giants Franklin Roosevelt and Winston Churchill a remarkable action. On August 7, 1941, without letting the still-neutral American nation know what was going on, the unorthodox and purposeful president had arrived … on the Newfoundland coast … . Two days later the equally resourceful prime minister of Britain

1 On this point, see Wilkerson, *Caste*.

2 For liberal critiques of British imperialism and its consequences, see Priya Satia, *Time's Monster: How History Makes History* (Cambridge, MA: Harvard University Press, 2020); Adom Getachew, *Worldmaking after Empire: The Rise and Fall of Self-Determination* (Princeton, NJ: Princeton University Press, 2019); Mahmood Mamdani, *Neither Settler Nor Native: The Making and Unmaking of Permanent Minorities* (Cambridge, MA: Harvard University Press, 2020); Roderick Matthews, *Peace, Poverty, and Betrayal: A New History of British India* (London: Hurst, 2021); Sathnam Sanghera, *Empireland: How Imperialism Has Shaped Modern Britain* (London: Penguin, 2021); Lisa Ford, *The King's Peace: Law and Order in the British Empire* (Cambridge, MA: Harvard University Press, 2021).

3 See Hobson, *Imperialism*, p. 218.

4 For an illuminating historical treatment of American irresponsibility during this period, see Kagan, *The Ghost at the Feast*.

arrived in the same port."[5] In addition to discussing their military intentions, they issued "one of the most important statements about human rights, trade, the freedom of peoples and democratic purpose. The statement, soon termed in the press, 'The Atlantic Character,' was issued after the two leaders had secretly returned home."[6] A year later, on 14 August 1942, after the U.S. had declared war on Japan (December 8, 1941) and Germany (December 11, 1941), President Roosevelt issued the following message, commemorating the first anniversary of the Atlantic Charter:

> A year ago today the nations resisting a common barbaric force were units or small groups fighting for their existence. Now these nations and groups of nations in all the continents of the earth have united. They have formed a great union of humanity dedicated to the realization of the common programme of purposes and principles set forth in the Atlantic Charter through world-wide victory of their common enemies. Their faith in life, liberty, independence and religious liberty, and in the preservation of human rights and justice in their own as well as in other lands, has been given form and substance as the United Nations.[7]

In his earlier state of union address on 6 January 1941, asking Congress to support lend lease, Roosevelt spoke about the foundations of a healthy and strong democracy, listing:

> Equal opportunity for youth and others.
> Jobs for those who can work.
> Security for those who need it.
> The ending of special privilege for the few.
> The preservation of civil liberty for all.
> The enjoyment of the fruits of scientific progress in a wider and constantly rising standard of living.[8]

He then went on:

> In the future days, which we seek to make secure, we look forward to a world founded upon four essential freedoms.
>
> The first is freedom of speech and expression—everywhere in the world.

5 See Paul Kennedy, "Joined with Single Purpose," *Wall Street Journal*, August 28–29, 2021, C7, C9 at C7.

6 See ibid., C7.

7 See "The Atlantic Charter," www.nato.int/cps/en/natohq/official_texts_16912.htm.

8 "The Four Freedoms," https://voicesofdemocracy.umd.edu/fdr-the-four-freedoms-speech-text/, p. 10.

> The second is free of every person to worship God in his own way—everywhere in the world.
>
> The third is freedom from want—which, translated into world terms, means economic understandings which will secure to every nation a healthy peacetime life for its inhabitants everywhere in the world.
>
> The fourth freedom is freedom from fear—which, translated into world terms, means a world-wide reduction of armaments to such a point and in such a thorough fashion that no nation will be in a position to commit an act of physical aggression against any neighbor—anywhere in the world.[9]

Two nations, separated for a long period, now came together in the terms of the political liberalism that they now experience as visibly at threat, and the terms of their common liberalism is not uniquely British or uniquely American, but "a great union of humanity" around the four freedoms, which include both civil liberties and social democratic values, "everywhere in the world."[10] There were extraordinary consequences both in the U.K. and the U.S. of their victory over fascism in terms of, in the U.K., social democracy when Labour takes power in 1945–51, and, in the U.S., the leadership played, among national institutions after the war not by Congress or the executive, but initially by the U.S. Supreme Court as, for the first time in its institutional history, it exercises its *Marbury* powers in fact to protect the human rights of racial/ethnic minorities, and later anti-war demonstrators, second wave women, and advocates of gay rights.

We now turn to the impact of World War II on institutional developments both in British and American constitutionalism, developments that arose from the felt need in both nations that their liberal constitutionalism had to be rethought and readjusted to deal with new challenges to the values of human rights they now recognized, more strongly than ever, that they shared, and that institutional changes were required better to secure the protection of human rights. The consequence was an American and British constitutional constructivism, very much in the spirit of Burke, that would reflect on historical experience of a political liberalism more at lethal threat than it had ever previously been, and that would construct new forms of national, transnational, and international constitutional institutions that would address these threats in the interest of the protection of human rights. Roosevelt thus makes quite clear in his commemoration of the Atlantic Charter that the United Nations is one such institutional development, to be followed by the Universal Declaration of Human Rights of 1948.

9 Ibid., pp. 11–12.

10 For two recent studies of these events and their significance, see David McKean and Bart M. J. Szewczyk, *Partners of First Resort: America, Europe, and the Future of the West* (New York: Brookings, 2021); Michael Kluger and Richard Evans, *Roosevelt and Churchill: The Atlantic Charter* (Annapolis, MD: The Naval Institute, 2021).

In the wake of World War II, both Britain and the U.S. played important roles in creating the United Nations system and the Universal Declaration of Human Rights of 1948 and shared alliances (including NATO) during the Cold War against communism in Soviet Union and China. And Britain played a central role in the design and implementation of the European Convention on Human Rights, as A. W. Brian Simpson writes in his important book on this development.[11] How does one square this with the classic British view reminiscent of Burke on "real" human rights stated by the Lord Chancellor, Lord Simon: "It is the existence in this country of these effective practical remedies of procedure which have secured these important rights, and not any declaration at all"[12] and the view, as Simpson put it, that "Britain had invented human rights"[13] and had nothing to learn from anyone else. Simpson later observes: "I was a law student in Oxford, from 1951 to 1954, and do not recall it [the European Convention] ever being mentioned. Indeed up to the time I left Oxford, in 1972, there was no such things as a course on human rights, and there was no professor in the subject until 1999."[14]

Britain's role in drafting and supporting the European Convention on Human Rights required the British to work with Europeans in those European countries who, in the wake of the fascist attack on liberal democracy and human rights, had decided that the protection of human rights could not be limited to the various European written constitutions after World War II, like the German Basic Law, but required as well as transnational convention and related institutions (the European Court of Human Rights) that would tie the U.K. and European nations into a normative consensus on the basic human rights they all shared, eventually allowing citizens in countries bound by the convention to appeal to the European Court to test whether laws in their jurisdiction complied with the guarantees of human rights in the convention. It was this enterprise that marked the opening of British constitutionalism to comparative constitutional law, which the very enterprise of the European convention required, as the British and Europeans had to find common ground in the normative traditions of human rights they shared, itself an exercise in comparative constitutional law. The European Union was a yet further development in this enterprise, as in time it gave rise to yet further protections of human rights, including the EU Charter of Fundamental Rights.[15]

11 See A. W. Brian Simpson, *Human Rights and the End of Empire: Britain and the Genesis of the European Convention* (Oxford: Oxford University Press, 2001).

12 Ibid., p. 213.

13 Ibid., p. 345.

14 Ibid., p. 809.

15 On this point, see Paul Craig and Grainne De Burca, *EU Law: Text, Cases, and Materials*, 7th ed. (Oxford: Oxford University Press, 2015), pp. 414–62.

With the U.K. Human Rights Act of 1998, Britain took the further step of incorporating the European Convention into its law that takes two forms. First, U.K. courts, in exercising their common law powers to interpret statutes, must give appropriate weight in their interpretation to the decisions of the European Court of Human Rights. Second, if the U.K. courts find that they cannot reasonably exercise their interpretive powers in light of decisions of the European Court, they must issue a declaration of incompatibility that the parliament and executive are bound to resolve.[16] There is ongoing controversy in the U.K., even by liberal judges like John Laws, over whether British courts have too closely followed European Court decision when they are not bound to do so, but that they are bound in some cases is now settled law.[17]

Comparative constitutional law now plays, for this reason, an important role in the interpretive process of the U.K. courts in exercising their common law powers, including in the interpretation of parliamentary statutes, including the rather demanding principle of proportionality review used by the European Court of Human Rights, a standard of review like the more demanding standards of judicial review that the U.S. Supreme Court has developed both in the protection of rights like free speech and religious liberty and the equal protection review of suspect classes and fundamental rights. Comparative constitutional law is, for this reason, very much a feature of the study of human rights in the U.K., and there is now a growing literature comparing how various jurisdictions interpret the human rights their written constitutions guarantee. Sandra Fredman's important book, *Comparative Human Rights Law*,[18] thus explores fascinating analogies and disanalogies in the protection of human rights in diverse jurisdictions in the areas of capital punishment, abortion, the right to health, the right to housing, freedom of speech, the right to an education, and freedom of religion. Some of these rights are familiar to the historical understanding of constitutional rights in the older constitutionalisms of the U.K. and the U.S., but others (the rights to health, housing, and education) are not. For a constitutional lawyer in the U.K. and the U.S., the study of more recent written constitutions that protect such rights, and indeed where the judiciary has played an important role in enforcing them (South Africa and India are notable examples of both[19]), require one to think outside the box of one's conventional understanding both of constitutional rights and the role of the judiciary in protecting them, and to ask

16 See Aileen Kavanagh, *Constitutional Review under the UK Human Rights Act* (Cambridge: Cambridge University Press, 2009).

17 John Laws, *The Constitutional Balance* (Oxford: Hart, 2021), pp. 125–26.

18 See Sandra Fredman, *Comparative Human Rights Law* (Oxford: Oxford University Press, 2018).

19 See, e.g., Sandra Fredman, *Human Rights Transformed: Positive Rights and Positive Duties* (Oxford: Oxford University Press, 2008), pp. 204–40. But for doubts about the role of the Indian Supreme Court responding to the illiberal populism of Modi, see Wojciech Sadurski, *A Pandemic of Populists* (Cambridge: Cambridge University Press, 2022), pp. 42, 93, 147, 160, 162.

the kinds of fundamental questions both about human rights and judicial powers that are rarely raised, let alone discussed. Perhaps, they should be.

The other pull on the U.K. after World War II was its wartime alliance with the U.S., based on the common ground of political liberalism that the U.K. and the U.S. acknowledged in their alliance first against fascism (the Atlantic Charter) and later Stalinist communism in the U.S.S.R., leading to the Marshall Plan and NATO. Unusually able leadership in the U.S. during and after World War II did not repeat the nation's catastrophic mistakes in not only entering World War I (a war essentially between competing European imperialisms, only two of which, the U.K. and France, approximated to anything like a democracy: women, for example, could not vote in either nation), but agreeing to a retributive peace treaty that humiliated Germany, sowing the seeds of the even more catastrophic World War II, and then not joining the League of Nations, which did not constrain the aggressive violence of fascist Italy and Germany. Both the Marshall Plan and NATO and the United Nations show the unusual wisdom of America's post-war leaders who also followed George Kennan's shrewd understanding of the politics of the communist U.S.S.R. as well as the containment policy he recommended, ending in the peaceful collapse of the Soviet Union that Kennan had predicted.[20] In forging these institutions, the Americans and British worked very much along the lines of Burke's conception of constitutional constructivism, starting from established institutions that worked and then reforming them from within in light of the experience of threats to them, including institutions (national, transnational, and international) that protect "real" human rights. In his last book, Richard Nixon—the pre-eminent American cold warrior against the Soviet Union—urged, after the fall of the U.S.S.R., that a comparably generous Marshall Plan be extended to the Russian Federation (including admission to NATO), worrying prophetically that the failure to do so might so humiliate the Russians that, like the Germans after World War, they would turn from democracy to authoritarian dictatorship and nationalistic aggression.[21]

The same quality of leadership was not in evidence as the U.S., at the time of the end of the imperialisms of France in Vietnam and of Britain in the Middle East, uncritically accepted an imperialist role both in Vietnam and the Middle East, leading to the disastrous Vietnam War and the Iraq War as well as the Iranian theocracy and the Afghanistan War. Many of these ventures were supported by the U.K., reflecting the pull of the Anglo-American alliance that had been so successful earlier. Unfortunately, the brilliance of America's policies in containing the U.S.S.R. did not carry over to these other ventures, and the U.K. though there was certainly opposition in Britain to its support of these American policies, usually went along.

20 On this historical period, see Louis Menand, *The Free World: Art and Thought in the Cold War* (New York: Farrar, Straus & Giroux, 2021).

21 See Richard Nixon, *Beyond Peace* (New York: Random House, 1994), pp. 55–82, 98–99.

It is now 80 years since the Atlantic Charter, and the question now arises, in light of "the great union of humanity" to which it appealed, whether the constitutional institutions that developed in each nation better to recognize universal human rights have achieved their purposes, or require rethinking. In his speech on the four freedoms, Roosevelt described the fourth freedom in the following terms:

> The fourth freedom is freedom from fear—which, translated into world terms, means a world-wide reduction of armaments to such a point and in such a thorough fashion that no nation will be in a position to commit an act of physical aggression against any neighbor—anywhere in the world.[22]

Roosevelt was thinking, of course, about state aggression, exemplified by fascist Germany and Italy, but both the U.S. and the U.K. have been confronted by such aggression not by state actors but by terrorist groups, whether the IRA or Islamic terrorism, some of which have been independent actors though sometimes supported by governments (e.g., the Taliban government in Afghanistan giving refuge to Al-Qaeda). The social-psychological roots of terrorism are now well understood. In *Terror in the Mind of God: The Global Rise of Religious Violence*, Mark Juergensmeyer interprets the global rise of fundamentalist violence as a response to perceived insults to manhood:

> Nothing is more intimate than sexuality, and no greater humiliation can be experienced than failure over what one perceives to be one's sexual role. Such failures are often the basis of domestic violence; and when these failures are linked with the social roles of masculinity and femininity, they can lead to public violence. Terrorist acts, then, can be forms of symbolic empowerment for men whose traditional sexual roles—their very manhood—is perceived to be at stake.[23]

The terrorism of Islamic fundamentalism exemplifies the toxic combination of technological know-how with extreme religious intolerance, most obviously, anti-Semitism, but also, in the IRA, the intolerance of Protestants and Catholics in Ireland (a legacy of British imperialism). Most believers in Islam condemn such terrorism, but there is a larger problem that makes such fundamentalism possible. In terms of democratic values, the political culture of most Islamic nations is problematic on two scores: its lack of separation of church and state and its sexism.[24] These are interdependent problems. Any religion can

22 Ibid., pp. 11–12.

23 Mark Juergensmeyer, *Terror in the Mind of God: The Global Rise of Religious Violence* (Berkeley: University of California Press, 2000), p. 195.

24 On these points, see Bernard Lewis, *What Went Wrong? Western Impact and Middle Eastern Response* (Oxford: Oxford University Press, 2002).

be corrupted to unjust ends when used by political leaders to entrench and legitimate their own power. Islam is only the most notable contemporary example of a phenomenon that has, at earlier historical periods, afflicted other religions, the various forms of Christianity before constitutional developments called for some form of the separation of church and state. It would be a great mistake to suppose that these nations are still not afflicted by sectarian religious, ethnic, and gender intolerance (see, for example, Chapter 7's critique of new natural law) or to overlook the fact that such intolerance sometimes drives ethnocentric forms of imperialism. And there is no reason to think that believers in Islam cannot reasonably free themselves of the corrupt politicians who afflict them. One place to start would be by taking seriously the feminist voices of Islamic women.[25]

Conversely, we can see what motivated the violence of Islamic fundamentalism in one of its founding martyrs, Sayyid Qutb, who warred both on the separation of church and state and on the sexual freedom of women. Qutb had turned his back on marriage in Egypt because "he hand been unable to find a suitable bride from the 'dishonorable' women who allowed themselves to be seen in public." If the problem in Egypt was that women were not traditionally patriarchal enough, what threatened Qutb in his 1948 visit to the U.S. was, above all, the freer sexuality of American women and, more generally, an American sexual permissiveness that he took to be established by the Kinsey Report, including the reported high incidence of homosexual relations among American men.[26] Qutb advocated Islamic fundamentalism as a response to the freer sexual of women in Egypt and the U.S., and out of this swamp emerged the ideology and terror of Al-Qaeda and other terrorist groups (Isis and others).

It is at least understandable how the constitutional advances on a range of issues in the U.K. and the U.S. (including race and class, religion, gay rights, and gender), when imagined by Qutb and others to explain imperialist injustices to Islamic nations, became the irrationalist targets of Islamic fundamentalism. It is a quite different question how well nations like the U.S. and the U.K. dealt with them, notably, the war in Afghanistan, followed by the war in Iraq. Some way of stopping Al-Qaeda by military means when supported, as it was, by the international community seems to me clearly in order, but nothing can justify the failure to focus on Al-Qaeda and the turn to the Iraq war, based on faulty intelligence, let alone the later military ventures against resurgent forms of Islamic terrorist groups incentivized by our focus on military as opposed to political solutions. Apparently, the intelligence of the American and British

25 See, e.g., Leila Ahmed, *A Border Passage: From Cairo to America* (New York: Farrar, Straus and Giroux, 1999).

26 Lawrence Wright, *The Looming Tower: Al-Quaeda and the Road to 9/11* (New Yori: Alfred A. Knopf, 2006), pp. 9, 12.

approach to the threat from a nation, the U.S.S.R., quite failed us when it comes to these terroristic groups.

The U.K. and the U.S. learned something important from the experience of the aggressive violence of fascism from Germany, Italy, and Japan in World War II, namely, that fascism was never a coherent political theory, but rather a violent political psychology and ideology arising from a sense of humiliated manhood that was at war with the political liberalism that its leaders came to believe had humiliated them.[27] To this extent, the recent forms of Islamic and other terrorisms share a common political psychology and ideology with fascism as well as the violence of Stalinist totalitarianism. Neither the U.K. nor the U.S. understood what they were facing in fascism (among British leaders, only Churchill is one of the few exceptions), and thus did not take the measures that might have held the violence of political fascism in check before its full irrational violence almost destroyed civilization as we know it, including the culture of liberal constitutionalism that we have been studying in their American and British forms in this book. What the Atlantic Charter reflects is the recognition of the U.K. and the U.S. when it was almost too late that they had made a catastrophic mistake in not seeing that fascism was in its nature an irrationalist war on political liberalism, and that British temporizing and American isolationism failed to understand that their central values, the values of political liberalism to which Roosevelt appeals in his four freedoms, were now at credible threat, and would later see a similar threat from the Soviet Union. All of the institutional innovations earlier mentioned—the Marshall Plan, NATO, the United Nations, the Universal Declaration of Human Rights, the European Convention on Human Rights—reflect this common understanding. And there were, as we have seen, domestic institutional developments in both the U.S. and the U.K. that reflect what we learned, namely, the role of the U.S. Supreme Court in protecting minorities, and the revival of the common law in the U.K., including the Human Rights Act, 1998.

Such threats continue, and not only the threats of Islamic fundamentalisms. I want at the conclusion of this argument, to reflect on two such threats: first, Brexit and the politics that led to it; and second, the worrying forms of reactionary anti-liberal politics that have emerged in the U.K., the U.S., the European Union, and Russia after the fall of the Soviet Union (including Russia's invasion of Ukraine). In particular, populist politics in both the U.S. and the U.K. have introduced illiberal threats to their liberal constitutionalism, and I want in conclusion to consider these threats, their sources and the way to deal with them.

27 On this point, see Paxton, *The Anatomy of Fascism*; Gilligan and Richards, *The Deepening Darkness*, pp. 232–40.

7 Patriarchal Religion in U.S. and U.K. Constitutional Law

Originalism as "Political Religion" (Burke) Unmasked

There have been two important contemporary developments in the U.S. and the U.K. both cutting back the constitutional protection of human rights—the opinion of the Supreme Court in *Dobbs v. Jackson* (overturning *Roe v. Wade* in relation to abortion) and in the U.K. the Johnson government's proposal to repeal the Human Rights Act of 1998 (which brought the European Convention on Human Rights into the national law) and replace it with The Bill of Rights Bill, that would dilute the protection of rights in the Human Rights Act, 1998. Both developments reflect the influence of a group of conservative Catholic thinkers, the so-called new natural lawyers.

In 2008, Nicholas Bamforth, Queens College, Oxford University, and I published with Cambridge University Press, *Patriarchal Religion, Sexuality, and Gender: A Critique of New Natural Law* (hereinafter *Patriarchal Religion*) criticizing at length the views of the so-called new natural lawyers concerning the law's treatment of contraception, abortion, and LGBTQ sexuality as improperly sectarian in a liberal constitutional democracy, and not supported by secular arguments. We pointed out that high-profile members of this group—particularly John Finnis (Oxford and Notre Dame) and Robert George (Princeton)—played influential roles both in the academy and in practical legal and political advocacy. At the time we wrote that book, however, their views had had no impact on the U.S. Supreme Court (which had constitutionalized both the rights to contraception and abortion services and indeed gay rights, decriminalization in 2003 and, eventually, in 2015, gay marriage). And, their views had had no impact in the U.K. either (parliament had also decriminalized, and would come to accept gay marriage as well).

However, views of members of the group have now had a demonstrable impact on the U.S. Supreme Court in *Dobbs* (in which a brief by Finnis and George and another article by Finnis—former PhD supervisor to Justice Gorsuch—are cited)[1] and on the Johnson government's and perhaps next government's

1 See *Dobbs v. Jackson*, 142 S.Ct. 2228 (2022), opinion for the court by Justice Alito, p. 2249, n. 24, citing "Brief for Scholars of Jurisprudence" by Finnis and George, and pp. 2254–55, n. 38, citing article by Finnis.

DOI: 10.4324/9781003410966-7

proposal to amend the 1998 Human Rights Act.[2] As such, it is important to highlight these practical developments as a basis for questioning the approach both of the Supreme Court and of strands in political debate in the U.K.

To frame my discussion of both developments, I will show that Burke's brilliant analysis of the violence of "political religions" is here very much at work. On Burke's analysis of this political psychology, such "political religions" use the mask of utopian ideology (as in the French Declaration of Human Rights) to mobilize and enforce a reactionary shame-driven political psychology, the Terror, that wars on liberal conscience, forging forms of anti-democratic illiberal repression. I argue that the political appeal of new natural law in the U.S. and U.K. is that of a "political religion" in Burke's sense.

7.1 New Natural Law in the U.S. Supreme Court

In *Patriarchal Religion*, Nicholas Bamforth and I develop and defend four criteria for when arguments are improperly sectarian: (1) it rests on religious content; (2) epistemically, its premises or conclusions, or both, can only justified by religious considerations (scripture, or revelation); (3) an essential part of the argument is motivated by religious considerations; and (4) historically the argument can be traced genetically to cognitive beliefs that are religious (*Patriarchal Religion*, pp. 46–52). We argued at some length that all the arguments that the new natural lawyers make condemning contraception, abortion, and LGBTQ sexuality are sectarian, and do not meet the standard of reasonable secular justification to all required in a liberal constitutional democracy (see, e.g., pp. 116–24, 190–278). Indeed, their arguments, on close examination, demonstrably rest on the patriarchal religious teaching of the Roman Catholic Church, in particular, the papacy.

We go on to observe in our book that we had no wish to accuse the new natural lawyers of acting in bad faith. Nonetheless, since we believed our arguments about the sectarian religious basis of their views are true, it raises the question of how persons of deep religious conviction might think themselves to be presenting a secular argument when they are, as a matter of logic, defending a religious (including a specifically doctrinal) position not shared by many other Christians, Jews, other religions, let alone non-believers. At this point, we introduced a distinction. While the new natural lawyers may be acting in good faith, there would appear to be a degree of audience sensitivity in the way in which they present their law-related arguments: for it seems clear that they have been careful to articulate some of their positions in a purportedly secular fashion

2 See Statement of Deputy Prime Minister Dominic Raab to the House of Commons, "Bill of Rights," Volume 716, debated on Wednesday, June 22, 2022, and Bill of Rights Bill, Bill 117; see also "Bill of Rights: European Convention on Human Rights Memorandum, Summary of Bill" and "Draft Bill of Rights, Impact Assessment," Ministry of Justice.

when addressing audiences that are not predominantly or exclusively religious (one such audience being legal theorists as well as the American judiciary and the British parliament), while invoking God, the Bible, or church authorities when discussing exactly the same arguments before clearly religious audiences sometimes in Rome, appealing to the patriarchal authority of the papacy on these issues. The first method of presentation might be termed "exoteric" and the second "esoteric," different modes of presentation that pervade their works (*Patriarchal Religion*, pp. 146–48).

John Finnis' recent treatment of abortion clearly illustrates his use of exoteric argument instead of the esoteric sectarian religious arguments that he not only believes but, like other new natural lawyers, has defended at length in his works. In his April 2021 article in *First Things*, "Abortion Is Unconstitutional,"[3] Finnis nowhere discusses his actual sectarian moral views for why abortion (like contraception and LGBTQ sexuality) is a homicidal aggression against his clearly religiously sectarian "one-flesh union" conception of marriage (all such sexual unions *must* lead to having children, condemning all gay sex and many forms of straight sex, including those using contraceptives) he dogmatically holds and defends. It is a view that may once have made secular sense when children were desperately needed to work on the farm in a largely agrarian society with high rates of infant and adult mortality, but makes little sense today in a largely industrial and post-industrial culture threatened by overpopulation and other looming disasters. Within the Christianity (Catholic and Protestant) derived from Augustine of Hippo, the view of the new natural lawyers may be traced to Augustine's deeply personal, proto-psychoanalytic argument in *The Confessions* that only celibacy opens the psyche to God's love (see *Patriarchal Religion*, pp. 308–20), conceding non-celibate sexuality, as Thomas Aquinas does, only on terms of strict procreational control and support of the celibate clergy (see *Patriarchal Religion*, pp. 152–66).

Finnis, however, engages none of these arguments, arguments that make his views at least understandable (over my years of teaching the constitutional privacy cases dealing with these issues, increasingly NYU law students can barely understand them). It is of interest that at least one constitutional theorist, Adrian Vermeule, who shares Finnis' commitment to Catholic moral orthodoxy (a version of neo-Thomism), sharply repudiates originalism as a mode of reasonable constitutional interpretation,[4] in part at least because it fails to give weight to historical traditions over time of what Vermeule calls common good constitutionalism, in which at least some ideas of human rights play an important role. Vermeule thus shares the view of more secular critics of originalism, like Erwin Chemerinsky, that certainly do not agree that neo-Thomism should play

3 See John Finnis, "Abortion Is Unconstitutional," *First Things* (April 2021): 29–38.

4 Adrian Vermeule, *Common Good Constitutionalism* (Cambridge, MA: Polity Press, 2022).

the central role in constitutional interpretation, but, like Vermeule, criticize originalism for its epistemological difficulties, as well as its incoherence, its abhorrent results, and its hypocrisy.[5]

In contrast, Finnis' defense of Catholic moral orthodoxy in constitutional interpretation is now put completely in quite narrow historical terms, more particularly, in the originalist terms that the Supreme Court was shortly to use in *Dobbs* as its ground for overruling *Roe v. Wade* (the reasonable expectations of the generation that wrote and ratified a constitutional text about how it should be applied freezes constitutional interpretation forever). In contrast, however, to Justice Alito's opinion for the court in *Dobbs*, Finnis does not limit his originalist appeal to arguing that *Roe*'s decriminalization of abortion services is wrong, but argues that abortion constitutionally must on originalist grounds be criminal because fetuses are persons under the Fourteenth Amendment.

Linda Greenhouse has recently argued that *Dobbs* clearly rests on sectarian religious views.[6] In effect, as the novelist Margaret Attwood anticipated in *The Handmaid's Tale*, "the dominant 'religion' is moving to seize doctrinal control, and religious dominations familiar to us are being annihilated."[7] If so, why and how is this not seen?

I have come to believe that it is precisely Finnis' strategic move from esoteric to exoteric argument at this point that has made his views so attractive to the conservative majority that now dominates the Supreme Court, all of whom—Chief Justice Roberts and Justices Alito, Barrett, Thomas, Kavanaugh, and Gorsuch—were raised Catholic (though Gorsuch now worships with his wife and daughter in the Episcopal Church).[8] It would have been unthinkable for the justices of the Supreme Court to embrace Finnis' moral theology explicitly as the ground for overruling *Roe v. Wade* not least because it would so fragrantly flout the first two civil liberties under the First Amendment of the 1791 Bill of Rights, "Congress shall make no law respecting an establishment of religion, or prohibiting the free exercise thereof." If they are effectively enforcing an esoteric moral theology in which most Americans do not reasonably believe, *Dobbs* would not only be illegitimate, but scandalously so. Is the key perhaps that the majority in *Dobbs* sees the issue through the same patriarchal lens as Trump himself?[9] Its version of originalism may, if problematic, suggest as much.

5 See Erwin Chemerinsky, *Worse Than Nothing: The Dangerous Fallacy of Originalism* (New Haven, CT: Yale University Press, 2022).

6 See Linda Greenhouse, "Religious Doctrine Drove the Abortion Decision," *New York Times*, July 24, 2022, SR9; Linda Greenhouse, "Justice Alito's Call to Arms to Secure Religious Liberty," *New York Times*, August 14, 2022, SR8.

7 Margaret Attwood, *The Handmaid's Tale* (New York: Anchor, 1998), p. xvii.

8 On this point, see Linda Greenhouse, *Justice on the Brink* (New York: Random House, 2021), p. xviii. Justice Sotomayor, a liberal, was also raised Catholic.

9 On this point, see Carol Gilligan and David A. J. Richards, *Darkness Now Visible: Patriarchy's Resurgence and Feminist Resistance* (Cambridge: Cambridge University Press, 2018).

The question is whether the brand of originalism the conservative majority has embraced not only in *Dobbs*, but in its gun rights opinion[10] and two opinions on issues of anti-establishment and free exercise[11] and others is reasonable, or so unreasonable in *Dobbs* that the opinion, as Justice Breyer argues in his dissent, is illegitimate, perhaps scandalously so. This is the question I will explore below.

Almost all sides of serious debate about the interpretation of the U.S. Constitution—liberal and conservative—acknowledge there is an important role for history in interpreting the text of the oldest written constitution in the world but one that means to endure for generations to come, a topic on which I earlier touched in Chapter 2's discussion of Madison's argument with Jefferson that it was better for the longer term cause of human rights if the constitution was not, as Jefferson argued, rewritten every 19 years, but rather enjoyed a Burkean weight of history reminding future generations of the role of human rights in the legitimacy of the constitution. But, meaning may be ascribed to the often abstract text of the U.S. Constitution in quite different ways, some ascribing different levels of connotative meaning (some more abstract, others more concrete), and others staying close to the denotative meaning—the things in the world to which the founding generation would have regarded as the things they meant to include and others they would have excluded (Founders' denotations). Of all these approaches, that of Founders' denotation, consistently adopted only by Raoul Berger,[12] is the most implausible because it would delegitimate many (perhaps most) important Supreme Court opinions that cannot be fit into Founders' denotations (including *Brown v. Board of Education*[13] and *Loving v. Virginia*[14]) thus not fitting perhaps the most enlightened opinions in American history that are legitimate if any opinions are legitimate. If there is a case for this approach to constitutional interpretation in any particular case, it must be made with powerful intellectual and normative force.

Justice Alito's opinion for the court in *Dobbs* does not meet this standard of highly reasonable justification. While he cites John Hart Ely's theory of rectifying representational unfairness in support of the court's result (Ely is skeptical women should be a suspect class at all now that they have the vote, and could decriminalize abortion politically), Alito's view that the issue of abortion is best left to democracy does not appeal to Ely's view of representational fairness but to a highly problematic view that voting by states on this issue best approximates contemporary democratic voice on this issue, which it does not; his interest in Ely is only in the fact that Ely, a secular progressive politically in

10 *New York State Rifle & Pistol Association, Inc. v. Bruen*, 142 S.Ct. 2111 (2022).

11 *Carson v. Makin*, 142 S.Ct. 1987 (2022); *Kennedy v. Bremerton School District*, 142 S.Ct. 2407 (2022).

12 See Raoul Berger, *Government by Judiciary* (Cambridge, MA: Harvard University Press, 1977).

13 *Brown v. Board of Education*, 347 U.S. 483 (1954).

14 *Loving v. Virginia*, 358 U.S. 1 (1967).

favor of the right of abortion, is a secular critic of *Roe*,[15] and does not engage the failure of Ely's theory to explain the central place among American constitutional rights of the rights protected by the religion clauses and other rights, nor its understanding of constitutional democracy. Rather, the decision focuses entirely on Founders' denotations, namely, that some form of abortion, either before or after quickening, was criminal in all states in 1868, and thus nothing in the text of the normative clauses of the Fourteenth Amendment of 1868 can be regarded as applying to decriminalizing abortion services. There are several problems with this analysis.

The constitution draws its legitimacy and appeal from reasonable justification not just to the generation that approved it, but from later generations, which is why more connotative interpretations of the constitutional text have had the appeal for the Supreme Court and others they historically have had and Madison argued they should have for this reason,[16] at least until at least five members of the court have now embraced, apparently exclusively, the denotative approach. At Breyer bluntly puts the point, "the Court reverses course today for one reason and one reason only, because the composition of this Court has changed."[17] Breyer acidly observes of Alito's argument that it refers "to the 'people' who ratified the Fourteenth Amendment: What rights did those 'people' have in their heads at the time [Founders' denotations]? But, of course, 'people did not ratify' the Fourteenth Amendment. Men did."[18] And his discussion of the mode of the court's originalist argument expresses an almost Swiftian black humor (for Swift, Britain warring on the humanity of the Irish;[19] for Breyer, the Supreme Court on women): "On the one side of 1868, it goes back as far as the 13th century (the 13th!) century,"[20] and in claiming "we must read our foundational charter as viewed at the time of ratification (except that we may also check it against the Dark Ages), it consigns women to second-class citizenship."[21] In effect, "the majority would allow States to ban abortions from

15 See John Hart Ely, *Democracy and Distrust* (Cambridge, MA: Harvard University Press, 1968); John Hart Ely, "The Wages of Crying Wolf: A Comment on *Roe v. Wade*," *Yale Law Journal* 82 (1973): 920–49. For a cogent critique of the role democracy plays in Alito's argument, see Melissa Murray and Katherine Shaw, "Dobbs and Democracy," *Harvard Law Review 127 (2024): forthcoming.*

16 For a fuller defense of this position, see David A. J. Richards, *Foundations of American Constitutionalism* (New York: Oxford University Press, 1989); Ronald Dworkin, *Law's Empire* (Cambridge, MA: Harvard University Press, 1986).

17 *Dobbs*, Breyer, dissenting, pp. 2319–20.

18 Ibid., p. 2324,

19 See Jonathan Swift, "A Modest Proposal for Preventing the Children of Poor People in Ireland from Being a Burthen to Their Parents or Country, and for Making Them Beneficial to the Public," in *A Modest Proposal and Other Satirical Works* (Garden City, NY: Dover, 1996), pp. 52–59.

20 *Dobbs*, Breyer, p. 2323.

21 Ibid., p. 2325.

conception onward because it does not think forced childbirth at all implicates a woman's rights to equality and freedom."[22] But, Justice Breyer might have gone on to observe that the rights of women to equality and freedom have not only been constitutionalized by the 19th Amendment (conferring the right to vote on women), but by the many opinions of the Supreme Court interpreting the Equal Protection Clause that have struck down the use of gender as suspect for reasons analogous to the suspectness of race[23] (though the text of Section 2 of the Fourteenth Amendment apparently expressly limits its terms to men, a fact that infuriated the abolitionist feminists who had worked to secure ratification of the Thirteenth Amendment, and led to suffrage feminism[24]). Whatever normative weight the human rights of women should have, at least on the issue of abortion, disappears by the court so framing the issue that women are invisible because the court's originalism focuses on one thing, and only one thing, the views of the patriarchal men of 1868, and nothing else for them has any constitutional weight whatsoever. The court thus frames its argument in the same originalist terms as John Finnis did, and to similar effect, apparently avoiding the otherwise plausible accusation of sectarian moralism or misogyny if they, like Finnis, were honest about the ground for their possibly sectarian and even patriarchal views about contraception, abortion, and LGBTQ sexuality. Women, as free moral agents, are invisible under patriarchy because women exist normatively only in service of the gender hierarchy of patriarchal men, ruling men lower in the hierarchy and all women. This pattern evidently persists in the many ways women are still not represented in data bearing on their rights and interests,[25] a pattern Carol Gilligan observed to me some years ago in studies of human development that did not include women, more than half the human species, as if women were not human, leading to her own continuing empirical work on the development of girls (personal communication).[26] It persists, anachronistically, in *Dobbs*: seeing the world through a patriarchal prism leads here, as elsewhere, to the invisibility of women as real people and moral agents with minds and bodies, convictions and relationships, authentically their own and thus bearers of the human rights owed all persons.

22 Ibid., p. 2323.

23 On this point, see the opinions of Justice Brennan in *Frontiero v. Richardson*, 411 U.S. 677 (1973); *Craig v. Boren*, 429 U.S. 190 (1978).

24 For an opinion of the Supreme Court that gives weight to this text on the issue of depriving ex-felons of the right to vote, see *Richardson v. Ramirez*, 418 U.S. 24 (1974). For an originalist, the same textual historical argument might be used against the opinions on gender as a suspect classification, yet it has not been raised in that context, showing a more connotative approach to constitutional interpretation.

25 On this point, see Caroline Criado Perez, *Invisible Women: Data Bias in a World Designed for Men* (New York: Abrams Press, 2021).

26 See, e.g., Lyn Mikel Brown and Carol Gilligan, *Meeting at the Crossroads: Women's Psychology and Girls' Development* (Cambridge, MA: Harvard University Press, 1996)

The disappearance of the human rights of an entire class of persons, as normatively and constitutionally invisible, strikes me as quite like another putatively originalist and shocking opinion, *Dred Scott v. Sanford*,[27] in which Chief Justice Taney claims to resolve the national crisis between the then various competing forms of abolitionist and proslavery constitutionalisms by paying no attention whatsoever to the human rights of people of color (think of Lincoln on this point: "if slavery is not wrong, nothing is wrong;"[28] or Garrison, the proslavery constitution as "a covenant with death and an agreement with hell"[29]). Taney resolved nothing, unleashing the most destructive war in American history both in terms of American lives lost and its legacy. There is a similar narcissist arrogance in Alito's opinion for the court in *Dobbs*, serving a reactionary patriarchal politics that with Trump took ideological power in both the presidency and the Senate,[30] all in the name of resolving neutrally the divisive politics of abortion. In fact, like Taney, he has resolved nothing, and has made matters much worse.

There is in *Dobbs* a failure of textual and historical analysis (putting aside, for the moment, its normative problematics) in the originalism the court claims to honor. The great normative clauses of the Fourteenth Amendment, reflecting the abolitionist thought to which they self-consciously give effect, contain the Privileges and Immunities Clause that I believe (with Justice Thomas) is the more interpretively defensible way to think both of the incorporation of the rights in the Bill of Rights as well as rights beyond the Bill of Rights (I come, however, to quite different conclusions from Thomas, myself regarding the constitutional privacy cases he condemns as "demonstrably erroneous decisions"[31] as wholly justified both textually and historically, appealing, as the second Harlan did in *Poe v. Ullman*, to the right to marriage as an instance of the right to intimate life; on this view, constitutional privacy starting in the right to marriage in *Griswold* ends in the highly principled application of the right to gays and lesbians in *Obergefell*, assuming, as I do, following Dworkin, that the legitimacy of the U.S. judiciary's *Marbury* powers rests on its reasonable interpretation of arguments of principle of the basic human rights of all persons owed to all persons as equals, including despised minorities).[32] With respect to

27 19 How. (60 U.S.) 393 (1857).

28 Quoted in David A. J. Richards, *Conscience and the Constitution: History, Theory, and Law of the Reconstruction Amendments* (Princeton, NJ: Princeton University Press, 1993), p. 62.

29 Quoted in ibid., p. 53.

30 On the political psychology of this development, see Carol Gilligan and David A. J. Richards, *The Deepening Darkness: Patriarchy, Resistance, and Democracy's Future* (Cambridge: Cambridge University Press, 2009), and *Darkness Now Visible*. For a recent book coming to quite similar conclusions, see Ivan Jablonka, *A History of Masculinity: From Patriarchy to Gender Justice* (London: Allen Lane, 2019).

31 See *Dobbs*, Thomas, J., concurring, p. 2301.

32 For a full exposition and defense of this position, see Richards, *Conscience and the Constitution*, pp. 217–32.

the latter, there is a rich history of the atrocity of American slavery taken very seriously by both the abolitionist movement and the Reconstruction Congress, and any reasonable attention to both text and history must take it seriously. Alito does neither.

There are two remarkable books, both by women of color, that offer relevant history on this point. The first is by my colleague, Peggy Davis, *Neglected Stories*;[33] the second is by Dorothy Roberts, *Killing the Black Body*.[34] Both point to the moral horror of abolitionists not only or mainly at the denial to people of color of the right to free labor, but to abridgment of the inalienable right to marriage (a right clearly understood as a basic right by leading Founders in 1787[35]); slaves in Protestant America, in contrast to Catholic Latin America, were not permitted to marry. There is a quite good reason why this right would not have been explicitly textually guaranteed by the Bill of Rights of 1791: the Bill of Rights was to apply only to the federal government that, under the federal system, had no jurisdiction over marriage, an issue for the states. The Fourteenth Amendment was expressly understood to fill the lacuna, acknowledged by Madison himself,[36] of the failure of the constitution to protect human rights violated by the states, and the atrocity of American slavery was one glaring example of this failure, taken seriously by abolitionists, in particular, by abolitionist women, black and white. The consequence of this for the people of color held in slavery was the traumatizing and heart-breaking experience that their mothers or fathers, husbands or wives, sisters or brothers, aunts or uncles, children, et al. could be and in many cases would be sold South as slavery was less economically lucrative in Virginia than further South. Persons held in American slavery were, in effect, cattle or, even worse, things, commodities.[37]

The denial of the inalienable right to marriage to any group is, I have come to think, one of the crucial ways by which culturally entrenched irrational prejudices like racism and anti-Semitism dehumanize whole classes of persons, a brilliant point that Justice Kennedy suggests at the beginning of his opinion for the Supreme Court in *Romer v. Evans*,[38] analogizing the first Harlan's dissent in *Plessy v. Ferguson* condemning the construction of a racist caste system in the U.S. to the abridgment of basic rights to Colorado Amendment Two, which strips homosexuals of all basic rights (thus, constructing yet another caste system).[39] Justice Kennedy does not there focus on the abridgment of the right

33 See Peggy Cooper Davis, *Neglected Stores: The Constitution and Family Values* (New York: Hill & Wang, 1997).

34 Dorothy Roberts, *Killing the Black Body: Race, Reproduction, and the Meaning of Liberty* (New York: Vintage, 1997).

35 On this point, see Richards, *Conscience and the Constitution*, p. 226.

36 On this point, see ibid., pp. 23–24.

37 On Southern racist rationalizations for such atrocities, see ibid., pp. 226–27.

38 517 U.S. 620 (1996).

39 On caste systems, see Isabel Wilkerson, *Caste: The Origins of Our Discontents* (New York: Random House, 2020).

to marriage specifically, but the analogy is very much at work when later in *Obergefell v. Hodges* he argues, in defending the extension of the inalienable right to marriage to homosexuals as a matter of principle, that the denial of this right to homosexuals "demeans gays and lesbians,"[40] enforcing the homophobic view that their loving intimate lives are, like the similar anti-miscegenation laws directed at people of color and Jews, subhuman.

Both Peggy Davis and Dorothy Roberts in their important books focus on the role of the right to intimate life and, more fundamentally in Lockean terms, to the right to the body in abolitionist thought. Abridgment of these rights rationalized on racist grounds allowed slave-owners violently to force women of color held in slavery to procreate, regarding the children as valuable additional commodities for work, sexual exploitation, or sale.[41] Such control over procreation extended to control as well over what "Southern medical journals occasionally documented," namely "the abortion practices that planters found so disturbing."[42] It is against this background that both textual and historical analysis, the heart of any plausible forms of originalism, would or should condemn the proposition Breyer ascribes to the majority in *Dobbs*, "the majority would allow States to ban abortions from conception onward because it does not think forced childbirth at all implicates a woman's rights to equality and freedom."[43] State criminalization of abortion is exactly the "forced childbirth" that abolitionist thought condemned as among the central evils of American slavery. It surely cannot be that such an evil is only an evil when the product of racism, for in fact the kind of patriarchal control over black sexuality is the same patriarchal control that any good historian of the history of American abortion laws would have identified as an important strand in the role of the American medical profession in securing anti-abortion laws in 1868, a point another of my colleagues, Sylvia Law, made in her amici brief for American historians in *Planned Parenthood v. Casey*.[44] What makes the opinion of the *Dobbs* court even more historically illiterate is that the real consequence of its opinion will bear most harshly on black women of color in Mississippi, precisely the women of color both Peggy Davis and Dorothy Roberts show should be at the heart of a historically informed opinion of the views of the Reconstruction Congress. Alito cannot see this history because his version of originalism regards it as irrelevant though it alone explains the complex cultural history of abortion in America, including the state of the law in 1868.

40 See Noah R. Feldman and Kathleen M. Sullivan, *Constitutional Law*, 20th ed. (St. Paul, MN: Foundation Press, 2019), p. 586.

41 See Davis, *Neglected Stories*, pp. 174–81.

42 Roberts, *Killing the Black Body*, p. 47.

43 Ibid., p. 12.

44 See *Planned Parenthood v. Casey*, 1992 U.S. S. Ct. Briefs, Lexis, 291.

Dorothy Roberts makes the case at some length in her book that a wide range of laws and practices dealing with the sexuality of women of color should be understood as continuous with the dehumanization of people of color under slavery, including what she calls the dark side of birth control (eugenics), Norplant and contraceptive vaccines imposed on women of color, criminal laws directed at pregnant black women who use drugs, and discriminatory welfare laws. She concludes, like Peggy Davis, that a woman's control of her body and sexuality, is an aspect of the constitutional conception of equal liberty, and what we should learn from the experience of women of color under slavery and after slavery is that abridgment of such control dehumanizes, rationalizing injustice, indeed, rendering such injustice invisible. Perpetuating such invisibility is, from this perspective, the point of Alito's version of originalism, in this respect, quite like *Dred Scott*—in *Dred*, people of color, in *Dobbs*, women. In the one case, the invisibility is in the name of property rights in slaves, in the other, the denial of property rights of women, as Roberts points out, in their own bodies. Americans don't like to think of themselves as having a continuing problem with patriarchy, a problem Carol Gilligan and I have argued in our two books as the greatest threat to democracy, as artists in democracies like Aeschylus have seen since *The Oresteia*.[45] *Dobbs* illustrates how painfully wrong they are.

In contrast, Chief Justice Roberts, though he concurs with the majority in its result (overruling viability), takes an altogether more reasonable line. Roberts acknowledges that there is a constitutionally protected interest in access to abortion, but argues that, in view of that interest, women must be allowed a reasonable period of exit from carrying the fetus to term.[46] But, the Mississippi law he upholds on this ground allows three months, and my question is whether, in view of the experience of women of color in Mississippi and elsewhere, this is reasonable. Apparently, it is not and this consideration persuaded the majority in *Roe* to move the constitutional line from the first trimester to viability.[47]

What is this constitutionally protected interest? Both Peggy Davis and Dorothy Roberts show us what it is, the right to intimate life and to the body. Having a child is one of the most intimate choices in anyone's life and it is, as Carol Gilligan has shown in her work with girls and young women, in its nature a relational right, whether one will have or form a relationship to a child with all that means for women and for children and for all of us. Only women have this experience and their experience should have decisive weight in a reasonable

45 See Gilligan and Richards, *The Deepening Darkness* and *Darkness Now Visible*.

46 See *Dobbs*, Chief Justice Roberts, concurring, pp. 2310–17.

47 See James D. Robenalt, "The Unknown Supreme Court Clerk Who Single-Handedly Created the *Roe v. Wade* Viability Standard," www.bunkhistory.org/resources/the-unknown-supreme-court-clerk-who-single-handedly-created-the-roe-v-wade-viability-standard; Joan Biskupic, "How the Supreme Court Crafted Its *Roe v. Wade* Decision and What It Means Today," www.com/2021/009/23/politics/roe-v-wade.history/index.html.

view of the scope of exit, which may be the real justification for *Roe*'s appeal to viability (in contrast, say, to birth), a symbolic bright line allowing a robust right to women of exit but, by allowing prohibition in the third trimester, distinguishing abortion from infanticide (birth, as the line, would arguably have been too close in popular perception to infanticide, and few, one philosopher excepted,[48] would want to extend the right of exit of abortion and the reasons for exit to killing young infants). There is also the view taken by the plurality three justices in *Planned Parenthood v. Casey*, who uphold viability as the line for exit, appealing to what sounds to me very much like a free exercise argument about what gives life meaning ("At the heart of liberty is the right to define one's own concept of existence, of meaning, of the universe, and of the mystery of human life. Beliefs about these matters could not define the attributes of personhood were they formed under compulsion of the State."[49]) There is, in fact, a close doctrinal relationship between free exercise and constitutional privacy,[50] and the plurality opinion, which the Alito opinion with characteristic lack of humility dismisses, is on to something. It would not surprise me at all if the many religious women from traditions that reject conception as the moral line for permissible abortions, some rather regarding birth as the proper line, would bring such actions on the basis of free exercise, a right to which the current ideological majority on the Supreme Court gives greater normative weight than previous courts.

This brings us to the question of how far Alito and the others in the majority will carry their version of originalism. The three other cases I mentioned earlier—the gun rights opinion[51] and two opinions on issues of anti-establishment and free exercise[52]—suggest quite far indeed.

The religion clause opinions seem to me not plausibly originalist at all, one (*Carson v. Makin*, allowing state funding to a private religious school) and the other (*Kennedy v. Bremerton*, allowing a high school football coach to engage in prayer in midfield after a game). Neither acknowledges, let alone takes seriously, what may be one of the most insightful features of the constitutional liberalism of Thomas Jefferson and James Madison, namely anti-establishment, which the Supreme Court has correctly regarded as enforceable against the states under the Fourteenth Amendment. We need to remind ourselves of just how path-breaking the thought of Jefferson and Madison on this point was.

48 See Michael Tooley, *Abortion and Infanticide* (Oxford: Oxford University Press, 1985).

49 *Planned Parenthood of Southeastern Pa. v. Casey*, 505 U.S. 833 (1992), in Feldman and Sullivan, *Constitutional Law*, pp. 531–38 at 532.

50 See John Sexton, "Note, Toward a Constitutional Definition of Religion," *Harvard Law Review* 91 (1978): 1056.

51 *New York State Rifle & Pistol Association, Inc. v. Bruen, 142 S.Ct.* 2111 (2022).

52 *Carson v. Makin*, 142 S.Ct. 1987 (2022); *Kennedy v. Bremerton School District*, 142 S.Ct. 20220).

Rooted in Locke's argument for toleration, Jefferson, in drafting the Virginia Bill for Religious Freedom that forbids state tax money to go to or otherwise support religious teaching, argues "but where he [Locke] stopped short, we may go on,"[53] not only arguing for a more expansive scope for free exercise than Locke endorsed (excluding Catholics and atheists), but forbidding state support for religious teaching as such. The idea, for Jefferson and Madison, was not so much to protect the state from religion, but religion from the state, having in mind the long history of how, under Constantine and later political leaders, the establishment of Christianity as the church of the Roman Empire had corrupted what Protestants took to be the humanism of the non-violent teachings of Jesus, leading to the Inquisition, the Crusades, religious wars among Christians, religious anti-Semitism, absolutism, and the like. None of the originalist opinions about the religion clauses even acknowledges the weight of the thought of Jefferson and Madison on these issues, and cannot, for this reason, be regarded as rooted in text and history. This is originalism without foundations, sectarian religious ideology untethered by any sense of reasonable constitutional interpretation of the oldest written constitution in the world to which, paradoxically, these originalists claim to pay homage.

It is bad enough that the case for interpreting the Second Amendment to protect gun rights was so textually and historically weak, as the dissenters cogently argued in both *District of Columbia v. Heller*[54] and *McDonald v. City of Chicago*;[55] if there is a more plausible argument for some degree of constitutional protection, it lies in the area of unenumerated rights as Justice Stevens argued in his dissent in *McDonald*, namely, the right of self-defense of "say, an elderly widow who lives in a dangerous neighborhood and does not have the strength to operate a long gun."[56] But, the current ideological majority on the court is, following, so it appears, Justice Scalia, hostile to such rights. In contrast, the originalism of the current majority foists on the nation with the worst incidence of gun violence among comparable advanced nations sheer anachronism (looking to gun use in 1791 as fixing meaning at least as the required constitutional starting point). If *Dobbs* is not enough to suggest patriarchy drives the current majority, as it strips women of constitutional rights, *Bruen* reveals a majority correspondingly and irresponsibly enhancing the often patriarchal powers of men prone to violence,[57] a far cry from Justice Stevens' humane focus on the right of self-defense of "an elderly widow." The issue of gender seems, in the context of the

53 Quoted in David A. J. Richards, *Toleration and the Constitution* (Oxford: Oxford University Press, 1986), p. 112.

54 554 U.S. 570 (2008).

55 561 U.S. 742 (2010).

56 See Feldman and Sullivan, *Constitutional Law*, p. 479.

57 See James Gilligan, *Reflections on a National Epidemic* (New York: Vintage, 1997).

court's originalism, inescapable though, through the patriarchal prism of their originalism, invisible.

It was a philosopher, Judith Jarvis Thompson, who first pointed out how difficult it was to imagine any man who would tolerate the kind of burdens that coerced pregnancy imposes on women.[58] Thompson's example had to be a kind of fantasy (a man, hooked up to a great violinist for 9 months, and required to endure that demand) because such demands are so far from men's experience, and that lack of experience or what comes to the same thing, experience idealized through a sectarian religious prism of women's appropriate sexuality, may, better than anything, explain the psychology of the *Dobbs* majority and the quite unreasonable arrogance, the lack of humility, of its blinkered and unimaginative originalism.

Perhaps, at this point, we should turn not to philosophy, but to the cultural psychology of patriarchy in order to understand *Dobbs*. Carol Gilligan and Naomi Snider in a recent book trace the persistence of patriarchy to a developmental psychology under patriarchy in which "relationships of mutuality—the cornerstone of intimacy—are … exchanged for relationships of complementarity, relationships where each person unconsciously seeks to find in the other the thing they cannot admit to or accept in themselves,"[59] for women the desire for independence covered by an ideology of self-sacrifice, for men emotional vulnerability covered by an ideology of autarkic independence. From this perspective, the majority in *Dobbs* exemplifies indeed enforces such persistence—women required to sacrifice, men invulnerable to their real emotions and lives.

Closer to the subject under discussion in *Dobbs*, such patriarchal psychology is critically discussed by persons from within the Catholic tradition, who know its unreasonable demands, as women and men, at first hand. A former Catholic priest, Eugene Kennedy, and a nun, Sister Jackowski, have explored the idealization of mothers (as asexual) and the denigration of sexual women of the Augustinian tradition that requires celibacy of the priesthood. Augustine's developmental psychology from sexual man to celibate monk shows a process of traumatic loss of the woman he sexually loved and rejected and from his idealized mother at her death. Both Kennedy and Jackowski argue that the psychology of celibacy of Catholic priests often rest on intense, highly idealized relations to their mothers that reflects a lack of real relationships with them or to women generally, an idealization arising from loss and a wounded sexuality that angrily blames women for their misery (rationalizing misogyny) and accordingly rationalizes the unjust patriarchal authority of the priesthood in matters of gender and sexuality. This deeply patriarchal psychology idealizes a conception

58 Judith Jarvis Thompson, "A Defense of Abortion," *Philosophy & Public Affairs* 1:1 (1971): 47–66.

59 Carol Gilligan and Naomi Snider, *Why Does Patriarchy Persist* (Cambridge, MA: Polity, 2018), p. 70.

of self-sacrificing, indeed asexual motherhood (reflected in the role of the Virgin Mary in Catholic piety). In consequence, the resulting Catholic teaching cannot take seriously the decision of real women facing difficult circumstances and trying to do their best for the web of relationships in their lives, rather, transforming a responsible moral decision by women into murder in service of a sectarian conception of fetal life at conception that many reject and reasonably reject.[60] Margaret Attwood makes this point in pointing out why the women in her prophetic novel dress as they do:

> The modesty costumes work by the women of Gilead are derived from Western religious iconography—the Wives war the blue of purity from the Virgin Mary, the Handmaids wear read, from the blood of parturition, but also from Mary Magdalene ... Many totalitarians have used clothing both forbidden and enforced, to identify and control people—think of yellow stars and Roman purple—and many have ruled beyond a religious front. It makes the creation of heretics that much easier.[61]

The point is that these women act as sexual agents defying patriarchal controls on their sexuality, and must be punished.

This sectarian ideology, based in the Augustinian-Thomistic view that all sex must be procreational, thus wars on and indeed condemns the legitimate sexual freedom of women because abortion frees them from a just punishment (having a child) for exercising a sexual freedom women do not and should not have. For these sectarians, having an abortion is justly punishable precisely because women having abortions are exercising a sexual freedom that patriarchy condemns. That is the central point: women having abortions exercise a sexual freedom from patriarchal control that patriarchy must condemn, and they must be punished—patriarchy's war on women.

It is of historical interest that the views on sexuality and gender of the Roman Catholic Church, so rooted in Roman patriarchal structures since it became the established church of the Roman Empire in the early fourth century C.E., should have carried forward and, if anything, further enforced features of Roman patriarchy's concern with controlling the sexual freedom of women who challenged through adultery control of their personal lives, indeed, in the provisions of Constantius and Constans in 330 C.E., called for stricter enforcement of these laws, decreeing that adulterers be punished "as though they were manifest parricides," by being sewn up in a leather sack with a dog, a cock,

60 For further argument, see David A. J. Richards, *Fundamentalism in American Religion and Law: Obama's Challenge to Patriarchy's Threat to Democracy* (Cambridge: Cambridge University Press, 2010), pp. 131–52. For Jackowski on Augustine, see pp. 132–33; for Kennedy on idealization and abortion, see p. 151.

61 Attwood, *The Handmaid's Tale*, p. xvii.

a viper, and a monkey, and cast into a river or the sea.[62] It is surely important that new natural law effectively enforces the papacy's moral condemnation of all forms of non-procreational sex. In effect, an absolute monarchy of celibate men (women cannot be priests) enforces a moral orthodoxy on central matters of sexuality and gender not only on women, but on everyone. The comments of Eugene Kennedy and Sister Jackowski suggest an underlying psychology of the idealization of mothers that motivates such a sectarian moral orthodoxy, in which the experience of real women has, to say the least, paid no role. Yet, it is this anachronistic ideology tied to an anti-democratic moral absolutism of a papal absolutist monarchy of celibate men that justifies without any secular basis the punishment of women whose sexual freedom reasonably includes access to abortion services.

Consider, from this perspective, Alito's list of what may count as *rational* bases for anti-abortion laws:

> respect for and preservation of prenatal life at all stages of development …; the protection of maternal health and safety; the elimination of particularly gruesome or barbaric medical procedures; the preservation of the integrity of the medical profession; the mitigation of fetal pain; and the prevention of discrimination on the basis of race, sex, or disability.[63]

Fetal life is given apparently decisive weight "at all stages of development;" what counts as "gruesome or barbaric medical procedures" as a standard of law is about as "neutral" as the moral disgust that was once the measure of what could be prosecuted as obscene in the U.S.; and what counts for the court as discrimination ignores the fact that this decision bespeaks a misogyny that cannot see or acknowledge the harm it has inflicted on women in general and black women in particular. And it explicitly allows a state's punishment of women seeking abortions.

There is a conspicuous gap in Alito's conclusion between what is said to be and what is, the same kind of mystification that psychoanalysts see in analysands: "the patient learns not to know what the patient knows she knows but is not supposed to know."[64] Psychoanalysts often discover with their analysands the powerful role of parents in using language to mystify, leading to disassociation, masking what a person knows but is not supposed to know. What Alito does not see is that for him, like Finnis, the appeal of originalism is in the same way an ideological mask, a mask so powerful that he is unaware of what on some level is plainly obvious, that his sectarian religious views are the basis

62 On this point, see Gilligan and Richards, *The Deepening Darkness*, p. 42.

63 *Dobbs*, Alito, J., at p. 2284.

64 Edgar A. Levenson, "The Enigma of the Transference," *Contemporary Psychoanalysis*, Vol 45, No. 2, ISSN 0010-7530, pp. 163–78, at p. 168. I am indebted for this reference to Naomi Snider.

for legitimating the punishment of women who resist patriarchal constraints on their sexuality. Of course, in making this claim, I am moving from personal to political psychology, but the role the Supreme Court majority is playing in *Dobbs* is, if I am right, so masking its own sectarian commitments that it must mystify what it is in fact doing, acting as a theocratic not a secular parent to a nation, a personal psychology write large.

I have argued elsewhere that there is an important connection between the role of fundamentalism in religion and law, and tried to expose the similar role of patriarchy in both.[65] That book was inspired by my hopes in Barack Obama, whose autobiography quite conspicuously explores his own struggle with patriarchy in his relationship to his absent father and his coming to resist it both in his marriage and his politics.[66] It is, to say the least, unusual for a straight man, let alone an ambitious politician, even to see the psychological power of patriarchy in his own life, let alone resist it. The continuing power of patriarchy in American culture has for me only been confirmed by the reactionary politics his two terms as president apparently unleashed in American politics.[67] It has now been confirmed not only by Trump's victory but by his three appointments to the Supreme Court and their nakedly patriarchal originalism. We will only responsibly, as lawyers and citizens and Americans, deal with this problem when we see the problem.

Burke gave a name, "political religion," to the psychological role new natural law is playing in shaping both American and British constitutional law. "Political religion" was, as we saw (Chapter 1), central to Burke's analysis of the political psychology that had destroyed any possibility of liberal constitutionalism both in the English Civil War and the French Revolution. Both the Puritan sectarians in the English Civil War and the Jacobins in the French Revolution had abandoned the universalist humanism Burke regarded as central to Christianity for sectarian fanaticisms incapable of respecting deliberative secular reason, warring on those who disagree with them in terms, "unreal human rights," that conceal the motives of violent patriarchal repression that have historically motivated such anti-democratic ideologies, as they do now in the populist ideologies that threaten liberal constitutionalism. New natural law is a "political religion" in precisely this sense. Its normative claims are today not secular, and indeed widely regarded as unreasonable (Americans now support contraception, abortion access, and gay marriage); and it tracks the views of a now conspicuously patriarchal reactionary religion that enforces the shaming of legitimate sexual freedom (rationalizing sexist and homophobic violence of laws criminalizing such freedom); and its interpretive originalist claims are

65 See Richards, *Fundamentalism in American Religion and Law*.

66 See Barack Obama, *Dreams from My Father* (New York: Three Rivers Press, 2004).

67 On this point, see Gilligan and Richards, *Darkness Now Visible*.

incoherent. The distinguished legal theorist David Dyzenhaus sees it, as I do, as "profoundly reactionary,"[68] and goes on to observe:

> In fact, … it is so reactionary that it is plausible to view it as not only anti-liberal but as anti-legal, in much the same way that Carl Schmitt's theory is both these things. If my suggestion is correct, Finnis's theory is, unlike the command and Kantian theories, not even a candidate for a "political theory."[69]

Schmitt, of course, rationalized Hitler's exercise of executive powers to establish his totalitarian rule. From this perspective new natural law is, like Schmitt's constitutionalism, ideally suited to express and rationalize a populist politics that is both anti-democratic and anti-liberal, a role it has apparently played in both the U.S. and the U.K.

So, how could new natural law come to have the political force it came to have in Trump's populist politics, leading the Republican Party to endorse appointments to the Supreme Court that were to effect, at a minimum, the overruling of *Roe v. Wade*? New natural law rests on an anachronistic moral theory of a right to enforce the Catholic Church's prohibition of non-procreational sex regarded by its coreligionists as rights, for example, of a fetus to life and women's culpable lack of maternal self-sacrifice, and thus abortion is morally the same as murder. Like any "political religion," its utopian ideology rests on unreal rights and duties and draws its political appeal by mobilizing a shame-driven repressive violence directed at any upsetting of traditional patriarchal gender roles (persons, men and women, shamed by the questioning of patriarchal gender roles by feminists and so many others, including the rights of women to sexual liberty and autonomy). A reactionary shame-driven politics, humiliated by the questioning of the gender binary and hierarchy central to patriarchy, thus turns its mindless collective rage, encouraged by the lies and distortions of a deeply patriarchal man, on one of the best qualified presidential candidates in American constitutional history, Hillary Clinton.[70] There evidently were sufficient numbers of persons not only to elect Trump but, in his attempt to retain power, members of the Republican Party to support the right-wing appointments to the Supreme Court that gave us what they were put there to do, overrule *Roe v. Wade*, for the most specious of reasons, an originalism rooted in misogyny, in effect, working patriarchy's revenge on women's sexual freedom, legitimating state punishment of women seeking abortions

68 Dyzenhaus, *The Long Arc of Legality: Hobbes, Kelsen, Hart*, p. 435.

69 See ibid., p. 436.

70 On this point, see Gilligan and Richards, *Darkness Now Visible*. See also Michael J. Diamond, *Ruptures in the American Psyche: Containing Destructive Populism in Perilous Times* (Bicester: Phoenix, 2022).

It is striking that it was at the point, when these appointments had been made, that new natural law plays the role it does in *Dobbs*, allowing justices to give expression to personal religious views rooted in a patriarchal tradition they had never seriously questioned, a tradition never acknowledged as playing the role in the opinion it clearly does. New natural law gave them a way of masking such unconstitutional motives in the form of an originalism that in fact betrays Madison's ambition of a written constitution that would speak to later generations about human rights and how to realize and enforce them, an ambition centered by Jefferson and Madison on a Lockean secular state innovated well beyond Locke in both the free exercise and anti-establishment clauses of the First Amendment of the Bill of Rights (see Chapter 4).

In Chapter 2, I examined Madison's response to Jefferson's proposal that the constitution be amended every 19 years. Madison objected to such frequent amendment in *Federalist* No. 49 in the most Burkean argument Madison ever made, defending the proper role of history in constitutional interpretation as an alternative to frequent amendment:

> It may be considered as an objection inherent in the principle that every appeal to the people would carry an implication of some defect in the government, frequent appeals would, in great measure, deprive the government of that veneration which time bestows on everything, and without which perhaps the wisest and freest government would not possess the requisite stability … . The reason of man, like man himself, is timid and cautious then left alone, and acquires firmness and confidence in proportion to the number with which is it is associated … . In a nation of philosophers, this consideration ought to be disregarded. A reverence for the laws would be sufficiently inculcated by the voice of an enlightened reason. But a nation of philosophers is as little to be expected as the philosophical race of kings wished for by Plato. And in every other nation, the most rational government will not find it a superfluous advantage to have the prejudices of the community on its side.[71]

For Burke, political forms must be tested by cumulative historical experience over time, and he wrote about the proper weight of history in constitutionalism in exactly the same way Madison did:

> We are afraid to put men to live and trade each on his own private stock of reason, because we suspect that this stock in each man is small, and that the individuals would do better to avail themselves of the general bank and capital of nations, and of ages. Many of our men of speculation, instead of

71 See Alexander Hamilton, James Madison, and John Jay, *The Federalist Papers* (Garden City, NY: Dover, 2014), p. 247.

> exploding general prejudices, employ their sagacity to discover the latent wisdom, which prevails in them. If they find what they seek, and they seldom fail, they think it more wise to continue the prejudice, with the reason involved, than to cast away the prejudice, and to leave nothing but the naked reason; because prejudice, with its reason, has a motive to give action to that reason, and an affection which will give it permanence.[72]

Nothing in Madison's Burkean defense of the appropriate weight of history in constitutional interpretation supports the form of originalism that the current U.S. Supreme Court appeals to in *Dobbs* and other opinions, which accord a weight to history closer to Filmer than to Locke, denying precisely the Lockean weight each generation has to experience and give effect to liberal values by its own lights and experience through ascribing more abstract connotative meaning to quite generally stated written texts (free speech, anti-establishment and free exercise, due process, privileges and immunities, equal protection) responsive to both history and experience. It is not just, however, that the court's approach has no defensible roots in the Madison's Burkean idea of a written constitution for the generations, but, much more seriously, it ignores the embodiment of the deepest values of the Founders' liberalism realized and to be kept alive (against political factions) through the interpretation of the constitution that shows that "prejudice, with its reason, has a motive to give action to that reason, and an affection which will give it permanence." Those values are quite explicit in the text and spirit of the guarantees of both anti-establishment and the free exercise of conscience in the First Amendment of the Bill of Rights, probably the most important guarantees of political liberalism that Jefferson and Madison bequeathed to later generations of Americans and to the world, the requirement of a secular state. However, my argument shows that, on close examination, *Dobbs* flouts that argument, enforcing an unreasonable sectarian religious view on the nation at large. Thus, its illegitimacy.

7.2 New Natural Law in U.K. Politics

The new natural lawyers and their associates have played an increasingly important role in Britain in British debates over the repeal or watering down of the Human Rights Act recently proposed by the Johnson government or its successor. Their views are reflected in a number of articles in *Policy Exchange*, critical of the impact of opinions of the European Court of Human Rights, under the European Convention of Human Rights, on British policy (e.g., requiring the British government to change its views banning gay in the military) and the impact of the HRA on more aggressive judicial review by the British court on

72 Burke, *Reflections*, p. 90.

human rights and other issues (e.g., the Supreme Court of the U.K. striking down as unconstitutional Johnson's suspension of parliament). This is a live political issue in Britain because of the successful politics of Brexit, led as I write this by its now outgoing Prime Minister, Boris Johnson, and the two prime ministers that succeeded him, a politics that would release Britain as a nation to pursue its own way free of the constraints of its membership of the European Union. The Johnson government, consistent with its support of resurgent British nationalism, finds it politically popular to release Britain as well from European conceptions of human rights enforced by British courts under the HRA, although not yet advocating departure from the European Convention of Human Rights itself in which post-World War II Britain played an important role in designing and implementing, analogous to its role with the U.S. in supporting transnational institutions like the United Nations and NATO.[73] Britain is, of course, much more culturally and politically liberal (on issues like contraception, abortion, and LGBTQ rights, all of which were decriminalized by parliament, not the judiciary) than the U.S. and Finnis' arguments on these issues have had much less political resonance there than in the U.S., but his views have had an impact on the Johnson's government recent proposals regarding the HRA and, to the extent resting on indefensibly sectarian views of human rights, should be recognized and questioned in Britain on that basis.

The central figure is John Finnis, who in a number of articles not only supported Brexit, urged Britain's withdrawal from the European Court of Human Rights, and criticized the recent U.K. Supreme Court decisions in *R (Miller) v. Secretary of State for Exiting the European Union*[74] and *R (Miller) v. The Prime Minister and Cherry v. Advocate General for Scotland*,[75] all in alleged service of returning political power in Britain, including the protection of rights, to parliament alone.[76] Contra Finnis, these opinions illustrate how and

73 For a magisterial study, see A. W. Brian Simpson, *Human Rights and the End of Empire: Britain and the Genesis of the European Convention* (Oxford: Oxford University Press, 2001).

74 [2017] UKSC 5.

75 [2019] UKSC 41.

76 See John Finnis, "'Intent of Parliament' Unsoundly Constructed," *Judicial Power Project*, November 4, 2016, https://judicialpowerproject.org.uk/john-finnis-intent-of-parliament-unsoundly-constructed; "Judicial Power and the Balance of Our Constitution," *Policy Exchange*, http://judicialpowerproject.org.uk/wp-content/uploads/2018/01/Judicial-Power-and-the-Balance-of-Our-Constitution.pdf; "Brexit and the Balance of Our Constitution," *Judicial Power Project*, http://judicialpowerproject.org.uk/wp-content/uploads/2016/12/Finnis-2016-Brexit-and-the-Balance-of-Our-Constitution2.pdf; "Judicial Power: Past, Present and Future," *Judicial Power Project*, October 20, 2015, http://judicialpowerproject.org.uk/wp-content/uploads/2015/10/John-Finnis-lecture-20102015.pdf; "Judicial Usurpation and Human Rights," *Judicial Power Project*, March 8, 2018, https://judicialpowerproject.org.uk/john-finnis-judicial-usurpation-and-human-rights/; "Terminating Treaty-Based UK Rights," *Judicial Power Project*, October 26, 2016, http://judicialpowerproject.org.uk/wp-content/uploads/2016/10/Finnis-2016-Terminating-Treaty-based-UK-Rights-v2.pdf; "Terminating Treaty-Based UK Rights: A Supplementary

why such judicial power is needed to preserve the very legitimacy of parliamentary supremacy over executive abuses, as Paul Craig has convincingly argued.[77] Yet, allegedly wedded to parliamentary powers alone, Finnis questions a decision that protects and preserves such powers.

Finnis' defense of executive power in the *Miller* cases, so inconsistent with a traditional understanding of parliamentary supremacy, confirms Dyzenhaus' criticism of Finnis' theories as "reactionary," rationalizing precisely the executive powers that Schmitt constitutionally defended to legitimate Hitler's populist totalitarianism. Such a theory can barely be regarded, Dyzenhaus argues, as a *legal* theory at all since the rule of law does not play the central normative role it must and should.

Finnis' arguments, here and elsewhere, are no more coherent or well supported in law,[78] and indeed rest on originalist appeals to quite early British constitutional history that, in contrast to the U.S. quite old written constitution, make little sense in Britain with an unwritten constitution interpreted by a parliamentary supremacy justified by its flexible deliberative adjustments to contemporary circumstances.

Note," *Judicial Power Project*, November 2, 2016, http://judicialpowerproject.org.uk/wp-content/uploads/2016/11/Finnis-2016-Supplementary-Note-pg.pdf; "Terminating Treaty-Based UK Rights," *Constitutional Law Group*, October 26, 2016, https://ukconstitutionallaw.org/2016/10/26/john-finnis-terminating-treaty-based-uk-rights/; "Terminating Treaty-Based UK Rights: A Supplementary Note," *Constitutional Law Group*, November 2, 2016, https://ukconstitutionallaw.org/2016/11/02/john-finnis-terminating-treaty-based-uk-rights-a-supplementary-note/; "The Law of the Constitutional Before the Court," *Policy Exchange*, https://policyexchange.org.uk/wp-content/uploads/The-Law-of-the-Constitution-before-the-Court.pdf; "The Miller Majority: Reliant on European Perspectives and Counsel's Failings," *Judicial Power Project*, January 25, 2017, http://judicialpowerproject.org.uk/john-finnis-the-miller-majority-reliant-on-european-perspectives-and-counsels-failings/; "The Unconstitutionality of the Supreme Court's Prorogation Judgment," *Policy Exchange*, https://policyexchange.org.uk/publication/the-unconstitutionality-of-the-supreme-courts-prorogation-judgment/#:~:text=September%2028%2C%202019-,The%20unconstitutionality%20of%20the%20Supreme%20Court's%20prorogation%20judgment,the%20Government%20to%20prorogue%20Parliament; "Two Too Many," *Policy Exchange*, November 24, 2016 https://policyexchange.org.uk/john-finnis-two-too...

77 See Paul Craig, "Constitutionality, Convention, and Prorogation," in *The UK Supreme Court Yearbook, Volume 10* (London: Appellate Press), pp. 1–26; "The Supreme Court, Prorogation and Constitutional Principle," *Public Law* (Apr. 2020): 248–77; "Response to Loughlin's Note on Miller; Cherry," *Public Law* (April 2020): 282–86. See also Paul Craig, "Judicial Power, the Judicial Power Project, and the UK," *University of Queensland Law Journal* 36 (2017): 355–74; "Legislative Intent and Legislative Supremacy: A Reply to Professor Allan," *Oxford Journal of Legal Studies* 24:4 (2004): 585–96; "Ultra Vires and the Foundations of Judicial Review," *Cambridge Law Journal* 57:1 (1998): 63–90; "Public Law, Political Theory and Legal Theory," *Public Law* (2000): 211; "Political Constitutionalism and the Judicial Role: A Response," *International Journal of Constitutional Law* 9 (2011): 112.

78 For a further critique along these lines, see Craig, "Judicial Power, the Judicial Power Project and the UK."

My interest here is in how Finnis' quite bad arguments in these articles reflect the same exoteric quality of his arguments for new natural law that conceal, on examination, what is for him really at stake, his esoteric defense of the sectarian religious doctrines of the Papacy. It is striking surely that in the initial debate over these issues Finnis published a 2019 *Daily Telegraph* article, "Only one option remains with Brexit—prorogue parliament and allow us out of the EU with no deal,"[79] joining populist forces very much defended by the newspaper in question, urging precisely the position the executive was to take and that the U.K. Supreme Court would unanimously strike down for compelling constitutional reasons. Supporting such populist forces on one issue masks, as is common in Finnis' work, sectarian arguments with much less appeal.

Finnis has made quite clear, in his lecture on judicial power, that he regards the opinions of the U.S. Supreme Court on the right to abortion as well as gay marriage as non-judicial. The abortion decisions were "disreputable, legally indefensible, and even as showing no sense of an obligation to be constitutionally sound in adjudication,"[80] and the decisions legitimating gay marriage "as so defective in legal argumentation as to be almost unreadable by professionals,"[81] a decision, as I earlier argued, that is a highly principled elaboration of the constitutional right to marriage. But, Finnis then does on to criticize decisions of the European Court of Human Rights, in particular, their interpretation of the basic rights of the European Convention as "living interpretation"[82] requiring closer scrutiny of their proportionality.[83] Finnis' conservative critique of such judicial review should be contrasted with the left-wing critique of John Griffith and others,[84] concerned to cabin judicial interpretations that have historically limited the ends of socialism.[85]

What is, in fact, Finnis' concern is the role that the European Court of Human Rights played in *Dudgeon*,[86] holding the criminalization of gay sex in Northern

79 John Finnis, "Only one option remains with Bexit—prorogue parliament and allow us out of the EU with no deal," *Daily Telegraph*, April 1, 2019, at www.telegraph.co.uk/politics/2019/04/01/one-option-remains

80 Finnis, "Judicial Power and the Balance of Our Constitution," p. 37.

81 Ibid., p. 38.

82 Ibid., p. 56.

83 On this point, see John Finnis, "Judicial Law-Making and the 'Living' Instrumentalism of the ECHR," in N. W. Barber, Richard Elkin, and Paul Yowell (eds.), *Lord Sumption and the Limits of the Law* (Oxford: Hart, 2016), pp. 73–120.

84 See J. A. G. Griffith, *The Politics of the Judiciary*, 5th ed. (New York: Harper Collins, 1997). For a recent critique along these lines, see Martin Loughlin, *The Case of Prorogation: The UK Constitutional Council's Ruling on Appeal from the Judgment of the Supreme Court* (London: Policy Exchange, 2019), pp. 5–22.

85 On this critique, see Richard Elkins and Graham Gee, *Judicial Power and the Left: Notes on a Sceptical Tradition* (London: Policy Exchange, 2017), and Harlow, "Judicial Power, the Left, and the LSE Tradition," pp. 20–25.

86 *Dudgeon v. United Kingdom*, ECHR5, (1982) 4 EHRR.

Ireland inconsistent with Article 8 of the European Convention, and the impact of the European Union in recognizing that discrimination on the basis of sexual orientation on the same basis as such discrimination on the basic race/ethnicity, religion, and gender,[87] let alone the decision of the European Court of Human Rights in *Smith v. Grady v. United Kingdom*,[88] that unanimously found the exclusion of gays from the U.K. military unconstitutional because inconsistent with the right to a private life under Article 8 of the European Convention and not proportional in the pursuit of legitimate state interests. It is precisely this higher level of proportionality review for abridgment of basic rights, long familiar in the protection of rights in the U.S. (least restrictive alternative analysis) and the European Court of Human Rights and its growing impact on the British judiciary (an impact that would survive any successor to the Human Rights Act, 1998[89])—always in the protection of rights that do not comply with papal moral theology—that Finnis rhetorically condemns with conclusory labels ("disreputable") as non-judicial, as if, contrary to fact, arguments of principle play no legitimate role in judicial interpretation of basic rights when, in fact, such arguments play, as Dworkin has shown, a crucial role in understanding the scope and limits of judicial power certainly in the U.S. and now in the work of the European Court of Human Rights and, as John Laws has argued, in the work of the British judiciary.[90]

7.3 Populism in the U.S. and the U.K.: How Should Liberal Constitutionalists Respond?

The impact of the new natural lawyers both in the U.S. and U.K. was made possible by two different kinds of populist leaders and their political successes, Donald Trump in the U.S. and Boris Johnson in the U.K. Of the two, Trump is much more psychologically and politically problematic and his continuing political appeal even more so.[91] Before the 2016 election psychiatrists, including my colleague the psychiatrist James Gilligan, warned Americans of a psychopathic and deeply patriarchal male narcissism in Trump that was dangerous,[92] and the recent events of January 6 at the U.S. Capitol now have rendered that analysis

87 See Craig and De Burca, *EU Law: Text, Cases, and Materials*, pp. 228, 597, 598–99, 947–48, 966, 970.

88 (1999) 29 EHRR 493.

89 On this point, see Nicholas Bamforth, "Articles 13 and 35(1), Subsidiarity, and the Effective Protection of European Convention Rights in National Law," *European Human Rights Law Review* 5 (2016): 501–17.

90 See Laws, *The Constitutional Balance*.

91 See Bandy X. Lee, *Profile of a Nation: Trump's Mind, America's Soul* (New York: World Mental Health Coalition, 2020); Steven Hassan, *The Cult of Trump* (New York: Free Press, 2019).

92 See Bandy Lee, *The Dangerous Case of Donald Trump* (New York: Thomas Dunne Books, 2017), in particular pp. 163–73.

no longer doubtful. Americans as a people are quite tragically left with the possibly enduring constitutional legacy of his essentially thoughtless and cynical appeal to his base, a Supreme Court dominated by conservative ideologues and a Republican Party that supinely facilitated it.[93] Johnson is certainly narcissistic but not psychopathic as he apparently can distinguish truth from falsity in a way Trump and his followers, when faced we defeat, cannot, and the more flexible British parliamentary system has ended his rule in a way the American constitutional procedures of impeachment, twice reasonably brought against Trump, could not. To the extent the new natural lawyers have played the role they have in a populist politics so hostile to constitutionally protected human rights, they must be seen for what they are—serving, however unintentionally even unconsciously, some of the darkest populist forces of resurgent ethnic and religious nationalism scapegoating minorities that threaten liberal constitutionalism everywhere, free women and gays in the U.S., and immigrants in the U.K. both used as scapegoats upsetting the hierarchal patriarchal order of things.

How should liberal constitutionalists respond? In the U.K., the British parliamentary system, which has already gotten rid of Johnson, may be better positioned to deal with the issue than the U.S. at least staying within the parameters of our current constitutional system. My own argument here has been confined to arguments among modes of constitutional interpretation under *Marbury*, but the constitutional crisis has led to serious reflection about reforms of the constitutional system itself among which Roosevelt's court-packing proposal has been seriously, among others, revived.[94] And there have been more radical suggestions that the very liability of the system to distortion by anti-constitutional populists like Trump and the lawyers who have served him calls for more radical rethinking, some of which suggest aspects of the British parliamentary system.[95] We should remind ourselves that the British parliament abolished slavery peacefully with compensation in 1833, adopted socialism in 1945–51 and retained much of it through cross-party consensus until Thatcher and still even then retained the NHS (universal health care), abolished the death penalty, and decriminalized contraception, abortion, and gay sex, and then recognized gay marriage all through democratic politics. Radical proposals to rethink U.S. constitutionalism along such lines because no longer in service of political liberalism should not be dismissed.

93 See Jackie Calmes, *Dissent: The Radicalization of the Republican Party and Its Capture of the Court* (New York: Twelve, 2021); Linda Greenhouse, *Justice on the Brink: The Death of Ruth Bader Ginsburg, the Rise of Amy Coney Barrett, and Twelve Months That Transformed the Supreme Court* (New York: Random House, 2021).

94 For a fuller discussion of various proposals, see *Presidential Commission on the Supreme Court of the United States Final Report* (December 2021).

95 See, e.g., Ryan D. Doerfler and Samuel Moyn, "Liberals Need to Change the Rules," *New York Times*, August 21, 2022, at SR9.

Americans should remind themselves that the long abolitionist American struggle against race-based slavery and, after the Civil War, the neo-abolitionist struggle against our intractable cultural racism as well as cognate populist irrational prejudices like sexism, religious prejudice (anti-Semitism), and homophobia, criticized current constitutional law by appeal to a deeper value of political liberalism, and was only successful within limits after World War II. Part of its limited success was the growth in a more expansive and muscular conception of free speech, which facilitated various resistance movements, not least Martin Luther King, Jr.'s non-violent civil disobedience (leading to the Civil Rights Act of 1964 and the Voting Rights Act of 1965) and the anti-Vietnam War movement and second wave feminism and gay rights. Resistance to injustices wrought by constitutional law is not a new American story. It is the American story.

8 Concluding Reflections on Burke on Liberalism and the Political Psychology of Anti-liberal Violence

As already seen, views of members of the new natural lawyers have now had a demonstrable impact on the U.S. Supreme Court in *Dobbs* and on British politics. I find Finnis' originalist arguments deeply unreasonable for the reason that most such arguments are unreasonable, namely, they would freeze constitutional interpretation to the measure of views in 1787 or 1791 (Bill of Rights) or 1868 (Fourteenth Amendment), periods when women were not yet accepted as bearers of constitutional rights and homosexuals were regarded as subhuman.

Of course, the next step in this kind of argument would be to embrace, as the measure of human rights today, Blackstone's views on homosexuality. It is important to remember exactly what Blackstone opined on the matter in all its cruel and anachronistic erasure of gay people as subhuman, parroting sectarian religious views now widely discredited among Christians and others. Blackstone can barely discus why male consensual homosexuality (lesbianism is evidently not condemned) is criminally wrong, indeed he gives no reasons, rather explicitly echoing and appealing to a long-standing Judeo-Christian view of unspeakability and unknowability, marked by moving from English to Latin, and, as to punishment, with sanguinary ferocity:

> I will not act so disagreeable part, to my readers as well as myself, as to dwell any longer upon a subject, the very mention of which is a disgrace to human nature. It will be more eligible to imitate in this respect the delicacy of our English law, which treats it, in its very indictments, as a crime not fit be named: "*peccatum illud horribile, inter christianos ... not nominandum* [that horrible crime, not to be named amongst Christians]." A taciturnity observed likewise by the edict of Constantius and Constans: "*ubi scelus est id, quod not proficit scire, jubemus insurgere leges, armari jura gladio utore, ut exquisitis poenis subdantus infames, qui sunt, vel qui future sunt*" ["Where that crime is found, which is unfit even to know, we command the law to arise armed with an avenging sword, that the infamous men who are, or shall in future be

DOI: 10.4324/9781003410966-8

guilty of it, may undergo the most severe punishments" (in footnote)]. Which leads me to add a word concerning its punishment.

Thus the voice of nature and of reason, and the express law of God, determine to be capital. Of which we have a signal instance, long before the Jewish dispensation, by the destruction of two cities by fire from heaven: so that this is an universal, not merely a provincial, precept. And our antient law in some degree imitated this punishment, by commanding such miscreants to be burnt to death, though Fleta says they should be buried alive: either of which punishments was indifferently used for this crime among the antient Goths. But now the general punishment of all felonies is the same, namely, by hanging: and this offence (being in the time of popery only subject to ecclesiastical censures was made single felony by the statute 25 Hen. VIII. c. 6, and felony without benefit of clergy by statute 5 Eliz. C 17. And the rule of law herein is, that, if both are arrived at years of discretion, *agentes et consentientes pari poena plectantur* [the perpetrator and consenting party are both liable to the same punishment].[1]

Finnis' argument for the unconstitutionality of abortion liberalization in the U.S. is no better than the argument he would make against homosexuality, and shows, I believe, exactly the dimensions of his reactionary moral views that motivate his and his followers' exoteric attempts to reject gay rights as constitutionally protected rights, let alone rights to abortion services and contraception. And, it is no better than the indefensible arguments he has made supporting Brexit and proposing U.K. withdrawal from the European Convention on Human Rights, all in an attempt to withdraw Britain from its distinguished achievements in recognizing gay rights as constitutional rights through the European Declaration and European Union.

At this point, we should turn again to Burke, whose liberalism may have been inspired, as I argued in Chapter 1, by giving voice to his own love for another man, exposing the irrational terror and mob violence surrounding this issue in his lifetime. Bentham's contemporary views were even more highly developed (condemning both the criminalization of gay sex and homophobia), but he is silent, not publishing his path-breaking critique. Burke is not, though his very speech is censured in contemporary newspapers in starkly sexist and homophobic terms: "Every *man* applauds the spirit of the spectators, and every *woman* thinks their conduct right. It remained only for the patriotic Mr. Burke to insinuate that the crime these men committed should not be held in the highest detestation than ignominious death."[2] And one of the common caricatures of Burke during this period portrays his opposition to the French Revolution not as the act of

1 William Blackstone, *Commentaries on the Laws of England: Book IV* (Oxford: Oxford University Press, 2016), p. 143, secs. 215–16.

2 Crompton, *Byron and Greek Love*, p. 33.

liberal conscience it was, but as the divided conscience of two old ladies.[3] So, no person, holding such views, can be a real man, or a real women, exposing the central role in the cultural psychology of such illimitable violence of the patriarchal conception of gender roles that wars on any threat to such gender roles. It confirms this understanding of Burke's brilliant insights into the political psychology of anti-liberal violence that, when he first explores the contrast of the sublime and terror to the beautiful and love in *A Philosophical Enquiry into the Sublime and the Beautiful*, the contrast is so highly gendered, men at one polarity, women at the other, very much in line with what Carol Gilligan and Naomi Snider argue is the cultural psychology of patriarchy in which "relationships of mutuality—the cornerstone of intimacy—are ... exchanged for relationships of complementarity, relationships where each person unconsciously seeks to find in the other the thing they cannot admit to or accept in themselves,"[4] for women the desire for independence covered by an ideology of self-sacrifice, for men emotional vulnerability covered by an ideology of autarkic independence. What Burke sees in addition is the role of violence, personal and political, in enforcing the masculine polarity, a violence he himself experienced when, in exposing the violence of London women murdering gay men because of their deviation from male gender roles, he is himself condemned as not a man. Only a man, himself moved to question conventional gender roles (in my experience, by his enduring love for another man or anyone finding love outside the boundaries of patriarchal categories of gender hierarchy), could have this insight into the role political violence plays in patriarchy's war on a liberalism challenging such roles, an insight he carries over into British unjust humiliation of the Irish, the Americans, and the Indians (all leading to violence) and the French transmogrification of human rights into illimitable violence on anyone who would disagree with them. This both explains and clarifies why, in *Reflections on the Revolution in France*, the humiliation of Marie Antoinette by violent mobs of women who dehumanize her should play so central a role in Burke's astonishing anatomy of the psychology of the illimitable violence of the French Revolution, ending in a Roman-style patriotic militarism, European imperialistic wars, and dictatorship. It also explains his insights into the psychology of the London homophobic mobs and the larger insights into "political religions" that he discovered and that I, very much in the liberal tradition he bequeathed to us, have used to understand the populist appeal of the misogyny and homophobia of the new natural lawyers, still very much alive.

My argument illustrated the depth of Burke's understanding of both liberalism and the political psychology of anti-liberal violence by its convergence with the insights of Hannah Arendt into twentieth-century totalitarianisms and

3 See Robinson, *Edmund Burke*, p. 136.

4 Carol Gilligan and Naomi Snider, *Why Does Patriarchy Persist* (Cambridge, MA: Polity, 2018), at p. 70.

James Gilligan's views on violence and political violence, in which Burke's analysis of terror that "so effectually robs the mind of all its powers of acting and reasoning"[5] plays a central role in the psychological deadening of conscience and resistance to injustice. Both Hitler's fascism and Stalin's communism illustrate this psychology as well as its war on liberal values of freedom of thought, conscience, and speech, exactly what Burke saw quite early in the French Revolution and its dynamic leading, as he foresaw, to terror, imperialist militarism, and dictatorship. What distinguishes the French Revolution is its ostensible celebration of human rights in contrast to Hitler's crackpot scientific racism/anti-Semitism and Stalin's equally crackpot theory of historical inevitability, but the Burkean psychology is, remarkably, the same.

There was to be, as Lynn Hunt has shown,[6] quite a historical gap between the ostensible values of human rights of the French Revolution, discredited among Europeans by Napoleon's violent imperialism, and the rebirth of serious interest in what Burke would have called "real" human rights after World War II in the Universal Declaration of Human Rights of 1948 and the other national, transnational, and international institutions earlier discussed. Both Burke's liberalism and his political psychology clarify both these developments, including the forms of constitutional constructivism, by the U.S., Britain, and many others, that led to new institutions constitutionally to protect "real" human rights.

My focus has been on the two eighteenth-century constitutionalisms that endured, the British and the American, the first represented by Burke, the second by Madison, who share so much, as we have seen, in understanding the construction of liberal constitutionalism, the unwritten version of the U.K., the written version of the U.S. The interest for me was Burke's deep understanding not only of the legitimacy of the American Revolution, but of its constitutionalism, which learned from British historical experience as well as the experience of many other peoples (Chapter 2). Burke's cautionary warning to the Americans was, so I have argued, correct (Chapter 3): the violence of the American Revolution may have been justified against British imperialism and the abridgment of the rights Americans were owed as Britons, but its justice as against the British with all its liberal idealism covered the injustices inflicted on people of color held in slavery and the Amerindians, both of which injustices would lead to wars, including the American tragedy, the Civil War, the subject of which, slavery, the British had abolished with compensation through parliamentary deliberation in 1833.

Such inconsistency in their liberalism of the American constitutionalists (including Madison), leading to political violence Burke understood and in part predicted, took place by British constitutionalists in their dealings with their first colony, Ireland, as well as with America and, finally, India and its other colonies

5 Burke, *A Philosophical Enquiry into the Sublime and the Beautiful*, p. 47.

6 See Lynn Hunt, *Inventing Human Rights: A History* (New York: W. W. Norton, 2007), pp. 176–214.

(Chapter 4). Burke worried throughout his life that British unjust treatment of Irish Catholics, in violation of principles of liberal toleration, would, particularly inspired by the French Revolution, lead to violent uprisings and even terror, and he was right. There were comparable atrocities by the British in other colonies, including India. What is of interest, however, is that it was outsiders, Gandhi in India, Martin Luther King, Jr. in the U.S., who would with their informed understanding of the contradictions in both British and American constitutionalism (a constitutional liberalism and Christianity in tension with racist violence—Amritsar in India, lynchings in the U.S.) discover a non-violent strategy, Satyagraha, which would persuade both nations to more just treatment both of the Indians, as a people, and people of color in the U.S. Yet, the legacy of British injustice in India (divide and conquer) led to the enduring trauma of partition, and both Gandhi and King would be murdered by those they challenged, unleashing yet again patriarchal violence against liberal voice.

It is simply not defensible, on examination along several parameters of comparison, that the U.S. Constitution of judicial review enjoys a better record on human rights than the U.K. (Chapter 5). The American experience, not least recent ideologically conservative appointments to the Supreme Court, shows a judiciary that only since World War II has protected the human rights of minorities, and that is now very much at threat. Even the liberal record of the U.S. Court has been plausibly questioned on grounds of effecting liberal policies in fact,[7] and constitutional courts in other jurisdiction have been questioned on similar grounds.[8] In contrast, such critics have documented a much better record of the judiciary on issues of progressive social change not in the U.S. or U.K., but in India.[9] There is much to be learned both from the experience of Britain with its unwritten constitution and the U.S. with its written constitution about which model or mixture of models better secures the aims of political liberalism. Some forms of populism may be consistent with and indeed in service of a more democratic constitutionalism (Franklin Roosevelt in the U.S., for example[10]), but certainly those that attack democratic governance of repeat play by parties over time and constrain a democratic majority within limits from prevailing cannot be justified.

7 See Gerald N. Rosenberg, *The Hollow Hope: Can Courts Bring about Social Change*, 2nd ed. (Chicago: University of Chicago Press, 2008); Stuart A. Scheingold, *The Politics of Rights: Lawyers, Public Policy, and Political Change*, 2nd ed. (Ann Arbor: University of Michigan Press, 2004).

8 Ran Hirschl, *Towards Juristocracy: The Origins and Consequences of the New Constitutionalism* (Cambridge: Harvard University Press, 2004).

9 Gerald N. Rosenberg, Sudhir Krishnaswamy, and Shishir Bail, *A Qualified Hope: The Indian Supreme Court and Progressive Social Change* (Cambridge: Cambridge University Press, 2019).

10 On this point, see Tushnet and Bugaric, *Power to the People*. For a discussion of Franklin Roosevelt in general and his proposal of court packing in particular, see pp. 159–62, 172–76.

My colleague Samuel Issacharoff has made a compelling case along these lines in his important recent book, *Democracy Unmoored: Populism and the Corruption of Popular Sovereignty.*[11] Issacharoff studies and criticizes anti-constitutional forms of political populism not only in the U.S. (Trump) and the U.K. (Brexit), but in the broad range of other constitutional democracies where it has arisen and, in some cases, democratically entrenched its power (Poland and Hungary) against opposing political voices and parties. The common theme in such populism is its hostility to the institutional forms of constitutional democracy (including free speech) that protect the democratic governance of alternative political parties taking power over time in representative government. Both Trump's false claims of voter fraud, undermining democratic procedures, and the use of a referendum in Brexit illustrate this dynamic, unleashing angry populist political irrationalisms against the familiar scapegoats of racial, sexist, religious, and homophobic prejudice, all of which remain much too alive in democratic politics. Issacharoff calls not only for strengthening existing institutional constraints on populism, but rethinking those that exist (including the power of social media) to address the threat to democracy from a formerly mainstream party (the Republican Party) that now is dominated by an anti-constitutional populism supported by some such media that sponsor blatant lies, known to be untruths.[12] How far should such rethinking go? Perhaps, even current American doctrines of protected speech and even state action must be rethought to the extent they protect such corrosive lies.[13]

British and American constitutionalism, separated since the successful American Revolution and Treaty of Paris of 1783, rejoined in terms of common values in response to the challenge of the fascist aggression of World War II to political liberalism everywhere (Chapter 6). Very much in the spirit of Burke's conception of liberal constitutional constructivism, the Americans and British forge new forms of constitutionalism in Germany, Italy, and Japan, new transnational institutions like the European Convention on Human Rights in which Britain plays a very important constructive role, as well as the European Union, NATO, the Marshall Plan, the United Nations, and others. By Burkean constructivism, I mean the close attention to historical experience, including the imperialistic wars of World War I and the aggressive ethnic imperialist war and genocide of fascism in World War II. It is from these European tragedies that the Universal Declaration of Human Rights arises, and the construction of

11 On this point, see Samuel Issacharoff, *Democracy Unmoored: Populism and the Corruption of Popular Sovereignty* (New York: Oxford University Press, 2023).

12 For a further discussion along these lines, see Issacharoff, *Democracy Unmoored*, pp. 185–224.

13 For a compelling normative argument to this effect, see Seana Valentine Shiffrin, *Speech Matters: On Lying, Morality, and the Law* (Princeton, NJ: Princeton University Press, 2014). For the U.S. Supreme Court's view that knowingly false statements of fact cannot be criminalized, see *United States v. Alvarez*, 567 U.S. 709 (2012).

new European institutions better to protect what Burke would have called the "real" rights of persons. The problem of endless European wars was at the center of these deliberations, which only Burke and Kant in the late eighteenth century had taken seriously, and which the new institutions aim to address by forging new transnational institutions, including the European Union, very much modeled on the American federal union based on Montesquieu argument for common markets as the key to peace among nations.

It is against the background of these institutions that the argument turned to the threat posed to constitutional liberalism in both the U.S. and U.K. by the impact of patriarchal religion both on American constitutional interpretation and British politics, weakening the HRA (Chapter 7). Patriarchal religion has always played a historically significant role in the construction and enforcement of patriarchal hierarchies of ethnicity/race, gender, class, sexual orientation, and the like,[14] and my argument has, I believe, shown that their views have played an important role both in the U.S. and the U.K. in supporting forms of originalism that are indeed hostile to contemporary political liberalism. Burke's liberalism and political psychology of illiberal violence arose, so I have argued, from his own understanding as a man in a long-term loving relationship to another man of the role of patriarchally enforced terror on any such relationships, a war on any public voice resisting such injustice. What is so remarkable, indeed astonishing, about Burke is that he spoke, uniquely in his period, in such a public voice, not only about the violence directed against gay men, but about the violence against Irish Catholics, against the Americans, and against Indians, and the French against any dissent, all based on the centrality to liberalism of free voice and conscience, centered in love. These threats remain very much alive, in particular, in the ways they war in fact on the basic values of political liberalism. The psychological root of the violence Burke studied throughout his life was violence against liberalism itself in which the hierarchies of race, ethnicity, gender, religion, and sexuality have no place. History, to which Burke turned constantly for close study, shows us the consequence of nationalisms or fundamentalisms that demand violence in some form whenever at threat from liberal voice and resistance. It is in fact the history of Europe since the French Revolution culminating in World War II. We need, now more than ever, Burke's sense of a liberalism based on what such history tells us, a liberalism not terrorized by not being a patriarchal man or woman, but by standing on "real" rights, the rights to be human.

I regard such arguments, whether in the U.K. or the U.S., as of a piece with a wider reactionary populist politics that we see even within the nations in the European Union (e.g., Poland and Hungary) that have demonized advocacy of gay rights and thus gay people as equal citizens and bearers of human rights,

14 On this point, see Wilkerson, *Caste*.

as well as the use of the issue to similar ends in Russia and Turkey, and other nations, including the homophobic savagery of Uganda's recent laws against LGBTQ persons, expressed in the imposition of the death penalty.[15] Russia under Putin has certainly not adopted the democratic constitutionalism that we had hoped for in the wake of the end of the U.S.S.R., but rather turned to a form of authoritarianism at home with no respect for free speech (in particular, speech by homosexuals), let alone real democratic dissent, and a foreign policy that supports violently illiberal regimes (Syria) and takes actions, illegal under international law, against Ukraine (seizing Crimea and supporting anti-government militias in Ukraine, and now invading Ukraine). And what we had hoped for in putative links between economic and political liberalization in China has not yet taken place; instead, the state's repression of any open discussion of its role in quashing through state violence the democratic dissent in the 1989 Tiananmen Square protests has been followed by an increasingly authoritarian one-party state, that, like other authoritarian states, regards dissent as treason or terrorism, explaining its extraordinary repression of civil liberties in Hong Kong, a last bastion of British liberalism in China, let alone its unjust treatment of the Uyghurs in Xinjing. What we need and have not yet had in the U.K. and U.S. is anything like the wise policies of containment of the U.S.S.R. that leaders in both countries developed and executed that ended without violence the threat to human rights, domestically and internationally, of the U.S.S.R. The turn to military solutions against such imagined threats in Vietnam, Iraq, and Afghanistan has ended badly, and certainly has not advanced the ends of political liberalism.[16] Though European nations refused to follow the U.S. in its Vietnam misadventure,[17] they supported its Iraq and Afghanistan policies. We know better leadership is possible and feasible (we saw it in the response of the U.K. and U.S. to the catastrophe of World War II and its legacy).[18]

Brexit reflects a loss of confidence in the U.K. about its institutional turn to Europe and the resulting Burkean invention of new constitutional forms, including the European Convention of Human Rights and the European Union, in both of which Britain played an important constructive role very much in the Burkean tradition (Chapter 6), a return to its more traditional stance of sovereign independence and its alliance with the U.S. It remains an open question how far Britain will carry the reactionary forces that led to Brexit. Aileen McHarg and Alison L. Young have thus asked whether Brexit might carry with it an attempt

15 For an illuminating recent study of Poland and Hungary along these lines, as well as of Brazil, India, the Philippines, and Venezuela, see Wojciech Sadurski, *A Pandemic of Populists* (Cambridge: Cambridge University Press, 2022).

16 On this point, see Samuel Moyn, *Humane: How the United States Abandoned Peace and Reinvented War* (New York: Farrar, Straus and Giroux, 2021).

17 On this point, see McKean and Szewczyk, *Partners of First Resort*, p. 30.

18 For a further discussion of what steps have been and should be taken in future, see ibid.

to reverse many of the constitutional developments in the U.K. since World War II that we have discussed in this book[19] and what Vernon Bogdanor called "the new British Constitution,"[20] including the revival of common law judicial scrutiny of executive actions, the Human Rights Act 1998, devolution, hung parliaments, a reformed House of Lords, use of referenda, a new government of London, and toward a written constitution.

I began this book in the preface by asking what we should make of Dicey's proposal in an 1897 article, as the title put it, "A Common Citizenship for the English Race"[21] between England and the U.S. Is there anything to it but late Victorian racism? I noted that is my question, or one of my questions. I can now give my answer, occasioned by Britain's decision to leave Europe and draw closer to the U.S. and what Churchill would have called "English-speaking peoples." Whatever Brexit means, it cannot and should not be taken to mean that the U.K. and the U.S. stand on some common ethnic ground, as my own personal history shows. I trace my ancestry from Southern Italy, and am therefore an Italian American and, like Burke in Britain, an outsider to the dominant American majority that once forbade my ancestors entry to the U.S. as what Theodore Roosevelt and Woodrow Wilson, political enemies, condemned as "hyphenated Americanism"[22]; my response has been resistance, publishing books dealing with both American and Italian racism and anti-liberalism as well as the operatic art of Giuseppe Verdi, decidedly an Italian liberal and lover of an anti-patriarchal free woman, whose operatic art of tragic voices (e.g., that of a woman in *La Traviata*, and a man in *Rigoletto*, both tragedies of love under patriarchy) I have long cherished as piercing portraits of the struggles of an Italian liberal against the protofascism of Italian patriarchy[23] (my beloved father was both a civil engineer, his occupation, and a gifted opera singer, his expressive soul, wedded in love to a remarkable working woman (a hospital pharmacist) in an egalitarian marriage). And my interest in gay rights is the expression neither of race nor ethnicity nor religion, but an expression of my now 45-year love for and relationship to another man, Donald Levy, a philosopher, across the

19 Aileen McHarg and Alison L. Young, "The Resilience of the (Old) British Constitution," UK Constitutional Law Association, https://ukconstitutionallaw.org/2021/09/08/aileen-mcharg-and-alison-l-young-the-resilience-of-the-old-british-constitution/.

20 See Vernon Bogdanor, *The New British Constitution* (New York: Hart, 2009).

21 Dylan Lino, "The Rule of Law and the Rule of Empire: A.V. Dicey in Imperial Contest," *Modern Law Review* 81:5 (2018): 739–64 at 749.

22 On this point, see David A.J. Richards, *Boys' Secrets and Men's Loves: A Memoir* (Bloomington, Ind.: Xlibris, 2019), p. 286. See also Daniel Okrent, *The Guarded Gate: Bigotry, Eugenics, and the Law That Kept Jews, Italians, and Other European Immigrants Out of America* (New York: Scribner, 2019), p. 220.

23 See David A. J. Richards, *Italian-American: The Racializing of an Ethnic Identity* (New York: New York University Press, 1999), and *Tragic Manhood and Democracy: Verdi's Voice and the Powers of Musical Art* (Brighton: Sussex Academic Press, 1988).

boundaries that, *because* we resisted them, did not divide but united us—my Will Burke. My interest in Burke, which motivated writing this book, is that the moral passion that drove his political liberalism had psychological and cultural roots not unlike my own. His life and work spoke to me, not least that he regarded constitutionalism as a constructive work of man's art, and "Art is man's nature."[24] For him and for me, liberal constitutionalism, born in Britain and America, is a work of culture on which all can responsibly work and pass on to future generations.

The American problem may be redeemed by the role of the judiciary in the U.S. since World War II, although the recent ideologically conservative appointments to the Supreme Court put that in some doubt; and recent developments in the U.K. suggest a rethinking of these issues as its judiciary adopts more demanding interpretive tests for the role of ministers and officials in service of statutory demands, including the increasingly important role of comparative public law, although attempts to revise the Human Rights Act put that in doubt as well. Britain may still be an island, perhaps more so after Brexit, but its commitment to respect for human rights is no longer insular, but attends to human rights as a universal concern for liberal constitutional democracies everywhere they exist. There is now a dialogue—comparative public law—over the meaning of universal human rights, exemplified by the fact, as have seen, that the constitutional recognition of gay rights has arisen in diverse contexts, suggesting that the right in question is deeply human, as deep as the place of love in our human natures. The U.K. and the U.S. now join others in that dialogue, teaching and learning, as they have learned from one another and today learn as much as teach from others who have joined them in the deeply human enterprise, based on dialogue between free and equal persons, of democratic constitutionalism—as Burke saw, one of the greatest cultural achievements of the mind in human history, all the more so, because open to reform and rethinking in light of "real" human rights.

24 Burke, "An Appeal from the New to the Old Whigs," p. 496.

Bibliography

Books and Articles

Adams, Charles Francis (ed.), *The Works of John Adams*, vol. 4 (Boston, MA: Little, Brown, 1851).

Adams, Willi Paul. *First State Constitutions*, trans. Rita and Robert Kimber (Chapel Hill: University of North Carolina Press, 1980).

Adorno, T. W., E. Frenkel-Brunswick, D. J. Levinson, and R. Nevitt Sanford. *The Authoritarian Personality* (New York: Wiley, 1950).

Ahmed, Leila. *A Border Passage: From Cairo to America* (New York: Farrar, Straus and Giroux, 1999).

Allan, T. R. S. *Constitutional Justice: A Liberal Theory of the Rule of Law* (Oxford: Oxford University Press, 2003).

Allan, T. R. S. *Law, Liberty, and Justice: The Legal Foundations of British Constitutionalism* (Oxford: Clarendon Press, 1993).

Allan, T. R. S. *The Sovereignty of Law: Freedom, Constitution, and Common Law* (Oxford: Oxford University Press, 2013).

Altmeyer, B. *The Authoritarian Spectre* (Cambridge: Harvard University Press, 1996).

Appiah, Kwame Anthony. *The Honor Code: How Moral Revolutions Happen* (New York: W. W. Norton, 2010).

Arendt, Hannah. *Eichmann in Jerusalem: A Report on the Banality of Evil* (New York: Penguin, 1963).

Arendt, Hannah. *The Jewish Writings* (New York: Schocken, 2007).

Arendt, Hannah. *Lectures on Kant's Political Philosophy*, ed. Ronald Beiner (Chicago, IL: University of Chicago Press, 1992).

Arendt, Hannah. *The Life of the Mind* (San Diego, CA: A Harvest/HBJ Book, 1971).

Arendt, Hannah. *On Revolution* (New York: Penguin, 1963).

Arendt, Hannah. *The Origins of Totalitarianism* (New York: Harcourt Brace Jovanovich, 1973).

Arendt, Hannah. *Responsibility and Judgment*, ed. Jerome Cohn (New York: Schocken, 2003).

Arendt, Hannah. *Thinking without a Banister: Essays in Understanding 1953–1975* (New York: Schocken, 2018).

Aristotle. "Politics," in Jonathan Barnes (ed.), *The Complete Works of Aristotle*, vol. 2 (Princeton, NJ: Princeton University Press, 1984).

Aschcraft, Richard. *Locke's Two Treatises of Government* (London: Allen & Unwin, 1987).
Aschcraft, Richard. *Revolutionary Politics and Locke's Two Treatises of Government* (Princeton, NJ: Princeton University Press, 1986).
"The Atlantic Charter," www.nato.int/cps/en/natohq/official_texts_16912.htm
Attwood, Margaret. *The Handmaid's Tale* (New York: Anchor, 1998).
Augustine. *The City of God*, trans. Henry Bettenson (Harmondsworth: Penguin, 1972).
Ayling, Stanley. *Edmund Burke: His Life and Opinions* (New York: St. Martin's Press, 1988).
"Bagehot: The Great Reversal," *The Economist*, August 7–13, 2021, p. 47.
Bailey, D. S. *Homosexuality and the Western Christian Tradition* (London: Longman, 1955).
Bailyn, Bernard. *The Ideological Origins of the American Revolution* (Cambridge, MA: Harvard University Press, 1967).
Bamforth, Nicholas. "Articles 13 and 35(1), Subsidiarity, and the Effective Protection of European Convention Rights in National Law," *European Human Rights Law Review* 5 (2016): 501–17.
Bamforth, Nicholas. "Sado-masochism and Consent," *Criminal Law Review* (1994): 661–64.
Bamforth, Nicholas, and David A. J. Richards. *Patriarchal Religion, Gender, and Sexuality: A Critique of New Natural Law* (Cambridge: Cambridge University Press, 2008).
Barbu, Zevedei. *Problems of Historical Psychology* (New York: Grove Press, 1960).
Baron de Montesquieu. *The Spirit of the Laws*, trans. Thomas Nugent (New York: Hafner, 1949).
Bauer, Bob, et al. *Presidential Commission on the Supreme Court of the United States Final Report* (December 2021).
Benedict, Ruth. *The Chrysanthemum and the Sword: Patterns of Japanese Culture* (Boston, MA: A Mariner Book, 2005, originally published 1946).
Benedict, Ruth. *Patterns of Culture* (Boston, MA: Houghton Mifflin, 2005, first published 1934).
Bentham, Jeremy. *Of Sexual Irregularities, and Other Writings on Sexual Morality*, eds. Philip Schofield, Catherine Pease-Watkin, and Michael Quinn (Oxford: Oxford University Press, 2014).
Berger, Raoul. *Government by Judiciary* (Cambridge, MA: Harvard University Press, 1977).
Biskupic, Joan. "How the Supreme Court Crafted Its *Roe v. Wade* Decision and What It Means Today," www.com/2021/009/23/politics/roe-v-wade.history/index.html
Blackstone, William. *Commentaries on the Laws of England*, Book 4 (Oxford: Oxford University Press, 2016).
Blackstone, William. *Commentaries on the Laws of England*, vol. 1 (Chicago, IL: University of Chicago Press, 1979).
Blight, David W. *Race and Reunion: The Civil War in American Memory* (Cambridge, MA: The Belknap Press of Harvard University Press, 2001).
Boas, Franz. *Kwakiutl Ethnography* (Chicago, IL: University of Chicago Ethnography, 1966).
Boas, Franz. *The Mind of Primitive Man* (n.p.: Forgotten Books, 2012, originally published 1922).
Bogdanor, Vernon. *The New British Constitution* (New York: Hart, 2009).

Boni, Albert et al. *The Compact Edition of the Oxford English Dictionary*, vol. 2 (Oxford: Oxford University Press, 1971).

Bourke, Richard. *Empire and Revolution: The Political Life of Edmund Burke* (Princeton, NJ: Princeton University Press, 2015).

Boyd, Julian P. (ed.). *The Papers of Thomas Jefferson 1789*, vol. 15 (Princeton, NJ: Princeton University Press, 1958).

Boyd, Julian P. (ed.). *The Papers of Thomas Jefferson 1789–1900*, vol. 16 (Princeton, NJ: Princeton University Press, 1961).

Bradley, F. H. *Ethical Studies* (Oxford: Clarendon Press, 1876, 1988).

Bray, Alan. *Homosexuality in Renaissance England* (New York: Columbia University Press, 1995).

Bromwich, David. *The Intellectual Life of Edmund Burke: From the Sublime and Beautiful to American Independence* (Cambridge, MA: Harvard University Press, 2014).

Brown, Christopher. "Later, Not Now," *London Review of Books* 43:14 (2021): 25–28.

Brown, Lyn Mikel, and Carol Gilligan. *Meeting at the Crossroads: Women's Psychology and Girls' Development* (Cambridge, MA: Harvard University Press, 1996).

Bubb, Alexander. *Meetings without Knowing It: Kipling and Yeats at the Fin de Siecle* (Oxford: Oxford University Press, 2016).

Bucholz, Robert. *Foundations of Western Civilization II: A History of the Modern Western World Course Guidebook* (Chantilly, VA: The Teaching Company, 2006).

Burke, Edmund. *A Philosophical Enquiry into the Sublime and Beautiful*, ed. Paul Guyer (Oxford: Oxford University Press, 2015).

Burke, Edmund. *The Parliamentary History of England from the Earliest Period to the Year 1803*, vol. 21 (London: T. C. Hansard, 1814), cols. 388–89.

Burke, Edmund. *Revolutionary Writings*, ed. Iain Hampsher-Monk (Cambridge: Cambridge University Press, 2014).

Buttrick, David. *Speaking Jesus: Homiletic Theology and the Sermon on the Mount* (Louisville, KY: Westminster John Knox Press, 2002).

Caimmi, Michele. "When Hitler Ordered the Destruction of Germany," https//medium.com-wgat-i-ve-learned/when-hitler-ordered-the-destruction-of-germanyb34540ea1500

Calmes, Jackie. *Dissent: The Radicalization of the Republican Party and Its Capture of the Court* (New York: Twelve, 2021).

Canellos, Peter. *The Great Dissenter* (New York: Simon & Schuster, 2021).

Carter, Zachary D. *The Price of Peace: Money, Democracy, and the Life of John Maynard Keynes* (New York: Random House, 2021).

Chandler, Daniel. *Free and Equal: What Would a Fair Society Look Like?* (London: Allen Lane, 2023)

Chemerinsky, Erwin. *Worse Than Nothing: The Dangerous Fallacy of Originalism* (New Haven, CT: Yale University Press, 2022).

Clayton, Tim. *James Gillray: A Revolution in Caricature* (New Haven, CT: Yale University Press, 2022).

Colley, Linda. *Britons: Forging the Nation 1701–1837* (New Haven, CT: Yale University Press, 2020).

Colley, Linda. *The Gun, the Ship, and the Pen: Warfare, Constitutions, and the Making of the Modern World* (New York: Liveright, 2021).

Colley, Linda. "The Radical Constitutional Change Britain Needs," *New York Times*, September 13, 2022 at A22.

Colman, John. *John Locke's Moral Philosophy* (Edinburgh: Edinburgh University Press, 1983).

Cone, Carl B. *Burke and the Nature of Politics: The Age of the American Revolution* (Lexington, KY: University of Kentucky Press, 1957).

Cone, Carl B. *Burke and the Nature of Politics: The Age of the French Revolution* (Lexington, KY: University of Kentucky Press, 1964).

Cook, Matt (ed.). *A Gay History of Britain: Love and Sex between Men since the Middle Ages* (Oxford: Greenwood World, 2007), pp. 77–144.

Cooke, Jacob (ed.). *The Federalist* (Middletown, CT: Wesleyan University Press, 1961).

Corbett, K. *Boyhoods: Rethinking Masculinities*. New Haven, CT: Yale University Press (2009).

Cowie, Jefferson. *Freedom's Dominion: A Saga of White Resistance to Federal Power* (New York: Basic Books, 2022).

Craig, Paul. "Constitutionality, Convention, and Prorogation," in ed. Daniel Clarry, *The UK Supreme Court Yearbook*, vol. 10, pp. 1–26 (London: Appellate Press, 2018–2019)

Craig, Paul. "Judicial Power, the Judicial Power Project, and the UK," *University of Queensland Law Journal* 36 (2017): 355–74.

Craig, Paul. "Legislative Intent and Legislative Supremacy: A Reply to Professor Allan," *Oxford Journal of Legal Studies* 24(4) (2004): 585–96.

Craig, Paul. "Political Constitutionalism and the Judicial Role: A Response," *International Journal of Constitutional Law* 9 (2011): 112.

Craig, Paul. *Public Law and Democracy in the United Kingdom and the United States* (Oxford: Clarendon Press, 1990).

Craig, Paul. "Public Law, Political Theory and Legal Theory," *Public Law* (2000): 211.

Craig, Paul. "Response to Loughlin's Note on Miller; Cherry," *Pubic Law* (2020): 282–86.

Craig, Paul. "The Supreme Court, Prorogation and Constitutional Principle," *Public Law* (2020): 248–77.

Craig, Paul. *UK, EU and Global Administrative Law: Foundations and Challenges* (Cambridge: Cambridge University Press, 2015).

Craig, Paul. "Ultra Vires and the Foundations of Judicial Review," *Cambridge Law Journal* 57(1) (1998): 63–90.

Craig, Paul, and Grainne De Burca. *EU Law: Text, Cases, and Materials*, 7th ed. (Oxford: Oxford University Press, 2020).

Craig v. Boren, 429 U.S. 190 (1978).

Crewe, Tom. *The New Life: A Novel* (New York: Scribner, 2023).

Crick, Bernard. *George Orwell: A Life* (London: Sutherland House, 1980).

Crompton, Louis. *Byron and Greek Love: Homophobia in 19th-Century England* (Berkeley, CA: University of California Press, 1985).

Crosland, Anthony. *The Future of Socialism* (London: Constable, 1956, 2006).

Crotty, James. *Keynes against Liberalism: His Economic Case for Liberal Socialism* (London: Routledge, 2019).

Dangerfield, George. *The Strange Death of Liberal England* (Stanford, CA: Stanford University Press, 1935, 1997).

Darwall, Stephen. *The Second-Person Standpoint: Morality, Respect, and Accountability* (Cambridge, MA: Harvard University Press, 2006).

Davis, Peggy Cooper. *Neglected Stores: The Constitution and Family Values* (New York: Hill & Wang, 1997).

De Vos, Pierre. "A Judicial Revolution: A Court-Led Achievement of Same-Sex Marriage in South Africa," *Utrecht Law Review* 4 (2008): 161–74.

Dewey, John. "Individualism Old and New," in Jo Ann Boydston (ed.), *The Later Works of John Dewey, 1924–1953*, vol. 5 (Carbondale, IL: Southern Illinois University Press, 2008), pp. 41–123.

Diamond, Michael J. *Ruptures in the American Psyche: Containing Destructive Populism in Perilous Times* (Bicester: Phoenix, 2022).

Dicey, A. V. *Introduction to the Study of the Law of the Constitution* (Indianapolis, IN: Liberty Fund, 1982).

Dickens, Charles. *Barnaby Rudge* (London: Penguin, 2003).

Dodds, E. R. *The Greeks and the Irrational* (Berkeley, CA: University of California Press, 1959).

Doerfler, Ryan D., and Samuel Moyn. "Liberals Need to Change the Rules," *New York Times*, August 21, 2022 at SR9.

Dorrien, Garry. *American Democratic Socialism: History, Politics, and Theory* (New Haven, CT: Yale University Press, 2022).

Du Rivage, Justin. *Revolution against Empire: Taxes, Politics, and the Origins of American Independence* (New Haven, CT: Yale University Press, 2017).

Dunn, John. *The Political Thought of John Locke* (Cambridge: Cambridge University Press, 1969).

Dwan, David, and Christopher J. Insole. *The Cambridge Companion to Edmund Burke* (Cambridge: Cambridge University Press, 2012).

Dworkin, Ronald. *Law's Empire* (Cambridge, MA: Harvard University Press, 1986).

Dworkin, Ronald. *Taking Rights Seriously* (Cambridge, MA: Harvard University Press, 1977).

Dyzenhaus, David. *The Long Arc of Legality: Hobbes, Kelsen, Hart* (Cambridge: Cambridge University Press, 2022).

Eaton, Joseph W., and Robert J. Weil. *Culture and Mental Disorders: A Comparative Study of the Hutterites and Other Populations* (New York: Free Press, 1955).

Elkins, Caroline. *Imperial Reckoning: The Untold Story of Britain's Gulag in Kenya* (New York: Owl Books, 2005).

Elkins, Caroline. *Legacy of Violence: A History of the British Empire* (New York: Alfred A. Knopf, 2022).

Elkins, Richard, and Graham Gee. *Judicial Power and the Left: Notes on a Sceptical Tradition* (London: Policy Exchange, 2017).

Ely, John Hart. *Democracy and Distrust* (Cambridge, MA: Harvard University Press, 1968).

Ely, John Hart. "The Wages of Crying Wolf: A Comment on *Roe v. Wade*," *Yale Law Journal* 82 (1973): 920–49.

Encarnacion, Omar G. *The Case for Gay Reparations* (New York: Oxford University Press, 2021).

Euripides. *Medea and Other Plays*, trans. Philip Vellacott (London: Penguin, 1963).

Farrand, Max (ed.). *Records of the Federal Convention*, vols. 1 and 2 (New Haven, CT: Yale University Press, 1966).
Fawcett, Edmund. *Conservatism: The Fight for a Tradition* (Princeton, NJ: Princeton University Press, 2020).
Fawcett, Edmund. *Liberalism: The Life of an Idea*, 2nd ed. (Princeton, NJ: Princeton University Press, 2018).
Feldman, Noah R., and Kathleen M. Sullivan. *Constitutional Law*, 20th ed. (St. Paul, MN: Foundation Press, 2019).
Fink, Zera S. *The Classical Republicans* (Evanston, IL: Northwestern University Press, 1945).
Finneran, Richard J. (ed.). *The Collected Works of W. B. Yeats, Volume I: The Poems* (New York: Scribner, 1997).
Finnis, John. "Abortion Is Unconstitutional," *First Things* (April 2021), pp. 29–38.
Finnis, John. "Brexit and the Balance of Our Constitution," *Judicial Power Project*, December 20, 2016.
Finnis, John. "'Intent of Parliament' Unsoundly Constructed," *Judicial Power Project*, November 4, 2016.
Finnis, John. "Judicial Law-Making and the 'Living' Instrumentalism of the ECHR," in N. W. Barber, Richard Elkin, and Paul Yowell (eds.), *Lord Sumption and the Limits of the Law* (Oxford: Hart Publishing, 2016), pp. 73–120.
Finnis, John. "Judicial Power and the Balance of Our Constitution," *Policy Exchange*, February 2, 2018.
Finnis, John. "Judicial Power: Past, Present and Future," *Judicial Power Project*, October 21, 2015.
Finnis, John. "Judicial Usurpation and Human Rights," *Judicial Power Project*, March 8, 2018.
Finnis, John. "The Law of the Constitution before the Court," *Policy Exchange*, February 2, 2018
Finnis, John. "The Miller Majority: Reliant on European Perspectives and Counsel's Failings," *Judicial Power Project*, January 25, 2017.
Finnis, John. "Only One Option Remains with Brexit: Prorogue Parliament and Allow Us Out of the EU with No Deal," *Daily Telegraph*, April 1, 2019, www.telegraph.co.uk/politics/2019/04/01/one-option-remains-brexit-prorogue-parliament-allow-us-eu/
Finnis, John. "Terminating Treaty-Based UK Rights," *Constitutional Law Group*, October 26, 2016.
Finnis, John. "Terminating Treaty-Based UK Rights," *Judicial Power Project*, October 26, 2016.
Finnis, John. "Terminating Treaty-Based UK Rights: A Supplementary Note," *Constitutional Law Group*, November 2, 2016.
Finnis, John. "Terminating Treaty-Based UK Rights: A Supplementary Note," *Judicial Power Project*, November 2, 2016.
Finnis, John. "Two Too Many," *Policy Exchange*, November 24, 2016.
Finnis, John. "The Unconstitutionality of the Supreme Court's Prorogation Judgment," *Policy Exchange*, March 5, 2020

Ford, Lisa. *The King's Peace: Law and Order in the British Empire* (Cambridge, MA: Harvard University Press, 2021).
Ford, Paul Leicester (ed.). *Pamphlets on the Constitution of the United States Published during Discussion by the People 1787–1788* (Brooklyn, NY: n.p., 1888).
Forsyth, Christopher (ed.). *Judicial Review and the Constitution* (Oxford: Hart, 2000).
Foster, R. F. *Modern Ireland 1600–1972* (London: Penguin, 1989).
Foster, R. F. *W.B. Yeats: A Life II, The Arch-Poet 1915–1939* (Oxford: Oxford University Press, 2003).
"The Four Freedoms," https://voices of democracy.umd.edu/fdr-the-four-freedoms-speech-text
Fredman, Sandra. *Comparative Human Rights Law* (Oxford: Oxford University Press, 2018).
Fredman, Sandra. *Human Rights Transformed: Positive Rights and Positive Duties* (Oxford: Oxford University Press, 2008).
Freud, Sigmund. "Civilization and Its Discontents" in *The Standard Edition of the Complete Psychological Works of Sigmund Freud Volume XXI (1927-1931)*, trans. James Strachey (London: The Hogarth Press, 1961), pp. 59–148.
Fromm, Erich H. *The Art of Loving* (New York: Harper Perennial, 2006, first published 1956).
Fromm, Erich H. *Escape from Freedom* (New York: Henry Holt, 1965, first published 1941).
Fromm, Erich H. *Man for Himself: An Inquiry into the Psychology of Ethics* (New York: Henry Holt, 1990, first published 1947).
Fromm, Erich H. *The Sane Society* (New York: Henry Holt, 1990, first published 1955).
Gentles, Ian. *The New Model Army: Agent of Revolution* (New Haven, CT: Yale University Press, 2022).
Gerodimos, Roman (ed.). *Interdisciplinary Application of Shame/Violence Theory: Breaking the Cycle* (Cham: Palgrave Macmillan, 2022).
Getachew, Adom. *Worldmaking after Empire: The Rise and fall of Self-Determination* (Princeton, NJ: Princeton University Press, 2019).
Gilligan, Carol, and David A. J. Richards. *Darkness Now Visible: Patriarchy's Resurgence and Feminist Resistance* (Cambridge: Cambridge University Press, 2018).
Gilligan, Carol, and David A. J. Richards. *The Deepening Darkness: Patriarchy, Resistance, and Democracy's Future* (Cambridge: Cambridge University Press, 2009).
Gilligan, Carol, and Naomi Snider. *Why Does Patriarchy Persist* (Cambridge, MA: Polity, 2018).
Gilligan, James. "Terrorism, Fundamentalism, and Nihilism: Analyzing the Dilemmas of Modernity," in Henri Parens, Alaz Mahfouz, Stuart W. Twemlow, and David E. Scharff (eds.), *The Future of Prejudice: Psychoanalysis and the Prevention of Prejudice* (Lanham, MD: Rowman & Littlefield, 2007), pp. 37–59.
Gilligan, James. *Violence: Reflections on a National Epidemic* (New York: Vintage Books/Random House, 1997).
Gilligan, James. *Why Some Politicians Are More Dangerous Than Others* (Cambridge, MA: Polity, 2011).
Gilligan, James, and David A. J. Richards. *Holding a Mirror Up to Nature* (Cambridge: Cambridge University Press, 2022).

Gilmore, David A. *Manhood in the Making: Cultural Concepts of Masculinity* (New Haven, CT: Yale University Press, 1990).
Grant, Ruth W. *John Locke's Liberalism* (Chicago, IL: University of Chicago Press, 1987).
Green, T. H. *Lectures on the Principles of Ethics*, eds. Paul Harris and John Morrow (Cambridge: Cambridge University Press, 1986).
Green, T. H. *Prolegomena to Ethics* (Oxford: Oxford at the Clarendon Press, 1883, 2012).
Greenhouse, Linda. "Alito's Call to Arms to Secure Religious Liberty," *New York Times*, August 11, 2022 at SR8.
Greenhouse, Linda. *Justice on the Brink: The Death of Ruth Bader Ginsburg, the Rise of Amy Coney Barrett, and Twelve Months That Transformed the Supreme Court* (New York: Random House, 2021).
Greenhouse, Linda. "Religious Doctrine Drove the Abortion Decision", *New York Times*, July 24, 2022 at SR9.
Griffith, J. A. G. *The Politics of the Judiciary*, 5th ed. (New York: HarperCollins, 1997).
Grosskurth, Phyllis. *John Addington Symonds: A Biography* (London: Longmans, 1964).
Hamilton, Alexander, James Madison, and John Jay. *The Federalist*, ed. Terence Ball (Cambridge: Cambridge University Press, 2007).
Hampsher-Monk, Iain (ed.). *Burke: Revolutionary Writings* (Cambridge: Cambridge University Press, 2014).
Hand, Learned. *The Bill of Rights* (New York: Atheneum, 1968).
Harris, Ellen T. *Handel as Orpheus: Voice and Desire in the Chamber Cantatas* (Cambridge, MA: Harvard University Press, 2001).
Harris, J. W. *Property and Justice* (Oxford: Oxford University Press, 1996).
Hassan, Steven. *The Cult of Trump* (New York: Free Press, 2019).
Hennessy, Peter. *Never Again: Britain 1945–1951* (New York: Pantheon Books, 1993).
Hirschl, Ran. *Towards Juristocracy: The Origins and Consequences of the New Constitutionalism* (Cambridge, MA: Harvard University Press, 2004).
Hobhouse, Leonard. *Liberalism and Other Writings*, ed. James Meadowcroft (Cambridge: Cambridge University Press, 2006).
Hobson, John Atkinson. *Imperialism* (Cambridge: Cambridge University Press, 1902, 2010).
Honoré, Tony. *Sex Law* (London: Duckworth, 1978).
Hoock, Holger. *Scars of Independence: America's Violent Birth* (New York: Crown, 2017).
Hulliung, Mark. *Citizen Machiavelli* (Princeton, NJ: Princeton University Press, 1983).
Hume, David. *Essays Moral, Political, and Literary* (Oxford: Oxford University Press, 1963).
Hunt, Lynn (ed.). *Eroticism and the Body Politic* (Baltimore, MD: The Johns Hopkins University Press, 1991).
Hunt, Lynn. *Inventing Human Rights: A History* (New York: W. W. Norton, 2007).
Hutchinson, William T., and William M. E. Rachal (eds.), *The Papers of James Madison 1783*, vol. 6 (Chicago, IL: University of Chicago Press, 1969).
Hyneman, Charles S., and Donald S. Lutz. *American Political Writing during the Founding Era 1760–1805*, vol. 1 (Indianapolis, IN: Liberty Press, 1983).
Isay, R. W. *Becoming Gay: The Journey to Self-Acceptance* (New York: Vintage, 1966).
Isay, R. W. *Being Homosexual: Gay Men and Their Development* (New York: Vintage, 1989).

Isay, R. W. *Commitment and Healing: Gay Men and the Need for Romantic Love* (New York: Wiley, 2006).

Israel, Jonathan. *Revolutionary Ideas: An Intellectual History of the French Revolution from the Rights of Man to Robespierre* (Princeton, NJ: Princeton University Press, 2015).

Issacharoff, Samuel. *Democracy Unmoored: Populism and the Corruption of Popular Sovereignty* (New York: Oxford University Press, 2023).

Jablonka, Ivan. *A History of Masculinity: From Patriarchy to Gender Justice* (London: Allen Lane, 2019).

Jefferson, Thomas. *Notes on the State of Virginia*, ed. William Peden (New York: W. W. Norton, 1954).

Jensen, Merrill. *The Articles of Confederation* (Madison, WI: University of Wisconsin Press, 1970).

Jensen, Merrill (ed.). *Documentary History of the Ratification of the Constitution*, vols. 1 and 2 (Madison, WI: State Historical Society of Wisconsin, 1976).

Juergensmeyer, Mark. *Terror in the Mind of God: The Global Rise of Religious Violence* (Berkeley, CA: University of California Press, 2000).

Kagan, Robert. *The Ghost at the Feast: America and the Collapse of World Order, 1900–1941* (New York: Alfred A. Knopf, 2023).

Kant, Immanuel, "Critique of Practical Reason," in Mary J. Gregor (ed.), *Practical Philosophy* (Cambridge: Cambridge University Press, 1999), pp. 133–271.

Kaplan, Bert, and Thomas F. A. Plaut. *Personality in a Communal Society: An Analysis of the Mental Health of the Hutterites* (Lawrence, KS: University Press of Kansas, 1956).

Kavanagh, Aileen. *Constitutional Review under the UK Human Rights Act* (Cambridge: Cambridge University Press, 2009).

Kennedy, Paul. "Joined with Single Purpose," *Wall Street Journal*, August 28–29, 2021, C7, C9 at C7.

Keynes, John Maynard. *The Economic Consequences of the Peace* (New York: Harcourt, Brace and Howe, 1920).

Klug, Heinz. *The Constitution of South Africa: A Contextual Analysis* (Oxford: Hart, 2021).

Kluger, Michael, and Richard Evans. *Roosevelt and Churchill: The Atlantic Charter* (Annapolis, MD: The Naval Institute, 2021).

Knights, Mark. *Trust and Distrust: Corruption in Office in Britain and Its Empire 1600–1850* (Oxford: Oxford University Press, 2021).

Kohler, Joachhim. *Zarathustra's Secret: The Interior Life of Friedrich Nietzsche* (New Haven, CT: Yale University Press, 2002).

Koskenniemi, Martti. *To the Uppermost Parts of the Earth: Legal Imagination and International Power 1300–1870* (Cambridge: Cambridge University Press, 2021).

Kramnick, Isaac (ed.). *The Portable Edmund Burke* (New York: Penguin, 1999).

Kramnick, Isaac. *The Rage of Edmund Burke: Portrait of an Ambivalent Conservative* (New York: Basic Books, 1977).

"La Marseillaise: History, Lyrics, and Translation," www.britannica.com/topic/La-Marseillaise

Langmuir, Gavin I. *Toward a Definition of Antisemitism* (Berkeley, CA: University of California Press, 1990).

Larson, Edward J. *American Inheritance: Liberty and Slavery in the Birth of a Nation, 1765–1795* (New York: Norton, 2023).

Laws, John. *The Constitutional Balance* (Oxford: Hart, 2021).

Lee, Bandy. *The Dangerous Case of Donald Trump* (New York: Thomas Dunne Books, 2017).

Lee, Bandy X. *Profile of a Nation: Trump's Mind, America's Soul* (New York: World Mental Health Coalition, 2020).

Levenson, Edgar A. "The Enigma of the Transference," *Contemporary Psychoanalysis* 45(2) (2009): 163–78. , ISSN 0010-7530.

Levin, Yuval. *The Great Debate: Edmund Burke, Thomas Paine, and the Birth of Right and Left* (New York: Basic Books, 2014).

Levinson, Daryl, and Richard Pildes. "Separation of Parties, Not Powers," *Harvard Law Review* 119 (2006): 2311–86.

Levy, Leonard. *Blasphemy: Verbal Offense against the Sacred, from Moses to Salman Rushdie* (Chapel Hill, NC: University of North Carolina Press, 1993).

Levy, Leonard W., and Dennis J Mahoney (eds.), *The Framing and Ratification of the Constitution* (New York: Macmillan, 1987).

Lewis, Bernard. *What Went Wrong? Western Impact and Middle Eastern Response* (Oxford: Oxford University Press, 2002).

Lincoln, Abraham. "Speech to the Young Men's Lyceum of Springfield (1838)," https://constitutioncenter.org/the-constitution/historic-document-library/detail/abraham-lincoln-speech-to-the-young-mens-lyceum-of-springfield-1838

Lino, Dylan. "The Rule of Law and the Rule of Empire: A.V. Dicey in Imperial Contest," *Modern Law Review* 81:5 (2018): 739–64.

Lock, F. P. *Edmund Burke, Volume 1: 1730–1784* (Oxford: Oxford University Press, 1998).

Lock, F. P. *Edmund Burke, Volume 2: 1784–1797* (Oxford: Oxford University Press, 2006).

Locke, John. *An Essay Concerning Human Understanding*, ed. Alexander C. Fraser, 2 vols. (New York: Dover, 1959).

Locke, John. "Fundamental Constitutions of Carolina," in *The Works of John Locke,* vol. 10 (London: Thomas Tegg, 1823), pp. 175–99.

Locke, John. *A Treatise of Civil Government and Letter Concerning Toleration* (New Yor: Appleton-Century-Crofts, 1937, originally published 1690).

Locke, John. *Two Treatises of Government*, ed. Peter Laslett (Cambridge: Cambridge University Press, 1960).

Loewald, Hans W. *The Essential Loewald: Collected Papers and Monographs* (Hagerstown, MD: University Publishing, 2000).

Loughlin, Martin. *Against Constitutionalism* (Cambridge, MA: Harvard University Press, 2022).

Loughlin, Martin. *The Case of Prorogation: The UK Constitutional Council's Ruling on Appeal from the Judgment of the Supreme Court* (London: Policy Exchange, 2019).

Lukes, Steven and Nadia Urbinati. *Condorcet: Political Writings* (Cambridge: Cambridge University Press, 2012).

MacPherson, C. B. *Burke* (New York: Hill & Wang, 1980).

MacPherson, Sir William of CLUNY. "The Stephen Lawrence Inquiry Cm4262-I," https://assets.publishing.service.gov.uk/uploads/attachment_datafile/27111/4262.pdf

Madison, James. *Notes of Debates in the Federal Convention of 1787* (Athens, OH: Ohio University Press, 1966).

Mahmood, Mamdani. *Neither Settler Nor Native: The Making and Unmaking of Permanent Minorities* (Cambridge, MA: Harvard University Press, 2020).

"Marie Antoinette and the French Revolution," www.pbs.org/marieantoinette/life/tranon.html

Marshall, T. H., and Tom Bottomore. *Citizenship and Social Class* (London: Pluto, 1992).

Massing, Michael. *Fatal Discord: Erasmus, Luther, and the Fight for the Western Mind* (New York: Harper, 2018).

Matthews, Roderick. *Peace, Poverty, and Betrayal: A New History of British India* (London: Hurst, 2021).

McCloskey, Robert Green (ed.), *The Works of James Wilson*, 2 vols. (Cambridge, MA: The Belknap Press of Harvard University Press, 1967).

McDonald, Forrest. *E Pluribus Unum* (Indianapolis, IN: Liberty Press, 1965).

McHarg, Aileen, and Alison L. Young. "The Resilience of the (Old) British Constitution," *UK Constitutional Law Association*, September 8, 2021, https://ukconstitutionallaw.org/2021/09/08/aileen-mcharg-and-alison-l-young-the-resilience-of-the-old-british-constitution

McKean, David, and Bart M. J. Szewczyk. *Partners of First Resort: America, Europe, and the Future of the West* (New York: Brookings, 2021).

Meade, J. E. *Efficiency, Equality and the Ownership of Property* (New York: Routledge, 2020).

Meeks, Wayne A. *The Moral World of the First Christians* (Philadelphia, PA: Westminster Press, 1986).

Menand, Louis. *The Free World: Art and Thought in the Cold War* (New York: Farrar, Straus, and Giroux, 2021).

Mill, John Stuart. "On Liberty," in *On Liberty, Utilitarianism, and Other Essays* (Oxford: Oxford University Press, 2015), pp. 5–112.

Mill, John Stuart, and Harriet Taylor Mill. *Essays on Sex Equality*, ed. Alice S. Rossi (Chicago, IL: University of Chicago Press, 1970).

Montgomery, Jonathan. *Health Care Law*, 2nd ed. (Oxford: Oxford University Press, 2013).

Morgan, Edmund S. *Inventing the People: The Rise of Popular Sovereignty in England America* (New York: W. W. Norton, 1988).

Moyn, Samuel. *Humane: How the United States Abandoned Peace and Reinvented War* (New York: Farrar, Straus and Giroux, 2021).

Murray, Melissa, and Katherine Shaw, "Dobbs and Democracy," *Harvard Law Review* 127 (2024): forthcoming.

Nietzsche, Friedrich. *On the Genealogy of Morals*, trans. Douglas Smith (Oxford: Oxford University Press, 1996).

Nixon, Richard. *Beyond Peace* (New York: Random House, 1994).

Norman, Jesse. *Edmund Burke* (New York: Basic Books, 2013).

Obama, Barack. *Dreams from My Father* (New York: Three Rivers Press, 2004).

O'Brien, Conor Cruise. *The Great Melody: A Thematic Biography of Edmund Burke* (Chicago, IL: University of Chicago Press, 1992).

O'Hagan, Timothy. *Rousseau* (London: Routledge, 1999).

Okrent, Daniel. *The Guarded Gate: Bigotry, Eugenics, and the Law That Kept Two Generations of Jews, Italians, and Other European Immigrants Out of America* (New York: Scribner, 2019).

O'Leary, Kevin C. *Madison's Sorrow: Today's War on the Founders and America's Liberal ideal* (New York: Pegasus, 2020).

O'Neill, Daniel. *Edmund Burke and the Conservative Logic of Empire* (Berkeley, CA: University of California Press, 2016).

Orwell, George. *Essays*, intro by John Carey (New York: Everyman's Library, 1996).

Ovid. *Metamorphoses*, trans. David Raeburn (New York: Penguin, 2004).

Palmer, Matthew S. R., and Dean R. Knight. *The Constitution of New Zealand: A Contextual Analysis* (Oxford: Hart, 2022).

Palmer, R. R. *The Age of the Democratic Revolution*, vol. 1 (Princeton, NJ: Princeton University Press, 1959).

Paxton, Robert O. *The Anatomy of Fascism* (New York: Vintage Books, 2004).

Perez, Perez. *Invisible Women: Data Bias in a World Designed for Men* (New York: Abrams Press, 2021).

Piaget, Jean. *The Moral Judgment of the Child* (New York: The Free Press, 1997).

Plato. "Republic," in John M. Cooper (ed.), *Plato: Complete Works* (Indianapolis, IN: Hackett, 1997), pp. 971–1223.

Pocock, J. G. A. *The Ancient Constitution and the Feudal Law* (Cambridge: Cambridge University Press, 1957).

Pocock, J. G. A. (ed.). *Political Works of James Harrington* (Cambridge: Cambridge University Press, 1977).

Rakove, Jack N. *The Beginnings of National Politics: An Interpretive History of the Continental Congress* (Baltimore, MD: Johns Hopkins University Press, 1979).

Rawls, John. *Lectures on the History of Political Philosophy*, ed. Samuel Freeman (Cambridge, MA: The Belknap Press of Harvard University Press, 2007).

Rawls, John. *A Theory of Justice* (Cambridge, MA: Harvard University Press, 1971).

Regis, Amber K. *The Memoirs of John Addington Symonds: A Critical Edition* (London: Palgrave Macmillan, 2016).

Reiss, Hans (ed.). *Kant's Political Writings* (Cambridge: Cambridge University Press, 1977).

Richards, David A. J. *Boys' Secrets and Men's Loves: A Memoir* (Bloomington, Ind.: Xlibris, 2019).

Richards, David A. J. *Conscience and the Constitution: History, Theory, and Law of the Reconstruction Amendments* (Princeton, NJ: Princeton University Press, 1993).

Richards, David A. J. "Dignity and Free Speech," in Salman Khurshid, Lokendra Malik, and Veronica Rodriguez-Blanco (eds.), *Dignity in the Legal and Political Philosophy of Ronald Dworkin* (New Delhi: Oxford University Press, 2018), pp. 277–99.

Richards, David A. J. *Disarming Manhood: Roots of Ethical Resistance* (Athens, OH: Swallow Press/Ohio University Press, 2005).

Richards, David A. J. *Foundations of American Constitutionalism* (New York: Oxford University Press, 1989).

Richards, David A. J. *Free Speech and the Politics of Identity* (Oxford: Oxford University Press, 1999).

Richards, David A. J. *Fundamentalism in American Religion and Law: Obama's Challenge to Patriarchy's Threat to Democracy* (Cambridge: Cambridge University Press, 2010).

Richards, David A. J. *Identity and the Case for Gay Rights: Race, Gender, Religion as Analogies* (Chicago, IL: University of Chicago Press, 1999).

Richards, David A. J. *Italian-American: The Racializing of an Ethnic Identity* (New York: New York University Press, 1999).

Richards, David A. J. (with Nicholas Bamforth). *Patriarchal Religion, Gender, and Sexuality: A Critique of New Natural Law* (Cambridge: Cambridge University Press, 2008).

Richards, David A. J. *The Rise of Gay Rights and the Fall of the British Empire* (Cambridge: Cambridge University Press, 2013).

Richards, David A. J. *Sex, Drugs, Death and the Law: An Essay on Human Rights and Decriminalization* (Totowa, NJ: Rowman & Littlefield, 1982).

Richards, David A. J. *A Theory of Reasons for Action* (Oxford: Clarendon Press, 1971).

Richards, David A. J. *Toleration and the Constitution* (New York: Oxford University Press, 1986).

Richards, David A. J. *Tragic Manhood and Democracy: Verdi's Voice and the Powers of Musical Art* (Brighton: Sussex Academic Press, 1988).

Richards, David A. J. *Why Love Leads to Justice: Love across the Boundaries* (Cambridge: Cambridge University Press, 2015).

Richards, David A. J. *Women, Gays, and the Constitution: The Grounds for Feminism and Gay Rights in Culture and Law* (Chicago, IL: University of Chicago Press, 1998).

Richardson v. Ramirez, 418 U.S. 24 (1974).

Robenalt, James D. "The Unknown Supreme Court Cleak Who Single-Handedly Created the *Roe v. Wade* Viability Standard," *Washington Post*, November 29, 2021, www.washingtonpost.com/history/2021/11/29/viability-standard-abortion-supreme-court-hammond

Roberts, Dorothy. *Killing the Black Body: Race, Reproduction, and the Meaning of Liberty* (New York: Vintage, 1997).

Robinson, Nicholas K. *Edmund Burke: A Life in Caricature* (New Haven, CT: Yale University Press, 1996).

Rosaldo, Michelle Z. *Knowledge and Passion: Ilongot Notions of Self and Social Life* (Cambridge: Cambridge University Press, 1980).

Rosaldo, Michelle Z. "The Shame of Headhunters and the Autonomy of Self," *Ethos* 11(3): 135–51.

Rosenberg, Gerald. *The Hollow Hope: Can Courts Bring about Social Change?* 2nd ed. (Chicago, IL: University of Chicago Press, 2008).

Rosenberg, Gerald N., Sudhir Krishnaswamy, and Shishir Bail. *A Qualified Hope: The Indian Supreme Court and Progressive Social Change* (Cambridge: Cambridge University Press, 2019).

Rousseau, Jean Jacques. *Constitutional Project for Corsica* (n.p.: Kessinger Publishing, n.d.).

Rousseau, Jean-Jacques. *The Government of Poland*, trans. Willmoore Kendall (Indianapolis, IN: Hackett, 1985).

Ryan, Alan. *John Dewey and the Hide Tide of American Liberalism* (New York: W. W. Norton, 1995).

Sadurski, Wojciech. *A Pandemic of Populists* (Cambridge: Cambridge University Press, 2022).

Sager, Lawrence G. "Insular Minorities Unabated: *Warth v. Seldin and City of Eastlake v. Forest City Enterprises*," *Harvard Law Review* 91 (1978): 1373–425.

Salome, Lou. *Nietzsche*, trans. Siegfried Mandel (Redding Ridge, CT: Black Swan Books, 1988).

Sanghera, Sathnam. *Empireland: How Imperialism Has Shaped Modern Britain* (London: Penguin, 2021).

Satia, Priyal. *Time's Monster: How History Makes History* (Cambridge, MA: Harvard University Press, 2020).

Saunders, Cheryl. *The Constitution of Australia: A Contextual Analysis* (Oxford: Hart, 2011).

Scanlan, Padraic X. *Slave Empire: How Slavery Built Modern Britain* (London: Robinson, 2020).

Scanlon, T. M. *What We Owe to Each Other* (Cambridge, MA: The Belknap Press of Harvard University Press, 1998)

Scheingold, Stuart A. *The Politics of Rights: Lawyers, Public Policy, and Political Change*, 2nd ed. (Ann Arbor, MI: University of Michigan Press, 2004).

Sedley, Stephen. *Lions under the Throne: Essays on the History of English Public Law* (Cambridge: Cambridge University Press, 2015).

Sexton, John. "Toward a Constitutional Definition of Religion," *Harvard Law Review* 91 (1978): 1056–89.

Shiffrin, Seana Valentine. *Speech Matters: On Lying, Morality, and the Law* (Princeton, NJ: Princeton University Press, 2014).

Simmons, A. John. "Inalienable Rights and Locke's *Treatises*," *Philosophy & Public Affairs* 12 (1983): 175.

Simpson, A. W. Brian. *Human Rights and the End of Empire: Britain and the Genesis of the European Convention* (Oxford: Oxford University Press, 2001).

Skocpol, Theda. *States and Social Revolutions* (Cambridge: Cambridge University Press, 1979, 2015).

Stenner, Karen. *The Authoritarian Dynamic* (Cambridge: Cambridge University Press, 2005).

Stokes, Eric. *The English Utilitarians and India* (Oxford: Clarendon Press, 1959).

Storing, Herbert J. *The Complete Anti-Federalist* (Chicago, IL: University of Chicago Press, 1981).

Strauss, Leo. *Thoughts on Machiavelli* (Chicago, IL: University of Chicago Press, 1984).

Sunstein, Cass R. *The Second Bill of Rights: FDR's Unfinished Revolution and Why We Need It More Than Ever* (New York: Basic Books, 2004).

Swift, Jonathan. *A Modest Proposal and Other Satirical Works* (Garden City, NY: Dover, 1996).

Symonds, John Addington. *A Problem in Greek Ethics* (n.p.: Pen House Editions, 1901).

Symonds, John Addington. *A Problem in Modern Ethics* (Frankfurt am Main: Outlook Verlag, 2020).

Taruskin, Richard. *Music in the Seventeenth and Eighteenth Centuries, Volume 2, The Oxford History of Western Music* (Oxford: Oxford University Press, 2010).
Tawney, R. H. *Equality*, 4th ed. (n.p.: Capricorn, 1961).
Taylor, D. J. *Orwell: The Life* (New York: Henry Hold, 2003).
Thiruvengadam, Arun K. *The Constitution of India: A Contextual Analysis* (Oxford: Hart, 2017).
Thompson, Judith Jarvis. "A Defense of Abortion," *Philosophy & Public Affairs* 1(1) (1971): 47–66.
Tooley, Michael. *Abortion and Infanticide* (Oxford: Oxford University Press, 1985).
Trumbach, Randolph. *Sex and the Gender Revolution, Volume One: Heterosexuality and the Third Gender in Enlightenment London* (Chicago, IL: University of Chicago Press, 1998).
Tully, John. *A Discourse on Property: John Locke and his Adversaries* (Cambridge: Cambridge University Press, 1980).
Tushnet, Mark. *The New Fourth Branch: Institutions for Protecting Constitutional Democracy* (Cambridge: Cambridge University Press, 2021).
Tushnet, Mark, and Bojan Bugaric. *Power to the People: Constitutionalism after Populism* (Oxford: Oxford University Press, 2021).
Vermeule, Adrian. *Common Good Constitutionalism* (Cambridge, MA: Polity, 2022).
Vile, M. J. C. *Constitutionalism and the Separation of Powers*, 2nd ed. (Indianapolis, IN: Liberty Fund, 1998).
Waldron, Jeremy. "The Core of the Case against Judicial Review," *Yale Law Journal* 115 (2006): 1346.
Waldron, Jeremy. *One Another's Equals: The Basis of Human Equality* (Cambridge, MA: The Belknap Press of Harvard University Press, 2017).
Walzer, Michael. *The Revolution of the Saints* (Cambridge, MA: Harvard University Press, 1965).
Washington v. Glucksberg 521 U.S. 702 (1997).
Watt, Watt. *UK Election Law: A Critical Examination* (London: Routledge, 2016).
Webb, Beatrice, and Sidney Webb. *Soviet Communism: A New Civilization?* (New York: C. Scribners' Sons, 1936).
Webb, Sidney, and Beatrice Webb, *Industrial Democracy: New Edition in Two Volumes Bound in One* (Indianapolis, IN: Alpha Editions, 2020).
Webber, Jeremy. *The Constitution of Canada: A Contextual Analysis* (Oxford: Hart, 2021).
Wechsler, Herbert. "Toward Neutral Principles of Constitutional Law," *Harvard Law Review* 73 (1959): 1.
Whitehouse v. Lemon, [1979] 2 WLR, or *Whitehouse v. Gay News Ltd.* [1979] AC 617, HL.
Wikipedia. "Assisted Suicide in the United Kingdom," https://en.wikipedia.org/wiki/Assisted_suicide_in_the_United-Kingdom
Wikipedia. "Judicial Appointments Commission (U.K.)," https://en.wikipedia.org/wiki/Judicial_Appointments_Commission
Wikipedia. "Martyrs of Compiegne," httprs://en.wikipedia.org/wiki/Martyrs_of_Eompi%C3%A8gne

Wikipedia. "Northcoe-Trevelyan Report," https://en.wikipedia.org/wiki/Northcote%E2%80%93Trevelyan_Report

Wikipedia. "Referendums in the United Kingdom," https://en.wikipedia.org/wiki/Referendums_in_the-United-Kingdom

Wikipedia. "Scarman Report," https://en.wikipedia.org/wiki/Scarman_Report

Wikipedia. "Select Committee (United Kingdom)," https://en.wikipedia.org/wiki/Select_committee_(United_Kingdom)

Wikipedia. "Tuition Fees in the United Kingdom," htpps://wikipedia.org/wiki/Tuition_fees_in_the_United)Kingdom

Wikipedia. "Yes Minister," https://en.wikipedia.org/wiki/Yes_Minister

Wilkerson, Isabel. *The Origins of Our Discontents* (New York: Random House, 2020).

Williams, David (ed.). *The Enlightenment* (Cambridge: Cambridge University Press, 1999).

Wolfe, Naomi. *Outrages: Sex, Censorship, and the Criminalization of Love* (London: Chelsea Green, 2020).

Wood, Allen W. *Kant's Ethical Thought* (Cambridge: Cambridge University Press, 1999).

Wood, Gordon S. *The Constitution of the American Republic, 1776–1787* (New York: W. W. Norton, 1969).

Wood, Gordon S. *The Radicalism of the American Revolution* (New York: Vintage, 1991).

Woodhouse, A. S. P. (ed.) *Puritanism and Liberty* (London: Dent, 1938).

Woodward, C. Van. *Reunion and Reaction: The Compromise of 1877 and the End of Reconstruction* (New York: Oxford University Press, 1966).

Wormuth, Francis D. *The Origins of Modern Constitutionalism* (New York: Harper & Row, 1949).

Wright, Lawrence. "The Apostate: *Paul Haggis v. The Church of Scentology*," *New Yorker*, February 14 and 21, 2011.

Wright, Lawrence. *The Looming Tower: Al-Quaeda and the Road to 9/11* (New York: Alfred A. Knopf, 2006).

Wyatt-Brown, Bertram. *Southern Honor: Ethics and Behavior in the Old South* (Oxford: Oxford University Press, 2007, originally published 1982).

Young, Julian. *Friedrich Nietzsche: A Philosophical Biography* (New York: Cambridge University Press, 2010).

Young, Michael. *The Rise of Meritocracy* (New Brunswick, NJ: Transaction, 2008).

Young-Bruehl, Elisabeth. *Hannah Arendt: For Love of the World* (New Haven, CT: Yale University Press, 1982).

Case Law

Britain

Airedale NHS Trust v. Bland [1993] AC 789.

Anisminic v. Foreign Compensation Commission [1969] 2 AC 147.

Associated Provincial Picture Houses Ltd. v. Wednesbury Corporation [1948] 1 KB 223.

Regina v. Brown [1993] UKHL 19.

R (Factortame Ltd) v. Secretary of State for Transport (No. 2) [1991] 1AC 603.

Ridge v. Baldwin [1964] AC 40.

R (Miller) v. The Prime Minister and Cherry v. Advocate General for Scotland, [2019] UKSC 41.
R (Miller) v. Secretary of State for Exiting the European Union [2017] UKSC 5.
Shaw v. Director of Public Prosecution, House of Lords [1962] A.C. 220.

European Commission and European Court of Human Rights

Dudgeon v. United Kingdom, ECHR5, (1982) 4 EHRR.
Gay News Ltd. and Lemon v. United Kingdom [Eur Comm HR] 5 EHRR 123 (1982), App. No. 8710/79.
Lautsi & Ors v. Italy, [2011] ECHR Application No. 30814/06 (18 March 2011).
Smith v. Grady v. United Kingdom (1999) 29 EHRR 493.
Whitehouse v. Lemon, [1979] 2 WLR, or *Whitehouse v. Gay News Ltd.* [1979] AC 617, HL.

India

Justice KS Puttaswamy v. Union of India, Writ Petition (Civil) No 494 of 2012, 24 August 2017.
Navtej Singh Johar & Ors. v. Union of India, Writ Petition (Civil) No. 572 of 2016, 6 September 2018.

South Africa

Minister of Home Affairs v. Fourie, Cases CCT 60/04 and 10/05, 2006 (1) SA 524, paras [78], [79], [82], [114], [117], [118], [120] (Sachs J); see also [164] (O'Regan J).
National Coalition for Gay and Lesbian Equality v. Minister of Home Affairs, CCT 10/99, 2000 (2) SA 1, paras [57], [97].
National Coalition for Gay and Lesbian Equality v. Minister of Justice, CCT 11/98, 1999 (1) SA 6.

United States

Brown v. Board of Education, 347 U.S. 483 (1954).
Buckley v. Valeo, 424 U.S. 1 (1976).
Carson v. Makin, 142 S.Ct. 1987 (2022).
Church of the Lukumi Babalu Aye v. City of Hialeah, 508 U.S. 520 (1993).
Citizens United v. Federal Election Commission, 558 U.S. 310 (2010).
Craig v. Boren, 429 U.S. 190 (1978).
Cruzan v. Director, Missouri Dept of Health, 497 U.S. 261 (1990).
District of Columbia v. Heller, 554 U.S. 570 (2008).
Dobbs v. Jackson, 142 S.Ct. 2228 (2022).
Dred Scott v. Sanford, 19 How. (60 U.S.) 393 (1857).
Frontiero v. Richardson, 411 U.S. 677 (1973).
Griswold v. Connecticut, 381 U.S. 479 (1965).
Kennedy v. Bremerton School District, 142 S.Ct. 2407 (2022).

Lawrence v. Texas, 539 U.S. 558 (2003).
Lochner v. New York, 198 U.S. 45 (1905).
Loving v. Virginia, 358 U.S. 1 (1967).
McDaniel v. Paty, 435 U.S. 618 (1978).
New York State Rifle & Pistol Association, Inc. v. Bruen, 142 S.Ct. 2111 (2022).
New York Times Co. v. United States [The Pentagon Papers Case], 403 U.S. 713 (1971).
Obergefell v. Hodges, 576 U.S. 644 (2015).
Planned Parenthood of Southeastern Pa. v. Casey, 505 U.S. 833 (1992).
Plessy v. Ferguson, 163 U.S. 537 (1896).
Poe v. Ullman, 367 U.S. 497, 523 (1961).
Richardson v. Ramirez, 418 U.S. 24 (1974).
Roe v. Wade, 410 U.S. 113 (1973).
United States v. Alvarez, 567 U.S. 709 (2012).
United States v. Ballard, 322 U.S. 78 (1944).
Washington v. Glucksberg, 521 U.S. 702 (1997).

Index